Labor and the American Left

ALSO BY MEL VAN ELTEREN

*Americanism and Americanization: A Critical History
of Domestic and Global Influence*
(McFarland, 2006)

Labor and the American Left

An Analytical History

MEL VAN ELTEREN

McFarland & Company, Inc., Publishers
Jefferson, North Carolina, and London

LIBRARY OF CONGRESS CATALOGUING-IN-PUBLICATION DATA

van Elteren, Mel.
    Labor and the American left : an analytical history /
Mel van Elteren.
      p.   cm.
    Includes bibliographical references and index.

    ISBN 978-0-7864-6487-6
    softcover : 50# alkaline paper ∞

    1. Labor unions—Political activity—United States—History.
2. Socialist parties—United States—History.   3. Labor unions
and socialism—United States—History.   4. United States—
Politics and government. I. Title.
HD8076.E48   2011
322'.20973—dc23   2011030523

BRITISH LIBRARY CATALOGUING DATA ARE AVAILABLE

© 2011 Mel van Elteren. All rights reserved

No part of this book may be reproduced or transmitted in any form or by any means, electronic or mechanical, including photocopying or recording, or by any information storage and retrieval system, without permission in writing from the publisher.

Front cover design by David K. Landis (Shake It Loose Graphics)

Manufactured in the United States of America

McFarland & Company, Inc., Publishers
  Box 611, Jefferson, North Carolina 28640
    www.mcfarlandpub.com

To my beloved Nancy, poet and fellow traveler

Acknowledgments

I had the opportunity to test out some of my ideas at annual conferences of the Netherlands American Studies Association and the Midwest chapter of the Popular Culture Association/American Culture Association. My special thanks go to the late Ray B. Browne, founder and former president of PCA/ACA; Gary Burns, president of PCA/ACA; Tom Discenna, Midwest PCA/ACA area chair on Working-Class Culture; and Kees van Minnen, director of the Roosevelt Study Center, Middelburg, the Netherlands. Last but not least I am indebted to my life partner, Nancy A. Schaefer, for helping me to bring this project to fruition.

Contents

Acknowledgments	vii
Introduction	1
1. The U.S. Political System and Institutional Constraints on Labor-Based Politics	9
2. Organized Labor, Socialist Parties, and Early Efforts to Establish a Labor Party	36
3. Labor and the Left during the New Deal and the Onset of the Cold War	73
4. Corporate Assaults on the Labor Left and the Limits of Postwar Liberalism	103
5. Labor Renewal and the Issues of Immigration, Globalized Production and Erosion of Workers' Rights	130
6. The Legacy of U.S. Labor Politics and Challenges Facing the Left	163
Notes	191
Bibliography	213
Index	231

Introduction

A severe financial crisis, triggered by a credit crunch in the U.S. banking system, brought the U.S. financial and global systems to the brink of collapse in 2008, causing far-reaching spiraling effects that plunged the nation into the deepest recession since the Great Depression. The bursting of the housing bubble and the wave of home foreclosures (many predicated on weak if not fraudulent mortgage underwriting practices), as well as the drop of the value of 401(k) plans and other pension investments, have eroded what tenuous economic security American working- and middle-class people had attained by then. Moreover, average unemployment and underemployment rates have increased to reach the highest levels since peaking in the 1930s. There are, however, great disparities between the various income groups; while Great Depression–type figures can be found among the nation's low-income workers today, close to a full employment condition prevails among the most affluent at the time of this writing (February 2011).[1]

The financial meltdown was rooted in a series of deregulations from the 1980s onward and widespread failures in what remained of government regulation, along with corporate mismanagement, reckless risk taking and massive fraud by investors on Wall Street.[2] The U.S. Treasury and Federal Reserve have taken steps to rescue, stabilize and eventually reform the financial architecture and construct a stimulus package to offset the reduction in private-sector demand caused by the crisis. A multi-trillion dollar bailout went to the very elite financial firms that were heavily implicated in producing the dismal state of affairs in the first place. A comparatively much smaller amount was granted to citizens through economic incentives, first-time home owner tax benefits, auto purchase credits, and to help guarantee the loans of certain lenders. Importantly, this package was freighted with business-friendly tax cuts while too thin on labor-intensive projects designed to put people to work right away, reflecting a stubborn refusal to advance serious public works programs.

Meanwhile, all across the nation populist anger against "big government" and "irresponsible spending of taxpayer money" has emerged, which "needs to be understood, harnessed, and channeled in egalitarian and anti-imperialist ways by genuinely progressive and democratic activists" as observers on the American left have noted (Street and DiMaggio 2010: 4–5). But this has not happened thus far. Instead, the right has captured the mood and, aided by corporate-owned mainstream media, has seized the opportunity to spread its message. Pundits and political figureheads (including Glenn Beck, Rush Limbaugh, Sean Hannity, Michael Savage, Bill O'Reilly, Sarah Palin, Newt Gingrich, and Michele Bachmann) and members of the Tea Party movement appeal to anxious and oppressed people who indeed have real grievances. They accuse self-professed "New Democrat" President Barack Obama and his corporate-friendly fellow Democrats of "socialism" (even "socialist tyranny") and other allegedly "radical leftist" preoccupations. Ironically, this occurs while the Obama administration through its bailouts has actually continued the George W. Bush administration's policy of granting massive taxpayer transfers to big American banks and has refrained from thorough structural reform of the financial industry (including refusing to nationalize and/or cut down the "too-big-to-fail" financial institutions), leaving the country's economy and politics pretty much in the grip of concentrated wealth and power.[3]

This tendency is further reinforced by deficit-increasing tax cuts for the rich that (in December 2010) Obama agreed to endorse and pass along from his predecessor, now rhetorically repackaged to the American public as necessary to create jobs and expand economic recovery. In addition, the Obama administration struck a deal in its 2009 U.S. auto industry bailout that eliminated tens of thousands of livable wage union jobs and caused a cascade of wage and pension cuts for current and retired autoworkers. And capital flight was awarded by allowing the establishment of new manufacturing plants abroad as part of the reform plan.

For the time being, the Obama administration also keeps funding the military-industrial complex at record-setting levels through extensive U.S. military presence abroad and intensified warfare, both overt and covert, especially in the Middle East, while largely abandoning American workers and the poor. Even the "health care reform" bill it has passed is heavily tilted in favor of the corporate insurance and pharmaceutical industries, after eliminating the prospects of a single-payer program of publicly-financed health care for all, and backing off from a more modest public option that could compete with profit-oriented health care insurance (Street 2010b: 10–15, 219–220; 2011).[4] All of this certainly does not represent a left-wing political agenda by any stretch of the imagination. But the phrase "socialism for the rich and capitalism for the poor" or the term "lemon socialism" (a system in which losses are public but gains are private) might be highly appropriate with regard to some of the above-mentioned infusions of government capital and the huge CEO bonuses that some bailout recipients have received.[5]

In the meantime, Republicans allied with elite business interests—newly emboldened by their midterm electoral gains in 2010—have stepped up their attacks on major public services and social provisions at all levels of government in seeking to diminish huge governmental budget deficits. (Excluded from their discourse, too, is any mention of tax increases for the wealthy, corporate welfare and tax evasion and cutbacks on services such as defense and security.) Furthermore, in states across the country, elected officials and right-wing pundits are cracking down on organized labor, demanding cuts to wages, pensions, and benefits of government employees. In several states—mostly those with Republicans in control of the governor's mansion and both chambers of the statehouse—they are also pushing new legislation to curb, if not break, the power of unions in collective bargaining and politics (Greenhouse 2011a).

What is most interesting, however, is that the current right-wing "populism" with its absurd take on Obama's and other corporate-friendly Democrats' political orientation contradicts a wealth of public opinion data indicating that the majority of Americans hold center-left attitudes regarding key domestic and foreign policy issues.[6] Given the pacification and co-optation of already weakened left-progressive movements by the Obama administration, those potential voters appear to lack an adequate political outlet to act on their majority progressive opinions and on their rising populist resentment. This problem is further exacerbated by the left's invisibility in the public arena, one that is dominated by conservative media, as well as its virtual absence in electoral politics (Street 2010a; Selfa 2010a). What makes it even more remarkable, in light of many years of anti-socialist propaganda and red-scare mongering in this country, is that recent opinion polls show significant support of "socialism" among American adults. These include self-identified Democrats (44 percent positive) and another key group, the "millennial generation," those between eighteen and twenty-nine (43 percent positive) who grew up during the heyday of neoliberalism and reached political age in an era of mostly Republican rule.[7] There is also increased interest in the revitalization of socialist ideas and practices among American public intellectuals, academics, politicians, social activists and laborites at a time when many people are anxiously searching for effective remedies to the existing societal problems associated with rampant capitalism and alternatives in terms of social justice and economic democracy.[8]

Meanwhile, the United States has undergone a significant decline in union membership over the past few decades, down to a general union density of about 12 percent (only 7 percent in the private sector, but still 36 percent in the public sector—labor's last bulwark at a time of massive anti-unionism).[9] This is noteworthy given the fact that historically, socialist and other labor-based parties tend to be closely related to trade unions in industrial societies. It seems to be a timely moment to take a fresh look at the history of socialism and labor politics in America in order to better understand these developments and what alternatives might look like.

This means partly a revisit to what was seen as "American labor exceptionalism" in twentieth-century scholarship, which originated in the question first posed by Werner Sombart, "Why is there no socialism in the United States?" (1906). His answer to this question, and later elaborations by Selig Perlman in the 1920s and Louis Hartz in the 1950s, established an orthodox view of American labor exceptionalism that emphasized the lack of class consciousness and class conflict throughout American history and the failure of socialism ever to attain a significant foothold in American politics (Perlman 1928; Hartz 1955). The conventional exceptionalism thesis assumes an ideal working-class consciousness and socialist engagement in Europe as a frame of reference for comparison with the United States, which is questionable. With regard to the United States, this thesis ignores the high degree of state and employer violence and does not take racial conflict into account. Problematic is the assumption that Europe in the late nineteenth and early twentieth centuries was characterized by a strong monolithically class-conscious working class, with strong socialist trade unions and political parties, in contrast to an America of business unionism and two-party machine politics. This overlooks significant dissimilarities in class formation, articulation of class consciousness, and in the forms in which the economic, political, and cultural demands of workers were expressed ideologically or organizationally. As historian Mary Nolan points out,

> France had syndicalist unions and a multiplicity of socialist parties, which weakly coalesced only after the turn of the century. British trade unions did not begin to break their alliance with the Liberals until the 1890s, and the Labour Party was small, weak, and most definitely not Socialist after World War I. If any country was exceptional in the size and strength of its Socialist Party and trade unions, it was Germany. And there, as well as elsewhere, large numbers of workers supported political Catholicism, voted for bourgeois liberal parties, or remained distant from political organizations and electoral politics. In the interwar years, when welfare states first developed, there was similar diversity. In the 1920s, the laissez-faire United States looked different from Germany with its well-developed social policy, but New Deal America differed more from Britain. In the post–World War II decades, patterns of class politics and welfare states shifted again, but there was never a single European model, deriving in teleological fashion from a shared feudal past and statist and communitarian values [Nolan 1997: 771–772].

References to relevant issues in this long-standing debate will be made only when absolutely necessary. This book focuses on the distinctive features and historical trajectory of U.S. labor and politics *without* embracing any form of "American exceptionalism" whatsoever.

American workers clearly did not always accept the conditions they were faced with. Social and labor historians have pointed to the vitality of a tradition of collective resistance to capitalism that was manifested in a variety of social and political movements. These include the plebeian radicalism of the Workingmen's parties of the 1820s and 1830s; the first great labor movement in the wake of the Civil War and its struggle for the eight-hour workday; and the militancy at the point of production of the Industrial Workers of the World and kindred radical syndicalist groupings in the early twentieth century until World War I, which resurfaced after the war until the mid-1920s. Other manifestations of such collective action are the sit-down strikes of industrial workers in the 1930s; the massive strike wave of 1945–1946 and into the 1950s, during which unions sustained a high level of strike activity until 1955; and the upsurge of labor militancy from the mid-1960s until 1974.

American workers were often the most militant in the labor market. Until the late twentieth century, American strike levels have been generally higher than those in Europe; the violence of industrial disputes has also been greater than in Europe. However, the intensity of conflict in the workplace was not expressed in politics by a strong and enduring labor or socialist party (Moody 2007: 98–100; Lipset and Marks 2000: 272–273). The question put simply is why did American workers respond to capitalism and economic exploitation in the ways they did? Why was militancy in the labor market and workplace seldom translated into the politics of class? The answer in bold strokes is that American workers' preoccupations centered on control of the workplace rather than creating a working-class presence in politics (Montgomery 1979; Green 1980). Therefore the issue of the weakness of socialism in America becomes "a problem of explaining the *disjuncture* of industrial relations and political practice in the United States" (Foner 1984: 60). This study focuses on that disconnection and the various efforts to establish an independent labor-based party over the course of time, updating the story to include the Reagan revolution and beyond, up to the present.

Socialism, as commonly construed, is not synonymous with social democracy, which is at the center-left on the classic political spectrum. The former concerns a political movement that seeks to fundamentally transform capitalism, aiming for collective or governmental ownership and administration of the means of production and distribution of goods. This includes socialization of basic industries and establishing publicly owned utilities, as well as some form of industrial democracy or even a more radical version of workers' control.

Originally social democracy referred to a political movement advocating a gradual or peaceful transition from capitalism to socialism by democratic means. Over the course of time the emphasis came to rest on mobilizing working people on behalf of state intervention, planning and social priority within capitalism (thus aiming for some type of mixed or social-market economy), and building a democratic welfare state that incorporates both capitalist and socialistic practices (Crouch 1997). Somewhat confusingly, however, social democracy has sometimes been called "reform socialism," in contrast to various forms of revolutionary or left-wing socialism. Neither socialism nor social democracy has ever become an enduring mass-based movement in the United States.

It should be noted that the question about the lack of an enduring, electorally viable socialist party in the United States has been conflated with a number of related issues. These include the question about why there is no labor-based party in the United States, as well as questions about the absence of a more class-conscious labor movement, and why no revolutionary labor-based party sunk deep roots here. In the extensive literature on these questions, the distinctions between them have become blurred. One must be aware, too, that the "failure of socialism" in America is not unique. There are other advanced capitalist societies that likewise failed to establish a social democratic or socialist party or lacked a very class-conscious labor movement (let alone a revolutionary party or movement). It is only with regard to the absence of an enduring labor-based party that the American experience is distinctive (Archer 2007: 3). This is taken as a starting point for examining the relevant developments at critical junctures from the 1870s onward.

The book is structured as follows. The first chapter outlines the U.S. political system, and more particularly the institutional constraints of the state structure and the party system on labor-based politics. It discusses the early expansion of white male suffrage and its impact on worker constituencies before the arrival of socialist parties in U.S. politics. It also looks at the electoral system with its winner-take-all principle and single-member districts, which is contrasted to proportional representation systems in Europe that are typically more hospitable to third-party efforts. The chapter further considers the nature of the major parties' duopoly and its ramifications for labor politics. The final section highlights changes in the rules of American electoral and legislative politics from the mid–1970s onward that have tilted the political system even more in favor of corporate interests in recent history.

Chapter 2 examines labor politics in the United States from the 1870s to the 1920s. It sheds light on the exclusive (craft) unionism of the American Federation of Labor (AFL) that came to dominate the American labor movement, after having been challenged for a while by the inclusive unionism of the Knights of Labor. The chapter looks at the involvement of several AFL unions in the movement toward establishing a farmer-labor party in the early 1890s, which was ultimately halted by AFL president Samuel Gompers and his allies. This is followed by an analysis of the attempts at independent class politics by proponents within the AFL in the early twentieth century, against the increasing hostility of the Federation's leadership to such initiatives. The next section highlights labor militancy at the point of production as practiced by the Industrial Workers of the World, and contrasts its inclusive national unionism to the "pure and simple" unionism practiced by the AFL. Subsequently the effort by moderates within the Socialist Party at establishing a labor party is discussed. Afterward the chapter considers the involvement of AFL unions in third-party efforts (especially of the farmer-labor kind) both at the state and the national level in the aftermath of World War I, ending with the 1924 presidential campaign of the Progressive Party candidate Robert La Follette, backed by both the AFL and the Socialist Party. The chapter concludes with a discussion of the implications for labor politics of the rift between the Socialist Party and mainstream unions.

Chapter 3 begins with an attempt to define the basic features of the so-called first and second New Deal, respectively. It illuminates the promising grassroots movement in the 1930s for a new labor party, and explains how and why it was terminated by powerful union leaders. It also considers the causes of failed attempts to establish an independent labor party during World War II. The National Labor Relations Act (1935) is discussed in terms of the opportunities and constraints it presented to labor. The chapter also describes the Congress for Industrial Organization's (CIO's) political action committee launch through which the political alliance between its industrial unions and the Democratic Party was to take hold. Next the major determinants of the postwar defeat of the larger ambitions of the labor left are summarized. Finally, the chapter takes a closer look at the Taft-Hartley Act (1947) and its far-reaching consequences for union power, labor politics and socialism in America.

Chapter 4 outlines the postwar campaigns against an emerging "laboristic society" that drew employers' concern, in support of "free enterprise" as part of concerted efforts by corporate businesses intent on countering the expansion of the New Deal order. It also regards the pattern of AFL-CIO interventions in politics that became established in the 1950s. Next the spotlight is on the Landrum-Griffith Act (1959), which because of its double-edged character was used both in right-wing assaults on labor and, to a lesser extent, by rank-and-file movements within unions seeking union democracy. The chapter further examines the possibilities and limits of postwar liberalism as manifested in President Lyndon B. Johnson's Great Society programs and the period immediately afterward. The ensuing section focuses on organized labor's responses to the new social movements that emerged in the 1960s, and particularly its conflicted relations with New Left activists involved in the upsurge of workplace militancy and rank-and-file democratization movements within unions. The final part makes the transition to the next chapter with a discussion of the rise of the corporate culture movement in the 1980s, along with "flexible specialization" and team-based production, and their impact on working conditions and unionism.

Chapter 5 provides an analysis of organized labor's development during the past three decades with an emphasis on the challenges facing the AFL-CIO's new reformist leadership (since 1995). It describes the growing number of workers' centers that constituted an important medium for immigrant low-wage workers to organize and act, and proved to have the potential of bringing black and immigrant workers together as well. The chapter also outlines the new strategies in the inclusive approach of union organization, along with the central labor councils that have been significant agencies in broader movements aimed at strengthening workers' economic power in various sectors and geographic regions. It signals the problems that social movement unionism experienced within a labor movement whose predominant ideology and practices still continued to be those of business unionism. The chapter further looks at the alternative to business unionism's approach to politics, a labor party, toward which a new major effort was launched in the mid–1990s, but that ultimately went nowhere. It also scrutinizes organized labor's dealings with corporate globalization and the various dilemmas that arose in the global campaigns, cross-border alliances and movements in which American unions were involved. Lastly, the chapter discusses proposals and actions to counter the further erosion of workers' rights and union power by critical observers among the labor left.

The final chapter considers the long-lasting effects of mainstream labor's ideological heritage and political practices on labor-based party efforts. It also looks at the various stances that today's socialists take toward the Democratic Party. Next the chapter reviews an alternative to the electoral trajectory to change the course and outcome of the political process as desired by the labor left, which is social movement activism with mass disruption, defiance, and demonstrative protest as preferred strategies. Currently, however, it is the right-wing Tea Party movement rather than a progressive grassroots movement that is mobilizing larger numbers of discontented Americans. The chapter examines the basic features of the Tea Party insurgency and its challenges to the left. It also assesses the potential of mobilizing the existing center-left majority (regarding major economic and social issues, at least according to opinion polls) for a large-scale progressive movement. The chapter closes with a discussion of the limits and possibilities facing anti-capitalists in America who want to take aim at global capitalism in transnational alliances with kindred groupings abroad.

1

The U.S. Political System and Institutional Constraints on Labor-Based Politics

Our starting point is that, in principle, structure and agency together shape political life. If politics rests on some exercise of agency by the political actors involved, it is also true that structures restrict agency, and it is this dimension of labor politics that is the focus of this chapter. It outlines the structural arrangements of the U.S. political system that have put constraints on labor-based politics, but also left open some options for labor and political leaders. There were particular historical junctures when they had at least some latitude so that their choices mattered in shaping the course of events. The following chapters will identify the options available for labor and the left at critical moments and examine how and to what extent they used those opportunities. Here we look at institutional features that worked to stymie, if not prevent, the establishment of a labor-based party over a longer period. Some concern the constitutional division of power, others the incentives and disincentives generated by the electoral system. Another characteristic of the U.S. political system that deserves attention is the nature of the major parties' duopoly. There have been changes in the rules of U.S. politics over the past thirty years or so that have tilted the political system increasingly in favor of corporate interests, which will be addressed as well.

Federalism

The Founding Fathers deliberately created a political system in which power was diffused horizontally and vertically. Horizontally, the separation of powers (between the executive and legislature) and the system of checks and balances (embodied by the judiciary in particular) ensured the absence of a powerfully concentrated center of political authority. The exception to this arrangement is the presidency, whose incumbents can exercise executive power on certain occasions, by referring to both constitutional authority and a popular mandate. Often such power is exercised more effectively with regard to foreign policy than domestic reforms. Vertically, the power is diffused through federalism. Each of the states has its own constitution and set of laws; each elects politicians. Federal authority in constitutionally defined domains and the U.S. Constitution always trump state law when they clash, but as a whole the federal system is an institutional arrangement that contributes to a weaker national state (González and King 2003: 43–44). The separation of sectional-based interests into separate governments with constitutional guarantees of separateness produces what Theodore Lowi has called "a form of balkanization." The distribution of governmental powers into separate governmental units was deliberately intended by the Founders as a way of permitting the prevailing interest in any section of the country to be dominant in its own section without being able to impose itself by majority vote on other sections (Lowi 1984: 375–376).

The authors of the Constitution set up an elaborate division and balance of powers within an intricate governmental structure "designed to make parties ineffective ... [because they] would lose and exhaust themselves in futile attempts to fight their way through the labyrinthine framework" (Schattschneider 1942: 128, qtd. in Piven 1992: 242). This reflected the Founders' fear of the populace that could be mobilized by parties at a time when the protection once provided to the propertied elites by the armies of the British Crown was gone and radical democratic currents stirred by the revolutionary war were fermenting among a still-armed population. It would be unwise to ignore democratic aspirations, but these could be blunted and diffused by a system of "checks and balances" that effectively divided authority for key policies between the Congress, the presidency, and the courts, and also made these decision-making centers at least partially independent of each other. Another implication of these safeguards against direct majority power was that they limited party influence over officials in government. They encouraged shifting and flexible alliances and made it difficult to translate election victories into policy (Lipset and Rokkan 1967: 31–32). The long-term effect was not only to fragment the central government's authority but also to put up enduring obstacles to coherent party organization.

At the same time, post-revolutionary elites aimed to constrain the new central authority they were creating, partly because of the highly diverse economies of the thirteen colonies, as infamously codified in the constitutional compromise over slavery (in which slaves were counted as three-fifths of a person). The more general compromise, which was to have lasting effects, was to structurally decentralize power. This happened in two ways. First, the authority of the new national government was limited to constitutionally specified policies, thus leaving a huge reservoir of unspecified power to the state legislatures. Second, the system of electoral representation was designed to give great weight to regions as opposed to persons, both in representation in the Senate and in the arrangement of the Electoral College by which the president was chosen.

The American Constitution assigns a critical role to various mechanisms of checks and balances in the political system. One is the interaction of the president and Congress and different methods of appointment to the two branches of the legislature: Senate and House. The independence of the courts is another. In the American system of government, the formation of legislation results from an interaction of executive and legislative power. Often one party holds a majority in one or both branches of the legislature, while the other party holds the presidency, a situation called a "divided government." Divided government tends to produce policy moderation, that is, a middle-of-the-road approach. Middle-of-the-road voters can also "create" a divided government with the aim to keep in check what they consider as very extreme policies. One aspect of this moderating effect is the midterm electoral loss of the party holding the presidency. Of course, we must realize that this is all in terms of the American political spectrum, which leans to the right of the middle-of-the-road position of contemporary European democracies.

Further, certain institutions, especially the Senate, were created with the express purpose of protecting property rights (Alesina and Glaeser 2004: 90, 255). The Senate is one of the basic institutional arrangements that is seriously biased because of a crucial democratic deficit: the senators' clout is disproportionate to population numbers. Today senators from twenty-six states, with representing less than 20 percent of the population, have more than 50 percent of the votes used to determine the congressional legislative agenda. But one should also take into account that institutions with enormous financial-economic power, like the Federal Reserve, are outside any democratic political control whatsoever (Harvey 2005: 205).

Due to the institutional fragmentation within Congress, individual members have a much larger degree of power than in any other democratic system in the world. This has been achieved because the U.S. Congress chose to protect its institutional prerogatives through the creation of an elaborate committee system that delegates political authority for particular policy decisions to individual committees and subcommittees—what has been called "committee government." At the beginning of every Congress, each chamber creates permanent standing committees that are empowered to receive, write, and report legislation and conduct investigations. Thus all major legislation originates in the detailed investigative and legislative work undertaken by congressional committees. This diffusion of powers offers many opportunities to block change. Legislation and its administration aimed at progressive reform can be held up almost indefinitely by such diversions and procedures as delay, filibuster, veto, court invalidation, and resistance of executive agencies. Under Dixiecrat control, for example, the House Rules Committee, with the help of Senate filibusters, tied up civil rights legislation for many years, when a bipartisan conservative coalition of southern Democrats and northern Republicans dominated Congress (Sexton 1991: 162–168).

The decentralization of government power also fostered the growth of the local clientelist political organizations that have played such a significant role in American politics, and that put a heavy stamp on working-class politics particularly during the first decades of industrialization. This meant that local government did many things with relative autonomy, and could yield enormous patronage resources. At the same time, the wide distribution of the (male) franchise meant that nineteenth-century artisans and laborers attracted the organizing efforts of clientelist parties. These working men could deliver the votes that could lead to victories for the parties and control over the patronage resources that local or state government handed out. Thus, when an industrial working class emerged, powerful local organizations were already in place that appealed to workers on the basis of ethnic, religious, and individual advantage.

Last but not least, a fragmented and decentralized state also fueled interest group politics even as it inhibited the party development that might counter interest group influence. This is partly explained by a government system with multiple points of access that was more exposed to well-organized groups with the resources and tenacity to pursue influence.

> Interest groups could operate in the several branches of government or at different levels of government to promote the policies they favored or to block policies they opposed. Moreover since the very structural arrangements which exposed the state to well-organized interests also ensured the fragmentation of political parties and their consequent lack of a strategic or programmatic center, there was little resistance from party leaders to the demands of well-organized interest groups [Piven 1992: 244].

Generally, American political institutions have shown more historical continuity than their European counterparts have done. However, one should avoid considering American institutions as set in stone since the nation's foundation. It is not possible simply to refer back to the Founding Fathers and the prevailing ideas and practices at the nation's inception in order to determine its basic characteristics once and for all. Political rhetoric has often exaggerated U.S. institutional stability, in which historical continuity was assigned to modified institutional arrangements and political opponents were discredited as proponents of radical change.[1] In reality, many American political institutions have undergone changes over time. No branch of government today even faintly resembles its counterpart in 1789. For example, over the period from 1800 to 1835, the U.S. Supreme Court established itself as a powerful third branch of government. During and after the Civil War, as well as in the 1960s, power was reallocated between states (particularly in the South) and the federal government. Major changes in the rules concerning suffrage occurred as late as the 1960s, when, as a result of the civil rights movement, African Americans in the South finally had access to the voting booth on a large scale. More generally, all branches of government have expanded steadily over America's entire history.

American institutions only appear to be static in comparison to the massive changes that took place in Europe (and also influenced several former colonies and other countries within European political orbits). As Alberto Alesina and Edward Glaeser correctly point out, in the early twenty-first century there was no country in Western Europe whose institutions looked even remotely like those in 1789. Yet, in 1890, most European countries had hereditary monarchies and limited franchises. By 1917, Europe still consisted largely of hereditary monarchies, which in most cases were, even then, only mildly constitutional. As late as 1945, most of continental Europe was ruled by authoritarian, if not totalitarian dictatorships. Portugal, Spain, and Greece remained in this predicament until the 1970s, while communist regimes dominated Eastern Europe until 1989. Although many European institutions have their origins before 1945 — for example, some legal systems are characterized by strong continuity — one cannot seriously maintain that Europe is a continent of stable democracies with enduring institutions.

> While James Madison would probably recognize that America still adheres to many aspects of its Constitution, Louis XIV, Clement von Metternich, and Otto von Bismarck would surely be appalled by the changes in the government of their own countries [Alesina and Glaeser 2004: 96–97].

Federalism has been conceived both as a source of weakness for third parties, especially socialist ones, and as a component of the political system that can foster the emergence of viable minor parties. Two main arguments have been given for the first perspective. First, federalism, with its division of powers among the presidency, Congress and the judiciary made the national state an ineffective instrument for economic and social change. Because federalism dispersed authority between so many different political units, it made it nearly impossible to capture sufficient government authority to effectuate fundamental economic or social change. Second, federalism weakened efforts to generate working-class consciousness or support socialist criticisms of American society as a whole because institutional-political power was fragmented into states. The states had jurisdiction over many of the questions that were of most concern to unions, and so a labor-based party could only achieve decisive, systematic reform if it gained control over many different state governments at once. But this was extremely unlikely.[2] The second perspective asserts that federalism may actually facilitate third-party efforts, since it provides smaller and therefore more accessible political units for third parties that have little chance for success in the national political arena. According to this reasoning, federalism offered a favorable environment to the establishment of a labor-based party in several ways. It lowered the threshold concerning entry into the political system by increasing the number of points of access for a new party. It also created political units in locations where such a party might have been able to secure an initial basis. This offered a labor-based party the opportunity to first establish itself in those states and regions where the concentration of socialists and the strength of the labor movement were greatest. And finally, it enabled the labor movement to engage in strategic experimentation, by offering a wide variety of opportunities—at federal, state, and local levels—to try out different political models. In short, the multiplicity of political units may have stymied radical society-wide reforms, but at the same time, it increased the opportunities for those seeking to establish a political foothold (Archer 2007: 85).

Federalism indeed has a dual face for minor parties. It fragments political-institutional power that is detrimental to third-party politics at the national level, but it also divides executive authority into smaller political units that can be targeted by minor parties, including labor-based ones, as evidenced by developments in Canada and Australia. If a minor party at the national level succeeds in positioning itself as the leading or second party at the regional level, it can break out of the wasted-vote dilemma confronting third parties. Federalism in America offered electoral potential for labor-party advocates and socialists in so far as it divided the country into small constituencies. For example, the Socialist Party in the early twentieth century faced an enormous challenge trying to convince its potential supporters that it had a real chance in presidential elections, but this was not necessarily the case in state or city elections. In light of the geographical concentration of socialist support in just a few states, socialists could and did at times argue that votes in these political units could give them control of influential executive and legislative positions. Some state and city socialist parties and factions, in fact, had an impact over extended periods of time (Lipset and Marks 2000: 53–57).[3]

Early Suffrage

A classic line of argument to help explain the absence of an enduring mass-based socialist or labor party in the United States revolves around the achievement of the suffrage of the vast majority of white male American workers from the late 1820s onward — well before the advent of the industrial revolution. By the 1890s, universal male suffrage for whites had been a long-established part of American social life. In Europe, by contrast, property qualifications and other class-related measures were still deployed to deny voting rights to a large proportion of working-class men. By denying workers the equal political status of full citizenship, European states helped to generate a class-based political grievance around which a labor-based party could mobilize support. This was in sharp contrast to the U.S. scene, where the formation of a large industrial working class took place after property qualifications had been removed. Consequently, American labor lacked the crucial mobilizing issue that in most of

Europe superimposed economic conflicts within the emergent capitalist class structure onto the struggle of the disenfranchised to wrest the rights of citizenship from the ruling classes. In England, for example, class consciousness was fostered, at least in part, by the struggle for the vote by the Chartist mass movement, while the exclusion of workers from suffrage strengthened the sense of a class-divided society developed at the workplace (Archer 2007: 73; Lipset and Marks 2000: 267).

On closer inspection, however, the early "gift of the suffrage" appears to be an unconvincing explanation for the general weakness of socialism in America. The more common comparison with Europe is often overdrawn. Some European countries had abandoned property qualifications by the late nineteenth century, while others maintained such qualifications, which had the potential to reinforce divisions between skilled and unskilled workers. In Europe, labor-based parties emerged both in countries where workers were enfranchised early, and in countries where they were enfranchised late. Tellingly, when compared with Australia, most like the United States in this case, the argument about the importance assigned to early male suffrage falls apart based on the evidence. At the start of the nineteenth century, almost all American states restricted the right to vote to those who met various property qualifications. Because electoral law was solely a matter of individual states, change came unevenly. However, most states dropped their property qualifications in the 1820s, 1830s, and 1840s, although many installed instead the requirement that voting be restricted to taxpayers. Usually the amount of tax required was small, but it still prevented voting by the poor and it demonstrated that the principle of universal (white) male suffrage had not yet been fully accepted. This proved to be a transitional matter, though, as by the mid-nineteenth century universal male suffrage for whites (or at least something very close to it) was the norm in the United States. However, by the end of the 1850s, universal male suffrage was likewise the norm in all but two Australian colonies.

Full acceptance of universal male suffrage might have left American labor leaders and socialists without the opportunity to appeal to a democratic cause that many European socialists exploited to great effect. Yet in both the United States and Australia (and other countries with early universal male suffrage, for that matter), other actions of the state continued to generate major class-based grievances. Labor leaders in both societies could still appeal to democratic demands and the defense of classless suffrage rights to help mobilize support for independent labor-based politics (Archer 2007: 74–77). After all, American political rights, including suffrage, were protected more (if by no means entirely) and at an earlier stage (at least with regard to the male white vote) than in many other countries. But the pivotal issue in the United States is the long-standing lack of labor rights against the background of political repression of militant labor and the left (Goldstein 2010: 315).

Indeed, early male suffrage for white males did not necessarily diminish socialist mobilization. The timing of a mature and broadly based party system, rather than male suffrage in itself, is crucial. Take for example Australia and Switzerland. Although widespread suffrage was achieved relatively early in those two countries, it did not lead workers to identify with non-working-class parties. Given its similarity to the United States as a new society and a former British colony, the case of Australia is most revealing. In 1891, the New South Wales Labor Electoral League won over 20 percent of the vote, and by the first decade of the twentieth century, labor parties had been part of every state government except that of Victoria. These efforts were rewarded by the electoral results of the Australian Labor Party, when in 1910 it attained half of the national vote. In Australia there was no stable party system before a federal polity was formed at the beginning of the twentieth century; instead there was a diversity of weakly institutionalized parties based on shifting allegiances and cleavages that varied from state to state. Efforts on the part of the existing protectionist and free-trade parties to bring local organizations together into national coalitions were strongly impeded in the years before Australia became united. The dominant political issue up to the early 1890s, when labor parties were first established, was land redistribution, which never became the focus of a stable pattern of party-political division. Due to the late stabilization of party loyalties, the development of a stable party system followed, rather than preceded, the establishment of labor parties (Farrell 1985: 126–127).

The Swiss experience reinforces the conclusion derived from the Australian example. Universal male suffrage was in place in Switzerland by 1848, well before the emergence of a large urban working class. Yet the Swiss Social Democratic Party performed quite well in national elections, receiving 6.9 percent of the popular vote in 1896, rising steadily to 20.1 percent in the last election before World War I, and ranging between 20 and 30 percent since 1918. This party development was aided (as in Australia) by the fact that no cohesive party system developed in the decades following the introduction of male suffrage. The Swiss party system reflected the decentralized character of the political system (with a key role assigned to "cantons," the member states of the Swiss federal state), and the orientation of political parties varied from one canton to another. The Social Democratic Party, founded in 1888, was the first party to be organized along national lines (Bucher 1971: 48).

In the United States, by contrast, the Democratic and Republican parties were already deeply entrenched in the social life of urban workers by the time socialist parties were established. Because male suffrage was introduced prior to the creation of working-class parties in the 1880s, socialists had to compete for the allegiance of workers who had developed party-political loyalties in an established party system. The strength of the two major parties among organized labor and their city-based political machines, as well as the relative weakness of class division, narrowed the political wiggle room available to the Socialist Party in the early twentieth century. American workers were incorporated into a party system based on ethnicity, religion, and residential community rather than on class, occupation or work setting. They came to take part in the pragmatic game of coalition building in a polity dominated by two diverse and permeable political parties that competed for their votes by appealing across class lines to a variety of non-class sources of loyalty.[4]

The Electoral System

The Founding Fathers, fearful of what they saw as an excess of democracy, established rules that favor political elites capable of mobilizing political resources across broad geographical areas and at the multiple levels of federal, state, and local politics. As the historian Richard Oestreicher puts it, "These rules essentially disenfranchise any political tendency or political interest unwilling or unable to reach accommodation with the political elites who control a governing coalition" (Oestreicher 1998: 30). The crucial constitutional features that are tilted in favor of powerful elites include the apportionment of legislative seats to single-member geographic districts; the election within those districts by winner-take-all plurality; a bicameral legislature with the Senate allocated two seats for each state regardless of population; and, lastly, the separation of legislative elections from the presidential election. The rules rarely change because the Constitution makers set up severe barriers. For instance, a constitutional amendment can only be enacted by first obtaining two-thirds majorities of both houses of Congress and then by receiving the endorsement of three-quarters of the state legislatures.

The U.S. electoral system is based on the plurality principle in which parties do not receive any representation unless they gain more votes than any other party within a constituency. Contrary to European electoral systems that facilitate the emergence of a multiparty system, the U.S. single-member plurality system reinforces the two main existing parties and puts up tough obstacles to thwart any third party from gaining seats in the legislature. The non-parliamentary government established by the U.S. Constitution ensures that candidates not put up by one of the two governing parties are easily beaten in elections. This is because the simple-majority single-ballot system favors the two-party system; it hurts small parties if their limited support is spread across many constituencies. Single-member geographically based districts, combined with the winner-take-all system, means that candidates who seek power at any level of American electoral politics must be able to produce an electoral majority in a specific geographic location. A minority showing — no matter how large, even up to 49.9 percent of the vote in a district — usually yields absolutely nothing. Moreover, a large minority showing across many districts is equally fruitless. A socialist or labor party may draw 5, 10 or even 15 percent of the national vote — enough to be a major national player under different rules such as proportional representation or a parliamentary system — and still be left empty-handed in the United States (Oestreicher 1998: 30–31). Voters who might otherwise have supported a small or new party are held back from doing so because they realize that a vote for it is most likely to be wasted. Their support for a third party may actually be self-defeating if it reduces support for the major party they prefer as the "lesser evil" (Duverger 1954: 217).

No wonder the third-party record in the United States "is one of nearly total failure; for anyone seeking to form a third party, this historical fact should be ... a melancholy prospect to contemplate" (Dahl 1966: 62). The United States has a longer history of continuous rivalry between two major parties than any other two-party system. No case exists in American history where a third party has pushed aside a major party and won a national election. When the Whigs split internally over slavery, the Republican Party merely replaced it rather than competed with it. Since the Civil War, just nine non-major party candidates in thirty-three elections have drawn more than 5 percent of the national vote in any presidential election. And only one third party ever managed to obtain more than 5 percent of the total popular vote in two successive congressional elections: the Populists in 1894 and 1896. There was no lack of contenders, though. By the end of the twentieth century, some eleven hundred local, regional, and national parties had contested national or state elections since 1824, of which at least seventy-eight defined themselves as "workers'," "labor," or "socialist" (Burnham 1974: 718–719; Lipset and Marks 2000: 43).

While geographically based, winner-take-all districts create a structural bias in favor of cross-class political coalitions and raise the threshold to enter the political arena, the bicameral structure of Congress and the method of electing the president reinforce these tendencies. Since all legislation must pass both houses of Congress, a few dozen senators from sparsely populated rural states can veto any program even if the overwhelming majority of the electorate favors it. Needless to say, working-class and pro-labor votes concentrated in large industrial states are systematically underrepresented. Until a series of Supreme Court decisions in the 1960s, most state legislatures manifested similar extreme imbalances in representation between urban-industrial and rural areas.

Presidential elections constitute an additional impetus toward cross-class coalition politics. "The president functions like a constitutional monarch elected in a national plebiscite," Oestreicher writes. He also signals significant historical changes:

> A credible presidential campaign always demanded a national political base (both because of the scale of the campaign and the choice by the Electoral College) and vast amounts of money. The rise of mass media further increased the price of an admission ticket to the presidential sweepstakes. Only national political parties can raise such resources, and even they are ever more dependent on large financial backers [Oestreicher 1998: 32–33].

The absence of proportional representation at the national level in the

United States is surprising, given the fact that the idea first circulated widely in this country. The proportional representation movement took off in the mid-nineteenth century and drew substantial support both in the United States and Britain. In the 1860s and 1870s, Charles Buckalew, a Pennsylvanian Democrat who served in the U.S. Senate and later in the U.S. House, advocated proportional representation at the national level as a means of ensuring the enfranchisement of African Americans in the post-bellum South. Newspaper editor and reformer Horace Greeley likewise supported this voting system as a means of enfranchising a wider group of minorities (including women). But the positive impact that proportional representation would have had (at least theoretically) on minority representation was the very reason why the system never took hold. The idea gradually faded to the background of political debate. During the Progressive Era, when electoral reforms such as direct primaries, the referendum, and the recall were central in the public discourse and policy making, proportional representation never became a major issue. Although Progressives brought about major institutional changes, such as eliminating the indirect election of senators, proportional representation at the national level never came close to being adopted. Local proportional representation (especially at the municipal level), which had become quite common by the 1930s, was generally rolled back after the war.[5] By the 1950s, during the heyday of the Cold War, opponents emphasized a link between proportional representation and the communist threat.

The failure of proportional representation to catch on in the United States in the late nineteenth and early twentieth centuries is due to two major factors. First, the majority of white, native-born Americans feared that such a system would grant too much power to the large, new immigrant population and African Americans. Second, powerful conservative forces within the United States had no intention of allowing drastic reform. The courts, often a bulwark of conservatism, struck down proportional representation in California and Michigan. The socialist movements and left-wing uprisings that played a decisive role in adopting proportional representation in many European countries had much less clout in the United States.[6] By associating proportional representation with both Nazism and communism and relying on American nationalism, the right managed to defeat this reform movement (Alesina and Glaeser 2004: 97–100).

Did the electoral system also play a decisive role in hindering the emergence of a labor-based party in the United States during the late nineteenth and early twentieth centuries? A broader comparison with other countries is helpful in trying to answer this question. Countries like Australia, Britain, New Zealand, and Canada all had plurality electoral systems, but in all of them labor parties were established that consolidated themselves either as one of two main parties (as in Australia, Britain, and New Zealand), or as a permanent third party (as in Canada). Even more important for us here is that when European socialist and social democratic parties first emerged, proportional representation had not yet been introduced in the countries concerned. In Denmark and Sweden, these parties entered parliament to become an important political force under single-member plurality systems like those in the Anglophone countries. In Germany, Austria, Italy, the Netherlands, and Norway, social democratic or socialist parties likewise became part of parliament under single-member majoritarian systems that required two or more ballots with only two candidates in the final round and hence an absolute majority for the winner. In France, socialists also consolidated themselves under a similar two-ballot system, but without the requirement of an absolute majority in the final ballot. These two-ballot systems shared many of the features that make plurality systems inhospitable to third parties. Especially important among these shared features are the single-member districts that put up a high threshold for entry into the legislature. Moreover, while they avoided some of the "wasted-vote" effects of plurality systems, they all (except France) imposed an even higher threshold than plurality systems by insisting that a winning candidate gain 50 percent of the vote.

By imposing a high threshold, single-member plurality (and majority) systems undeniably place more obstacles in the way of insurgent parties than proportional representation systems. But in the late nineteenth and early twentieth centuries, such systems were rarely used either in the English-speaking world or in continental Europe. Indeed, before 1900 no European country used proportional representation for national elections. And no large European country used it before the end of the First World War.[7] It was Belgium that had the distinction as the first European country to use a proportional system in the general election of 1900 (Rose 1974: 53–54). Therefore, these sorts of obstacles, far from being unique to the United States, were actually the norm during the early formative period of socialism in Europe and the Anglophone world. Moreover, whatever effect these obstacles might have had on other parties, labor-based parties repeatedly demonstrated that they were able to draw the electoral support that they needed to become political players.

A single-member plurality electoral system will not obstruct an emerging party if its potential supporters are sufficiently geographically concentrated to cross the threshold in a number of electoral districts. The historical evidence shows that the potential support for labor-based parties in other countries was sufficiently concentrated not only in the most highly industrialized countries such as Germany and Britain but also in many that were far less industrialized. As one of the most industrialized countries in the world in the late nineteenth century, the United States was at the upper end of this range. This would suggest that the electoral system alone is not a significant factor in the explanation of the weakness of socialism in the United States.

There are two basic strategies that can offset the disadvantages for third parties arising from plurality electoral systems. First, third-party activists can focus their efforts selectively on constituencies in which they have some special source of strength such as coal mining areas and districts with heavy concentrations of industrial workers. Secondly, they can avoid splitting the left vote (in the case of progressive third parties) by making an electoral deal with the major party at the local level closest to them ideologically so that they do not compete over the same constituency. Finally, the wasted-vote effect may not apply if voters do not have a strong preference for either major party or if they consider voting to be a symbolic or expressive act rather than a means to influence election outcomes directly. This means that the effects of electoral systems on voting are not an automatic outcome but depend on party strategy and individual orientations, and these vary across time and place. For example, independent presidential candidate Ross Perot continued to gain votes as the election drew nearer during his revived 1992 campaign. According to survey data, his supporters did not have a strong preference for either major party's candidates and therefore felt no pressure to abandon Perot when it came to voting (Lipset and Marks 2000: 45–48; Sexton 1991: 164).

Presidentialism

It is not the electoral system alone, but rather its interaction with presidentialism that helps explain the failures to establish a viable socialist or labor party.[8] The plurality system fosters a two-party system in presidential (and gubernatorial) elections. While in a parliamentary system a third party might win the balance of power and share control of the executive, in the U.S. political system only one person can win the presidency (or the governorship of a state), and for that purpose his or her party must be able to attract widespread support across the country (or state). The geographical concentrations of electoral power that would win a number of legislative seats for a third party would not be of much benefit to it in a presidential election. And the problems facing a third party would be compounded by a strong psychological effect: third-party voters are likely to expect that a vote cast for their party would be wasted and may even help to elect their least preferred candidate (Archer 2007: 86).

The election to the executive branch combines two features that together pack a one-two punch to third-party aspirations: the principle of plurality and the aggregation of national votes through the Electoral College. The United States however is not unique in this regard. Britain, Canada, and other former Commonwealth countries also have plurality elections, and France has adopted a presidential election system based on two rounds of voting at the national level.[9] But among modern democracies, only the United States combines those two features, electing its executive via a plurality electoral system with a single round of voting. This makes it difficult, if not impossible, for a third party in the United States to achieve national success by cooperating with other parties to limit competition or by building on geographical concentrations of support. The first strategy is severely thwarted because the presidency is a unitary institution that cannot be easily divided among parties. Taking advantage of local pockets of support (as happens in parliamentary systems) is almost certainly doomed to fail because the effective constituency for the presidential election is the country as a whole. Even though there is the mathematical possibility for a third party to gain a balance of power in electoral votes if the major parties are closely matched, this has never happened in reality. The Electoral College method endows voters with unequal power based on where they live, can defeat the winner of the national popular vote, and sidelines the majority of voters who do not live in the dozen or so "swing states" today (Richie 2007: 4). The upshot is that close popular elections can be turned into landslide margins of victory for either major party. This leads to extremely disproportionate representation and skewed rewards in presidential elections. Logically, the influence of the wasted-vote effect should be weaker as one moves from presidential elections down to congressional and then to local elections. This is also what election results reveal more in general.

Given the separation of the executive and legislative branches of government in the United States, third parties are denied any executive influence as a coalition partner. The electoral system exerts severe pressure toward party consolidation, so factional coalitions have always been formed within, rather than between, political parties. Thus, the American presidential system epitomizes an extreme version of the winner-take-all principle: the winning ticket attains a monopoly of the executive for four years (Lipset and Marks 2000: 48–49).

Under a parliamentary system, votes for minor parties are much less likely to be lost than under the presidential system, because minorities often share power in coalition governments, contribute to the selection of government leaders, and make or break a coalition government. Parliamentary governments are in effect creatures of parliament: coalitions patched together by simple legislative majorities. When a party with the largest number of seats fails to get a majority, it must rely on smaller parties to achieve one. By providing the balance of power between two larger parties, a small party can gain a disproportionately greater influence. In such a system, third, and even fourth or fifth, parties often make sense, because at times they can exert substantial political influence.

The efficacy of European third parties is based on a system in which there is no distinction between the legislative and executive branches, and in which the party membership is ideologically coherent, especially when compared with the American major parties. In a parliamentary system, the prime minister is the head of the government who serves at the majority's discretion. A minor party (or a minority of small parties) in a ruling coalition can overthrow a government by withdrawing support in a vote of no confidence, which gives considerable power to the small parties in coalition governments. There are also possible drawbacks to proportional representation, of course; it can contribute to extreme instability of coalition governments, and it can allow very small minor parties to determine government policies. These risks can be lessened however by limiting the eligibility of small parties through the creation of an electoral threshold (Sexton 1991: 163, 165–166).

There can be little doubt that the practice of electing chief executives (presidents and governors) strongly reinforces the influence of the winner-take-all electoral system. The electoral college method of choosing the presidency helps entrench the two-party system. In order to win the presidency, a candidate needs a majority of electoral votes, which means winning a plurality across a wide geographic area. Given this situation, it seems only rational to practice vote maximization strategies; according to this argument, a third-party candidate with no chance of winning a majority would be a waste of time (Lowi 1984: 374–375). The majoritarian system not only sets serious barriers to third parties getting started, but also overrepresents low-density, non-industrial states. Given these structural constraints, it has been extremely difficult for a nascent socialist movement to have much if any influence on national elections (Alesina and Glaeser 2004: 121).

Class-Related Electoral Obstacles

Another set of structural arrangements that constrained the political influence of large segments of the working classes evolved a century after the writing of the Constitution. Elites everywhere were alarmed by the participation of southern blacks and poor whites in the Populist movement as well as new immigrants' interest in socialism and the Democratic city-based political machines. Northern Republicans forged a lasting political bond with southern economic elites and their representatives in the Democratic Party, which effectively demobilized Populism and poor Democratic voters in the South. During the closing decades of the nineteenth century, industrialists and Republicans in the North, in tandem with planters and Democrats in the South, introduced a series of "reforms" into state electoral laws and procedures that disenfranchised many workers and farmers. These efforts were particularly rigorous in the South, where the disenfranchisement of black males was linked to the stability of the plantation economy and the serf labor on which it relied. New literacy and poll tax requirements, together with personal voter registration requirements (including literacy tests and residency requirements), were incorporated into state constitutions and rapidly disenfranchised almost all blacks and most poor whites (about half of the white electorate). A similar effort swept the North, driven less by the race issue and more by elite reactions against insurgent farmer and industrial movements. The result was the same, although less drastic: Northern states reintroduced literacy tests that had been abandoned half a century earlier, in some states along with a poll tax. Meanwhile, elaborate and obstructive requirements for personal and periodic registration were implemented, at first mainly in the big cities where the immigrant working class and the local political machines (dependent on immigrant working-class support) were concentrated (Piven 1992: 245). The political influence of Catholics and new immigrants and their descendents was further curtailed by other tactics — malapportionment, redistricting, and gerrymandering. This ensured that Anglo-Protestant rural districts held the lion's share in Congress between 1910 and 1964, the year in which the Supreme Court broke the power of a bipartisan conservative coalition of Anglo-Protestant rural representatives by ordering House redistricting (Kaufmann 2004: 253–256).

The process of gaining access to ballots became more complicated and time consuming in some states when new regulatory measures were enacted.[10] In the early twentieth century, a number of electoral reforms were introduced that sometimes made split-ticket voting more difficult, and often had the effect of reinforcing the position of the two major parties and weakening the position of third parties. While major-party candidates were automatically listed on ballots, minor parties were confronted with a series of regulations and barriers adopted by individual state legislatures dominated by the major parties. Simply placing candidates on ballots became increasingly difficult as many states introduced complex petitioning rules and other restrictions on third parties' access to the ballot (Archer 2007: 88–89).

At the same time, the local parties, which might otherwise have aimed to counter or subvert these restrictions, came under attack by reformers who worked to divest those parties of their patronage resources, and to further fragment the local and (sometimes) state government they controlled. These reforms emerged in the context of the 1896 electoral alignment that reduced party competition in much of the country. Progressive reformers saw local elites and their party machines as the major obstacles to reform.[11] As discontent with this political system increased, these reformers began to insist that major party candidates be subject to the direct vote of party members. This was part of a more general push for a set of institutional reforms specifically designed to take power away from the then current political elites and the parties they controlled. The reform proposals also included the Australian ballot (secret ballot), recall elections, citizen initiatives on state ballots, voter registration reform, and the direct election of U.S. senators. This movement was spearheaded by Robert M. La Follette, Wisconsin's future Progressive Republican senator who in 1897 called for direct primary elections, a reform that was adopted in Wisconsin in 1903 when, under his leadership, this state enacted one of the first direct primary laws. However, the earliest direct primary law was passed in Mississippi a year before, in a context of white supremacy that certainly did not improve the predicament of African Americans. By 1910 two-thirds of the states (mostly in the West) had adopted the system whereby candidates were nominated for office by popular vote in direct primaries. By 1917 they were generally in place across the country (Sexton 1991: 168–169; Weinstein 2003: 251–252).

Collectively, these various reforms had a negative effect on voter participation after all. On the one hand, restrictive rules and procedures made voting difficult, and clientelist local parties had fewer resources to help voters through the process. On the other hand, uncompetitive elections ultimately diminished the motive of voters to vote or of parties to enlist them. Voter turnout, which had been consistently high for most of the nineteenth century, steadily declined after the turn of the century, dropping to barely half of the nationwide electorate by the 1920s (Piven 1992: 245–246).

The election rules have generally become more restrictive over the years. After World War II, state laws—or the way they were enforced—set ever more barriers for minor parties to get on the ballot. Today, the United States has some of the most restrictive ballot access laws in the world. Requirements for official party ballot status are often set very high, and state legislatures have a track record of increasing requirements when faced with potential historical challenges. These hurdles contrast sharply with the often simple filing requirements common in many other countries (Reynolds 2000: 53). A number of states (including California, Montana, and Oklahoma) demand that minor parties gain the signatures of 5 percent of the state's registered voters. Some states (for example, Tennessee) require an absolute number of signatures, and others, including New York, require a certain number of signatures from each county.[12] In South Carolina, signatories are obliged to list their precinct and voter registration numbers. On top of this, the deadlines for meeting such requirements vary from state to state, which is another source of frustration for minor parties conducting national campaigns. Petitions have to be circulated by one date and filed by another—in some cases several months before the election itself, in other cases only shortly before.

Consequently, a third party may have to deal not with one national nomination process, but with almost as many as there are states to be contested, each with its own bureaucratic peculiarities. Because these provisions are enforced by hostile major-party supporters, minor parties run the risk of being denied access to the ballot on a technicality. This happened, for example, to the Socialist Party in New York in 1946, when petitions collected in each county of the state with the requisite fifty signatures were considered invalid because the canvasser in some instances had misstated his own district. It was the Democrats who threw the Socialist Party off the ballot in New York, which fits a general pattern of exclusion. Because the Democratic Party usually had the most to lose when Socialists were on the ballot, it was also the Democratic Party rather than the Republican Party that most frequently sought to deny the Socialist Party a place on the ballot (Sexton 1991: 166; Lipset and Marks 2000: 63–64). Similarly, in recent years, more often than not it has been the Democratic Party that has fought to deny the Green Party, Naderites (supporters of Ralph

Nader), and other third parties and independent candidates on the left access to state ballots.

Major-Party Flexibility

The American political system also works against third parties by providing strong incentives for ideological diffuseness (albeit within the limits of liberal capitalism) inside the major parties. The combination of the electoral system, the separation of the executive branch from the legislature, and the primary nomination system have encouraged major parties to undermine minor parties by adopting parts of their platforms when they threaten to be successful.

The formation of majority government in any democratic society requires forming coalitions among competing interests and value groups. The American system offers a strong impetus to make those coalitions within parties before elections rather than between parties after elections, as is customary in political systems with proportional representation. Given the high degree of geographical, ethnic, and social diversity of American society, this coalition building has been instrumental in producing open and opportunistic political parties. Of course, such parties are not unique to the United States; all political parties operating in a plurality electoral system undergo the pressures mentioned above. However, from a comparative perspective the Democratic and Republican parties in America are characterized by a high degree of ideological diffuseness, permeable channels of recruitment, internal disagreement and electoral opportunism. These features are the result of particularly the separation of the executive and the legislature and the primary nomination system. Because the executive and legislative branches are divided, party unity in the legislature is not necessary to sustain the government in office. In contrast to parliamentary systems where parties tend to be much more disciplined to support their leaders and policies, the division of powers in America gives legislators much leeway to follow their own preferences and vote as they wish, in reaction to their constituents and financial sponsors.

In America, congressional politics is essentially local. Members of Congress tend to represent the interests or value groups that predominate in their individual constituencies, even if this brings them into conflict with others in their own party. In contrast to other plurality electoral systems, in the United States the electoral pressures toward building diverse coalitions have not been countered by attempts at building coherent, tightly disciplined parties to sustain a parliamentary majority to keep the executive in office. This tendency has been reinforced by the introduction of the popular nomination primary in the early twentieth century which provided opportunities for political activists to join and take over segments of either party. In the United Sates, party elites are not able to control access to the spoils of party candidacy. In aiming for the broadest possible supports, they must allow diversity of opinion within their ranks. Here lies an opportunity for frustrated minor party candidates (or potential ones) to campaign for political office within one of the major parties. In addition, it may be more rewarding for an ideological minority group to proceed under the label of a major party than to run its own candidate.

This strategy has been used successfully by activists who sought to organize a party within one of the two major parties as in the case of North Dakota's Nonpartisan League in 1915–1916, when it saw an opportunity in the Republican Party there, captured the label of the party, and elected a governor and the major state officials. Such cases are rare, however, and none of the options available in the American political system have produced results comparable with those of the labor left in many other democracies. Similar left-wing movements within the major parties achieved temporary electoral success. These included the Farmer Labor League in Oklahoma in 1923, the Commonwealth Federations in Oregon and Washington during the 1930s, and Upton Sinclair's End Poverty in California (EPIC) gubernatorial campaign in 1934. Each consisted of a reformist coalition that was prepared to operate within one of the major parties, rather than as a separate party, and thus won one or more state-level primaries. Basically, American communists followed a similar strategy in expediently operating among the Democrats in the 1930s and 1940s, as have a number of small groups that emerged from the New Left (Lipset and Marks 2000: 65–66, 179). Since the 1980s, the radical Christian right has likewise targeted the Republican Party as a vehicle through which to advance its agenda (Schaefer 2009: 299–300), as does the Tea Party movement today, both at the state and the federal level. However, up until today this particular use of direct primaries has never led to a mass-based socialist faction within either of the two dominant parties.[13]

A significant contributing factor to the ideological incoherence of parties in Congress was the conservative bipartisan coalition that emerged in response to the New Deal of the 1930s and that remained influential until the 1990s. This coalition, which included conservative Democrats, mostly from the South, and Republicans, repeatedly blocked progressive legislation after 1937 (Brinkley 1995: 140–143). From the mid-1960s, onward conservative Democrats from the South were gradually replaced in Congress by Republicans while a large part of the northern white working class (particularly Catholics) switched to the Republicans, as a result of which the conservative coalition across the parties largely disappeared. This contributed to a tightening of the ideological coherence of the two parties. Another cause of increased ideological coherence was the "Republican revolution" of 1994 when Republicans regained control of the Senate that they had lost in 1986, and gained a majority in the House of Representatives for the first time in forty years.

Even though the two parties are broad coalitions that involve politicians of various stripes, the party labels nevertheless remain meaningful to many voters in providing general information about a candidate's broad approach to policy making. Today it is reasonable to assume that a Republican supports more conservative policies overall than a Democrat (Mason 2003: 95-96).

The Major Parties' Duopoly

Basic features of the U.S. political system — federalism, the presidency, the plurality electoral system and primaries — foster and sustain a party duopoly at the national level. Given the ideological diffuseness, the lack of party discipline in Congress (at least until more recently) and the institutional porousness of the major parties, third parties have faced formidable competition at every level of American government. In no other democracy has the duopoly of the two major parties over political representation been so complete. Moreover, both of the two major parties are sympathetic to liberal capitalism, and neither has inherited or developed a socialist or social democratic vision of society (Lipset and Marks 2000: 261; Moody 2007: 154-155).

Historically, the two-party system has functioned as a "shock absorber," blocking or co-opting "restive segments of the electorate" (Selfa 2008: 88). The two major parties have proved remarkably adept at absorbing and defusing protest, through adopting demands of reformers in diluted forms, as a result of which those on the left have felt obligated to choose in elections between the "lesser of two evils." This created insurmountable barriers to radical change (Husbands 1976: xx-xxi). In nineteenth-century America, the same two parties repeatedly fought elections that virtually excluded minor parties. During most of the late nineteenth century, political alignments usually tended to be stable. In America there was no pattern of incessant fissions and fusions among bourgeois political parties as one finds in Germany, for example, in the last three decades of the nineteenth century, which made it easier for the German Social Democratic Party to gain a foothold in German politics.[14] There were no sharp class divisions between Republicans and urban Democrats; the two parties tended to represent ethnic and community rather than class interests (Moss 1993: 411). From the 1880s through the early twentieth century, the working class divided its loyalties between the Republicans and Democrats, although for two decades after 1901, the Socialist Party drew significant support among workers and poor farmers. Native-born Protestant workers tended to support the Republicans, while immigrant workers, often Catholics from Ireland, Italy, or Poland, allied to the Democratic urban political machines that solidified in northern cities at the turn of the twentieth century. This pivotal division in the U.S. working class lasted until the eve of the New Deal, with repercussions that were detrimental to the development of class consciousness (Selfa 2008: 44-45; Davis 1986: 26).

As Werner Sombart correctly observed, Democrats and Republicans alike recruited numerous party activists from the ranks of the working class. To an extent unknown in Europe (at least during the early stages of the Industrial Revolution), promising working-class leaders were co-opted into the system through the seductive appeal of elective or appointive office. The absence of a national party identified with workers made it easier for mainstream politicians to act this way. The two major parties were often highly adept at incorporating the demands and the potential leadership of labor-based political groups, whereas the early achievement of political democracy gave workers a vested interest in the existing political order. Thus, national politics diluted rather than reinforced the class consciousness that developed in the local workplace and union. American workers, it is argued, developed a strong sense of their rights in both polity and workplace, but did not see the need for launching direct national political attacks on capital (Sombart 1976: 50–51; Montgomery 1972; Dawley 1976: 209–217, 233–239). The co-optation of individual labor leaders was facilitated by the transformation of American city government that occurred in the 1880s as an aspiring social stratum of Irish — and occasionally German — descent began to take municipal power from old Yankee elites. It led to a symbiosis between labor leadership and the patronage machinery of the Democratic Party. Beginning with the victories of Irish mayoral candidates in New York (1880) and Boston (1884), this new group of politicians was instrumental in disseminating a Tammany Hall model of political brokerage based on a captive Catholic working-class vote in major northern cities (Davis 1986: 32–33).

Significant third-party movements have generally emerged in the United States when certain groups or factions thought they were being ignored by both major parties — that neither party was the "lesser of two evils." After such political minorities demonstrated their support base, they always ran the risk that one or both of the major-party coalitions would respond by co-opting elements of the minor-party program or by nominating candidates who deployed an appropriate rhetoric of protest. Third parties have typically had the ambiguous experience of gaining some of their legislative demands while losing the basis for continued organization as a separate party — for this phenomenon Richard Hofstadter used the metaphor of the bee that dies after having stung (Hofstadter 1972: 97). For example, when the Workingmen's parties that emerged in the late 1820s demanded the ten-hour workday, major-party administrations of states with concentrations of artisans and workers (Rhode Island, New Hampshire, Maine, New Jersey, and Connecticut) passed this demand into law. More generally, the Jacksonian Democrats responded to the electoral success of this third-party movement by showing greater concern for the various reform provisions (aimed to improve equality of opportunity) of the Workingmen's program and adapting their politics in those cities where the third party had strength. But while maintaining a mass following based on near-universal suffrage of white males, Jacksonian democracy also maintained its reactionary, slave-based core. The Democrats' populist rhetoric of anti-monopolism and producerism attracted the "producing classes" (yeoman farmers, workers, self-made men, and immigrants) opposed to "parasites" and "bloodsuckers" (bankers, lawyers, and speculators) while uniting diverse Democratic bases with the slavocracy. The slaveholders in the South, in turn, had their own reason to oppose industrial capital, represented in the antebellum era by the Whig Party. In 1872, the Democratic presidential candidate Horace Greeley, social reformer and member of the pre–Civil War Fourierist socialist movement, undermined the effort of the National Labor Union (the American affiliate of the First International) to run their candidate, David Davis, for the presidency (Lipset and Marks 2000: 67).

There were times when Republicans stood for liberal reforms, as was the case with Presidents Abraham Lincoln and Theodore Roosevelt and Wisconsin Progressive senator Robert La Follette. But over most of the last hundred years—and especially since the New Deal era—it was the Democratic Party to which progressive movements have tended to look for support. This support has come with strings attached and without necessarily having these movements' best interest at heart. This history of Democratic co-option begins with what can be seen as a dress rehearsal for the twentieth century—the collision between the Democrats and the Populists and the subsequent transformation of the People's Party into a more conventional electoral machine. This led to a moderation of this party's radical 1892 Omaha program (and a campaign to fight for free coinage of silver, a late nineteenth-century panacea of middle-class reformers) and fusion with the Democratic Party, culminating in William Jennings Bryan's run for the presidency on a Democratic ticket during the 1896 election. Although Bryan lost this election to the Republican candidate, William McKinley, he won most of the Populist vote. The People's Party collapsed in the wake of this spectacular defeat, and the Populists would never recover as an independent party (Smith 2006: 48–49; Selfa 2008: 89–93).

Another eminent example is Franklin D. Roosevelt's successful strategy of co-opting in his own rhetoric—and, to some degree, in policy—many of the demands of various alternative political movements and labor-oriented third parties. He absorbed the leaders of these groupings into his following and turned several of those third parties into satellites of the Democratic Party. These were conscious efforts to undermine left-wing radicalism, to save capitalism. In a parliamentary system, those third parties could have maintained their identities more easily and entered coalitions with Roosevelt, from which they might even have emerged stronger afterward. But the structural constraints of the major party duopoly and the presidential system frustrated such attempts (Davis 1986: 69–71; Lipset and Marks 2000: 71–78).[15]

Crucial Changes in the Rules of the Political Game and the Pivotal Role of Money Power

The U.S. political system has been tilted in favor of business in good times and hard times. But corporate money has been a crucial influence since the Gilded Age and has obtained even more political leverage over the past thirty or so years through changes in the rules of the political game. This process was enhanced by institutional changes in the mid–1970s that altered the electoral and legislative rules of U.S. politics. In the aftermath of the Watergate affair, Democrats increased their majority in the House vis-à-vis Republicans from 239 v. 192 in 1973 upward to 291 v. 144 in 1975 to 292 v. 143 in 1977. This lopsided majority enabled them to initiate reforms of both campaign finance and the internal structure of Congress itself. Both were well-intended reform efforts initiated by liberal Democrats.

The drive to reform campaign finance was a response to the disclosure of Nixon's secret fund-raising of some $20 million among wealthy friends and friendly corporations. The Federal Election Campaign Act (1974) created the Federal Election Committee to keep track of political money, to establish public funding for presidential nominating and general elections, and to set limits on campaign contributions, while requiring corporations and unions to establish PACs to collect and pay out funds. PACs, which had been introduced by organized labor (the CIO) in July 1943, were now also required for businesses that wanted to contribute to candidates or parties, which most did. The overall effect, however, was to draw corporate business ever deeper into funding presidential and congressional candidates. Both the number of corporate PACs and the amount of total corporate campaign contributions increased significantly in subsequent years, greatly outspending labor and anti-corporate groups.

Importantly, individual contributions became the largest part of campaign funding for congressional candidates as parties, interest groups, and candidates learned how to collect large numbers of individual contributions through direct mail and later the Internet. Corporate lobbyists and others elevated the practice of "bundling," that is, collecting individual contributions and handing them in bulk to candidates, first developed by Mark Hanna in the 1896 presidential election to defeat Democrat William Jennings Bryan. Bundling became more important with the enactment of limits on contributions at the federal level and in most states in the 1970s. These bundlers were often awarded with honorary titles and, in some cases, exclusive events featuring the candidate (Moody 2007: 149–151).

All this corporate and pro-business money went not only to Republicans; Democrats certainly received their share too. In presidential contests, business funds did go disproportionately to Republicans. But in congressional elections, corporate and trade contributions typically went to incumbents in Congress, particularly those with important committee positions. It is at this point that the second reform of the mid-1970s becomes relevant. The effort to reform the committee system in Congress was intended to give the newcomers—a large part of the increased Democratic majority at the time — access to this organizational structure dominated by longtime southern members. However, this reform amounted to an expansion of the committee and subcommittee system so that more Democrats could become committee chairs, which also meant more incumbents for business to make contributions to.

For the better part of the last fifty years or so in which Democrats held a majority in the House and the nearly as many years in the Senate, they received a huge share of corporate and trade money. The percentage of corporate PAC funds going to incumbent Democrats in the House rose from 35 percent in 1978 to 51 percent in 1994. The total of corporate PAC money going to all Democrats in the House in those years rose from 45 percent in 1978 to 54 percent in 1994. When the Democrats lost control of the House, this amount dropped to 30 to 35 percent of the total from 1996 to 2002. For other kinds of PACs—trade and "non-connected" or ideological and issue-based PACs—the trends were similar, although less pronounced in the Senate, where somewhat more corporate and trade money went to Republicans (Jacobson 2004: 63–75). The result, as labor historian Kim Moody emphasizes, was that, particularly in the House of Representatives, labor was not simply opposing Republicans, but, since the mid-1970s, was competing with big business for the loyalty of Democrats with funds that could never match those from business. It is no coincidence, then, that the last bout of pro-labor legislation, such as the Occupational Safety and Health Act, was in the early 1970s (Moody 2007: 151).

Although the Republicans cut the number of subcommittees after taking over in 1996, the Congress of 2005–2007 still had twenty standing committees and ninety-one subcommittees in the House, along with sixteen standing committees and seventy-one subcommittees in the Senate. These committees and subcommittees are the channels through which legislation is amended, killed, or passed on for a vote. For business, with hundreds of its own lobbyists and thousands of "hired guns" to be had for the money, it was an opportunity. But for labor, with its limited legislative resources, this was a major challenge that its grassroots lobbying and district-level legislative action committee could not overcome. This helps explain why the neoliberal agenda laid out in the 1970s by the Business Roundtable had been passed down in detail by the mid-1990s, even though the Democrats had dominated the House since 1954 and the Senate most of the time. In other words, the system with its army of lobbyists with deep pockets was tilted against labor more than ever.

The problems regarding big business influence were further exacerbated by a few other factors. There was the growing weakness of the Democratic Party in relation to candidates that ran in its name. Increasingly, candidates ran as individuals with their own campaign organizations and raised their own funds. They had to prove themselves capable of raising substantial amounts of money and of gaining support from people in power. Fund-raising was put front and center of campaigns since the growing role of the mass media and the decline of the urban political machines meant that elections became more and more expensive and dependence on moneyed contributors much greater. Moreover, the exorbitant costs of elections spurred the growth of the Washington-based lobbying corps into a major industry. Campaign contributions buy "access" to elected officials, and if the donation is big enough it is typically the lobbyist who collects on the access promise. It is also in this context that the practice of bundling, coupled with the deployment of the latest computer technologies, became increasingly important (Moody 2007: 151–153; Kirkpatrick 2007).

These problems persist despite passage of the Bipartisan Campaign Reform Act (BCRA), also known as the McCain-Feingold Act, by the Congress in 2002. It was the first significant overhaul of federal campaign finance laws since the immediate post–Watergate years. In trying to address the flood of money into campaign coffers, the act prohibits all "soft money" donations to the national party committees.[16] Historically, "soft money" refers to contributions made to political parties for purposes of party building and other activities not directly related to the election of specific candidates. Previously these contributions had not been regulated by the Federal Election Campaign Act, as interpreted by the U.S. Supreme Court in *Buckley v. Valeo* (1976). The Supreme Court's decision held that limitations on donations to candidates were constitutional (because of the compelling state interest in preventing corruption or the appearance of corruption); however, limitations on the amount campaigns could spend constituted a curtailment on free speech under the First Amendment and therefore were unconstitutional. *Buckley v. Valeo* also held that only speech that expressly advocated the election or defeat of a candidate could be regulated. Thus organizations could spend unregulated soft money for a variety of activities, including "issue advertising," a broad term that included any advertising that stopped short of expressly advocating the election or defeat of a candidate through words and phrases such as "vote for," "support," "defeat," or "elect." Beginning in the late 1970s, parties successfully petitioned the Federal Election Commission for the right to spend soft money on non-federal party building and administrative costs. Soon, this use of soft money expanded to voter registration, get-out-the-vote efforts, and issue advertising. However, the BCRA also doubled the contribution limit of hard money, from $1,000 to $2,000 per election cycle, with a built-in increase for inflation.

An important consequence of the limitation on personal contributions from any one individual ($2,400 for each election, with a total of $4,800 for a primary and general election as of 2009) is that campaigns are more likely to seek out bundlers. Bundling grew in importance after the BCRA prohibited soft money contributions to political parties. It became much more structurally organized in the 2000s, spearheaded by the "Bush Pioneers" for George W. Bush's 2000 and 2004 presidential campaigns, and reached an unprecedented level during the 2008 presidential campaigns, particularly in the case of Barack Obama (Malbin 2009: 14–15).

"Soft money" also refers to unlimited contributions to organizations other than candidate campaigns and political parties (except, where legal, to state and local parties for use solely in state and local races). Organizations that receive soft money are often called "527s," for the section of the tax code under which they operate. Such organizations can legally engage in political activity, but funds from soft money contributions may not be spent on ads promoting the election or defeat of a specific candidate in the strict sense mentioned above. After the passage of the BCRA, many of the soft money-funded activities previously undertaken by political parties were taken over by various 527 groups, which funded many issue ads in the 2004 and 2008 presidential elections.

American politics continues to show the basic features of a money-driven political system that is the focus of Thomas Ferguson's "investment theory of party competition."[17] According to Ferguson, "rivalries and competition between major investor blocs provide the mainspring (but not the *only* spring) of partisan competition" and provide a better guide to understanding politics in countries like the United States than what he calls "the usual 'median voter' model." This is because "classical theories of democracy greatly underestimate the costs facing ordinary voters as they attempt to control the state" (Ferguson 1995: 379). Based on his analysis of New Deal case studies, Ferguson concluded that business elites, not voters, usually determine both the nature and course of electoral alignments:

> The fundamental market for political parties usually is not voters ... most of these possess desperately limited resources and — especially in the United States — exiguous information and interest in politics. The real market for political parties is defined by major investors, who generally have good and clear reasons for investing to control the state.... During realignments ... basic changes take place in the core investment blocs which constitute parties. More specifically, realignment occurs when cumulative long-run changes in industrial structures (commonly interacting with a variety of short-run factors, notably steep economic downturns) polarize the business community, thus bringing together a new and powerful bloc of investors with durable interests. As this process begins, party competition heats up and at least some differences between parties emerge more clearly [ibid.: 22–23].

Regarding the influence of the electorate, Ferguson has suggested that "only if the electorate's degree of effective organization significantly increases ... does it receive more than crumbs." Otherwise the situation looks grim from the perspective of democratic voter participation, because then "all that occurs is a change of personnel and policy that, because it may reflect nothing more than a vote of no confidence in the current regime, bears no necessary relation to *any* set of voting patterns or consistent electoral interests" (ibid.: 23).[18]

This investment theory of political change has become even more plausible after the U.S. Supreme Court decision in the 2010 landmark case *Citizens United v. Federal Election Commission* that dramatically changed the rules regarding corporate expenditures to electoral campaigns. The Court's ruling held that corporate funding of independent political broadcasts in candidate elections cannot be limited under the First Amendment. (The Court's ruling, in effect, also legalizes U.S.-based companies with substantial foreign ownership to participate in U.S. electoral politics.) The ruling was based partly on a reading of the First Amendment that assigns the right of free speech to corporations, judicially defined as "persons" according to the pivotal decision in the Supreme Court's 1886 *Santa Clara* case, which declared that the corporation should be considered "a person" entitled to the due process rights guaranteed to all persons by the Fourteenth Amendment (Derber 1998: 128–131). The Court struck down a provision of the McCain-Feingold Act that prohibited all corporations, both for-profit and not-for-profit, and unions from broadcasting "electioneering communication," which had been defined in that act as a broadcast, cable, or satellite communication that mentioned a candidate within sixty days of a general election or thirty days of a primary. However, the *Citizens United* case did not involve the existing federal ban on direct contributions from corporations or unions to candidate campaigns of political parties, which means that such contributions are still prohibited.[19]

The ruling was widely decried at the time; President Obama even directly confronted the Supreme Court about this decision in his State of the Union address. The Court assumed that "effective disclosure" was in place for the corporate expenditures it did authorize, in which it was wrong. An attempt by Congress to require public disclosure of corporate election expenditures was blocked by a 59–39 Republican Senate filibuster vote in September 2010.[20] It seems highly likely that this U.S. Supreme Court decision will greatly expand the role of corporate money in electoral politics, particularly through the financing of political advertisements in various electronic media outlets, and further increase the already tremendous power that corporate interests exert over the political process and political speech in America. Given organized labor's much weaker financial resources, it will not be able to seriously counterbalance this through its contributions to advertisements in political campaigns. Overall, this judicial intervention by the Supreme Court will certainly hurt the ability of political parties (such as socialist or left-wing labor parties) that on principle do not accept or by their very nature do not attract corporate contributions to compete in the political arena.

2

Organized Labor, Socialist Parties, and Early Efforts to Establish a Labor Party

Historically, a significant factor that may help explain the ups and downs of labor-based parties is the relationship between economic and political organization of working-class people. Although trade unions and working-class parties are separate organizations in Western industrial countries, they tend to be closely related. Unionization may, in fact, precede and support political organization and mobilization (Shalev and Korpi 1980: 50–51). This chapter focuses on the relationships between labor organizations and socialist parties with regard to various attempts to launch an independent labor party in America from the 1880s until the Great Depression.

The labor-based parties that emerged in the late nineteenth and early twentieth centuries differed in the various countries concerned. But what all these parties had in common was that they assigned a distinctly privileged position to workers in terms of their ideology and identity, their organizational structures, as well as the social groups they represented. This combination of defining features set them apart from other political parties. Most labor-based parties espoused a form of socialism. But in some cases—for example, Britain and Australia—labor-based parties were originally established without a socialist orientation, while in France, Italy, and Spain, anarchist and anarcho-syndicalist tendencies had a major impact. Notwithstanding differences in the specific content, all of these parties held a labor-based ideology. And their organizational structure assigned a uniquely privileged place to trade unions, which was manifested through the interpenetration of party and union organizations and the interlocks between the two (Bartolini 2000: 66–87, 241–262). In some cases the party dominated and in some others, the unions. In still other cases there was a level playing field between the two. But the defining feature of all labor-based parties was the central importance assigned to their organizational ties with unions, which were given priority over relationships with other organized groups. In particular cases, labor-based parties might appeal to other social groups such as small farmers or middle-class intellectuals, but workers always remained the most important group they represented.

A number of socialist and labor parties did emerge in the United States in the late nineteenth and early twentieth centuries. But these organizations never grew as strong as the labor-based parties established in the rest of the advanced capitalist world. The most important labor parties — the United Labor parties in 1886, the labor-Populist parties in 1894, and the farmer-labor parties after the First World War — were briefly able to attain significant electoral support, but they were not able to persist as viable parties in their own right. The most important socialist parties, the Socialist Labor Party in the late nineteenth century and the Socialist Party in the early twentieth century, were enduring organizations, but, with the exception of a few local successes, they were not electorally significant nationally (Archer 2007: 4–5). Still, good arguments can be made that the pre–1920 Socialist Party "developed a sizable, albeit minority, presence, within the working class" (Chester 2004: 209).

The Predominance of Exclusive Unionism

Each labor movement consists of some mix of two major types of unionism. Exclusive unionism is based on skilled groups of workers ("craft" workers) who attempt to improve their working conditions mainly by limiting the inflow of unskilled workers into their job territory (for example, by means of apprenticeship regulations). Inclusive unionism is based on less skilled workers who attempt to improve their working conditions by mobilizing large numbers to pressure employers and/or gain political representation. A distinctive feature of the American labor movement is the extent to which exclusive unionism has historically predominated over inclusive unionism.

Exclusive unionism was challenged for a time by the Knights of Labor (KOL), a broad reform and labor movement based on a loose alliance of local assemblies of skilled and unskilled workers. Founded in 1869, the Knights grew rapidly during the 1880s to include some 700,000 or more workers at its peak before its downfall in the early 1890s. The KOL sought to include workers at all skill levels across a variety of industries. They did not eschew American politics and considered political education and the exertion of political pressure on legislators natural growths of worker solidarity and the broad social alliance of "producers" (including workers, farmers, and small manufacturers), as opposed to the parasitic and exploitative class of financiers, speculators, bondholders, and capitalist monopolists (Stromquist 1990: 544; van Elteren 2003). In its early years, KOL's preferred strategy was as a "purist" organization to emphasize only collective action with a local focus — a strategy then also pursued by the Farmers' Alliance. The Knights refused to endorse any political party and largely ignored the partisan proclivities of its membership. Its premise was that members would exercise their rights as individual citizens and so as informed voters back candidates favorable to their cause.

But in the 1880s the KOL, in step with the Farmers' Alliance, shifted to a "friends and enemies" strategy in which it worked to elect whichever major-party candidates promised to provide the greatest support for its goals as a movement organization while maintaining the principle of flexible nonpartisanship. The Knights then sought political solutions to the problems faced by workers, pressing for various political reforms, including a graduated income tax (Grob 1961; Fink 1983; Sanders 1999: 30–31). In the same decade, local Knights and agrarian activists mounted a joint effort to establish an independent third party in the form of a labor-farmer alliance. In 1886, the same year in which the American Federation of Labor was founded, unions affiliated with the Knights and the AFL, along with various radical groups on the left, established United Labor parties which succeeded in electing several of their candidates on local tickets in eastern and midwestern cities. It seemed at the time as if American unions were ahead of those in Britain in advancing independent labor representation. However, the United Labor Party suffered from internal wrangling between Henry George, the party head who focused on the single-tax issue, and socialists. The expedient response of the major parties to enact labor laws that met several of the unions' immediate demands undermined the party further still.

As a movement organization, the KOL was highly decentralized and lacked the centralized control of strike funds of more durable unions that were being established in the AFL. The KOL was poorly equipped to resist an employers' backlash that intensified in the 1890s, and it fell in disarray under the heavy state repression of strikes. After the Knights' demise, the American labor movement once again became the domain of a small group of skilled workers, organized primarily along craft lines. As such it increasingly deviated from labor movements in other English-speaking and continental European countries. From the 1890s onward, unions in those countries became more inclusive as large industrial unions composed of unskilled workers expanded significantly next to older, more exclusive unions (Lipset and Marks 2000: 88–89, 100–101; Voss 1993: 277).

Several authors have attributed the absence of an enduring, electorally viable labor party in the United States to the weakness of the "new unionism." Proponents of this view usually make a comparison with the British case, where the rise of the Independent Labour Party was closely connected with the rise of the new unionism (Pelling 1963; 1965). In 1910, five of the ten largest unions in Britain were inclusive industrial unions (and seven of the top ten in Germany), while in the United States there were only two inclusive unions among the top ten: the United Mine Workers and the International Ladies Garment Workers. In 1912, these two unions and two other industrial unions—the Brewers and the Western Federation of Miners—constituted about 18.5 percent of AFL membership. From the establishment of the AFL in 1886 to World War I, at least three-quarters of the total membership of the Federation in any year consisted of exclusive craft unions. Due to the rapid postwar expansion of unionism among textile workers, steelworkers, and other workers in heavy industry, the proportion of craft unionists declined, but it still remained higher than two-thirds throughout the 1920s (Marks 1989: 88–89; Sanders 1999: 75; Lipset and Marks 2000: 89).

There are clear indications that the conflict among unions over independent political activity is indeed linked to these organizational differences within the labor movement. Powerful craft unions inside the AFL held on to the "business unionism" that dominated the labor movement as a whole. Industrial unions, which were more sympathetic to a class-based political party, remained a minority, albeit at times a very articulate one. They took the lead among unions campaigning for a third party and political regulation of the labor market.

Ethnic and racial cleavages also were a factor regarding internal division within the movement. At the turn of the twentieth century, American craft unions were dominated by second-generation Irish-Americans who often looked down on the newer Southern and Eastern European immigrants, Asians and African Americans who by 1910 represented the majority of the industrial working class. In addition, the hostility of the Catholic clergy to socialism was reflected in the political tendencies of the AFL dominated by Irish-American Catholics (Sanders 1999: 74; Karson 1965: 221–240). The AFL leadership responded to the massive influx of new immigrants by emphasizing its allegiance to an American sense of identity rather than solidarity among all members of a transnational or even domestic working-class alliance. Samuel Gompers and his allies strengthened a sense of craft unionism by distinguishing the "legitimate working class" composed of U.S. citizen-workers from the rest, thereby widening the gap between skilled and unskilled workers. In this sense, American citizenship was held up against working-class identity. However, the ideological rhetoric aimed at reinforcing this national-political consensus was often phrased in terms of a defiant Americanism that targeted the holders of corporate wealth and their lackeys among government officials as the enemy (Kazin 1998: 55–60).

Even though members of exclusive unions were often very conscious of their status as labor aristocrats, they did not dodge industrial conflict if their vital interests were at stake. Craft unions have been involved in long and bitter strikes. But their militancy was part of their struggle to remain above the unskilled proletariat, to preserve their niche in the division of labor rather than to abolish the division of labor itself. They were driven by the fear of losing their craft and being downgraded to the ranks of the unskilled.

In the period before World War I, craft unions in the AFL, led by the Carpenters, the International Typographical Union, and the Cigar Makers' International Union saw political activity as the strategy of last resort, to be undertaken only under exceptional circumstances. More generally, the AFL leadership recognized that workplace-related goals such as union organizational rights and the abolition of child labor required government intervention, for which they were willing to lobby and, occasionally, campaign as well (Sanders 1999: 30). To the extent that craft unions campaigned for legislation regulating working conditions, this was intended to complement rather than replace their efforts in the workplace and labor market. Craft unions firmly believed that they could achieve their goals through occupational organization in the labor market. It is in this narrow sense that they can be considered syndicalist.[1]

When such unions ventured into politics from the early twentieth century on, they did so primarily in self-defense. They felt compelled to engage in politics to ward off mounting threats from the courts, to counter the political mobilization of employers in the open-shop drive, and to restrict immigration. From the 1890s onward, state courts issued a series of injunctions against unions, restraining strikes on judicial grounds of "conspiracy." The legal instrument they used was the set of antitrust provisions of the Sherman Act (1890), which were interpreted by the courts to include union activities during strikes.

Before 1906 the preferred strategy of the AFL was similar to the "purist" organization strategy emphasizing collective action with a local focus of the KOL in its early years. In 1906, 1908, and 1918, the AFL deployed a nonpartisan "friends and enemies" strategy, as we shall see later. By the 1910s, unions in the United States, like those in Britain and Germany, were deeply involved in politics. But craft unions in the AFL, unlike their foreign counterparts, continued to hold a narrow instrumentalist view on political activity and to reject independent third-party endeavors (Lipset and Marks 2000: 90–92; Sanders 1999: 31). The AFL leadership's decision not to form a new electoral party of labor or to become affiliated with an existing third party was a manifestation of what has been called "conservative syndicalism" (Vale 1971: 26). Gompers's early philosophy was to confine trade unionism to the economic movement based on the conviction that any entanglement with the state would compromise labor's interests (Aronowitz 1998: 204–205).

Prioritizing Economic Strategy Over Political Strategy

Another significant factor that helps explain the AFL leadership's resistance to engage in independent party politics is that Gompers and his allies feared that left-wing factionalism threatened to destroy the unions. According to the either-or discourse that prevailed in 1894 during the debate about the establishment of a labor party, union-based and party-based strategies were seen as

2. Organized Labor, Socialist Parties, and Labor Party Efforts 41

mutually exclusive. Protagonists, however, did not always phrase their positions in quite such contrasting terms. At the turn of the 1890s, Gompers, for instance, still seemed to believe that a union-based strategy might prepare the ground for the eventual pursuit of independent labor politics (Kaufman 1987: 161). Occasionally, he even acknowledged that in Britain, an independent political movement of workers might be compatible with the maintenance of strong trade unions. Yet, underlying his position was the taken-for-granted notion that labor could only pursue either a union-based strategy or a party-based strategy, but not both at the same time.

This mindset was rooted in the ideological conflicts that beset the American section of Marx's International Workingmen's Association (IWA), in particular an American version of the debate between Karl Marx and Ferdinand Lassalle over the relative importance of economic versus political organization, which came to a head in the early 1870s. In 1872, following the European panic induced by the Paris Commune, Marx had moved the headquarters of the International Workingmen's Association, or the First International, from London to New York,[2] and the debates that were held under his auspices played a formative role for a small but strategically located group of American labor leaders. Those who prioritized trade union organization claimed to be following Marx's lead, arguing that enthusiasts for political organization were being led astray by Lassalle. (He maintained that it was not until workers had acquired electoral rights and used them to gain control of the state that trade unions could really benefit workers much.) Some advocates of political organization were indeed followers of Lassalle, but many claimed to be following Marx. As a result, the debate between these two groups increasingly centered on competing interpretations of Marx's writings. In particular, Samuel Gompers (who began taking part in these debates in the fall of 1872) soon became closely aligned with proponents of the union-based strategy (Kaufman 1973: 3–55, 131–135).

The ideological conflict over the relative importance of economic versus political strategy manifested itself in organizational form. The exponents of a union-based strategy formed the core of what eventually became the AFL, and the protagonists of a party-based strategy formed the core of what eventually became the Socialist Labor Party (SLP). The conflict was exacerbated by increasingly bitter faction fighting within the Cigar Makers' union in the early 1880s, between the AFL unions and the Knights of Labor in the mid-1880s, and between the leaders of the AFL and the SLP in the late 1880s and early 1890s (Archer 2007: 220). Gompers and his Internationalist fellow member Adolph Strasser founded the Social Democratic Workingmen's Party in 1874 upon the demise of the International Workingmen's Association. They emphasized the centrality of unions and came to advocate a form of organization based on the English "new model" craft unions. Their views would be picked up by the other father of "pure and simple unionism," Peter J. McGuire, who converted from Lassallianism to Marxism around 1880, after which he helped found the Carpenters' Union. Ironically, however, Marx and Engels were highly critical of the English craft unions precisely for the craft narrowness that Strasser, Gompers, and McGuire embraced as the recipe for stable organization (Moody 2008).

Gompers's and Strasser's transition from Internationalism to "pure and simple" exclusionary unionism is exemplified by their actions as leaders of the Cigar Makers' International Union (CMIU) in the 1870s and 1880s. This is surprising given that they began their labor careers by organizing cigar makers who had been barred from membership in New York's cigar makers' union by exclusionary codes and high dues. When their union, CMIU Local 144, was young and weak, the two leaders favored a highly inclusive policy that allowed cigar makers of all nationalities and both sexes to join. At that time the trade was rapidly becoming dominated by thousands of recent immigrants, especially Bohemian women, with extensive cigar-rolling experience, who therefore posed a threat to the union men's monopoly over high-grade cigar manufacturing. As production had moved from the factories into the tenements of New York's Bohemian quarter, skilled cigar makers lost their power to control the labor market through membership in their union. Out of mere self-interest, the cigar makers for a time became proponents of industrial unionism in the cigar industry.

This strategy was put to test during the great New York cigar makers' strike of 1877, when ten thousand cigar makers—men and women from various nationalities, both from factories and tenements—struck for the abolition of tenement outwork, but ultimately lost their battle due to the unity of the employers and the onset of winter. In the strike's aftermath a major rift began to emerge between the leadership and a large part of the union membership. Gompers and Strasser successfully beat back an attempt to steer the union toward adopting the party-based strategy. They moved to reform (and centralize) the union's administration and implement more effective business methods. The majority of the rank and file, especially tenement outworkers (who were mostly women and had become severely disillusioned with such trade union practices), moved into the socialist camp and pinned their hopes for relief and redress on the success of their independent labor politicians. Gompers and Strasser also looked to political action, but at meetings of the immigrant Marxists' faction within the IWA led by Friedrich Sorge, they had learned to mistrust the ballot box, cherished by the Yankee reformers within the International. Their goal was to protect the interests of the skilled hand-rollers who had chosen them to lead the cigar makers' union, not to build an independent workers' party. So, in 1879, instead of supporting their socialist members, they lobbied mainstream parties to pass a state anti-tenement labor bill, a law that if approved would drive female tenement workers out of the trade (Messer-Kruse 1998: 230–231). Of course, this lobbying was at odds with the resolution declaring that no union local "shall be permitted to aid, cooperate, or identify itself with any political party whatsoever" that the CMIU leadership had managed to pass (Kaufman 1986: 71–72, 139).

2. Organized Labor, Socialist Parties, and Labor Party Efforts

Gompers and Strasser took recourse to the same methods to keep control over the CMIU that Sorge had employed against the Yankees in the International. As part of the campaign to outlaw the manufacturing of cigars in tenements, the CMIU leadership tried vigorously to reelect the man who initiated the legislation, Republican Edward Grosse, a former member of the International Workingmen's Association. Members of the Socialist Labor Party in the union denounced the union leadership for backing a non-socialist for electoral office and demanded that association with mainstream politicians be renounced. Collectively they succeeded in defeating Gompers's reelection bid as president of Local 144 in 1882, replacing him with his Bohemian socialist rival, Samuel Schimkowitz. Gompers retaliated by running off with the union books and the treasury, while Strasser worked feverishly behind the scenes to annul the election results (on the formal grounds that Schimkowitz was an employer). Predictably, the socialist insurgents seceded and formed a competing union, the Progressive Cigar Makers' Union, whose membership soon outnumbered that of Local 144 (Messer-Kruse 1998: 231).[3]

The exodus of the socialists gave Gompers and Strasser the opportunity to further refine their business methods and try once again to build up the union through labor-market exclusion. They were able to do this by employing simple innovations such as the union label and consumer boycott. Within a decade the CMIU had been successfully transformed into a strong centralized organization composed of a skilled segment of tobacco workers who eagerly protected their labor-market niche against all other workers. The reality, however, was that about half of all cigar makers in New York were female and another large proportion worked in tenement shops or occupied the lower positions of the newly subdivided process of making cigars. Neither of these groups was allowed into the CMIU (Saxton 1971: 73–77; Kaufman 1986: 125).

Gompers in effect became the principal defender of an aristocracy of skilled white male labor. But this had not always been the case. Like the majority of the immigrant Marxists who surrounded him in his early years, Gompers adhered to the principle that workers should be organized regardless of their gender, race, or nationality. Gradually, he too reached the conclusion that this belief conflicted with the higher principle that the trade union movement was the primary expression of class conflict and the only practical basis for social and political improvement. Ultimately, Gompers deliberately tweaked his egalitarianism whenever the ideals of international brotherhood seemed to conflict with the growth and power of established trade unions. As president of the AFL, Gompers advocated organizing black workers, based on the principle that this was in the best interests of white workers, not on a larger sense of working-class solidarity or humanitarian principle. His line of argument was similar to that which the committee charged with formulating policy for the now-defunct National Labor Union had employed in the 1860s, namely that black workers posed a danger to the security of white workers, and the best way for white workers to counter this threat was to organize them into their own trade unions.[4]

Whenever the issue boiled down to a choice between the strength of the union and the higher principle of racially inclusive brotherhood, Gompers never hesitated to opt for the first. He did so in 1877, when he publicly advocated that any Chinese cigar makers who were brought to New York would be met with "violent action." Gompers embodied the hypocrisy of the mainstream American labor movement's attitude toward race, from the first convention in 1881 of the Federation of Organized Trades and Labor Unions, at which he urged all members to do their utmost to get rid of the "Chinese labor evil," through the early twentieth century, when he published telling examples of his racist malice, including *Meat vs. Rice: American Manhood against Asiatic Coolieism; Which Shall Survive?* (1902). As Gompers's AFL came to dominate the labor movement, it steadily abandoned women, ethnic minorities, African Americans and all those whose unskilled work gave them little power vis-à-vis their employers (Messer-Kruse 1998: 232–233).

It also took some time before Gompers abandoned labor-based party politics altogether. In 1886, he was involved in the campaign to elect Henry George as mayor of New York on a United Labor Party ticket that was backed by unionists and socialists. It was the most prominent of all the United Labor Party campaigns that year. When an attempt was made to establish a more permanent party organization in order to build on George's strong performance, a bitter struggle over the platform erupted between single taxers and socialists. George then moved to turn the party into a one-issue single-tax organization, and the socialists who had helped to establish it were expelled. In response, the socialists split from the Labor Party to form a second "Progressive" labor party. Neither party was successful at the polls and within a year both became defunct.

Similar problems arose in many other cities and states, where the establishment of a United Labor Party was also accompanied by intense struggles between advocates of different labor reform ideologies, which subsequently led to the party's failure and collapse. In Chicago, for example, a promising beginning was soon halted by fractious infighting. Here Terence Powderly, the national leader of the Knights of Labor, repudiated the party, which contributed to its failure. But attempts by Democrats to bend this party to their own ends also played a role in its demise. Ultimately, no fewer than three separate labor parties were established to compete for the support of workers in Chicago.

Gompers pointed to the conflict in the New York election as proof of the futility of forming a labor party when there were such great divisions between factions and solidarity was so weakly developed. Gompers became convinced that any effort to mobilize a young struggling union in politics would be disastrous, so he concentrated instead on union activity in the labor market, kicking the can of political action down the road. This approach led to bitter attacks by the Socialist Labor Party (and later by a number of leaders of the new Socialist

Party formed at the turn of the century). When in 1890 Daniel De Leon and the Socialist Labor Party insisted on affiliating with the AFL, this further aroused Gompers's suspicion that socialists sought to dominate the Federation and steer it toward political action. After Gompers's rejection, De Leon and the SLP went on to form a dual union, the Socialist Trades and Labor Alliance (ST&LA). It started, in 1895, with perhaps more than half of the remaining Knights of Labor's national membership and a number of socialists from defecting AFL locals behind them. Four years later, the ST&LA was crushed by the AFL, as former anarchists lined up with the AFL and a split-off group of moderate socialists joined them, leading to a division into two hostile factions. A contributing factor was De Leon's political rigidity that alienated him from many sincere union activists and more reform-minded socialists. The anti-AFL faction led by De Leon became a part of the Industrial Workers of the World at its founding in 1905 (Lipset and Marks 2000: 169–171; Archer 2007: 215–216; Buhle 1999: 58–60).

The AFL and the Movement Toward a Farmer-Labor Party in the Early 1890s

In the early 1890s, various developments combined to culminate in a new and unprecedented period of social unrest in the United States. Industry-wide unions of coal miners and railroad workers were established, followed by a series of major strikes in which state governments and the federal government deployed military force (state militias and federal troops) and local governments used police force to intervene on behalf of the employers, crushing the unions. There was also a sharp rise of agrarian radicalism among poorer farmers and sharecroppers, especially in the South and Southwest. Populist farmers established People's parties which made gains in several states and called directly for the support of organized labor. Meanwhile, the economy sank into a horrendous depression (Archer 2007: 14). It was in this historical context that the AFL came close to establishing a labor party.

In February 1892, delegates from several AFL unions, including the Mine Workers and Machinists, met in St. Louis with representatives from farmers' organizations and the Knights of Labor to express their support for the People's Party (also known as the Populist Party). The movement appealed most to economically distressed small farmers and artisans, and organized workers such as shoe workers, metal miners and machinists facing a similar threat due to the rapid introduction of machinery that undermined their autonomy, degraded their skills, and reduced their incomes (Rogin 1974: 149). In the same year, the AFL convention in Philadelphia adopted two planks of the People's Party platform: government ownership of the telegraph and telephone systems, and the popular initiative and referendum. The convention also instructed members of the Executive Council to do their best to carry on a vigorous campaign of education aimed to broaden the scope of the trade union's policy in the direction of political action. Gompers, however, flatly resisted Populism. He refused to have anything to do with the Farmers' Alliance and branded the People's Party as an organization "mainly of employing farmers without any regard to the interests of [agricultural wage labor] of the country districts or the mechanics and laborers of the industrial centers." He considered a union with the farmers impossible because it was fundamentally "unnatural." The agrarians, he admonished, "simply do not understand and are woefully ignorant upon the underlying principles, tactics and operations of the trade unions" (Gompers 1892). The position that Gompers took was clearly influenced by his residual Marxist view of farmers as "petit bourgeois" capitalists, thereby ignoring the plight of impoverished tenant farmers and debt-laden small farmers (Sanders 1999: 84).

At its next convention the following year, the AFL came close to establishing a labor political action committee along the lines of the still small but promising Labour Representation Committee in Britain. The delegates discussed a proposed "Political Programme," consisting of eleven planks, including demands for compulsory education; a legal eight-hour workday; abolition of sweat shops; municipal ownership of street cars and gas and electric plants; nationalization of telegraphs, telephones, railroads, and mines; the referendum; and even the "collective ownership by the people of all means of production and distribution" (Plank Ten), which was the most controversial of all. The program's preamble urged the AFL members to follow the example of British unionists in adopting the principle of independent political action. The program was to be referred back to the membership of individual unions, who would instruct their delegates on how to vote at the next convention.

During the ensuing months, the eleven planks drew support from many unions. Only the Bakers' Union rejected them outright, while the International Typographical Union was one of only two unions to reject Plank Ten. The favorable reception of the Political Programme gave a boost to those unionists who supported the idea of forming an alliance with small farmers, and saw the People's Party adopt most of the policy planks proposed, and then began to put this plan into practice.

Unions of miners and railroad workers were especially well positioned to provide a bridge between the labor movement and the Populists, since miners were frequently located in rural communities. It was not uncommon for farmers to supplement their income by working in the mines during the winter months, while miners worked in farmers' fields during the summer. Many miners also had close personal relationships with surrounding farming communities, which facilitated the rapprochement between their union and the Populists in fostering a labor-Populist alliance. Railroad workers were likewise located in many rural communities, where they too developed close personal and commercial ties. In order to run their steam engines, the companies needed to employ large con-

2. Organized Labor, Socialist Parties, and Labor Party Efforts 47

centrations of workers in junction towns, rail depots, and roundhouses, which had to be located at periodic intervals along the track. Although most worked full time for the railroad companies, some railroad workers—particularly unskilled construction workers—were also farmers or farm laborers.

The men who worked in the roundhouses and railroad workshops, the running crews that were based in them, and the construction and maintenance crews that moved throughout the region formed a significant base for unionism through much of rural America. Furthermore, a producerist notion of class was still strong in both the United Mine Workers (UMW) and the American Railway Union (ARU) in the early 1890s (as it had been earlier among the Knights of Labor), and both were prepared to embrace a Populist program, appropriately modified to include specific union demands. This is what both unions did in the wake of the disastrous industrial defeats of 1894. The Miners' president, John McBride, arranged such an alliance in Ohio, while the ARU became closely involved in a similar effort in Illinois.[5]

Despite this strong support for political action, the results of the 1894 AFL convention were ambiguous. Rather than submitting the program as a whole to a vote, the preamble and individual planks were considered one by one. With the exception of the preamble, which was rejected, and Plank Ten, which was amended to refer to the abolition of the monopoly system of landholding rather than public ownership, all the remaining planks were adopted. However, when the platform was voted on as a whole it was rejected by 1,173 votes to 735. The pressure for political independent action weighed heavily at this convention, evidenced by the fact that AFL president Gompers, who led the fight against independent political action, was defeated for reelection by John McBride, who had argued in favor of a labor party and backed the Populists at the elections in that year.

However, support for independent labor representation diminished as the labor-Populist movement fell apart, and the failure of the political program to win wholehearted AFL approval turned some leading socialists away from the organization. The 1895 AFL convention was dominated by "pure-and-simple" unionism again, and Gompers was reelected as president, the position he held until he died in 1924. With the AFL's position decided, the People's Party came under the control of its more conservative wing. The party then dropped most of labor's demands, and focused on the demand for the unlimited coinage of silver—presented as an all-encompassing panacea to recessionary ills.[6] The free-silver Populists merged with the Democratic Party, and a major realignment occurred in the elections of 1896, enabling the Republican Party to dominate national politics for most of the period until the New Deal (Lipset and Marks 2000: 100–103; Archer 2007: 15).

The political sociologist Robin Archer attributes the ultimate defeat of the Political Programme of 1894 to the sectarian styles of former and current Marxists. He points to the bitter factionalism of the debate between the two sides whose leaders had learned their strident "either-or" polemical style in the Marxist-dominated socialist movement of the 1870s and 1880s. The hostility of Gompers and his allies toward both the SLP and the effort to establish a new independent labor party in 1894 was in part influenced by a history of ideological and organizational ties with their very opponents. The key protagonists in the debate had once been members of the same Social Democratic Workingmen's Party, and their conflict showed all the signs of sibling rivalry (Archer 2007: 220–225). This may be true, but the unwillingness of the AFL leadership to take this first step toward a new labor party should be seen in a much broader perspective.

As Kim Moody points out, the whole project was overshadowed by the economic depression of 1893 that had reduced the unions' membership rolls dramatically. Notwithstanding the establishment of the United Mine Workers in 1890 and the Western Federation of Miners in 1893, and the huge Dockers' strikes in St. Louis and New Orleans in 1892, mass general unionism during this period was severely hampered by the depression, along with sustained political repression. In addition, there was another component of capitalist development that worked to the advantage of the craft unions, which was the protection afforded to the unions of building trades and local transport workers in the growing urban labor markets. Only the more conservative craft unions in construction and local transport held on as the urban building boom continued and their employment expanded (Moody 2008). Despite deep recessions, the number of construction workers rose steadily from 795,000 in 1870 to 2.7 million in 1910. These unions excluded most immigrants as well as blacks and constituted a solid base for Samuel Gompers and the development of business unionism (Montgomery 1987: 50–57, 176). This base enabled him to defeat subsequent moves toward an independent labor-based party. The survival of these craft unions further convinced Gompers and others that exclusive craft unionism was the only viable model of stable organization. So the playing field was heavily tilted in favor of craft unions rooted in expanding labor markets and against industrial organization by workers who were constantly on the move, frequently thrown out of work, and facing corporations whose wealth and power were expanding rapidly. But the relative abundance of lesser-skilled workers in itself also contributed to the predominance of exclusive, craft-oriented unionism over inclusive, industrial unionism by diminishing their value as allies to unionized skilled workers (Moody 2003: 354; Friedman 1988: 405).

Moreover, as Moody also indicates, the inability of the U.S. working-class formation in the 1890s to create mass, nationwide unions has much to do with the exceptional nature of the process of capital accumulation from the 1870s through the early 1900s. This process stood in stark relief to that of other industrializing nations in terms of the size and speed of industrial growth, as well as the geographic and demographic scale. From 1880 to 1900, the general popu-

2. Organized Labor, Socialist Parties, and Labor Party Efforts   49

lation grew by 51 percent, while the urban population grew by a whopping 174 percent. In the same twenty-year period, real gross domestic product (GDP) grew by 50 percent, while manufacturing output exploded by 138 percent. Unsurprisingly, the number of production workers in manufacturing almost doubled, while the value-added product more than tripled in real terms.

On the basis of these impressive figures, one might expect that this rapid industrialization should have laid the basis for mass industrial or general unionism. But the process did not entail a simple linear development. Every year thousands of businesses collapsed as the new trusts, cartels and (finally) corporations deploying new technologies and organizational structures destroyed old sites of unionism, creating an increasingly greater power imbalance between capital and labor in terms of organization and resources. Workers, millions of them first-generation immigrants (and lesser-skilled workers), were constantly on the move. This made the establishment of both enduring unions and political organizations on a national scale hard to achieve. The Knights of Labor and newer industrial unions like the United Mine Workers or the more radical Western Federation of Miners, which favored independent political action, might have provided the mass base in support of a labor party. But they were up against repression and economic depression, as well as the scale, scope, and spread of industry during the period, all of which made stable national organization extremely difficult (Moody 2008).

Other factors were also involved that stymied the establishment of a labor-based party. Since the dominant political order was incapable and unwilling to regulate the employers, it was harder to make the case for a social democratic or socialist party, which explains why a syndicalist perspective seemed more realistic to some laborites. As the historical sociologist Robin Blackburn has suggested, perhaps an even more important obstacle to labor-party efforts was the fact that the federal state was fiscally crippled, making projects for a welfare state impractical (unlike the social security system underway in Germany at the time). The Union's massive Civil War expenditures had been funded, in part, by a progressive income tax.[7] In 1872, the income tax was abandoned and, in 1895, declared unconstitutional by the Supreme Court. Ironically, the Fourteenth Amendment that had promised "all persons" the equal protection of the laws proved to be a dead letter so far as the freedmen were concerned, but the corporations—who had been assigned the legal status of "persons" in 1886— successfully invoked it against measures of corporate taxation and regulation. These developments might in themselves have increased the willingness of trade unionists to back a labor party, but this proved not to be the case. As we have seen above, many key craft union leaders had greater industrial bargaining power and feared that their organizations might be put at risk if they allied with those whom they saw as political adventurers (Blackburn 2010: 168).

Finally, we must note that during most of the period, a significant portion of the transient working class was barred from voting, due to lack of citizenship, strict residency requirements, and the emergence of disenfranchising rules imposed by racial segregationists in the South and elite urban reformers in the North. Notably, Progressive reforms ensured that much of the early twentieth-century working class was disenfranchised (Forbath 1999: 201).[8] Taken together, these were simply not the right conditions for the development of an effective working-class electoral strategy like that of Britain or Australia prior to World War I (Moody 2003: 357).

The Organizational Logic of AFL Politics

The chief purpose of making an independent political effort or endorsing Democratic or Republican candidates was to obtain favorable legislation. This was problematic since the American courts had decreed that many areas of labor relations were constitutionally outside the domain of federal law. This prompted organized labor to sponsor legislative campaigns in a multitude of states, which were likely to compete for industrial locations by denying labor claims. In the event that campaigns succeeded, the AFL had to apply constant pressure on executives to secure vigilant enforcement. Even when a legislative victory was won, the law in question could easily be annulled in the state or federal courts on the grounds that the constitutional right to contract was being infringed. From this perspective it made sense to union organizers to espouse a doctrine of "self-help," challenging business in the workplace by collective action there. Once the tenets of voluntarism were adopted, however, the AFL was locked into a distinct organizational logic that exacerbated its conservatism and marginality to national reform politics. At conventions, national and international unions were privileged over state and local federations, which were more inclined to political engagement, and the Executive Council was firmly controlled by craft unionists of the Gompers line (Sanders 1999: 73–74).

By 1900, the AFL and its most important affiliates had attained such a strong power base in many states that they were able to seriously weaken all attempts to organize the unskilled or engage in class-based politics. In other comparable countries, craft unionists existed who disliked political action and industrial unions as well, but they never established a labor organization with the AFL's power, partly because they did not achieve the centrality of the national arena in the twentieth century as the AFL under Gompers's leadership did (Olssen 1988: 435–436).

In eschewing national political-party commitments, the AFL leadership gave its local trade unions leeway to make their own accommodations to local power structures; that is, to form political alliances with city machines. In practice this meant that these unions could be Democratic in Democratic cities and Republican in Republican cities. Craft unions in decentralized and local-market industries—notably the building trades—had little interest in national politics.

For them good relations with city and state governments were necessary to enable them to control job access through favorable building codes, fire and sanitary inspections, licensing regulations, apprenticeship laws, issuances of building permits and conditions of work, and appointments of inspectors. Such ties also enabled union leaders on limited salaries to supplement their incomes by securing political appointments to city jobs or nominations to electoral office. The best practitioners of this pragmatic, local-oriented politics were the building-trade unions who by 1912 composed 29 percent of the AFL membership and held a commanding leadership position.

But this lucrative approach to local politics was pursued by other trade unions as well. For example, the Amalgamated Associates of Iron, Steel, and Tin Workers opposed independent labor politics in the core steel regions and exerted most of its political energies in support of the protective tariff, in alliance with the Republican Party. This collaboration gave a number of Amalgamated leaders the opportunity to secure political offices in Pennsylvania, Ohio, and New York and may have protected steel workers' jobs by limiting imports. Yet it also tied the craft union leadership to the great trust that decimated the union movement in the steel industry after the Homestead strike of 1892.

Likewise, the leaders of the four railroad brotherhoods formed an alliance with railroad executives, called the American Railroad Employers and Investors Association, to lobby against government limitations of rates and discrimination in favor of large corporations. In Pennsylvania, Illinois, and Ohio, the AFL non-partisan policy allowed leaders of mine workers' unions to reward sympathetic Republican politicians like Senator Marcus Hanna, with a reputation as an enlightened employer and advocate of cooperative labor-management relations. But the result of such relationships was also pressure to support conservative Republicans for Congress in opposition to labor tickets and to minimize labor struggles that might endanger Republican candidates. In San Francisco, building-trade unionists won local political dominance, developing a tight grip over construction after 1906, and creating their own independent political machine in the United Labor Party (ULP). This local labor government achieved considerable wage and hour benefits for its craft union constituency and supported some policies of broader interest to labor. However, the ULP only managed to do so through corruption, patronage, and campaigns of virulent race-baiting against Asian immigrants.

Because of its deliberate rejection of broad political organization of the working class toward local economic advantage, the AFL did not have the wherewithal to constrain unions' various accommodations to local political economy and ethnic group relations. AFL's policy strongly discouraged membership revolts against union leadership and refrained from interference in the internal affairs of unions. There was little chance that the national organization would step in to discipline union leaders who misbehaved, even when they accepted bribes from businessmen to pursue policies that worked against the best interests of members, or turned into highly authoritarian leaders. In practice, the voluntarism articulated by the AFL was not so much anti-political but politically opportunistic. The absence of a coherent ideology and political program allowed local labor leaders to make their own accommodations to the political and economic power structure, often to the disadvantage and discredit of the labor movement nationally. Needless to say, the hodgepodge of opportunistic, non-programmatic local accommodations and issue alliances made a large-scale political mobilization even more difficult, in the event such an effort became necessary.

As the slogan "labor for itself" of voluntarism became "each craft for itself" of business unionism, skilled workers' unions opted for what seemed to them the path of least resistance: collaboration with capitalists. At the top, AFL leaders set an example by joining the National Civic Federation alongside leading capitalists who repeatedly celebrated the merits of trusts in their declarations. At the lower level, individual union leaders were subject to the forces of the national political economy as the political significance of the tariff and other sectional issues enabled capital to entice a major segment of the labor movement, separating it from other political reform forces and ensuring its neutrality or acquiescence on regulatory issues. Preeminent examples are the metal workers who endorsed the tariff policy of their Republican employers, and the railroad brotherhoods who joined with management to oppose expanded regulation of railroad enterprise. Thus, by the early twentieth century, labor had become tied up in the political machinations of capital, in the context of the powerful polarization of American politics between export-oriented agrarianism and industrial capitalism (Sanders 1999: 75–77).

Advocates of Left-wing Politics Within the AFL

Between the 1890s and 1920s, many state AFL organizations called for independent class politics, but the AFL leaders became increasingly hostile to socialist or other third-party initiatives, especially at the national level. This strategy was partly a reflection of the leadership's recognition of the importance of ethnic political machines and local political alliances. But it also reflected a strong loyalty to the Democrats among many AFL leaders and even a desire to avoid antagonizing the Catholic hierarchy (Olssen 1988: 436).

Growing Socialist electoral strength from 1902 to 1912 went along with strongly fluctuating support within the AFL for independent labor representation. At the 1902 national convention, Max Hayes, a leading Socialist in the International Typographical Union, introduced a resolution requiring the AFL to "advise the working people to organize their economic and political power to secure for labor the full equivalent of its toil and the [overthrow] of the wage system, and the establishment of an industrial cooperative democracy."[9] It was narrowly defeated by a vote of 4,897 to 4,171, with 309 abstaining. The following year, similar resolutions were proposed but decisively rejected (Lipset and Marks 2000: 101–103).

By 1906, Gompers came to the realization that labor had to achieve political influence at the federal level or risk being crushed by the state at employers' behest. That year, the AFL Executive Council was panic-stricken by the Sherman Act, deployed to defeat the unions; court rulings under this law threatened the AFL's very survival. In response to increasingly restrictive court injunctions and virulent attacks by "open shop" employers (spearheaded by the National Association of Manufacturers), the AFL initiated a kind of class politics. The Executive Council urged affiliates to support labor's friends in the 1906 election, and, if necessary, run their own candidates against labor's foes. Many would have done so anyway but not at the Federation's instigation. Then a national move to align the unions with the Democratic Party began, as representatives from fifty-one AFL unions drew up a Bill of Grievances[10] and established a national organization to concentrate the movement's legislative activity. The AFL's focus on lobbying gave way to a mass mobilization grassroots effort to "reward our friends and punish our enemies."

Although the new national organization had the same name as that used by British unions—the Labor Representation Committee—the resemblance stopped here. The AFL participated in the election campaigns as a pressure group and, unlike the British Trades Union Congress (TUC), refrained from taking steps toward an independent party. British unions, on the contrary, ran their own Labour Party candidates in strongly working-class districts, while supporting labor-friendly major-party candidates (mainly Liberals) in constituencies they could not win alone (ibid.: 103–104). The TUC felt obligated to turn to politics mainly because of the *Taff Vale* decision in 1901, when the House of Lords ruled that a union, even though lacking a corporate status, could still be held liable for civil damages. Unlike the AFL, the TUC went so far as to back the creation of an independent labor party. But the Labour Party in Britain did not emerge because of widespread enthusiasm for state intervention; it originated in the desire of union officials to escape the encroachment of state authority they discerned in the *Taff Vale* ruling (Pelling 1963: 64).

In the United States, the failure of the AFL's effort to break Republican control of the House of Representatives in the 1906 congressional elections or to limit the use of injunctions seemed to increase the chances that a labor party could be created. After the Supreme Court's 1908 decision in the *Danbury Hatters* case, which ruled that the Sherman Antitrust Act extended to unions, even moderates within the AFL began to condone more drastic remedies. The AFL endorsed Bryan during his third presidential campaign in 1908 and publicly campaigned for him. In return, Gompers was vilified by critics across the political spectrum; Socialist- and Republican-leaning AFL members attacked him for not supporting their particular candidate. Meanwhile, there was an outcry among others over the propriety of his supposed attempt to "dictate" political choices to unionists. The upshot was that Gompers never again openly promised the Democratic Party that the AFL would "deliver the labor vote" (Cobble 1999: 193).

Afterward, Gompers and his allies in the AFL instead turned to more "elite politics," reverting to behind-the-scenes lobbying and high-level consultation. Although the AFL failed to get Bryan elected, its efforts helped energize working people, build an (uneasy) de facto alliance with the Democratic Party, and make the "labor question" central to American politics (Greene 1998). It took some time for many local unionists outside the South, however, to ally with the Democrats. Workers in the municipal building trades in cities like San Francisco, Chicago, and Philadelphia were accustomed to making mutually beneficial deals with whichever party was dominant in their cities. And a large and very heterogeneous minority of union members was still enthralled by socialist ideals. But after 1908, AFL unionists' predominant inclination was toward the Democratic Party (Kazin 1999: 190). Still, the call for independent labor presentation resounded at several AFL conventions in those years. The high point of this challenge to the AFL's "pure and simple" unionism coincided with the Socialist Party's peak in 1912.

Here it is worthwhile to pause momentarily to make a comparison with labor politics in Britain which initially had inspired American proponents of an independent labor party. The historian Ross McKibbin has argued that Sombart's question about the failure of American labor to adopt a Marxist perspective could just as well be applied to British labor before 1914 (McKibbin 1990). Before World War I, the British Labour Party (which was only formally organized by 1906) neither won a majority of workers nor was committed to the cause of socialism. Most British workers kept voting Liberal, and as late as 1910 the Labour Party (whose major purpose was to elect workers to parliament rather than to bring about a socialist transformation of the British economy) drew only 7 percent of the vote in national elections. In comparison, the more explicitly ideological American Socialist Party of Eugene V. Debs won 6 percent of the vote in the presidential election of 1912.[11] In that year, Max Hayes, Socialist and longtime advocate of independent labor representation, challenged Gompers for the presidency of the AFL and received almost one-third of the vote. Without ever getting a majority of AFL delegates behind the idea, supporters of a labor party found significant niches in some of the largest industrial unions (Gerber 1997: 259–260; Lipset and Marks 2000: 104).

Before the 1930s, five early industrial unions affiliated with the AFL — the United Mine Workers, the Brewery Workmen, the Amalgamated Clothing Workers, the Western Federation of Miners, and the International Ladies Garment Workers — provided most of the support for left-wing causes and independent labor-party initiatives. Together they regularly attained up to one-third of the votes at AFL conventions. However, in terms of their political tendencies, social policies, and organizational preferences, the continued agitation of Socialists and industrial unionists had little effect on the national direction of the AFL (Sanders 1999: 75). Unsurprisingly, Socialists fought for the introduction of industrial unionism as a general principle within the AFL. They were headed by James Maurer, the leader of the Socialist Party in Reading, Pennsylvania, and a prominent union activist. At the 1910 Socialist Party convention, he sponsored a minority left-wing motion, supporting the Socialist International's condemnation of "class collaborationist craft unions" and backing "Industrial Unionism as a principle and as an indispensable part of the class struggle without endorsing any particular organization" (Kipnis 1952: 238). He also defended the principle within the AFL and succeeded in getting the Pennsylvania Federation to endorse industrial unionism.

Next to the Socialist-leaning industrial unions, a few craft unions also engaged in independent labor politics. Various groups of artisans (especially boot and shoe workers, machinists and carpenters beleaguered by technological change and employer anti-union campaigns) experienced a drastic erosion of their skills, job control, and traditional work practices. The political engagement of these workers was to a varying degree a response to the failure of "pure and simple" unions to secure (and retain) a niche in the division of labor against the backdrop of dramatic economic-industrial change. Labor parties in the cities resulted from the activities of industrial unions and craft unions in retreat. In Milwaukee, the Brewery Workmen led the way; in Reading and Minneapolis, the Machinists; and in New York, the garment unions (Lipset and Marks 2000: 94). But the unions that provided the core support for class-based labor politics—inclusive unions of unskilled and skilled workers and unions of craft workers on the defense—continued to muster only a minority within the AFL.

Farmer-Worker Disconnections

Farmers and farm laborers still constituted a significant segment of the working population in this period. Yet persisting prejudice against farmers among the Gompersian AFL leadership stymied any further attempt to forge a farmer-labor alliance in the form of an independent labor-farmer party prior to World War I. A number of intellectuals within the Socialist Party likewise held the notion of farmers as petit-bourgeois capitalists. More orthodox Socialists in the northern industrial states looked disdainfully at the naiveté and religious fervor of their rural comrades within the Socialist Party. They were disturbed about the whole idea of socialist farmers, which they considered a contradiction in terms. Socialist organizers from the North who spent some time in the relevant regions in the Southwest soon came to a different conclusion, aware that these farmers did not belong to "the possessing class" (and certainly did not own the national "tools" of production and transportation) and that most had very low incomes. But many of the party's urban Marxists were never able or willing to adapt their ideological tenets to make room for a genuine outreach to farmers. Socialist theorists who supported the party's endorsement of "immediate demands" and a gradual transition to socialism did not act much differently either. At the Socialist Party's unity convention in 1901, the delegates voted 82 to 30 to include immediate demands in their platform, but they were seriously divided over a proposal to include a list of Populist-stamped farmer planks. The majority of delegates were convinced that every farmer belonged to the "possessing class" and that the interests of rural farmers and urban wage workers were by definition antithetical. Moreover, the midwestern and northeastern Socialists, many of whom were foreign-born, and the highly class-conscious Pacific states delegates knew farmers who were relatively prosperous, conservative, and often exploitative employers of wage labor (Sanders 1999: 62–63; Green 1978: 37, 45).

A group of southwestern and Wisconsin Socialists, along with farmer advocate Algie M. Simons, continued to lobby within the national Socialist Party for recognition of the farmer's plight and endorsement of programs geared to its improvement. But at the 1908 party convention, delegates voted 99 to 51 for a resolution pledging complete socialization of all land and urging the farmer to "study the economics of the cooperative social system." The 1908 platform was, in effect, a program geared entirely to the perceived needs of urban labor. It condemned private ownership of land and mentioned the farmer only once, as someone "indirectly" exploited by capital.[12]

In 1910, the southwestern Socialists again made an attempt to win the national party's approval for their farm program, particularly the one proposed by the Oklahoma Socialist Party, emphasizing that even the most revolutionary, class-conscious renters were "fighting tooth and nail to get forty acres of land." But most of the delegates opined that the southwestern program deviated from socialist principles, which simply required that "private property be wiped out for the farmers as well as for every other class" (Socialist Party 1910, qtd. in Sanders 1999: 64).

Two years later, the national convention proved somewhat more amenable to farmer demands. A new section in the platform's preamble acknowledged that farmers in every state were "plundered by the increasing prices exacted for tools and machinery and by extortionate rents, freight rates, and storage charges." The definition of "working class" was extended to include those who worked on the soil. And several farmer-oriented planks were added to the long list of immediate demands that constituted the Socialist Party's working program. One plank held that cities, states, or the federal government should take over all grain elevators, stockyards, and storage warehouses. The government should also take an active role in land reclamation and flood control. Finally, the Socialist Party program called for "the collective ownership of land wherever practicable" and, where not practicable, for "confiscatory taxation of the profits of land held for speculation" (Johnson 1978: 181–191, 207–211). However, significant parts of this "farm program" would already be abandoned by 1916. The election results showed that the program was not very competitive with what the Democratic Party offered the farmers. In addition, the Socialist Party in its midwestern and northeastern enclaves moved increasingly closer to AFL affiliates that continued to neglect both small farmers and lesser-skilled workers (Sanders 1999: 65, 71).

Labor Militancy at the Point of Production

Militant labor activism at the point of production was an important trend in the United States before, during, and immediately after World War I, and it was aggressively opposed by Gompers and other "pure-and-simple" union leaders. At its core were the direct forms of representation established in the workplace similar to (and influenced by) the British shop stewards' movement and the German revolutionary shop stewards. This current was widespread among industrial unions represented in the AFL and dominated in the early twentieth-century AFL's radical competitor, the Industrial Workers of the World (IWW), also called the "Wobblies."

The IWW, founded in 1905, emerged from the Western Federation of Miners (WFM) whose members were mostly immigrants from Northern and Western Europe. The WFM began as a conservative, job protective organization but radicalized as a response to strike experiences (Dubofsky 1969: 35; 1999: 368). What the IWW basically tried to do was to modernize the legacy of all-inclusive national unionism (bequeathed by the Knights of Labor) in light of industrial changes since the late nineteenth century. Its leaders called for the economic solidarity of all workers, which culminated in an attempt to create "one big union" of all workers, and envisioned governance of socialist production through industrial unions.[13] The IWW consequently adopted the format of a centralized union on the national level that could confront the centralized power of American monopoly capital. The central union would be subdivided into industrial unions to defend the specific interests of workers in each major industry and pave the way for the eventual takeover of production by those revolutionary unions. The IWW concentrated its efforts on economic action and organization while proclaiming its political neutrality. It prioritized industrial action within the revolutionary movement but did not oppose the participation of individual Wobblies in politics (Peterson 1983: 53–54, 58, 61–62).

Individual members of the IWW occasionally ran for local office, endorsed Socialist Party candidates, and regularly participated in "street politics" through free speech actions (Conlin 1969: 33; Kipnis 1952: 320). But they did not have any illusions that real societal change could be brought about through the electoral process (Dubofsky 1988: 83). The major value that politics might have for the Wobblies was in defending their presence at the point of production where capital and labor clashed head on. They saw the act of production as inextricably linked to the process of exploitation, and as such, it was on the job that workers were capable of mounting their most effective resistance against employers, by disrupting the exploitative process that yielded ever greater profits and power to their capitalist masters.

The key weapon in this battle was the self-activity of workers who deployed their collective power to halt production. Although the conception of the "general strike" was in theory part of the IWW arsenal, the more frequently utilized tactics included "soldiering" or striking on the job, slowdowns, work stoppages, sit-downs, and other forms of industrial sabotage. As the labor historian Howard Kimeldorf puts it,

> Such combativeness seemed only natural in a world that knew nothing of state-sanctioned collective bargaining, more than a decade before the establishment of the National Labor Relations Board (NLRB) when the law of the jungle still determined the winners and losers in most industrial disputes [Kimeldorf 2005: 547].

The Wobblies' practice of unionism can thus be understood as a kind of "practical syndicalism" (Kimeldorf 1999), which differed from the variety of syndicalism propagated at the time by European left-wing intellectuals premised on a theoretical antagonism to the state and a belief in the emancipatory power of the general strike (Conlin 1969: 9). Although both anti-statism and the general strike were part of official IWW doctrine, neither had any direct impact on its practice of unionism. Rather, the IWW's practical syndicalism was grounded in its rejection of the electoral arena as a terrain of struggle and a consequent privileging of the workplace as the site for class conflict (Kimeldorf 2005: 546). In this regard, the Wobblies were not all that far removed from mainstream organized labor. In 1916 the IWW even decided to stop using much of its revolutionary rhetoric in favor of a pragmatic approach that resembled "pure-and-simple" unionism in more ways than most of its members would have liked to admit (McCartin 1999: 347; Shor 1999: 68).[14]

It should be noted that the IWW never became a large union. The labor radicals and revolutionaries who united to plan what became the IWW had grandiose visions of labor's role and a belief in an egalitarian post-capitalist future very different from that of their AFL counterparts. However, only few of these radical visionaries remained in the IWW beyond its first three years. The very union that brought a substantial number of members into the IWW, the WFM, was already on its way out by 1907 and parted within a year. In print and speech, the IWW promised to treat new immigrants, non-whites, and women without discrimination and condescension. The membership of the IWW became increasingly more differentiated indeed to include native-born white Americans and Americanized immigrants from Western and Northern Europe (Irish and Finns especially), more recent immigrants from Eastern and southern Europe (South Slavs and Italians in particular), and small numbers of African Americans and Mexicans (Montgomery 1999: 357–358; Dubofsky 1999: 368).

But this should be put into proper perspective. As Melvyn Dubofsky points out, the founders of the IWW acted at precisely the moment that AFL unions and other non-affiliated "business unions" had completed the most successful organizing campaign in U.S. history, raising the number of union members from less than 500,000 in 1897 to almost 3 million by 1904. The International Brotherhood of Teamsters and the International Longshoremen's Association, both AFL affiliates, had more African-American members than the IWW would ever recruit. The United Mine Workers likewise organized more new immigrants than the Wobblies did. Moreover, the International Ladies Garment Workers Union, the Amalgamated Clothing Workers, and the Cloth, Hat and Cap Makers Union each had more female members than the IWW. And the AFL drew more Mexican-American and Mexican workers into its ranks than the IWW managed to do. On the other hand, the IWW was alone among labor organizations in welcoming Asian workers; however, only a few Chinese, Japanese, and Filipino workers actually joined.

After the WFM's withdrawal from the IWW, and prior to 1916, the IWW never counted more than 25,000 to 30,000 members; and at its peak between 1916 and 1918, it probably had just over 100,000 members.[15] Moreover, these numbers represent a highly fluctuating membership because workers moved in and out of the organization. There are two different interpretations for this revolving door. On the one hand, the tendency of workers to stay only a short time in the organization suggests that the IWW fostered only a minimal commitment among its recruits. On the other hand, the rapid membership turnover suggests that the IWW influenced many more workers than its reported membership might indicate, leading some analysts to claim that far more than a million workers passed through its ranks and learned a lasting lesson in solidarity (Dubofsky 2005: 538).

With the exception of the Western Federation of Miners in its early years, the IWW failed to win major union affiliates, although support was considerable within the United Mine Workers of America and the Brewery Workers. During its first two years of existence, the IWW was riddled with bitter internal squabbles, leading to stagnation. Its revival between 1908 and 1912 was due largely to the organizational dynamism that it developed among casual workers in the Far West (lumberjacks, agricultural laborers, dock workers, and hard rock miners), and to its strategic interventions in mass strikes of unskilled new immigrant workers in eastern manufacturing centers such as McKees Rocks, Pennsylvania; Lawrence, Massachusetts; and Paterson and Passaic, New Jersey; as well as Akron, Ohio, and Detroit in the Midwest.[16] During this period, the

IWW gave a clearer structure to industrial unionism and stimulated organizing along industrial lines in more traditionally craft-oriented unions (Stromquist 1990: 564).

As a result of vigilante actions and federal prosecutions (from July 1917 to 1920), the imprisonment of its top leadership and the criminalization of the organization because of its anti-war position and revolutionary character, the IWW was eliminated as a vibrant movement; by 1925 its membership had declined dramatically. But the legacy of strikes led by the IWW often resurfaced vigorously in settings where hardly any vestiges of the IWW remained. The cities of Lawrence, Paterson, and Passaic were all the scene of massive strikes again from 1916 through 1921. Workers struck in 1919 for a forty-eight-hour workweek with fifty-four hours' pay, manifesting a solidarity that matched that of the famous strikes of 1912–1913, while deploying similar styles of revolutionary mobilization. Strikers rejected the AFL, and many veterans of the earlier IWW strikes showed up in local leadership positions. Wobblies were also heavily involved in the great maritime strikes of 1923–1924 and the Sacco and Vanzetti strikes of 1927 (Montgomery 1999: 359).[17] The continued influence of the IWW legacy explains why Lawrence, Massachusetts, became by 1922–1924 the most important stronghold in the United States of the Canadian-based One Big Union (Goldberg 1988).

The Socialist Party and the Labor Party Question

This is the appropriate place to take a closer look at the ways in which various factions within the Socialist Party responded to the AFL and IWW and dealt with the labor party issue. The Socialist Party was formed in 1901 as a merger between Eugene V. Debs's Social Democratic Party[18] (founded in 1898) and a split-off from the SLP in New York, led by Morris Hillquit, who repudiated De Leon's ban on socialist membership in the AFL. Many in the Socialist Party rejected the AFL outright. Eugene Debs, the party's most prominent leader, had long fallen out with Gompers. Their personal enmity began during the Great Pullman Strike of 1894 when Debs, leader of the American Railway Union, called for a general strike against Gompers's wishes. Debs and his followers backed the IWW, when in 1905 it was established as a dual union competing with the AFL. Debs's membership in the IWW lasted only until 1908, but he continued to look for an alternative to the AFL throughout his career.

Most of the time, however, the majority of the Socialist Party backed operating within the AFL, hoping to move it toward socialism. Some major international AFL unions, such as the United Mine Workers, the United Brewery Workers, the Machinists' Union, and the Ladies Garment Workers Union, were influenced or controlled by Socialists. Throughout the AFL's early history, especially between 1900 and 1918, the socialist grouping within the Federation was the main opposition to Gompersism on all fundamental political questions. It was this faction that fought for industrial unionism and jettisoned the AFL's avowedly non-partisan approach to politics (Seidler 1961: 210; Lipset and Marks 2000: 171–172).

The Socialist Party was itself deeply divided between radicals and moderates, with the labor party being one of the contested issues. A third of the membership aligned with the radical left, and, prior to World War I, explicitly rejected the labor party perspective in favor of strengthening links to militant workers at the grassroots level. They were committed to building a political party that would not just focus on winning elections, but also would challenge the conservative leadership of the AFL in the workplace. Party moderates repudiated this approach, insisting that the Socialist Party should refrain from intervening in the internal affairs of trade unions, opting instead for garnering their support for the Socialist ticket. Moderates also stressed the importance of electoral victories in attaining the gradual reforms that would eventually bring about the socialist transformation of society (Chester 2004: xii, 206–207).

Many pre–World War I party activists were principally opposed to efforts to encompass unionists in a labor party, based on the idea that there was no need for a new party, since the Socialist Party was the American workers' party (Dick 1972: 62–64). Some went even further and denounced the notion of an inclusive labor party as a trap designed by the capitalists to halt the growing clout of the Socialist Party (Kipnis 1952: 125). The historical record shows several cases of successful Socialist opposition to such efforts in the first decade of the twentieth century, which were all driven by the fear that a broadly based labor party would not be radical enough in its program (Laslett 1970: 212–214). Opposition to the establishment of a labor party then became the dominant position within the Socialist Party.[19]

Efforts to create labor parties at the municipal level were generally seen as opportunistic (Shannon 1967: 16–17; Kipnis 1952: 427–428). Electorally successful Socialist parties such as those in Milwaukee, Minneapolis, Reading, and Schenectady were based on alliances with local labor movements. The Socialist Party's left wing found it hard to acknowledge that winning elections and holding office were not necessarily incompatible with socialist principles. They denigrated municipal socialism by dubbing it "sewer socialism," but the limited power of city governments offered Socialist officeholders little room to maneuver differently than pursuing short-term practical reforms, which they themselves were the first to recognize. Municipal Socialist organizations that managed to win office were often centers of opposition to the Socialist Party's left wing (Bassett 1973; Lipset and Marks 2000: 175–177).

There was also the homegrown socialism in the Southwest that had developed among agrarian radicals after the decline of Populism, and was further fueled by industrial-union organizing by the WFM and IWW. However, as noted earlier, attempts at creating socialist farmer-labor alliances were doomed to fail because the socialist ideology that dominated within the Socialist Party at the national level excluded the landowning small farmer from its definition of "working class." Except for a few years (1912–1916), its political program did not accommodate to this agrarian socialism — in contradistinction to state Socialist parties in those regions.

By 1909, the Socialist Party had grown to 40,000 members, with solid roots in several distinctive communities. However, socialism remained clearly a minority current within the working class and the labor movement. Most workers, as well as most trade union officials, remained attached to the two-party system. Increasingly frustrated, moderates among the Socialist Party leadership came to believe in a labor party as an alternative to an explicitly socialist party. Holding a reformist perspective, they envisioned a two-step process, beginning with the transformation of the Socialist Party into a more homogeneous organization. Calls for a socialist future would be downplayed, and the party would emphasize its support for a program of social reforms that could appeal to the craft unions of the AFL. Once this happened, a new, more moderate Socialist Party could play a key role in the formation of a labor party backed by a substantial segment of the established unions. This strategic plan took a small social democratic party in Britain, the Independent Labour Party (ILP), as its model. In 1901, the ILP, an organization of moderate socialists, joined with a coalition of trade unionists to form the Labour Representation Committee, later to be renamed the Labour Party. Importantly, the British Labour Party was a mass-based political party directly linked to the trade unions. It was originally formed on a platform that, by intention, was socialist, but it adopted only a vaguely socialistic statement of purpose in 1918. Shortly afterward the Labour Party became one of the two major parties in Britain; it would never be a genuinely socialist party (Chester 2004: 206).

Thus, influential moderates within the Socialist Party — particularly local leaders in New York and Milwaukee and a circle of social workers-reformers active in settlement houses in the larger cities of the Northeast and the Midwest — were intent on becoming a pressure group within a looser, less ideologically defined party linked directly to the AFL and its affiliated trade unions. Prominent figures such as Morris Hillquit, Victor Berger, Robert Hunter, John Spargo, Algie Simons and Job Harriman were convinced that this labor party would quickly become a major party and that Socialists would function as an important left-wing presence within it. However, before a sizable section of the AFL leadership would even consider such a plan, the Socialist Party would first have to be transformed, with its radical left wing marginalized and isolated. After having shed or at least contained its left-wing members, the party would be ready to make common cause with progressives within the AFL leadership to form a truly broad-based labor party. Once the AFL, or at least a substantial number of its larger affiliates, agreed to create a labor party, the Socialist Party would no longer nominate its own candidates but would act as a left-wing watchdog within the broader, new party.

But the Socialist Party leaders involved could not openly advance such a labor party perspective, as the overwhelming majority of the rank-and-file activists, whatever their political leaning, remained strongly committed to the party and were not at all interested in incorporating it into a broader, and less radical, political formation. Initial calls for the formation of a labor party evoked a series of hostile responses, not only from the radical left wing and its ally, Eugene Debs, but also from a renowned member like the journalist-social worker William English Walling who had little sympathy with either the IWW or direct action. Consequently, labor party advocates within the Socialist Party turned to the clandestine pursuit of their goal in the vain hope that their actions would pave the way to the formation of a mass labor party that could rapidly attract a majority of the working class. They hoped to convince progressive AFL officials to initiate a public call for a labor party.

Unsurprisingly, a furious debate erupted within the Socialist Party as these undemocratic tactics and secretive maneuvers became known to the general membership. Yet despite the personal intervention and official backing of reputed heavyweights such as Keir Hardie of the British Labour Representation Committee and Karl Kautsky, preeminent theoretician of the German Social Democratic Party, the moderates were pushed to abandon their project. In a coordinated attack on the left wing of the party, they did however succeed in having their primary target, Bill Haywood, leader of the IWW, ejected from the National Executive Committee at the 1912 national convention, which led to a significant outflow of radicals among the party membership (Chester 2004: 39–81). This seemed to ensure the moderates' domination of the party's leadership. At the same time, unions open to socialist ideas were gaining in strength within the AFL. At every level, opportunities for a new move toward a labor party opened up.[20] Yet, over the next five years, a series of events killed any effort toward such a formation, socialist activist and historian Eric Chester points out:

> In 1913, President Woodrow Wilson appointed William B. Wilson [no relation], a former secretary-treasurer of the United Mine Workers, to his cabinet as Secretary of Labor. Beyond this symbolism, Wilson did little to aid the cause of workers of trade unions, but AFL officials came to view themselves as insiders, with personal access to power. As World War I engulfed Europe, virtually every single union official, including most of the progressives, rallied behind the president. After April 1917, and U.S. entry into the war, the Socialist Party went from being a mass-based party with a significant electoral base to a hunted pariah. Gompers and most of the AFL leadership not only supported the war effort, they enthusiastically endorsed the federal government's draconian repression of the Socialist Party [ibid.: 83].

The Debsians within the Socialist Party continued to hold an anti–AFL stance. In 1914, Debs demanded that the United Mine Workers disaffiliate from the AFL and join a new industrial-union federation that would include all trade unions with industrial tendencies so as to transform the "reactionary federation of craft unions" (Lipset and Marks 2000: 171–172). But the Socialist Party failed to respond to the industrial uprisings of the immigrant factory workers between 1909 and 1919, such as those at McKees Rocks, Paterson, Lawrence and the great steel strike of 1919. (This also had to do with the Socialist Party's obsession with winning elections, and a tendency to measure the advance of socialism almost solely in terms of the ballot box at the expense of organizing between elections.) The IWW demonstrated that it was possible to organize these workers (mostly unskilled and semi-skilled). Despite sympathy for the IWW on the part of Debs and other left-wing Socialists, the two organizations took separate roads. Historian Eric Foner has described the fundamental problem of those years as follows:

> The militancy expressed in the IWW was never channeled for political purposes while socialist politics ignored the immigrant workers. Indeed, the Socialist Party's strength lay not among factory workers but in an unusual amalgam of native-born small farmers, skilled workers in certain cities, ethnic groups from the Russian Empire like Finns and Jews, and professionals and intellectuals.... [Its] thinness among the industrial working class was certainly among the Party's most debilitating weaknesses [Foner 1984: 71].

Third-Party Efforts and the AFL After World War I

The World War I experience weighed heavily on the relationships between leftist political parties, organized labor, employers, and government in the United States and Europe. In the war mobilization that occurred in Britain after 1914, the Labour Party often played a conciliatory role, while radical elements of the trade union movement more directly challenged capitalist employers. The Labour Party gained in strength and legitimacy during the war partly at the expense of the leadership of the unions because it supported the war effort and was seen by the Lloyd George government as a more responsible representative of workers' interests than much of the union leadership.

Conversely, in the United States, both the Socialist Party and the IWW took a firm stance against U.S. participation in the war and suffered severe repression as a result of their opposition to the "capitalists' war." The AFL, however, gained legitimacy because its leaders were willing to cooperate with the government's industrial mobilization (Gerber 1997: 265–266). This was the result of the bureaucratic lessons union officials had learned from the upsurge of mass strikes during the decade preceding America's entry into the war. Despite their minority status within the working class, the American unions had built an organizational network (including new forms of local and work-

2. Organized Labor, Socialist Parties, and Labor Party Efforts 65

place organizations) and enjoyed experience among workers that no other organization could beat. According to David Montgomery, their membership had almost doubled between 1912 and 1920, rising to some 5 million workers. This rate of union growth (92 percent) was about the same as that in Britain, which rose from 4 to 8 million members, overshadowed by those in France (143 percent, from 1 to 2.5 million) and Germany (188 percent, from 4.5 to 13 million) and dwarfed by that of Italy: 609 percent for the General Confederation of Labor alone (Montgomery 1983: 89). The war experience thus makes it clear that one needs to consider not only the strength of labor parties as a possible factor influencing employer attitudes toward collective bargaining, but also the relationship that existed between such parties and organized labor and the relative militancy of these two wings of the working-class movement.

After World War I there was much third-party activity in the United States as a number of labor organizations aimed to emulate the success of the British Labour Party in attaining a major-party status. The war experience revealed the possibilities of state control in various sectors of the economy. Industries of direct concern to the war effort, especially water and rail transport, the mines, and the telephone and telegraph systems, were brought under direct governmental control, and several others, including the ammunition industries, were subject to extensive regulation (Shapiro 1971). Several unions, including the United Mine Workers, the Railway Brotherhoods, and organizations in the needle trades came to demand the socialization of industry. In 1918 and 1919, the United Mine Workers and the Ladies Garment Workers supported the establishment of state labor parties in Illinois and New York, respectively.

At the initiative of these state parties, a national meeting to form a Labor Party of the United States was held in November 1919. Fifty-five affiliates of the AFL attended the convention, including the United Mine Workers, the Ladies Garment Workers, the Amalgamated Clothing Workers, the Brewery Workers, the Cigar Workers, Bricklayers, Carpenters, Painters and Molders, Bakers, Quarry Workers, Fur Workers, Glass Workers, and the sixteen unions of the independent Railroad Brotherhoods. The founding convention also attracted an unofficial delegation from an important organization of progressive farmers, the National Nonpartisan League. In an effort to broaden the appeal of the new party, the name Farmer-Labor Party was adopted at the national convention. The platform of the party consisted of a combination of liberal-progressive and socialist demands for equal rights for women, an inheritance and graduated income tax, proposals for federal action on unemployment, the eight-hour workday, a minimum wage, public ownership of the nation's utilities and resources, and "democratic management" of industry and commerce (Shapiro 1985; Dick 1972: 163–170).

The Farmer-Labor Party, with its primary base in the Chicago Federation of Labor and other local trade unions, failed to enlist the Progressive Republican senator Robert M. La Follette as its presidential candidate, mainly because he did not feel like running on a ticket that included socialist demands. Follette objected in particular to the demand for "an ever increasing voice for the workers in the management and control of industry." When the party leaders refused to budge on the issue, La Follette declined the nomination (Chester 2004: 91). In the presidential election of 1920 the Farmer-Labor Party received only 300,000 votes for its candidate, Parley Parker Christensen, a Progressive and relatively unknown Utah attorney, and his running mate, ex-Socialist Max Hayes. The Socialist Party, which had rejected an offer to join with the new party, received over three times as many votes (3.5 percent of the total) for its presidential candidate, Eugene Debs, who ran from a prison cell, convicted of sedition in 1918 for his anti-war activities.

The post–World War I endeavors to form a labor party were thwarted by the failure of all the efforts to forge industrial unionism in the basic and mass-production industries that the war had given a strong momentum. In addition, the older established industrial unions underwent sharp declines after the war. Both Socialists and syndicalists had pushed hard for amalgamation of AFL craft unions and the extension of the organization to include unskilled and semi-skilled workers as well ("all grades"), that is, industrial unionism. Toward the end of the war, however, a coalition of unions in meatpacking in 1918 and steel in 1919, pulled together by William Z. Foster (then a syndicalist inside the AFL and later a Communist leader), succeeded in organizing on an industrial basis. They were meant to be the first steps of an all-out assault on mass-production industries. But both major efforts failed, primarily for two reasons. The first concerned the quarreling and timidity of many of the craft unions that had initially joined the campaigns; the second was the racism of these unions, triggered by the "Great Migration" of African Americans from the rural South to northern industries.[21] These defeats were followed by either the retreat or complete collapse of unions in several other major industries in the aftermath of the biggest strike wave in U.S. history from 1918 to 1922. Total union membership dropped from just over 5 million in 1920 to 3.6 million in 1923. The AFL changed back to its core of craft unions in all but a few industries. The latter included the building industry, where unions even grew during the 1920s. For most of the decade the AFL craft organizations, with their conservative outlook regarding both internal and external matters, came to dominate the Executive Council and the conventions of the AFL, putting a heavy stamp on policy (Bernstein 1969: 86). The AFL repudiated attempts by radicals to join with moderate labor unions to resist the employer assaults on labor. By 1922 most leading AFL unions enacted constitutional amendments that barred Communists from holding union office and, in many cases, excluded them from membership (Aronowitz 2003: 66).

While a concerted effort to build a labor party lasted until 1923, its potential mass base had vanished by that time. Without it, there was no longer hope of breaking through the two-party system on a national scale or even in most states. In the presidential election of 1924 both the AFL and the Socialist Party backed Robert La Follette as an "independent." This was the first and only time that the AFL would support a third party. Two years earlier, the Socialist Party had altered its constitution to permit cooperation with a labor party. Morris Hillquit voiced the hope of many moderate Socialists that this marked the beginning of a new era of unity between the political and industrial wings of labor. Several unions that had been active in setting up a labor party in 1919 shared similar hopes. Both the United Mine Workers (within the AFL) and the Amalgamated Clothing Workers under Sidney Hillman (from outside the AFL) made large financial contributions to the effort (Lipset and Marks 2000: 105– 106). The AFL's tendency of jumping onto the independent political bandwagon while trying to steer it resembled much what craft unionists did elsewhere. But in countries where the unskilled were unionized, as in France, Britain, or New Zealand, workers proved more susceptible to revolutionary ideas, and this compelled most craft unions there to espouse revisionist socialism and a labor-based political party. That was the price they had to pay for survival (Olssen 1988: 436–37).

The Socialist Party's decision to support the La Follette campaign in 1924 was a major break from the socialist principles it had upheld until then. The Socialist Party had already backed the formation of a labor party, but this had been rationalized as support for a working-class party that could easily be transformed into an explicitly Socialist Party. La Follette's base of support rested with the small farmers of the Midwest. As an electoral expression of the Progressive movement, the 1924 campaign — even if it would have culminated into a permanent third party — could never have provided the basis for a socialist party. At this time, the Socialist Party was veering toward acceptance of liberal reformist politics; to legitimize this to its constituency, the party sought to link its electoral strategy to that deployed by the more progressive trade unions. This process began in 1921 when the Socialist Party joined with a coalition of railroad unions (led by Progressive AFL officials) in creating the Conference for Progressive Political Action (CPPA), and gathered further momentum during the La Follette campaign. It would crystallize during the 1930s, when the Socialist Party tacitly backed Firello La Guardia's campaign for mayor of New York (in 1937) and then joined the American Labor Party (Chester 2004: 207– 208).

But during the 1924 presidential election, the appearance of unity hid fundamental differences in goals between the unions and the Socialists. The AFL leadership considered their support of La Follette as a one-off to punish the Republican and Democratic parties for rejecting the AFL's Bill of Grievances and adopting tickets that were clearly unsympathetic to organized labor.[22] The candidates of both major parties were deemed unacceptable to labor and neither one could be considered "the lesser of two evils." Neither La Follette nor the AFL considered the electoral campaign of 1924 as the beginning of a permanent challenge to the two-party system. La Follette received five million votes or 16.6 percent of the national total, the second-highest share for a third party since the Civil War. (Theodore Roosevelt had received 27.4 percent of the national vote in 1912.) The Progressive Party won only one state, Wisconsin, and came in second in eleven other states, including California (Lipset and Marks 2000: 106).

With modest financial resources, La Follette had presented both major party candidates with a credible challenge. His candidacy could not be dismissed as isolated and irrelevant, as he brought a sharp anti-corporate message into the mainstream political discourse. From this perspective, the campaign was a success, particularly given its late start and the AFL's lukewarm support. But La Follette's campaign had been presented as the starting point for genuinely independent politics, so arguably from that perspective it was a great failure. La Follette had maintained his links to progressive politicians within the two major parties and had deliberately chosen to campaign as an independent candidate rather than as the nominee of a democratically controlled third party. Moreover, his coalition fell apart only a few months after the election (Chester 2004: 144–145). For most unions within the AFL, which judged the performance of the Progressive Party in terms of electing friends in high places, the endeavor was a failure as well.

For the Socialist Party majority, which had given unwavering support to La Follette, this third-party experience could also have led to a critical reassessment of the labor party strategy, as Eric Chester suggests:

> For the Socialist Party, the 1924 campaign had proven to be an unmitigated disaster. They had submerged their own distinctive identity into that of a liberal electoral formation, which had then disintegrated, leaving nothing. Trade unions close to the SP, especially those in the garment trades, had previously provided the Party with resources and funds. During the 1924 campaign, these unions had supported La Follette, and they were reluctant to return to a policy that linked them to the electoral fortunes of the Socialist Party. Unions such as the International Ladies Garment Workers Union (ILGWU) drifted into the Democratic Party, leaving the SP even more isolated than before [ibid.: 143].

Ultimately, the AFL unions had not gotten any closer to breaking their ties with the Democratic Party after the election.

Through the rest of the 1920s and the early 1930s, a few unions continued to voice their support for independent labor representation but never managed to gain the support of even one-third of the delegates at AFL conventions. The labor party question would remain a major issue for debate throughout the years of the Great Depression. From 1935 onward, the main sources of support for a labor party were located in the CIO, the newly formed Committee for Industrial Organization (later renamed the Congress of Industrial Organizations).

Implications of the Socialist Party-Unions Rift

According to Seymour Lipset and Gary Marks, an important negative consequence of the split between the Socialist Party and mainstream labor unions was that it severely weakened the party's membership and resource base, and therefore its organizational strength. Of all union federations in Western industrialized societies, the AFL was the only one that did not give its support to a labor-based political party. By contrast, Canada, Great Britain, Australia, and New Zealand had such parties that were eventually institutionalized with the support of the major unions. The Socialist Party was established autonomously from the AFL. It existed in isolation from the mass of organized workers, while the AFL craft unions did not involve the mass of unskilled and semi-skilled workers.

At the turn of the twentieth century, the AFL counted 750,000 members; by 1913 the figure skyrocketed to 2.5 million. The Socialist Party's membership never exceeded the number of 118,000 that it reached in 1912. The contrast is even greater when one considers that almost all unions built on occupational communities, close-knit groups of workers that shared certain norms and values. Some communities such as coal miners, for example, characterized themselves by distinctive ways of life. In the days before the enactment of labor legislation that enabled unions to legally enforce membership, the strongest unions were those based on occupational communities in which union membership could be inculcated as a social norm. The financial commitment (in the form of membership dues) of unionists also was much higher than that of party members. Undoubtedly American Socialists suffered from a split between their party and mainstream unions, given the latter's embeddedness in the working class, their extensive membership, and their relative financial strength (Lipset and Marks 2000: 68–71, 108).

This disadvantage was partly counterbalanced, however, by the fact that the AFL industrial unions and especially the IWW were much more inclusive than the mainstream unions, with self-identified Socialists in both. Several AFL unions were led by Socialists, including the Garment Workers and the Brewery Workmen. Many of the left wing of the Socialist Party sympathized with or had joined the IWW.[23] But the mainstream labor movement, representing skilled workers in specific trades and occupations, and the Socialist Party remained estranged for the most part.

In most industrial societies, workers' parties were the first mass organizations in the political arena. They sought to mobilize large numbers of supporters to compensate for the drawbacks of being outsider parties representing less privileged segments of the population. Labor-based parties closely allied to unions in Britain, Germany, Australia, and Sweden had human and financial resources at their disposal that were many times greater than those available to an isolated party. One effect was that the American Socialist Party remained a small and weak organization in an age of mass organizations and mass movements. In many countries, socialist parties once constituted a true subculture; they were part of a working-class community based in clubs, pubs, libraries, political meetings, and a diversity of social organizations, with labor unions at the core (Hanagan 1984: 32–35; Lipset and Marks 2000: 108–109). In the late nineteenth century and after, craft unions of the AFL (many of which were still linked to old artisan modes of production) created a somewhat comparable, albeit less inclusive and smaller, "working-class public sphere" (as Aronowitz calls it) through the "labor temples" they built in both smaller communities and big cities. These union halls housed the offices of affiliates of the local trades council and also provided space for routine union meetings, as well as public lectures and discussion groups (Aronowitz 2008: 228).[24] The American Socialist Party, however, was not part of an inclusive working-class community, except in places such as Milwaukee, Reading, New York City (the Lower East Side, Brownsville, and the Bronx) and Minneapolis, which remained centers of socialist or left-leaning third-party strength until the emergence of the New Deal and the CIO in the 1930s.

The absence of strong union-Socialist Party links in the United States also weakened class consciousness over the longer term because it undercut the possibility of a single labor movement that would integrate workers' economic and political concerns within one organization. The efforts of the AFL craft unions to segment labor organization into specific trades or organizations countered the Socialist Party's appeals to inclusive working-class consciousness. Craft unions attuned their organizations to the specifics of labor markets and pre-existing cultural loyalties and prejudices, especially between whites and blacks and native-born whites and new immigrants. Class consciousness was further weakened by the division between orientations in the workplace and residential communities. American workers rarely felt themselves part of a class subculture, nor did they partake in an encompassing labor movement based on a network of educational, leisure, and fraternal organizations reinforcing social class. On a variety of indices, including the volume and violence of strikes, American workers were as aggressive as—if not more militant than—workers in other Western societies in this period, but industrial conflict rarely deepened class consciousness. In the United States, social, economic, and political institutions undermined class consciousness by articulating the cleavages based on race, ethnicity, religion, region and ideology (Katznelson 1981: 71–72; Davis 1986: 21–29; Cowie and Salvatore 2008: 6).

The Crucial Role of American Liberalism in Co-opting Working-Class Movements

Last but not least, we need to consider the way in which liberalism evolved in America and responded to working-class and populist movements in comparison with liberalism in other countries. Throughout the nineteenth century in Europe and British North America, a rising liberalism found a natural stronghold among the bourgeois classes but was challenged by vestiges of declining monarchical power on the one hand and the increasing strength of working-class movements and organizations on the other. Occasionally, these struggles led to major political uprisings: in 1848 throughout Europe, in 1870–1871 along the Rhine and in Paris, and in Russia and various other places in the world between 1917 and 1919. Revolutionary communist organizations that emerged from these movements in turn evoked a social democratic response. This usually took the form of a labor or socialist parliamentary party, which was rooted in working-class politics and even influenced by Marxist ideas, and sought nonrevolutionary means to articulate working-class people's political aspirations.

Liberals found themselves caught between the new politics and the old, and their response to this challenge was neither uniform nor consistent. A certain liberal reformism at the end of the nineteenth century simultaneously reasserted its eighteenth-century roots and gravitated toward the petit bourgeoisie — rural or urban — as an alternative to the old aristocracy on one side and the socialists on the other. Liberalism in Europe remade itself between the two poles of Toryism (or its continental European counterparts) and social democracy, in some countries also vis-à-vis Catholic or Protestant social movements, unions, and workers' associations. In the United States, however, the social democratic impulse did not win enough support to become institutionalized in national politics. The Populist tradition also lacked sufficient political leverage to be able to act as a progressive force at the national level. Social democracy in America was so heavily suppressed as to be unable to do what it did elsewhere, that is, to incorporate working-class revolt into parliamentary politics. Instead it was liberalism, emerging from a patrician Progressivism, that co-opted working-class and populist movements into the sphere of congressional politics and governmental bureaucracy. This liberalism went into defensive mode, becoming an antidote to leftist tendencies. While immediately before World War I, the (largely Republican) Progressive movement led by Robert La Follette and Theodore Roosevelt had drawn significant support, it was Woodrow Wilson who became the leading exponent of this newly transformed liberalism. While he fought the monopoly trusts in the early twentieth century, he was also a determined opponent of socialism. This liberalism was quite at home with racism and class exploitation but responded to political pressures when deemed necessary (such as in the granting of female suffrage).

Liberalism came to play a pivotal, dual role of co-opting any progressive urge among the multiracial working class and repressing the same force when it turned into too much of a challenge to the power of capital or the liberal state. The true nature of this form of liberalism became apparent during and after World War I when President Wilson fought conservatives in the Senate to establish a League of Nations while at the same time his administration attacked socialists in the street and organized repressive detention against workers and labor organizers, as well as immigrants suspected of being in league with the enemy, deporting 2,500 American "reds" to Russia (Smith 2005: 36–39).

On the other hand, both left-wing Progressives and New Deal liberals had no qualms about working with Socialists such as Mother Jones, Florence Kelley, and Sidney Hillman, to their mutual benefit (Kazin 1995: 1510). After World War I, left-leaning Progressives (or "liberals" as they increasingly called themselves in the 1920s) took an active part in the construction of a progressive Americanism through popularizing the phrase "industrial democracy." Initially, they had been inclined to look sympathetically at the new forms of democratic governance that seemed to be emerging in revolutionary Russia. These liberals thought they had found an exciting version of extra-parliamentary, direct democracy in the form of "workers' control" in the "soviet." And they quickly began calling for a similar extension of the principles of political democracy to economic life in America. However, when the iron grip of Bolshevik control made the soviets increasingly appear too risky to experiment with in American circumstances, these liberals (spearheaded by Herbert Croly and his *New Republic* intellectual circle) turned toward the less radical form of industrial democracy advocated by British guild socialists such as Harold Laski and G.D.H. Cole and, from 1918 onward, by the British Labour Party itself. A series of strikes by American workers in 1919 struck these liberals with fear and made them more enthusiastic about the British way, as it seemed to them the only option that could possibly prevent a Bolshevik-style revolution in the United States (Gerstle 1994: 1053–1054).[25] It remains true, however, that a substantial part of liberal reform was deliberately designed to prevent or counter socialism, as we shall see in the next chapter.

3

Labor and the Left During the New Deal and the Onset of the Cold War

The New Deal was much indebted to the Progressive movement's strain of liberalism and not based on socialist principles by any stretch of the imagination. President Franklin Delano Roosevelt wanted to maintain a capitalist economy.[1] The New Deal did not transform American capitalism in any profound way. But the New Deal did drastically increase the statist element in American politics and gave further public support to the trade unions. A strong emphasis was placed on planning, the creation of basic welfare provisions, and on the role of the government as a major regulatory agency. This is why Richard Hofstadter concluded in his historical overview that this period brought a "social democratic tinge" to the United States for the first time in its history (Hofstadter 1972: 308). The government was now committed to providing at least minimal assistance to the poor, the unemployed, and the elderly. It also moved to protect the rights of workers and unions, stabilize the banking system, regulate the financial markets, and subsidize agricultural production, and it adopted many more tasks that had previously not fallen under the remit of the federal government.

As a result of the New Deal, American political and economic life changed considerably due to the increased opportunities for workers, farmers, consumers and others to press their demands upon the government, opportunities that in the past had been available only to corporate business. In this regard, the government acted as what has frequently been described as a "broker state," a state brokering the claims of numerous groups. The New Deal also literally transformed the American landscape through its vast public works and infrastructure projects. Ultimately, the New Deal drastically altered economic policy with its commitment to massive public spending as an antidote to recession, but this was only near its end. And the New Deal's most innovative projects, including work relief programs, community and national planning initiatives, community-building efforts, and public works agencies, did not survive the war (Brinkley 1998: 33–35).

A pervasive fragmentation of collective class identity remained a basic feature of American political life. Yet during the Great Depression, white working people coalesced into a coalition that would bring about a major breakthrough in collective working-class politics and organization. Several factors facilitated this development. Working people (including many second-generation "new immigrants"), attracted by an increasingly homogeneous popular culture, slowly ventured beyond their separate enclaves as their ethnic loyalties were no longer reinforced yearly after the Immigration Act of 1924 and ethnic welfare resources were exhausted. Group identity was also restructured due to the reorganization of production over the previous four decades through the introduction of Taylorist, Fordist, and other "rationalized" systems. Importantly, the distinction between skilled and unskilled workers leveled with the emergence of a broad category consisting of large numbers of semi-skilled workers. At the same time, the experience of welfare capitalism in the 1920s, in which employers provided social programs and benefits in lieu of union representation, broadened workers' conception of their rights in the wake of that system's breakdown early in the Depression. This, coupled with the severity of the Great Depression, helped foster a general sense of a shared fate and even national destiny.

Two additional transformations in the early years of the New Deal contributed to the breakthrough in collective working-class organization. New union leadership, committed to industrial unionism and militant tactics against management, sought to organize all workers in a given industry, including at times women and African Americans. (Although the war years brought a great influx of blacks and women into the working class, this did not lead to a significant integration of these newcomers into the class-conscious working class or its institutions.) [2] There was also the important role of government. For the first time in U.S. history, the federal government actively supported the right of working people to organize collectively to achieve their goals. The National Labor Relations Act (or Wagner Act) codified the right to organize and provided rules of conduct for, and oversight of, union elections (Cowie and Salvatore 2008: 6–8). This unprecedented set of legal protections was a double-edged sword, however, as we shall see later.

Section 7(a) of the National Industrial Recovery Act and Industrial Unions' Organizing Campaign

The New Deal's reorganization of the economy was aimed mainly at overcoming the immediate economic crisis and stabilizing the capitalist economy.

But it was also meant to quell the alarming growth of grassroots rebellion in the early years of the Roosevelt administration — organizations of tenants and the unemployed, movements of self-help, mass demonstrations, factory occupations and general strikes in several cities. The New Deal measures in this regard were aimed at giving enough relief to the lower classes to keep them from turning these rebellions into a full-fledged revolution. The creation of a so-called second New Deal, the expansion of the social wage (moving toward state-financed benefits such as pensions, unemployment insurance, and health care programs that comprise the modern welfare state), was foremost instigated by the industrial rebellions of the first half of the 1930s. This prompted "an extraordinary wave of social reform," beginning in 1935, from "a reluctant Roosevelt administration" (Aronowitz 2003: 77).

The 1933 National Industrial Recovery Act (NIRA) gave the federal government a mandate to play a more active role in achieving an economic recovery that market forces alone seemed unable to bring about. The National Recovery Administration (NRA) was designed to take control of the economy through a series of cartel-like trade codes agreed upon by management, labor, and the government, thereby fixing prices and wages, and limiting competition. But the NRA was dominated by corporate businesses and foremost served their interests. Consumers and members of the trade unions had little say in the organization of the NRA, or the formulation of basic policy.

The first two years of the first New Deal, 1933 and 1934, looked more like the pattern of the 1920s, when conservative national governments (lastly, the Hoover administration) had consistently ignored labor's calls for industrial justice. However, under pressure, the president had included Section 7(a) in the NIRA that recognized workers' right to organize unions "of their own choosing," but this was a non-enforceable provision. Only where organized labor was strong were concessions made to working people. In other cases, the Roosevelt administration could not withstand the pressures of industrial representatives to control the NRA codes (Preis 1972).

Both Socialists and Communists likened this first New Deal system to corporatism, the leading doctrine underlying fascist labor relations policy. Corporatism suppresses the structural antagonism between workers and employers and aims to defuse working-class discontent by incorporating workers into a program of cooperation between labor and capital. The industry boards under NIRA pitted a powerful association of employers that virtually set the terms of cooperation against a divided and largely disorganized labor movement.

Nevertheless, the leaders of some of the more viable industrial unions seized on Section 7(a) of the NIRA to launch a major organizing campaign across the country, in the coal fields, men's and women's apparel industries, and textiles. This resulted in the largest number of strikes since World War I and a dramatic increase in union membership. In the Northeast, some organizers ran the slogan "The President Wants You to Join the Union," which was a foreshadowing of the coming alliance between the new industrial unions, the Congress of Industrial Organizations (CIO), and the New Deal. The National Labor Relations Act that Congress passed in 1935 aimed to stabilize the social system in the face of labor unrest (Aronowitz 2003: 77–78; Goldfield 1989: 1273).

New Moves Toward a Labor Party Halted by the New Deal Coalition

Meanwhile, a new movement to create a labor party took shape among militant rank-and-file union activists who were less loyal to the Democrats or even to Franklin Roosevelt. Calls for an independent labor party reflected a newly confident working-class desire to fight on its own.[3] But they were also a response to the strikebreaking tactics that unions had faced under even the most liberal, pro-New Deal Democratic Party state and local governments. In the aftermath of the 1934 general textile strike in the South and New England, bloodily broken by militia called out by Democratic governors in twelve states, United Textile Workers leader Frank Gorman proposed one of a total of thirteen labor party resolutions at the 1935 AFL convention. (Ironically, Gorman helped to defeat the textile strike, but his experiences convinced him that a labor party was essential.) Despite considerable bureaucratic pressure by AFL leaders, his resolution lost by only four votes, 108 to 104 (Smith 2006: 105–106).

This pro-labor party sentiment threatened Roosevelt's and his secretary of labor Frances Perkins's plan to incorporate the labor movement into the New Deal coalition and defuse class struggle through its labor-relations machinery. Until the middle of 1935, Roosevelt had managed to draw support both from the majority of the unions and from the so-called "progressive" wing of corporate businesses (including the top managers of large corporations such as General Electric, U.S. Steel, the Rockefeller Standard Oil trust, and even the president of the U.S. Chamber of Commerce). He managed to create this fraught alliance by offering the AFL a more or less pro-union interpretation of the NRA codes in lighter, northern industries, as well as energetic relief measures. To big business, on the other hand, Roosevelt ceded an interpretation of the NRA codes in heavy industries that buttressed the company unions that had been installed to block genuine union organization.

This political maneuvering worked only for a time, as rank-and-file insurgency in the plants continued to grow despite the NRA codes, and corporations began to rethink their support for the New Deal. With a weakened base of business support (temporarily composed of anti–Wall Street segments of western and southern businesses), Roosevelt needed the powerful electoral support afforded by the influx of four million workers into the CIO during 1935–1937.

3. Labor and the Left During the New Deal and the Cold War

The mass desertion of business from the Roosevelt administration in 1935 pushed Roosevelt temporarily to seek the help of John L. Lewis and Sidney Hillman.[4] They, in turn, expected to benefit from the charisma of Roosevelt's backing and his political-judicial help to contain the rank-and-file CIO membership (Davis 1986: 62–63; Smith 2006: 117–119).

Thus, Lewis and Hillman pledged to throw CIO support behind Roosevelt in the 1936 election. For this political fix it was necessary to suppress pro-labor party sentiment among CIO members. This occurred within the context of their plan to dam the wave of rank-and-file labor militancy (led by defiant, often clandestine plant committees, autonomous from any of the official union apparatuses) that had developed in major manufacturing industries—auto, rubber, and electrical. This bottom-up movement with rudimentary tendencies toward an anti–Gompersian model of "class struggle unionism" carried the first CIO upsurge. It began with the "NRA" strikes following the passage of the 1933 National Industrial Recovery Act and would culminate in the sit-down strike wave of winter/spring 1936–1937.[5]

In their dealings with these labor insurgencies, Lewis and Hillman followed Lewis's own United Mine Workers' model of industrial unionism, characterized by tight central control, limited local autonomy, minimized rank-and-file participation and exclusion of radicals. Where industry-wide organization of shop committees or union nuclei were non-existent, as in steel and meatpacking, this structure was summarily put into place. Both the Steel and Packinghouse Workers' Organizing Committees (SWOC and PWOC) were strictly top-down operations, led by handpicked union officials (compliant to Lewis) who replaced existing local leadership. In industries where such a move was not possible (that is, where some form of national framework already existed, as in auto, rubber, electrical, and oil), Lewis created a dual structure of field representation and regional directors. The CIO staff worked closely together with New Deal officials to promote "responsible" regional settlements and to suppress the then-frequent use of the sit-down strike (Davis 1986: 55–56, 66–67).

In April 1936, Lewis initiated the formation of the Labor Nonpartisan League (LNPL), presented by its founders as a significant step in the direction of forming a labor party. But in reality this organization was nothing of the kind. It was primarily created to strengthen Roosevelt's reelection bid (to mobilize support and help in campaign financing), although it was also meant as the institutional instrument to exert union pressure on the Democratic Party. The union leaders also resorted to using vague threats that they would break away from the two-party system should the Democrats continue to ignore their concerns. But these threats were merely bluff, since the CIO leaders had no intention of breaking with the New Deal coalition. On the contrary, they saw President Roosevelt as a pivotal ally, and, as they publicly admitted afterward, their singular goal was to "reelect Franklin Delano Roosevelt." But in the same year (1936), the United Auto Workers (UAW) convention voted unanimously to actively support the establishment of a national farmer-labor party. Even more importantly, UAW delegates voted down a resolution supporting Roosevelt for president. CIO leaders threatened to remove funding for organizing the rest of the auto industry if the UAW did not rescind the vote and support Roosevelt. This intimidation proved effective, and the UAW delegates caved in at this crucial turning point, quickly passing a new motion in support of Roosevelt (Smith 2006: 121).

Other union leaders were just as cunning in gaining working-class votes for Roosevelt's reelection. Worried that socialist traditions among New York's garment workers would prevent them from voting Democrat, Hillman, leader of the Amalgamated Clothing Workers, led the formation of the American Labor Party (ALP) by the New York affiliate of the Labor Nonpartisan League in July 1936. Although its name suggested it was both national in scope and nonpartisan, in reality, the American Labor Party was neither. It operated almost exclusively in the state of New York in order to provide a more acceptable ballot line for socialists in local labor circles who voted for this "labor party" which actually funneled votes to Roosevelt. (When Hillman brought the idea to the board of his own union, he deployed rhetoric that portrayed the Democratic Party as the "lesser of two evils" compared with a Republican administration — rhetoric that would be repeated by labor leaders time and again in election years ever since.) New York state law mandated that a new party collect 12,000 signatures from around the state, with at least fifty coming from each of New York's sixty-two counties, as a prerequisite for ballot access. The needle trades unions provided the organizational resources for the new labor party. Since the needle trades were located primarily in New York City, collecting signatures in every county in the state was a daunting prospect. The nominally independent new party ended up relying on the Democratic Party apparatus to gain the necessary signatures from around the state to gain its standing as a certified political party (Chester 2004: 154–155; Smith 2006: 121–122).

By 1939, the entire range of tendencies that had debated the labor party question within the Socialist Party a few years earlier were represented within the ALP. The Socialist Party, the Social Democratic Federation and the Socialist Workers Party all had members within the ALP and shared a general consensus about strategy. Militants (a major faction in the Socialist Party), the "Old Guard" (who had left the Socialist Party in 1936), Trotskyists and Clarity supporters (members of the Clarity Caucus, a split-off from the Trotskyists) all cooperated to counter the influence of the Communist Party. But in true ALP fashion, none of these groups had any real influence on its policies. The ALP remained, as it had always been, a satellite of the Democratic Party (Chester 2004: 190).

It seems very unlikely that Lewis and Hillman could have consolidated their control over the CIO membership so easily without the aid of the Communist Party. Very soon after the UAW's victorious sit-down strike at General

Motors in Flint during the winter of 1936–1937, the Communist Party disbanded what was left over of its working relationship with the Socialists and moved toward a new alliance with Lewis (and subsequently, after his resignation in 1940, with Philip Murray and Hillman). Again this represented a highly calcultive alliance of convenience; the bureaucratic integration of the CIO into the New Deal coalition was much easier with active Communist cooperation, and Lewis also needed and used the excellent organizing talent that the Communists appeared to have in abundance. The Communist membership included an army of organizers ready to work long hours for little or no pay. Therefore it comes as no surprise that by 1937, Communist Party members held top leadership positions in 40 percent of CIO unions. On the other hand, the Communist Party's turn toward Lewis was a logical part of a broader strategy to legitimize the Communists as the left wing of the New Deal coalition. This went hand in hand with prioritizing the intra-bureaucratic struggle over the defense of rank-and-file democracy or the building of a mass socialist-oriented current in the unions. Communist criticism of Lewis (and later of Murray) was dropped while the call for an independent labor party was muted, and by 1938 the Communist Party's factory cells and plant daily papers were canceled (Davis 1986: 63–64; Smith 2006: 142–143, 150).

The impressive rise of the new industrial unions, which largely buttressed the Democrats, coincided with the emergence of alternative political movements and labor-oriented third parties. The list includes the Farmer-Labor Party in Minnesota, the Commonwealth Federations in Washington and Oregon, Upton Sinclair's End Poverty in California (EPIC) movement,[6] the Nonpartisan League in North Dakota, as well as the Progressive Party in Wisconsin continued by the La Follette family (Philip La Follette and his brother Robert La Follette Jr.), later fused with the state's farmer-labor movement. There were efforts from 1934 to 1936 to unite all these third-party movements into a single one that would prepare the launching of a new national party in 1936 or 1940. Known under the successive names "League for Independent Political Action," "National Farmer-Labor Federation," and finally "American Commonwealth Federation" (ACF), its leading protagonist was the Progressive Congress member from Wisconsin, Thomas R. Amlie. He was joined by John Dewey, Paul Douglas and other progressive liberals who tried to win the support of numerous farm organizations, trade unions, and statewide third parties to their program of "production for use." At its inaugural conference in Chicago in 1935, the ACF, backed by the garment and textile workers' unions, among others, envisioned it would win five to ten million votes in the 1936 elections and the presidency itself in 1940. The attempt ultimately failed, because at the heart of its entire strategy was sponsorship by the powerful Minnesota Farmer-Labor Party. When FLP governor Floyd Olson threw his support behind Roosevelt and the Democrats in 1936, it brought this whole movement for a progressive national party to a screeching halt (Gieske 1979: 206–208, 220–221).

At the same time, the surge of industrial unionism, confronted with the challenge of corporate and state repression, became politicized. In "feudal" steel towns in Ohio, Pennsylvania, Illinois, and Indiana, where steel barons exercised almost unrestricted local dictatorships, political mobilization was a necessary condition for union organization. Similarly, in centers of auto industries in Michigan (Lansing, Jackson, Flint and Saginaw), the sit-down strikes drove UAW militants to campaign against corporation-dominated local governments. Local after local of unions in the auto, electrical and garment industries voted for the concept of an independent labor party, a move that worried Lewis and Hillman. A Gallup poll taken in August 1937 following the wave of sit-down strikes indicated that 21 percent of the population supported the eventual formation of a national farmer-labor party as an alternative to the Democrats and Republicans. Gallup polls between December 1936 and January 1938 consistently showed that between 14 and 18 percent of respondents said they "would join a labor party." Among unionists this sentiment was even stronger than in the general population, particularly among workers at the forefront of struggle: namely the young workers in auto, rubber, textiles, and steel who had streamed into the CIO and also supported the concept of industrial unionism. At both the AFL and various CIO conventions in 1935 and 1936, resolutions supporting the formation of a labor party drew considerable support (Davis 1986: 66–67; Davin 1996: 122–123, 141–142; Smith 2006: 120).

Nevertheless, the convergence of politicized trade union militancy and all of these third-party deliberations failed to produce an enduring synthesis. One explanation is that the "leftward" turn of the New Deal in 1935 "stole the thunder" and co-opted the insurgent political movements. But the other explanation that sometimes has been given is that, contrary to the draconian repressive measures of predecessors Cleveland and Wilson, Roosevelt's tacit support for the CIO in 1936–1937 allowed him to appear as the savior of industrial unionism. Both of these explanations obviously have kernels of truth. But as Mike Davis has correctly pointed out, this two-factor line of argument clearly has its limits when one looks beyond the immediate conjuncture of 1935–1937 and the short-lived alliance of convenience between FDR and the CIO. First of all, the LNPL and the farmer-labor movements were not actually absorbed into the Democratic Party but became satellites and, especially in the case of the LNPL, little more than a captive campaign apparatus for Roosevelt and selected pro-labor Democrats. Secondly, a crisis of reform emerged in mid-1937 with the beginning of a second major economic dip in these months and the increasing defiance of the National Labor Relations Board by intransigent factions of capital (Ford, Dupont, Little Steel, and so on). Thirdly, in 1938, following the abysmal showing by liberals in the fall elections, a resurgent bloc of Republicans and conservative southern Democrats took control of Congress away from New Deal liberals.

Indeed, 1938 was a disastrous year for third-party and labor-party move-

3. Labor and the Left During the New Deal and the Cold War

ments, which instead of growing at the expense of the New Deal's crisis, virtually all collapsed. This paradox can be explained by the internecine war that erupted between the AFL and the CIO in 1937–1938. A resurgent conservative trade unionism became informally, but decisively, allied with the contemporary offensive launched by corporate capitalists. On a local level, the AFL cooperated with employers to preempt CIO organizing drives by signing "sweetheart" contracts or even the chartering of company unions. At the same time, AFL president William Green ordered a thorough purge of the CIO from local labor bodies, thereby splitting strategic labor councils in Detroit, Cleveland, and Akron. On the West Coast, the AFL teamsters countered the CIO's "March Inland" from its waterfront base with a wave of violence and secret agreements with employers. Even bloodier warfare erupted on the New Orleans docks between AFL and CIO longshoremen. Further collusion between the AFL and corporate business even included cooperation on a political plan to defend their contract deals by demanding the amendment of the Wagner Act (see below) to guarantee to the employer "free speech" to express his union preference. This was meant of course to put a halt to the growth of the CIO. By splitting the labor vote in this way, the AFL effectively undermined the base of state third-party movements, citywide labor tickets, and the left wing of the New Deal. In 1938, the AFL withdrew from the Minnesota Farmer-Labor Party, the Oregon Commonwealth Federation, and the New York American Labor Party, and also severed its remaining ties to the Labor Nonpartisan League (Davis 1986: 69–71).

Until the late twentieth century, this history of a promising yet ultimately unsuccessful collective movement pushing for the creation of an enduring labor party in the 1930s had been largely forgotten by historians. As Eric Leif Davin observes,

> So complete is the amnesia that neither labor and political historians nor even the children of the militants recall that it ever commanded the imagination, loyalty, and dedicated energy of so many working people for so long. Not only did labor's future belong to the Democrats, but the Democratic tide even claimed labor's past [Davin 1996: 158].

As the Democrats leaned more heavily on labor to get out the vote, labor increasingly identified its agenda with Democratic electoral victories. Mike Davis speaks of the "barren marriage" between labor and the Democratic Party when discussing the effects of the New Deal capture of the labor movement by the Democrats. This broadened the base of the party, but it certainly did not transform it into an analogue of European social democracy. The most striking manifestation of this was the discrepancy between labor's role in electoral mobilization and funding, and the meager legislative rewards it received in return (Davis 1986: 52–101). Labor historian Sharon Smith has argued that the failure to develop an enduring labor or social democratic party could have prevented "the repeated derailment of the working-class movement" by the Democrats in the decades that followed. With the benefit of hindsight, it seems unlikely that a labor party alone could have changed the overall outcome of the 1930s. But, Smith argues, it "could have exposed the corporate base of the Democratic Party and given workers the opportunity to develop a greater sense of independent class politics. This would have made a difference not only during the Depression but also in its aftermath" (Smith 2006: 152).

The 1938 shift in the national political power balance, combined with Roosevelt's paramount desire to win support for an increasingly interventionist foreign policy, blocked further reform initiatives or new concessions to labor. Moreover, it led to drastic cutbacks in public relief in 1939, which evoked widespread strikes and riots and renewed state repression of strike action and organizing drives (Davis 1986: 67–68). During the second New Deal term, Roosevelt, having obtained labor's support, no longer backed the CIO and other unions as before, CIO's leader John L. Lewis complained. Roosevelt also dealt strategically with those on his political right, including southern whites and Catholics, who together constituted a major part of his electoral and congressional support. For instance, he refused to press for measures—such as an anti-lynching bill— that would have alienated white southerners. Similarly, Roosevelt did not give in to the left's demand to support the Loyalist cause during the Spanish Civil War, as this would go against the pro-Falangist inclinations of the Catholic part of his coalition (Sexton 1991: 163–164; Lipset 2000: 77).

Ambiguities of the National Labor Relations Framework

In his overview of American trade unionism over the past century, labor historian Nelson Lichtenstein calls the National Labor Relations Act (NLRA) a "carefully drafted 'Magna Carta' for the labor movement":[7]

> The law was a radical legislative initiative because it was designed to put in place a permanent set of institutions within the very womb of private enterprise, which offered workers a voice, and sometimes a club, with which to resolve their grievances and organize themselves for economic struggle. It guaranteed workers the right to select their own union by majority vote, and to strike, boycott, and picket. And it enumerated a list of "unfair labor practices" by employers, including the maintenance of company-dominated unions, the blacklisting of union activists, intimidation and firing of workers who sought to join an independent organization, and the employment of industrial spies [Lichtenstein 2002: 36].

The newly established, federally administered National Labor Relations Board (NLRB) would hear employee complaints, determine union jurisdictions, and oversee on-site elections. Whenever a majority of a company's workers voted for a union to represent them, management was legally obliged to negotiate (although not to conclude an agreement) with that union alone over wages, hours, and working conditions. The Wagner Act banned any kind of management participation in or encouragement to a union, and it proscribed proportional representation, which could lead to more than one union representing the workers in a given trade or company. In contrast to the situation in countries like France, Britain and Sweden, the National Labor Relations Board, representing the U.S. government, would "certify" only one worker organization as the exclusive voice of the workers in a particular unit, which Senator Robert F. Wagner and like-minded advocates of the NLRA expected to have a company-wide character. The framers of the act were determined to ban company unionism, that is, employee organizations established or dominated by management. They saw those captive organizations as merely company efforts to thwart and corrupt the true voice of a firm's employees, and to divide, manipulate, and "speed up" their employees. It had been in periods of industrial turmoil during World War I and the first two years of the New Deal that industrialists had sponsored such schemes to co-opt and defuse the unionization impulse (Bernstein 1971: 318–339).

It should be stressed, however, that the industrial relations system in America had a Janus face. While historians such as Brody, Dubofsky, and Lichtenstein tend to highlight the benefits organized labor gained from the law (Brody 1993; Dubofsky 1994), other scholars emphasize the disadvantages that the National Labor Relations Act posed on workers. Members of the school of critical legal studies that emerged in the 1970s contend that the NLRA served as an instrument for "the manipulation of employee discontent and for the legitimation of existing inequalities of power in the workplace" (Van Wezel Stone 1981: 1517).[8] A closer look at the nature of the New Deal labor legislation and its modus operandi in the everyday praxis of the workplace offers strong support for this interpretation.

The Wagner Act was approved by Congress in the same year that the Supreme Court declared the National Industrial Recovery Act unconstitutional. The thrust of the new labor law was to make Section 7(a) of NIRA enforceable. The same-numbered section of the Wagner Act upheld the right of employees to form unions "of their own choosing" by establishing quasi-judicial procedures for ensuring the right of workers to organize and to bargain collectively through representatives they elected. The new Labor Board not only heard cases of unfair labor practices by employers, but also had the power to issue compliance orders against those not sticking to the rules; and employers could be penalized for non-compliance. The board was also empowered to resolve questions of jurisdiction between rival unions and determine appropriate units for the purpose of collective bargaining. It copied the American electoral system's secret ballot vote for union recognition and its winner-take-all system for certification. This meant that only one union could represent employees within a bargaining unit determined by the board. This provision was a clear break with the previous pattern of American labor relations, which made it possible for multiple unions to represent workers of the same employer. As noted earlier, it also differed markedly from many European labor relations practices that entailed proportional representation by competing unions, depending on their share of the vote (Aronowitz 2003: 78–80).

From the trade unions' point of view, the new law was first of all instrumental to union organizing and they welcomed the winner-take-all system. Most of their leaders thought it necessary to prevent company unions from gaining power in the plants. While most employers did not favor unions, the top managers of leading companies realized that workers could be better kept in check this way, and it would help stabilize the system undermined by wildcat strikes — the factory occupations of the rank and file — and the pickets and boycotts (Bellush 1976; Zinn 2003: 392–401). From the government's perspective, the Wagner Act was a tool to stabilize the economy. The Roosevelt administration exacted a price for giving up proportional representation and outlawing company unions. From now on, union autonomy would be constrained by a system of rules governing representation elections and by placing collective bargaining under the law. This tacit bargain would soon lead to government control over every aspect of labor relations (Klare 1978; Van Wezel Stone 1981).

The American Civil Liberties Union (ACLU) was among the few pro-labor organizations that recognized these tendencies toward greater state control over labor in the NLRA and was against its enactment.[9] Many socialists shared the ACLU's criticism, but no major organization on the left actively opposed the bill. At the time of its passage, the Communists and the Socialists attributed the enactment of the Wagner Act and the Social Security Act to Roosevelt's political need to make concessions to an insurgent working class. Generally, the left failed to acknowledge the downside of Roosevelt's "concessions," according to Stanley Aronowitz. While several other countries adopted national pension and health schemes and codes to protect health and safety conditions at the workplace, the American restrictions on labor's ability to deploy a wide array of methods to advance its interests was more typical of autocratic regimes than liberal democracies (Aronowitz 2003: 80).

Although the AFL supported the Wagner Act in 1935, it quickly became disillusioned. This was partly due to its historic reluctance to rely on government assistance (and more generally state intervention), which derived from the conviction that once labor became dependent on the state it could, and would, be oppressed by the state. From the AFL's perspective, the greatest legislative achievement to the benefit of the unions was not the Wagner Act but the 1932 Norris-LaGuardia Anti-Injunction Act, which declared the "yellow-dog contract"[10] unenforceable and greatly limited the use of injunctions and judicial orders that had thwarted so many strikes and boycotts (Goldfield 1989: 1258; Daniel 1980). The AFL disliked the National Labor Relations Board early on because this activist, powerful government agency tended to marginalize craft union claims in favor of the CIO-style bargaining units, regarding them as most in line with the industrial democracy idea that was the leitmotiv of this labor legislation. The AFL, in its efforts to mobilize opposition to the board and to revise the Wagner Act, even went so far as to ally itself with some of unionism's fiercest enemies — Republican congressmen, lawyers for the National Association of Manufacturers, and racist, labor-baiting legislators from the South (Lichtenstein 2002: 64–65; Bernstein 1985: 50).

The CIO, which benefited more than any other group from the New Deal labor legislation, nevertheless became dissatisfied as well. By the late 1930s, some CIO leaders (and much of the CIO rank and file) had reached the conclusion that the NLRB and the courts were using the Wagner Act also to limit labor's goals. The law had been deployed to institute an industrial relations system that protected collective bargaining over wages, benefits, and work rules, but implicitly, and at times explicitly, it also denied labor's right to challenge employers in any other way or on any other issues. This was epitomized by the new bureaucratic species that had emerged — the labor mediator, seen by many in the CIO as a grayish apparatchik committed merely to industrial stability and uninterested in, if not openly hostile to, the labor movement's larger aims. Thus, to those who envisioned that the CIO would become a vehicle for creating a new labor party or for attaining a significant share of control over the workplace (or possibly even for more radical forms of social change), the presence of the state in the center of labor conflicts had become a major obstacle (Brinkley 1995: 202–203).[11]

These discontented union members were aware of the dangers that were in the offing for the labor movement. During World War I the government had allowed control of economic-industrial mobilization to fall into the hands of corporate business leaders. Workers were offered only temporary benefits, which were almost all taken away, sometimes violently, in the immediate aftermath of the war. Labor unionists feared that World War II could turn out the same, reinvigorating capital and thwarting the labor movement's most ambitious and controversial aims. The war bureaucracy could accelerate the process the NLRB had already set in motion, which was speeding toward defining labor relations narrowly and entrenching labor mediators at the center of those relations.[12]

However, the CIO version of industrial democracy — whereby a rights-conscious citizenship became influential on the shop floor — was never hegemonic, even within unionized firms, since it encountered resistance from the very different model promoted by the craft unions of the AFL. They adapted the craft union idea to the new legal and political environment generated by the New Deal and the ensuing warfare state. By 1940 the AFL was larger than the CIO, and by 1955, when these federations reunited, the AFL would be even twice as big.

The unholy alliance between the AFL and right-wing groupings hostile to the Wagner Act soon made its impact felt. By 1941 Roosevelt had appointed men to the NLRB who paid their dues to craft union traditions, and Congress began to pass laws targeting the strikes and political activities of the industrial unions, although these were usually vetoed by the president. Government officials and legislatures increasingly turned against CIO-style unionism. The courts accommodated craft prerogatives but narrowed the capacity of the industrial unions to organize against employers unwilling to compromise (Lichtenstein 2002: 55, 65). Between 1937 and the end of World War II, the Supreme Court ruled that attempts to gain union recognition through factory occupations were illegal, while employers were granted the right to seek court injunctions restraining union members from mass picketing as they tried to prevent strikebreakers from performing their work (Aronowitz 2003: 86). In the aftermath of Pearl Harbor, in late 1941 and early 1942, an agreement was struck, whereby the leadership of both the AFL and the CIO, and most of the major unions in both organizations, promised to abstain from disruptive labor actions for the duration of the war. This "no-strike pledge" reflected the eagerness of labor leaders to demonstrate their support for the war effort along with their fear that if they did not take action to curb strikes, others would take much more draconian measures (Brinkley 1995: 209).[13]

In the summer of 1942, the War Labor Board reluctantly conceded a generalized "maintenance of membership" (quasi-union shop) and automatic union dues check-off. This was instigated by the administration's foremost concern to bolster the position of the labor bureaucracy in the face of internecine fighting between the AFL and CIO, as well as union decomposition (including outbursts of rank-and-file militancy and desertions within the CIO's own camp such as the UAW in 1942) and the consequent loss of control over the workforce. Increasing agitation against the no-strike pledge, as well as the reemergence of Lewis as an independent and possible recalcitrant force in the labor movement, pushed the government to reinforce the position of Murray and his associates. The result was a social contract that "conscripted" war workers into unions while at the same time denying the unions any capacity of significance to represent the economic interests of their members. This helped produce a dramatic increase in unionization, but with entirely different outcomes than those resulting from the struggles of the early thirties, as workers were now organized by the state into unions, rather than organizing themselves (Lichtenstein 1977: 228–235; Davis 1986: 76–77).

Constraints on Independent Labor Politics During World War II

After Roosevelt's third electoral victory in 1940, CIO leader John L. Lewis, who had opposed Roosevelt's reelection and advised the Republicans to nominate Herbert Hoover, came out in favor of a third-party venture, as did the

Communists active in the many CIO affiliates at the time. (Their new stance was due to the fact that after the Stalin-Hitler pact of August 1939, the Communists turned temporarily against Roosevelt, abandoning the antifascist Popular Front strategy they had been pursuing until then.) In the same year (1940), the CIO annual convention authorized its Executive Board to seriously consider formulating a program that would assure an independent political role for organized labor. But the growing conflict between Lewis and the pro-Roosevelt, pro-Allied majority of the CIO killed this initiative. After Lewis was replaced as CIO head, the Communists resumed their enthusiastic support of Roosevelt as well as their opposition to a labor party following Germany's invasion of the Soviet Union in June 1941 (Lipset and Marks 2000: 107).

Although the Roosevelt administration drew enormous domestic support for the war after Pearl Harbor, rank-and-file workers did show their widespread hostility to the no-strike pledge made by both the AFL and CIO leadership. In fact, the number of workers that went on strike during the four years the United States was at war soared. No fewer than 6,774,000 workers took part in a total of 14,471 strikes during the war — the vast majority wildcat strikes (Smith 2006: 163–164; Preis 1972: 25). The wartime insurgency against working conditions and the no-strike pledge often overlapped with racist attacks on new black workers. For example, between March and June 1943, over 100,000 man-days were lost in a wave of "hate strikes" against the upgrading of African-American workers. Unlike the 1933–1937 strike wave that had produced a profoundly unifying dynamic within the industrial working class, the participants in the 1943–1945 strikes vented frustration and anger without socializing the new workers into a common culture of struggle or assimilating their racial divisions (Davis 1986: 81–82).

John L. Lewis, pressured by his union's rank-and-file membership in the Pennsylvania coalfields, was the only leader of a major union to openly defy the no-strike pledge during the war. He led 530,000 miners (members of the UMW) out on strike three times in 1943. Roosevelt ordered "government seizure" of the mines, while the War Labor Board ordered the miners to return to work on the grounds that miners were working "for the government." The War Labor Board's tough stance against the miners had the approval of both its AFL and CIO representatives, no less. In contradistinction to UAW president R.J. Thomas's condemnation of the miners' strike as a "political strike against the president," an overwhelming number of rank-and-file autoworkers took the miners' side. Ultimately the miners won their demand for "portal to portal" pay. Their victory was the starting point for other workers to take strike action. These strikes were centered in the mass-production tire and auto industries, where 50 percent or more of all workers participated in wartime strikes in 1944 and 1945.[14] With the support of the War Labor Board, union officials took disciplinary action against strike leaders, including blacklisting known militants. Fear of reprisal did not stop labor militancy as its momentum continued to grow. The vast majority of the wildcat strikes were "quickie" work stoppages disputing working conditions, often involving just one or two departments within a plant, but often with far-reaching consequences elsewhere within the highly integrated mass-production industries involved (Smith 2006: 164–165).

Politically, this rebellion by the local leadership spawned renewed enthusiasm for the concept of a labor party. There was a strong sense in union ranks that the New Deal was in disarray and that the country was caught in a wave of reaction, exemplified by the 1943 Smith-Connally Anti-Strike Act (authorizing presidential takeovers of strike-torn industries and banning direct union political contributions). In the UAW, the Mazeyites, with supporters in fifty locals, were the strongest proponents of an independent labor party. (They were named after Emil Mazey, the leader of Briggs Local 212 in the auto industry, who had become a national rallying point for insubordinate shop stewards and local officials.) In 1943, they took over the virtually moribund Nonpartisan Labor League and revitalized it, with the declared purpose of creating a state labor party as soon as possible. The Dubinsky wing of the American Labor Party in New York, which was waging a fierce battle with the Hillman-Communist wing, worked for a state-by-state expansion of that party. David Dubinsky, head of the International Ladies Garment Workers, had no desire to challenge Roosevelt's national leadership, but he was dissatisfied with the subservience of the ALP to the New York Democratic Party. (This was due to the Communist Party's collaboration with Hillman in reducing the ALP to an uncritical and fully dependent appendage of the regular Democratic Party.) Dubinsky envisioned multiple labor parties that would allow the trade union bureaucracy to exert a more powerful and independent influence on local and state Democratic apparatuses. Although the Dubinsky group and the UAW dissidents were driven by different visions — Mazey and his allies were further to the left, tangentially influenced by Trotskyism — they shared an interest in fostering a more independent labor politics. This third-party agitation, closely connected with the massive grassroots upheaval against the bureaucratization and incipient state control of the unions, seemed to offer the best prospects since 1937 for the rebuilding of a socialist current among the working class.

Unfortunately, there was no large left cadre available in the industrial sector to coordinate the struggle against the no-strike pledge and to progress from the various initial impulses to independent political action. The Communist Party was adamantly opposed to the wildcat movement and to its political offshoots. The party had moved so far to the right since 1941 in support of the war effort and following the course charted by the Soviet regime that the traditional left-wing spectrum no longer accurately represented the real differences between factions of the CIO. The Communist Party under Earl Browder's leadership outdid the most conservative layers of the union bureaucracy in its advocacy of speedup of production and incentive pay in the war plants. And when rank-and-file workers struck for higher wages or against inhuman working conditions, the party was the first to defend the no-strike pledge. It also consistently supported the Murray-Hillman leadership in its efforts to clamp down on "divisive" third-party currents within the CIO (Davis 1986: 78–80).

The Democratic Party and the CIO's Political Action Committee

With the launching of the political action committee (PAC) as the CIO's new political campaign apparatus in July 1943, the political alliance between the CIO and the Democratic Party (dating from the formation of the Labor Nonpartisan League in 1936) took permanent hold. In this way, the CIO de facto sealed its refusal to form a labor party. The CIO-PAC would function as one of many competing interest groups within the Democratic Party in pledging to financially support Democratic candidates. The CIO-PAC was established to support Roosevelt's 1944 presidential campaign, but after the election, the CIO maintained the committee as its permanent political action apparatus. The CIO's dual nature of a trade union organizing center and a recruiting agency for the New Deal Democratic coalition limited the political action committee's historical potential (Selfa 2008: 98).

The PAC was created in response to parallel crises in the party and the CIO. The Democratic Party had suffered serious losses in the 1942 congressional elections due to the defection of most of the Midwest to the Republicans. For the New Deal coalition, the urban vote was more crucial than ever because the big-city Democratic machines could no longer reliably guarantee the delivery of the ethnic working-class votes. This was due partly to the depletion of their patronage resources following the increasing federalization of relief and employment, as well as to the success of industrial unions in weakening traditional patronage relationships between workers and ward heelers. Therefore Roosevelt and his chief political advisors gave priority to the creation of a trade union political apparatus that would compensate for the increasing electoral deficiencies of the ward system and also extend Democratic dominance to the newer industrial centers in the South and West.

The CIO leadership had given electoral politics a great deal of thought in the wake of the failure of its congressional lobbies and its relative marginalization in the councils of the war economy. The passage of the Smith-Connally Act in June 1943 made a new political strategy even more urgent. Murray and Hillman were well aware that the AFL's chief lobbyist, John Frey, had made a secret deal with a number of pro-AFL congressmen to vote with the majority to override President Roosevelt's veto. The CIO leaders saw the specter of an AFL-conservative alliance with the power to constrain or even roll back industrial unionism. But at the same time they had their doubts about the pro-labor party sentiments within their own ranks, especially those expressed by the same dissidents responsible for the wildcat movement. The Executive Board saw as the core of the CIO's political problems its failure to stimulate much more interest in electoral politics among its membership. Voter apathy was very high in the industrial working class, and the recomposition of the labor force during the war (when millions of rural migrants, women, and blacks entered the industrial labor market) exacerbated the situation. Therefore the CIO's goal in forming PACs on a national and local basis was to create a new "CIO voter" whose commitment to the New Deal wing of the Democratic Party would become as natural and reliable as that of a British Labour Party adherent or Western European social democrat. The PACs aimed to do this through massive voter registration drives and the creation of a permanent cadre of precinct workers.

At that time, the CIO leadership, the Communists and a broad spectrum of progressives all shared the idea that the formation of the PAC was part of a process of realignment that would eventually channel organized labor, New Dealers, and progressive Republicans into a single liberal party while forcing "Bourbon Democrats" (extremely conservative, southern Democrats) and the Republican mainstream to regroup in a second, conservative party. The prevailing opinion among the proponents of CIO's PAC was that such a realignment was the necessary precondition for resuming the progress of reform and breaking through the gridlock created by the alliance between southern Democrats and the Republicans since 1938.

The CIO invested much energy and large resources into building the PAC. The new grassroots campaign apparatus was vital to the Democrats and played an important role in the Democratic electoral success of 1944, but the CIO gained only little in exchange. This was partly due to the PAC's reluctance, under Hillman's direction, to actively defend the New Deal or to obtain any significant quid pro quo from Roosevelt. In the struggle between the right and liberal wings of the Democratic Party, Vice President Henry Wallace represented the beleaguered New Dealers. Virtually on his own in the Roosevelt administration, he continued to fervently defend regional planning, to make left-populist attacks on monopoly capitalists, and to advocate the CIO-sponsored proposal for an "Economic Bill of Rights." The Democratic Party's southern conservative wing (which supported James F. Byrnes, an influential politician from South Carolina)[15] and the big city machines (who supported Truman) were united in their opposition to Wallace's bid for renomination as vice president. Although the stakes were clear from the perspective of the labor left, the CIO leadership hesitated to openly challenge the power of the political machine bosses, and Hillman made no attempt to pressure Roosevelt on Wallace's behalf. This led to tacit CIO endorsement of Senator Truman, protégé of the corrupt Pendergast machine in Kansas City, and Wallace's elimination as candidate. The PAC's unwillingness to defend Wallace was a foreshadowing of a series of further defeats over federal reconversion policy, as the Seventy-ninth Congress repeatedly changed tax policy in favor of corporations and disabled welfare and employment legislation. Tax concessions were especially important, since they allowed corporations that showed losses after the war — as a result of strikes, for example — to claim rebates from their wartime excess profits tax (Davis 1986: 83–85).

Furthermore, in 1944, the anti–Stalinist members left the American Labor Party to form the Liberal Party. The ALP backed Henry Wallace in his 1948 presidential campaign (see below) and then gradually vanished from the political scene. With the support of David Dubinsky and other union officials involved, the Liberal Party replaced the ALP as the organizational mechanism for left-wing union pressure on the Democratic Party. It would survive until the early twenty-first century as a small ballot line engaging in a long series of electoral maneuvers. Needless to say, this wheeling and dealing was far removed from a truly independent politics (Chester 2004: 190).

Postwar Defeat of the Larger Ambitions of the Labor Left

By recruiting millions of unskilled and semi-skilled workers, the CIO's militancy had contributed in large part to the jump in total union membership between 1930 and 1940 from 3.4 million to 8.7 million, or from 11.6 to 26.9 percent of non-agricultural employment. Growth during the war was even greater, and was never matched before or since. By 1945 the total number of union members was 14.8 million, which was 35.5 percent of all non-agricultural workers and 21.9 percent of all workers (Patterson 1996: 40; Lichtenstein 1982). Unions, then, were a spearhead of American liberalism, even though they were not egalitarian in everything they said and did. Like other American institutions, unions had a generally poor record when it came to admitting women, blacks, and other minorities (Gabin 1990; Cobble 1991). But many union members, as well as other low-income Americans, had attained a sense of their rights as citizens during the New Deal. They supported a range of liberal social policies, voted for liberal office seekers, and exercised considerable political power within the Democratic Party.

In the immediate postwar period, many labor leaders and their labor-liberal supporters were attracted to social democratic ideas. Even though wartime government agencies like the War Labor Board (WLB) and the Office of Price Administration (OPA) had produced many disappointing decisions for labor, their existence nevertheless raised expectations for significant labor influence at the highest national level (as the Labour Party won in Britain after 1942) through tripartite structures for economic planning, involving representatives of the government, employers and organized labor. However, the strategy of big business during the Truman years revolved around the containment of industrial unionism within institutional constraints that fused collective bargaining with the restoration of managerial control over the labor process. At Truman's National Labor-Management Conference in October 1945, the business delegation accepted the utility of collective bargaining in the abstract, but it put "managerial inviolability" at the center of its program for postwar labor relations. Over a decade of intermittent rank-and-file insurgencies, including sit-down and wildcat strikes, had eroded the previously despotic powers of foremen and line supervisors. Rejecting the CIO's revived call for more "industrial democracy," the leading corporations in auto, steel, and electrical manufacture adopted an aggressive strategy that, they hoped, would ultimately force the unions to accept a tough trade-off between wage increases and control over working conditions. These corporations wanted in particular strong curbs on the role of rank-and-file leadership, the restriction of the right to strike and long, multi-year contracts (Davis 1986: 86).

At this point one should note the character of the Democratic Party when it had reemerged during the Great Depression as a party of labor. As Frances Fox Piven explains, given the highly decentralized nature of the American state structure, state and local party organizations have played a much larger and more independent role than in most other countries. Because of this distinctive feature and the unique restrictions on the franchise, the national Democratic Party was itself fragmented, without an effective center to formulate and deploy coherent party strategies. This condition fueled both the politics of the southern wing and the influence of well-organized business groups. Sectional and interest groups worked in turn to promote policies that inhibited the growth of the party's union allies and stunted the expansion of the welfare state programs that had drawn popular support for the Democrats in the 1930s. Although the Democrats were the party of northern labor since the New Deal, they continued to be the sectional party of the rural South, which was in fact an alliance with a quasi-feudal political formation. The decentralization of representation, particularly in the Senate and the Electoral College, gave this sectional political system a strong grip on the national government. And a system of divided powers in the national government meant that this grip could become a stranglehold on national policy, especially as powerful southern Democrats in the Congress allied themselves with northern Republicans (Piven 1992: 236, 246–247).

More than at any other time in American history, the union movement in 1945 defined the left-liberal limits of what was possible in the political arena. They were considerably more powerful at the time than left-wing organizations such as the Socialist and Communist parties. And other activist, progressive organizations, such as the Congress of Racial Equality, the NAACP, and the Southern Conference for Human Welfare, which sought to help poor and black people in the South, also met widespread resistance. None of these organizations were particularly influential in politics (Patterson 1996: 40–41).

The vision that the influential union leader Walter Reuther, president of the UAW, publicly expressed in 1945 incorporated much of what the liberal left was seeking to realize: a more elaborate welfare state with a governmentally guaranteed "annual wage," civil rights protection for abused minorities, federal legislation to promote better education and health care, and workers' involvement in key decisions about production and technological development (Zieger 1986: 100–101; Lichtenstein 1989; Milkman 1991: 135). But the larger ambitions of the labor left were defeated in the immediate postwar years by the two great conservative forces in American life hostile to union power. The first was corporate management, with its persistent hostility toward both the regulatory state and the power, or even the very existence, of trade unionism. The wartime experience of American business was also important in this regard, as Lichtenstein points out:

> Unlike their counterparts in continental Europe, or even the British Isles, who had been tarred with the brush of collaboration or appeasement, American business leaders found the wartime experience one of both commercial success and political advance. They felt in little need of the kind of state-sponsored labor-management collaboration that helped legitimize a mixed capitalist economy in Germany, France, and Italy in the immediate postwar era [Lichtenstein 2002: 109].

The second conservative force was the white ruling class in the South, which had backed many early New Deal initiatives, but came down on the unions with unprecedented ferocity. This happened when the link between CIO-style unionism and the mobilization of an increasingly self-confident black movement, which helped to undermine the existing institutionalized racism, became evident. Southern Democrats, unlike the Republicans, were neither against the expansion of New Deal power per se, nor against federal infrastructure spending or the regulation of the market. Indeed, southern agricultural interests in particular were staunch allies and beneficiaries of governmental policies that were part of New Deal state building in the South. The Tennessee Valley Authority projects, for example, had a major impact on four southern states while business benefited enormously from the military expenditures in the region during the Second World War and the Cold War decades afterward. But southern white elites strongly resisted any nationalizing attempt to democratize the region and bring its labor relations and racial norms more in line with those of the North and the West. And southern politicians proved to be highly successful in defusing those critical sides of the New Deal impulse. They did so in three ways.

First, the South's delegation in Congress comprised more than a third of the Democratic legislators, which gave them the power to exclude much of the region's people and industry from the scope of New Deal social legislation. Neither the Wagner Act nor Social Security covered agricultural labor or domestic service, which together employed more than 60 percent of the African-American labor force, and nearly 75 percent of those who were employed in the South. The federal governmental policies in the context of FDR's New Deal and Truman's Fair Deal were largely beneficial to whites (by now including first- and second-generation "new immigrants" as well), but they were by and large detrimental to blacks, Mexican-Americans and other U.S. citizens of color. Even in the North, veteran, education and housing benefits paid to people of color lagged behind those that whites received. The Fair Labor Standards Act of 1938 provided a minimum wage, maximum hours, and overtime protections to many U.S. wage workers, but again excluded domestic workers and farm laborers, who constituted a majority of both black and Mexican-American workers (Katznelson 2005; Williams 2003: 69–105; Roediger 2005: 206).

Of course, many whites were left out as well; some 40 percent were excised from Social Security in the 1930s (compared to 65 percent of African Americans nationally, and between 70 and 80 percent of blacks in various parts of the South), in a country that still was substantially agrarian. Southern legislators arranged that the minimum wage, first set by the Fair Labor Standards Act, did not interfere with pay scales in textiles, tobacco processing, lumber, and other typical southern industries. The same congressmen filibustered the Fair Employment Practices Commission so that it was not renewed in early 1946 (Lichtenstein 2002: 111; Katznelson 2005: 23–23, 43). At the same time, the Roosevelt administration institutionalized discriminatory practices that went further than white southerners requested. One notorious example is the New Deal's adoption of discriminatory housing policies that solidified the northern system of de facto segregation. Some New Deal programs even provided new opportunities for whites to enforce segregation on their own, again largely in the North. Recently established CIO unions in Detroit, Chicago, Cleveland and Pittsburgh, for instance, under the aegis of the Wagner Act, created seniority systems that confined African Americans to a narrow band of job categories (Boyle 1995; Nelson 2001).

Second, the South's white oligarchy maintained its conservative institutions and practices through a system of decentralized administration. Almost all of the New Deal's social wage legislation — including unemployment insurance, aid to families with dependent children, work relief and housing assistance, and support for veterans — was administered by state and local officials deeply hostile to black aspirations, by means of social and economic criteria largely determined by the ruling elites involved. This led to a situation in the Deep South in which welfare and unemployment payments were in some cases one-tenth of those in New England and New York. It was precisely because the Wagner Act was national in scope and standards that it met so much resistance in the South (Brown 1999: 99–134; Katznelson 2005: 23).

Third, in defending their power, the southern political and economic elites took recourse to one final measure. They simply nullified much New Deal social legislation, especially the labor law, when it empowered their opponents. Textile firms, tobacco processors, and independent oil producers were notorious violators of the labor law. It was southern textile interests that pioneered most of the legal and economic tactics that effectively annulled the Wagner Act: illegal firings, plant shutdowns, litigious delay, and managerial intimidation prior to an NLRB election. By the late 1950s, Texas, Georgia, and North and South Carolina were the nation's leading states in outright union busting (Lichtenstein 2002: 111–112).

Lastly, there was the postwar red scare that had triumphed by the mid–1950s, leaving anti–Communists—who tended to be more broadly opposed to any "socialistic" endeavor—in firm control of the American labor movement. For this and other reasons (to be discussed later), many unions from this period on operated more as special interest groups than as supporters of broad-based social liberal ideas (such as those emphasized by Reuther in 1945). Although unions were strong within the Democratic Party in industrial areas, they were captives too, unable to do much in politics without party backing. In non-industrial areas—and among the masses of blacks, working women, and other nonunionized Americans—unions had little influence. Committed social reformers in the United States realized that the stagnation of organized labor by 1950 "was both cause and consequence of a broader political stalemate that blocked liberal goals" (Patterson 1996: 54–55).

A Brief Interlude of Labor Party Explorations

In the immediate aftermath of the war there was an explosion of labor militancy that lasted from the late fall of 1945 to the end of 1946. Workers who had risked their lives in the war returned home to a recession economy and in many cases to find they had lost their jobs. Those who still had jobs dealt with much lower wages. In addition, four million women workers who had held industrial jobs during the war were laid off immediately afterward. In January 1946, auto, steel, electrical, and packinghouse workers were all on strike at the same time, hitting the industrial base of the economy. During the twelve months after V-J (Victory over Japan) Day, more than 5 million workers were involved in strikes, which lasted on average four times longer than those during the war (Smith 2006: 170–171). Truman responded by enjoining the miners, threatening to conscript the railroad workers, and calling for broad repressive powers. His anti-labor actions, reminiscent of Wilson's sharp rightward turn in 1919, coincided with the dismissal of Wallace (now secretary of commerce) and other former members of the New Deal inner circle in 1946. This temporarily disrupted the political strategy of the CIO and its liberal supporters. CIO leader Murray felt obligated to oppose the administration, albeit briefly. His former allies, the Communists, abandoning their long-held position that the Democratic Party was "the Popular Front," explored the possibility of a left-liberal third party supported by units of the PAC and its non-labor affiliates. Walter

Reuther, Norman Thomas, John Dewey and a number of other putative social democrats presented themselves in May 1946 as the (short-lived) "National Educational Committee for a New Party." Neither the Communists nor these social democrats proposed an immediate break with the Democrats, however. Instead, they counted on PAC successes in the 1946 congressional elections to shift the balance of power to the progressive pole. However, with a mere 30 percent of the electorate, CIO candidates were trounced, and the first Republican-dominated Congress since Hoover took office over the diminished ranks of the New Deal Democrats (Davis 1986: 87).

The idea of a labor party also resurfaced among other prominent figures within labor's orbit, including New York intellectuals such as Irving Howe and Daniel Bell; the Inter-Union Institute for Labor and Democracy, a group of labor officials and intellectuals led by the long-time labor journalist J.B.S. Hardman; and the Trotskyists in Max Shachtman's Workers' Party. They speculated that the CIO's political action committee would either transform the Democratic Party into a labor party or provide the nucleus for a third party. Each of these groups had a different political agenda, but at the time they all believed in labor's promise as a vanguard social movement (Geary 2001: 329).

The radical sociologist C. Wright Mills, who shared these groups' enthusiasm for labor's involvement in progressive politics, reported in his book *The New Men of Power* that 13 percent of AFL leaders and 23 percent of CIO leaders interviewed in 1946 favored formation of a labor party within the next two or three years.[16] When the timeline was stretched out to "eventually," implying ten years, those favoring a labor party rose to 23 percent for the AFL and 52 percent for the CIO (Mills 1948: 211–213). Needless to say, the longer view was much easier to maintain than a commitment to the short term. The UAW also took this non-committal approach in 1948 when, to counter the Progressive Party candidacy of Henry Wallace (backed by the Communist Party after yet another about-face in policy), they passed a convention resolution calling for a "genuine progressive political party" at some unspecified time after the election. The deepening institutionalization of their Democratic Party orientation and the connection of most unions with the Democrats killed virtually all labor party sentiment in the 1950s (Chester 1985: 116).

It was the CIO that had forged the basics of what would be labor's central political strategy, which was its alliance with and dependence on the Democratic Party. In the course of the New Deal and World War II, labor had abandoned the AFL's long-standing voluntarist ideology and its nonpartisan doctrine about "rewarding your friends and punishing your enemies" in favor of a semi-institutional alliance with the Democrats. By the late 1940s, the strategy had utterly failed by almost any account. Even before the capture of Congress by the Republicans in 1946 and the passage of the Taft-Hartley Act in 1947, labor was defeated by a Congress now dominated by the alliance of conservative southern Democrats and northern Republicans. In 1946 and 1947 the CIO's political and legislative connections lacked the wherewithal to expand the welfare state and prevent anti-labor legislation (Zieger 1995: 212–252).

The Taft-Hartley Act and Labor's Postwar Retreat

The 1947 Taft-Hartley Act codified much of labor's postwar retreat; it was a major vehicle in containing union power and reprivatizing collective bargaining. But Taft-Hartley was not a sudden sea change in American labor policy, as major parts of the bill had been developing in Congress since at least 1940. Moreover, judicial rulings and NLRB policy by the early 1940s had come to reflect the federal government's policy of subordinating workers' rights to the goal of achieving economic stability and industrial peace. Still, the enactment of Taft-Hartley marked a significant shift in labor policy (Gross 1981: 254–255; Tomlins 1985b: 247–252). Stanley Aronowitz rightly emphasizes that the Taft-Hartley amendments of 1947 should be seen as an extension of regulation imposed by the Wagner Act and by various Supreme Court decisions rather than as the key legislation that reversed labor's rights. He contends that labor's defeat originates in its leadership's embrace of the collective bargaining system of the Wagner Act (although the AFL leadership was clearly opposed to it initially and CIO leaders had second thoughts, as noted earlier). This move was associated with the incorporation of both wings of the labor movement into the Roosevelt coalition, an alliance that all but destroyed the emerging movement within labor's ranks for the formation of a labor party. With the arrival of the National Labor Relations Board and a growing open hostility of the courts to direct action, the Labor Board–supervised election gradually replaced the strike and other forms of direct action as the chief method in gaining union recognition. More importantly, the NLRA introduced a new dominant element in labor relations: the unions no longer relied upon direct intervention of workers themselves to solve grievance disputes and achieve economic gains (Aronowitz 2003: 85–88).

From this point of view — informed by a democratic syndicalist approach of labor activism predicated on rank-and-file control of unions — the regulation of labor relations meant a serious infringement upon basic labor rights. It restricted workers' freedom to withhold their labor when aggrieved and to prevent strikebreaking. It denied them the right to deploy effective means, that is, direct action in the form of factory occupations, mass picketing, obstructing truck and rail deliveries, and organizing collective self-activity and acts of solidarity such as sympathy walkouts, boycotts, and refusals to cross picket lines. Yet, as advocates of this approach to labor activism also emphasize, labor's weakening of power after World War II was not only the result of NRLA's integration into the dominant politico-economic order. The NLRA also played a role in aiding the U.S. Cold War objectives in foreign policy, which time and again moderated labor's activism and compromised the political independence of trade union leaders.

The Taft-Hartley Act required trade union officials to make anti-communist disclaimers, and outlawed sympathy strikes, secondary boycotts, and mass picketing. The president of the United States was given authority to impose an eighty-day "cooling-off" period on strikes that threatened the "national interest." Moreover, Taft-Hartley held union organizations and their leaders legally responsible for damages incurred by wildcat strikes or any other breach of contract. Taft-Hartley also codified the union-hostile status quo in the South and Southwest, especially after most states in those regions took advantage of Section 14(b) to ban the union shop and enact "right-to-work" statutes. Another Taft-Hartley revision of the Wagner labor law gave employers the right to "free speech" during NLRB elections as long as the speech did not contain a "threat of reprisal or promise of benefit." Section 8(c) opened the door to well-orchestrated union-avoidance campaigns. Given the highly uneven playing field between management wielding strong employer power and employees with only meager power resources, such campaigns normally were identical to intimidation.

The NLRA's purview, which already excluded agricultural, domestic, and public-sector workers, was narrowed further still. Independent contractors were placed outside the act's definition of employee, denying them the protection of federal labor law. But the most powerful instrument that became available to labor's opponents was the exclusion of foremen and supervisors from labor-law reach. With the rise of mass production and bureaucratic rationality during the late New Deal era, first-line supervisors had become a linchpin in the production process and the "man in the middle" caught between pressures from below and above by militant workers and managers (emphasizing efficiency and control) respectively. In the eyes of America's top managers, the unionization of foremen entailed union control of the shop-floor work environment. Seniority rights, grievance procedures, and union representation by foremen held the potential to subvert management authority, especially if lower-level supervisors were subject to strong social and psychological pressures from below. More generally, foremen organization undermined the unitary façade of management and opened the door to a much broader definition of what constituted a self-conscious working-class identity. The deunionization of foremen and their judicially forced return into the managerial realm was therefore a major contributor to insulating the union movement and the victory of management all along the white-collar boundary. The severity of this infringement on foremen's rights as workers became ever more apparent in later years when the unionization of finance, engineering, insurance, banking and other private-sector service industries turned out to be virtually impossible given the prohibition of supervisory unionism (Lichtenstein 2002: 114–122; Seitz 1984; Joyce 1987; DeChiara 1993).

Taft-Hartley also renewed the Smith-Connally Act's prohibition against union campaign contributions, which was an obvious attack on PAC operations. Both the AFL and the CIO initially wanted to boycott Taft-Hartley, but they soon concluded that it would also bar access to the National Labor Relations Board, to bargaining unit election procedures, and the remaining protections the labor law still provided against anti-union employers. Consequently their leaderships acquiesced to the new law, and the Communists who were influential in unions representing about a million workers were summarily expelled and sacrificed to the Cold War's increasing pressure toward political orthodoxy.[17] Taft-Hartley not only eliminated a political faction that was unpopular in many circles but also created the loss of the organic leadership that American Communists contributed to several movements that characterized mid-century social liberalism: opposition to the Cold War, trade union militancy, proto-feminism, and above all, the struggle for the liberation of African Americans. Importantly, the ejection of the Communists from much of American political life significantly diminished the role that issues of class and union power would play in the emergence of the civil rights movement and the New Left in the 1960s (Levy 1994: 111–127).

In 1948, CIO leaders resumed support for the Democrats and vigorously campaigned for Truman's reelection — largely based on his campaign promise to repeal Taft-Hartley, which he would fail to keep. The Communist Party's support of Wallace provided ammunition for the CIO's now open warfare against communism. The CIO's choice for a reconsolidation of its alliance with Truman and the national Democratic Party implied that the CIO became an integral part of the administration's escalating anti-communist crusade, paving the way for McCarthyism in the 1950s. The CIO's one-sided attachment to the presidential level of the Democratic Party also linked it to the twists and turns of American foreign policy and various forms of U.S. imperialism (Smith 2006: 172–73; Davis 1986: 88). The U.S. State Department, under the auspices of the Marshall Plan, enlisted the assistance of American labor leaders in crushing left-wing workers' movements in Western Europe.[18] In 1948, both the AFL and the CIO allied with British trade unions to form the anti–Soviet International Confederation of Free Trade Unions to advance the cause of pro-American (that is, opposed to radical) labor unions worldwide. In 1950, the CIO and the AFL started collaborating secretly with the CIA, a relationship that would last for decades and channel hundreds of millions of dollars to form and sustain anti-communist labor movements around the world. As Sharon Smith puts it, "CIO officials thus graduated from the role of 'labor statesmen' to international operatives for the U.S. government" (Smith 2006: 177; Preis 1972: 355).

The integration of the unions into the Cold War consensus went hand in hand with a new cultural cohesion within the postwar American working class, rooted in the rise of wartime nationalism. This new "Americanism" had been incubated during the thirties and brought to a fever pitch by the war mobilization. It was broadly inclusive regarding the white working class, but African Americans, Mexicans and Japanese Americans were excluded. This cultural cohesion was supported by strong material forces, including the job-generating capacities of the permanent war economy, and more generally the new structural position of the American working class within a postwar world dominated by U.S. capital. The American government acquired a powerful instrument for inculcating patriotic, anti-radical and pro-authoritarian attitudes in successive generations of workers by adopting universal peacetime military service in the late 1940s. This burden fell almost entirely on working-class youth via a system of class-based educational and occupational deferments.

Ironically, Popular Front leftists were among the most fervent advocates of the new nationalism. Unlike the First World War, when there was strong resistance to militarism, and especially to U.S. participation in the war, by the Socialist Party and the IWW, the majority of the left of the forties uncritically supported Roosevelt's wartime leadership. The Communists in particular went very far in using anti-fascism as legitimation to promote official nationalistic chauvinism, to the point of actively supporting the "relocation" of the entire Japanese-American population of the West Coast into internment camps in 1942. Their relinquishment of leadership in the wartime wildcat strikes even further weakened the left vis-à-vis the CIO bureaucracy once the new nationalism was redeployed in 1946–1947 as a virulent anti-communism.

Cold War jingoism, as Mike Davis has argued, probably had its most dramatic impact and settled most deeply in those sectors of the working class that had previously been most insulated from patriotic hysteria, namely Eastern European Catholics. The Red Army's entry into Eastern Europe late in the war had an alarming impact upon Slavs and Hungarians who comprised perhaps as much as half of the CIO's membership. The left-wing ethnic organizations that had played such a heroic role in the early years of the CIO, and had been one of the most important sources of radical influence on the industrial working class, either collapsed or became marginalized by a renewal of right-wing anti-communist nationalism in each ethnic community. This recasting of ethnic culture in a fervent patriotic mold was channeled to a great extent through the Catholic Church and its many organizations (ranging from the Association of Catholic Trade Unions to the Knights of Columbus) that permeated the daily life of the Catholic working class (Davis 1986: 89–90).

At its 1949 convention, the CIO passed its own anti-communist statutes, barring any member of the Communist Party from holding union office and giving the CIO the power to expel any unions with Communists in leadership positions. The convention next voted to remove two Communist-led unions, the United Electrical Workers and the Farm Equipment Workers. Soon afterward, Walter Reuther, in his role of vice president of the CIO, authorized CIO raiding of Communist-led unions. In 1950, the final purge took place when the convention voted to expel nine more of such unions. By then, the CIO had expelled roughly 20 percent of its membership, nearly 250,000 workers. Most of its rank and file showed relatively little concern about the expulsions, however unjust. The Communist Party had long since alienated those workers who would have fought hardest to defend union democracy (Preis 1972: 358, 401, 404–405; Guérin 1987: 176).

But the CIO purge went further than the removal of Communist-led unions. The remaining CIO unions forced out their own radical "troublemakers," thereby often collaborating closely with the House Un-American Activities Committee (HUAC) and other investigative committees. By 1954, fifty-nine out of a hundred unions had changed their constitutions to bar Communists from holding office, and forty unions had barred Communists from membership (Smith 2006: 190–192; Caute 1978: 353–354). Ultimately, the most important implications of the postwar red scare were the political domestication and containment of the everyday realities in factories and offices, schools, local libraries, radio stations, as well as of popular culture forms such as comic books, TV series and advertisements. Suspicion of "subversiveness" was extended from Communists to Socialists, labor activists, social liberals, progressive Democrats and New Dealers more generally. It can be safely concluded that the U.S. left was all but destroyed in the 1950s. In the labor movement, the purge of leftists (and those labeled as such) led to a historic depoliticization from which the U.S. trade unions would never fully recover. The defining legacy of this modern-day witch hunt was the foreclosure of radical options in general. Any politics that did not accommodate to the hegemonic version of "Americanism" was demonized, and the political center shifted to the right. This all occurred against the background of anti-colonial struggles in Indochina, Indonesia, the Philippines and West Africa; many were countries in which U.S. corporate interests had a major stake (Sexton 1991: 154–157; Marqusee 2004: 32, 54; Smith 2006: 194–195).

The restrictions imposed by Taft-Hartley encouraged workplace parochialism revolving around a defensive kind of firm-centered collective bargaining that gave capital a decisive advantage (Van Wezel Stone 1981; Tomlins 1985b: 258–281). Even the most left-liberal CIO unions felt obliged to adopt this type of private-sector collective bargaining in the context of the political defeat of almost all of Truman's Fair Deal legislative initiatives by the dominant conservative coalition in Congress (Hamby 1973: 293–310; Griffith 1989). Employers opposed social provisions funded by the tax system and administered by the state, which would have resulted in benefits that were likely to be universal, equitable, and inexpensive. Employers were against these because they would have had to carry a large portion of the financial burden through higher business taxes. And from the perspective of managerial control over worker behavior, a generous welfare state would empower workers; they could be less loyal to the company, switch jobs more easily, and draw an essential income even if they were ill, unemployed, or on strike. Legitimated by "pluralistic" industrial relations theory of power in the workplace, this shift amounted to the depoliticization of what had been the union movement's larger agenda, which extended to welfare arrangements such as pensions, medical provision, vacations, and supplemental unemployment insurance.

Thus, through the collective bargaining process, unions hoped to attain a private, firm-centered and job-dependent version of the more universal and sizable welfare systems that social democratic-oriented governments in Western Europe and other English-speaking countries were building. The privatization of contractual welfare arrangements led to institutionalized inequality in which health care and other provisions were job dependent, and workers (and their "dependents") drew benefits only to the extent that their employers offered them such coverage (Stevens 1990). This bargaining system was patriarchal and racially inflected. The segmented labor market put the majority of women and minorities in nonunionized jobs outside the industrial core. They did not obtain the social insurance that the skilled, unionized, and primarily male, white workers did. The drawbacks of this setup would be felt more fully in the late twentieth and early twenty-first centuries when many companies cut significant parts of the social benefits packages they gave to their employees (Lichtenstein 2002: 128; Levi 2003: 50; Smith 2003: 433).

Importantly, union leaders (with impressive rank-and-file support) did little to address racial or gender injustice, equal pay, or quality of work life, and made little effort to expand the labor movement and collective bargaining beyond the white, male, industrial sector during the New Deal order, which lasted until the early 1970s. Rather, they settled for the security that this regime offered: the rising wages that encouraged consumption and the legal and economic policies that promised secure, continuous employment. And as the American industrial relations system reinforced the economy's tendency to construct segmented and unequal benefit and compensation schemes at the firm level, it was instrumental in eroding solidarity by fueling envy and resentment within the working class. It also meant that over time, core working-class groups focused less on government for the provisions that would guarantee their security and more on the marketplace. In turn, a government that did less in this regard was less likely to generate trust or affection (Piven 1992: 253–254; Cowie and Salvatore 2008: 14; Lichtenstein 2002: 130). Here arguably lies a major cause of weak intra-class solidarity among workers, which made it very difficult for activists to draw broad support for a labor-based party seeking a social wage and universal coverage of major benefits as a primary goal.

4

Corporate Assaults on the Labor Left and the Limits of Postwar Liberalism

Despite the fact that business remained very powerful after the war, employers were highly concerned that the United States was becoming a "laboristic" society (Schlichter 1947: 35). By 1945 corporations had begun to pour much money into public relations, with the intent of fostering skepticism about unions and government, while selling "free enterprise." The same techniques that had facilitated the rise of mass consumption and mass politics, such as advertising, market research, and opinion polls, now were deployed to restore the public's faith in "free-market" capitalism and otherwise win people's hearts and minds for business's point of view. Many corporations spent vast amounts on lobbying, campaign finance, litigation, philanthropy, and funding research in efforts to broaden their influence. This was no monolithic affair, however; the National Association of Manufacturers (NAM), the leading conservative group, frequently clashed with slightly more liberal business lobbies such as the Committee for Economic Development and the U.S. Chamber of Commerce. Nevertheless, in most instances the leading corporate figures of the postwar era agreed in their opposition to expansion of the New Deal order (Patterson 1996: 58).[1] They actually pressed for a government that would largely follow the instructions of big business. One historian has called this "the largest and most systematic deployment of corporate power in the history of the United States" (Griffith 1989: 66).

Thus, from the late 1940s through the early 1960s, American corporations and employer organizations spent millions on ideological warfare against the twin evils of collectivism and statism. The Foundation for Economic Education, a conservative propaganda organization established in 1947, drew its membership from the huge manufacturing companies that were at the heart of CIO activity (Harris 1982: 162–198; McQuaid 1994: 18–35). That same year, the renowned Mont Pelerin Society was created by a small and exclusive group of passionate believers in neoliberalism. Its members included the political philosopher Friedrich von Hayek, the economist/philosopher Ludwig von Mises, the economist Milton Friedman, and even, for a while, the philosopher Karl Popper, author of *The Open Society and Its Enemies* (1945). They called themselves "liberals" (in the traditional European sense) because of their fundamental commitment to ideals of personal freedom. The neoliberal label indicated their adherence to those free-market principles of neoclassical economics that had emerged in the second half of the nineteenth century (through the work of Alfred Marshall, William Stanley Jevons, and Leon Walras) to displace the classical theories of Adam Smith, David Ricardo, and others. Yet they clung to Adam Smith's belief in the "hidden hand of the market" as the best device to attain prosperity for everyone. Neoliberal doctrine was deeply opposed to state interventionist theories, such as those fostered by John Maynard Keynes. Neoliberals rejected even more fiercely Marxist theories of centralized state planning. Importantly, in the decades that followed, Milton Friedman came to dominate the Department of Economics at the University of Chicago and to wield increasingly greater influence in the academy. By the 1970s he had moved center stage, and his ideas would influence many economists and policy makers for decades to come (Harvey 2005: 19–22).

Employers in both the union sector and nonunion sector turned their plants into front lines for the ideological crusade. Nonunion firms took the lead in developing new avenues for communicating their corporate values to their employees. Much of business's propaganda was aimed at the general public, although the workplace remained a vital target in the battle. Factories and offices were inundated with pamphlets, magazines, and books, including comic strips, filled with songs of praise of the virtues of free enterprise. Book racks brimming with anti-communist literature were placed in the plants where workers were also subjected to lectures and color movies explaining how to detect subversives. By the late 1950s, 84 percent of America's five hundred largest corporations were offering "practical politics" programs to their employees. In their public relations campaigns, employers also began using anti-union rhetoric that previously had been taboo in the mainstream discourse. Next to the marginalization of the CIO's left-wing unions, this was partly due to Taft-Hartley's free speech clause and the expansive interpretation given to it by Eisenhower's NLRB appointees, offering employers considerable leeway to express their views during trade union election campaigns and organizing drives. Taft-Hartley also required the Labor Board to treat unaffiliated (company) unions on equal footing as affiliated ones (Vogel 1978: 63; Fones-Wolf 1994; Jacoby 1997: 200–201).

Organized employers—like nonunion firms such as Kodak and Thompson Products before them — mailed letters and magazines to employees' homes and hosted corporate events such as family picnics to carry their ideological message into the workers' "private sphere." Throughout the 1950s, an important unionized employer such as General Electric ran a massive anti-union communications program that included dramatized "road shows" (some starring Ronald Reagan) and numerous publications. The program was based on survey research that informed General Electric's management about employees' beliefs, values, and attitudes.

During those years, right-wing fringe groups became more influential within the business community too. These groups ranged from specialized anti-union or isolationist organizations (e.g., the American Security Council and American Action) to multi-issue lobbying groups (the John Birch Society, the American Enterprise Association, and many others). Close ties existed with more established conservative organizations like the NAM and the U.S. Chamber of Commerce. In the late 1940s and 1950s, many members of the NAM's executive committee actively supported and gave substantial donations to ultraconservative groups. Nonunion employers were prominently associated with the extreme right, including executives from Eli Lily, DuPont, and Sears (Jacoby 1997: 232; Bell 1963; Burch 1973).

On the other hand, unionized employers encountered a massive propaganda effort by organized labor distributing newsletters and magazines and implementing educational programs. AFL unions like Local 3 of the Electrical Workers harkened back to the "new unionism" of the 1910s, when the Garment Workers sought to culturally uplift their immigrant members. The CIO developed its educational activities along similar lines, while also deploying new media like political action committees, radio broadcasts, and television shows. Amid the outpouring of information and propaganda, these unions continued to uphold their view of a "laboristic" America, thereby accommodating to the postwar situation. In the 1950s, unionized, urban, blue-collar workers voted solidly for the Democratic Party and showed little enthusiasm for their employers, according to surveys done at the time. Studies showed that many workers could simultaneously be loyal to both company and union, a phenomenon that mainstream social scientists in the 1950s called "dual allegiance" and hailed as a precursor to "the end of ideology." But this dual loyalty was an unstable disposition, subject to continual pushes and pulls, especially during strikes (Purcell 1960; Stagner 1954).

The CIO, purged of Communists and other leftists (or those branded as such), abandoned its broader vision of industrial democracy in favor of a philosophy that saw labor's exclusion from corporate decision making as a virtue and not as a failure of American unions. Generally, unions accepted the lines drawn by management and instead concentrated their efforts on issues where they met least resistance. This led to significant gains in wages and fringe benefits until the onset of a prolonged recession in 1957, at a time when imports were beginning to encroach more and more on U.S. markets. The next year a wave of bitter strikes (including a 116-day national steel strike) broke out that ushered in a period in which management took a tougher approach toward labor, including aggressive demands for greater flexibility and lower costs.

There was also renewed interest in asserting and extending management rights in the workplace (Jacoby 1997: 193–195, 228–243).[2]

The AFL-CIO and the Democrats and Assaults on Union Bureaucracy

Despite its failure, the basics of the CIO strategy toward the Democrats (outlined earlier) were fully adopted by the AFL-CIO upon its merger in 1955 when the Committee on Political Education (COPE) replaced the PAC. The AFL dominated the new leadership, since the AFL's membership at that time outnumbered the CIO's by two to one. AFL President George Meany (William Green's successor) assumed the presidency, while Walter Reuther became vice president. Meany, who would lead the AFL-CIO for its first twenty-four years, expressed his fervent belief in the "free-enterprise" U.S. capitalist system in a 1958 speech to the National Association of Manufacturers. He suggested that American trade unionists generally intended to preserve the system in their efforts at bettering workers' standard of living by improving the system itself. In pursuing business unionism to the extreme, Meany used influence peddling and power brokering as major strategies during the 1950s and 1960s (Smith 2006: 203). Historian Stephen Amberg describes organized labor's plight: "Union leaders in this era of philosophical complacency focused on strategy and tactics for moving the Democrats, and through them the American polity, toward support for labor's policy proposals. It was not to be" (Amberg 1998: 173).

In this period the modern pattern of AFL-CIO intervention in politics became established. The Federation had two arms to carry this out: the Legislative Department, which conducted its lobbying efforts, and COPE, which did its electoral work and raised money for political contributions, often for centrist candidates (whose closest approach to labor was voting for gigantic defense appropriations—tied to the endless arms race—as job creation for their districts). This strategy seemed to achieve a moment of modest success in the 1960s, when the Federation's leaders, notably Meany and Reuther, garnered much attention from Democrats. But this might well be attributed to the civil rights, anti-war, and women's movements rather than to the unions. And, even though Democrats dominated Congress and held the White House between 1961 and 1969, the labor movement won no significant pro-labor legislation that could reverse the overriding downward trend. Successful in helping to elect Democrats through the 1970s, COPE proved unable to prevent the party from moving ever more rightward (Moody 2007: 144–145; Smith 2006: 211).

In the second half of the 1950s, the labor movement fell under increasing public scrutiny. The McClellan Committee hearings of 1957 and 1958 marked a true shift in the public perception of American trade unionism and of the collective bargaining system to which it was yoked. These high-profile hearings had a devastating impact on the moral standing of the entire trade union movement. The trials and investigations uncovered corruption, autocracy, and nepotism among the leaders of numerous trade union locals, especially those on the New York docks, in the short-haul trucking industry, in some construction trades, and among unions that had organized bakeries, restaurants, and bars. Such union criminality was mostly concentrated in highly decentralized, multi-employer industries that gave individual union leaders, or their mob-connected deputies, the opportunity to misappropriate money from the pension fund, cut sweetheart deals, or run the local as a family business. Opinion polls showed waning trust in organized labor and growing hostility toward labor leaders.

Those who saw these labor corruption scandals as an opportunity to revive the assault on the union movement deliberately ignored most of the distinctions between mob-connected criminality, autocratic leadership, hard bargaining, and industry-wide negotiating strength. The 1959 Labor-Management Reporting and Disclosure Act (or Landrum-Griffin Act) was the legislative outcome of the McClellan Committee's work. It represented the anti-unionism of northern Republicans and southern Democrats who had enacted Taft-Hartley and then campaigned against "monopoly unionism" in the 1950s. One section of the new act tightened the restrictions of Taft-Hartley, outlawing the closed shop and secondary boycotts, and restricting picketing rights and other measures of solidarity. It also gave the Labor Department greater power to regulate union financial affairs. But another significant section of the Landrum-Griffin Act was a union member "bill of rights" which had nothing to do with the rising tide of civil rights activism of the black freedom movement and the NAACP Legal Defense Fund but entailed an essentially right-wing understanding of union dynamics, according to Lichtenstein. The major proponents of this union bill of rights were southern Democrats along with the Barry Goldwater wing of the Republican Party. When a potential link with the rights of non-white workers became public, northern Republicans did not hesitate to assure their southern allies that the legislation's provision for jury trials in cases brought under the law would preserve the "Southern way of life." Thus, Republican anti-unionism trumped the party's long-standing, yet increasingly perfunctory, claim as an upholder of African-American civil rights (Lichtenstein 2002: 162–165).

There was another side to the section known as the bill of rights, however, that appeared to offer democratic guarantees to the rank-and-file unionists. Although it did not guarantee reforms such as the direct election of union officers, it gave dissidents access to union membership lists, required officers to hold regular meetings, and mandated international union conventions at least every five years. It also gave individuals grievance rights regarding arbitrary and undemocratic actions of union officials handled by a special bureau of the Department of Labor. Yet other provisions in the act made it difficult for dissidents ever to reach the courts and claim such rights. Despite these limitations and the permanent risk of government involvement in the union's internal affairs, the bill of rights gave ordinary union members a minimal opportunity to protect themselves and their unions from the misbehavior of autocratic union leaders and their bureaucracies. It was up to members and their supporters to claim their rights.

This legislation drew the ire of the overwhelming majority of union officials because it required regular reports on union finances and health and welfare funds and, most of all, because of the bill of rights. The AFL-CIO lobbied hard against the bill and sought to soften its most draconian features, which was to no avail (Aronowitz 2008: 210). President Meany saw the bill of rights provisions as a direct assault on the kind of trade unionism that had enabled his own career and that he proudly identified with. He had to admit that violations of membership rights regularly occurred, but he insisted that it was labor's responsibility to clean its own house. On the surface, his arguments against government control seemed to have a militant tinge, but they proved to be mostly empty rhetoric, the effort of an autocratic leader to protect the chain of command of an established labor bureaucracy (Buhle 1999: 164–165).[3]

From the 1960s onward, employer anti-unionism would increasingly make use of the Landrum-Griffin Act rather than the Taft-Hartley Act to legitimate its attacks on labor. Corporate management's strategies shifted to the ostensible protection of the individual rights of workers against the undemocratic and bureaucratic unions in which they were enrolled. A national Right-to-Work Committee, funded by the National Association of Manufacturers and southern textile interests, focused on exploiting the new rights discourse in order to undermine the solidarity that was the very basis of trade unionism (Lichtenstein 2002: 166). On the other hand, there were also several cases in which rank-and-file reform movements against union oligarchies, often controlled by racketeers, availed themselves of the "infamous" Landrum-Griffin Act. For example, the Teamsters for a Democratic Union's successive campaigns for rank-and-file contracts (from 1976 onward) and its dramatic efforts to force a secret ballot direct-membership vote for national leaders, entailed the intervention of the federal government and the courts on the basis of the act, and especially in conjunction with the 1970 RICO law. This law gave the federal government extraordinary powers to intervene when a "private" organization, such as a labor union or a business, was subjected to racketeering (Aronowitz 2008: 214).[4]

Johnson's Great Society Programs and the Limits of Postwar Liberalism

Postwar liberalism had become intertwined with a fervent commitment to internationalism, and to the global fight against communism, which at times seemed to overwhelm everything else. Domestically, though, liberals adopted new goals as well, including a growing interest in the expansion of civil rights for individuals and groups, beginning with the struggle for racial justice for African Americans (Brinkley 1995: 269–270). The preeminent example of this liberalism was Johnson's set of Great Society programs that aimed to solve the problem of American poverty once and for all. Achieving this lofty goal would have required the Democratic Party to adopt European-style, social democratic policies involving extensive state interventions in labor and income markets, according to historian Ira Katznelson. But this alternative — espoused by the left wing of the New Deal and progressive elements of the labor movement — had already been headed off in the 1940s. Commercial Keynesianism had triumphed while the labor movement transformed from a social democratic insurgency into a mere interest group. In those years, race replaced social inequality tied to class as the great unsolved problem in American life. These transformations during the 1940s decisively shaped and limited the social programs of the 1960s.

Great Society policy makers were strongly influenced by economists professing commercial Keynesian doctrines that dismissed extensive state interventions in capital and labor markets as possible policies. And the labor movement showed little interest in using the War on Poverty to tackle the unequal distribution of income and power in American society. Due to the labor movement's reluctance on the one hand and the growing influence of the civil rights movement on the other, the War on Poverty became virtually entirely associated with the problems of urban African Americans. Although Great Society policy makers demonstrated great inventiveness and boldness in pushing the limits of the ideological framework in which they operated, they were unable to solve the problem of poverty — irrespective of skin color — without more extensive state regulations of capitalist institutions and markets. Moreover, their inability to undo the increasingly popular view that the Great Society was only aimed at helping blacks led to resentment against the Democratic Party among poor and working-class whites (Katznelson 1989). Steve Fraser and Gary Gerstle astutely summarize this interpretation:

> Great Society policymakers, imprisoned by the 1940s ideological framework they inherited, lacked the necessary intellectual autonomy and clarity. And even if they had somehow managed to step outside their own history and devise a set of wise social policies, they might have found their policies thwarted by the nation's strained economic base [Fraser and Gerstle 1989: xxiii].

Tensions within the Democratic Party over the issues of poverty and race augmented as the costs of defending the "free world," and in particular fighting the war in Vietnam, led to cutbacks in domestic social spending. The growing European and Japanese challenge to American economic superiority further strained the nation's resources and began generating a number of economic problems, including inflation, declining investment and productivity, unmanageable budget deficits, and negative trade balances. Politically, these pressures called into question two fundamental principles of the New Deal order: first, the adage that the benefits of consumer capitalism ought to be extended to ever more Americans; and, second, that the state, through its fiscal and monetary powers, should stimulate the production and distribution of economic abundance.

Pressured by a surging civil rights movement, the Johnson administration sought to extend the governmental regime that the New Dealers had helped to create to include African Americans and Latinos. This meant not only destroying Jim Crow, as important as that goal was, but also attacking racial discrimination in hiring practices and expanding welfare benefits (for both blacks and whites). In addition, by the summer of 1968, Johnson backed legislation designed to undermine discrimination in the housing market and thus foster neighborhood desegregation. These moves fueled a strong backlash among the white working class, with increasing numbers of Catholic voters deserting the Democratic Party. White working-class taxpayers were especially resentful about categorical programs identified with the minority poor. This may have been exacerbated by the fact that they shouldered the brunt of the highly regressive state and local taxes that helped fund those programs (Piven 1992: 253). When blue-collar whites complained during the late 1960s and 1970s that the liberals had left them behind, they had a point. New Deal-type liberal policy up until then had protected the racial, *relatively* privileged position of the white working class, with its high proportion of Catholics. Great Society policy makers indeed abandoned that restrictive framework.

After Johnson left the Oval Office, liberals pushed even harder on racial issues, endorsing the integration of northern school systems, cross-district busing, and affirmative action (Boyle 2008: 36). Many white workers, conscious of protecting the gains achieved through contractual agreements, heavily resisted what they saw as unwarranted attacks on their economic standing and neighborhood boundaries. As school busing moved to the forefront in northern cities after 1966, managed and enforced by federal courts, this anger exploded. A large number of northern working people then turned to more conservative political candidates, sharply leaning toward Republicans in presidential contests, as in Nixon's elections in 1968 and 1972 (Cowie and Salvatore 2008: 18).

Separate Spheres of Labor Rights and Civil Rights

The two legislative milestones that came to shape justice in the workplace were the NLRA (1935) and Title VII of the Civil Rights Act (1964). A coherent labor market policy aimed at occupational justice would have to confront both collective economic rights and the right to non-discrimination; however, these two pieces of legislation were products of separate historical eras and struggles, policy traditions, and judicial spheres. Unsurprisingly, they were often in tension, which helped solidify a division between race and class (even though they were lived as a unified social reality). As Paul Frymer argues, these two acts are products of "two vectors of power," and the failure to build a strong and diverse labor movement was foremost "the outcome of a political system that, in its effort to appeal to civil rights opponents, developed a bifurcated system of power that assigned race and class problems to different spheres of development" (Frymer 2008: 2–3).

With the benefit of hindsight, the two laws, and the trajectory of the movements that brought each about, tended to institutionalize the divisions rather than build bridges between them. By the 1970s, the division was growing into "an unbridgeable chasm." That decade brought forth a dual movement; the revolution in minority and women's occupational rights took place simultaneously with a counter-revolution in labor rights (Cowie 2010: 237, 239).

Contrary to the Wagner Act, whose power was restricted by subsequent laws and judicial rulings, Title VII opened the floodgate to a series of new laws, labeled "civil rights," that were crucial for the expansion of work rights in every domain, from factory, office, and school to salesroom. These laws included the Age Discrimination in Employment Act (1968), the Mine Safety Act (1969), the Occupational Safety and Health Act (1970), the Rehabilitation Act (1973), the Employee Retirement Income Security Act (1974), and the Pregnancy Discrimination Act (1978).[5] Through this extensive legislation, although highly contested at the time, issues that involved the hiring, pay, promotion, and layoff of employees became subject to governmental review and private litigation. Together, these laws went much further than anything that the union movement had achieved by collective bargaining, even during the heyday of the Wagner Act.

The civil rights approach was at right angles with the whole framework of organized labor and collective bargaining, let alone the idea of an industrial democracy in the workplace. According to Nelson Lichtenstein, this disjuncture between the civil rights approach and the unionizing impulse is distinctively American. He points out that the rights revolution of the 1960s (sometimes a decade or more delayed) strengthened social democratic movements and increased trade unions' density and power in parts of Western Europe, Canada, and even Poland, Spain, South Africa, and South Korea. In the United States, though, this was a time of relative union stagnation, divorced from the democratizing rights consciousness of the era (Lichtenstein 2002: 180–181). There were brief fusions of labor and civil rights struggles in the 1960s and 1970s—most notably the AFSCME Local 1733 strike by black sanitation workers in Memphis, where Dr. Martin Luther King Jr. was assassinated, and as expressed in the United Farm Workers' dual cries of "Viva La Huelga" (long live the strike) and "La Raza." However, the struggle for occupational justice was focused primarily on breaking down race and gender lines—gaining access to better and more skilled jobs for women and minorities—rather than marrying the project of integration to structural change. This emphasis on greater occupational opportunities for women and minorities gained momentum when the call for broad economic justice was in decline. As historian Jefferson Cowie points out,

> The result was heightened competition for dwindling opportunity. The political calculation shifted in the sixties and seventies from changing the division of the pie to making sure everyone had an equal chance to *compete* for a slice [Cowie 2010: 239].

It should not be forgotten, however, that the civil rights and feminist movements of the late 1960s and 1970s, in emphasizing the rights of people of color and women to equal opportunity and employment rights, first of all claimed access to many of the promises of the New Deal order: good wages, health care benefits, and Social Security, a voice and dignity at work, economic and political citizenship, housing, and a decent old age pension. Second, they momentarily reopened the struggle over the distribution of wealth. Third, as employers and courts actively worked to ensure that New Deal economic and social rights did not become firmly embedded in law and constitutional rights, these other social movements rushed in to address the core issues about what the basic human rights should be (Klein 2008: 45–46).

Labor, the New Social Movements and the New Left

Most of the AFL-CIO's top leaders remained entirely out of touch with the new social movements that emerged and invigorated left-liberal politics in the 1960s. The generation of trade unionists then in power had battled the Communists in the 1940s and accommodated themselves to the constraints of the Cold War and the narrow limits of the Taft-Hartley labor relations regime. The AFL-CIO had much internal strife coming to terms with deeply ingrained patterns of racial discrimination, not only against blacks but increasingly against Latinos as well. Labor markets in certain sectors and geographical areas felt the aftereffects when the Bracero program ended in 1964, which did little to interrupt the migratory patterns from Mexico to the United States but drove much more of the flows of laborers underground. Mexicans continued to cross the border, pushed by grinding poverty at home and pulled by the lure of jobs in the United States. This massive influx of agricultural workers also accelerated the urbanization of the Mexican population already settled in the United States. The existing Chicano farmers experienced severe competition from these newcomers. Like the small black and white sharecroppers from the South, many Chicanos went first to work in the arms industry, then construction, textiles, automobile assembly and finally the public sector (Daniels 1990: 305–307, 310–311).

The construction trade unions were very reluctant to open their doors to

4. Corporate Assaults and Limits of Postwar Liberalism 113

African-American and Latino workers, only conceding after severe legal assault. The International Ladies Garment Workers Union, the UAW, and the Textile Workers Union were criticized by the NAACP because of their failure to end de facto segregation in many locals and departments. In the 1960s, the UAW, for example, experienced a series of internal insurgencies by black workers who sought representation on the union's executive board as well as to transform power relations inside urban locals that were becoming increasingly multicultural. George Meany, AFL-CIO's president for a quarter century, was so hostile to the new liberalism that he withheld union backing from the 1972 presidential bid of progressive Democrat (and Vietnam War opponent) George McGovern. Meany and others among the AFL-CIO top leadership denounced peace demonstrators, ignored the new wave of feminism, and ridiculed gay demands for dignity and civil rights. Even Walter Reuther's UAW, which supported (financially and otherwise) both the civil rights movement and the early New Left, resisted moves to revitalize its institutions. Although Reuther did hire a significant number of ex-Socialists, ex-Trotskyists, ex-Communists and even some youthful veterans of the New Left, they were obliged to conform to a liberal regime that was autocratic and isolated from the insurgent movements of the decade (Lichtenstein 2002: 185–191).

In the 1960s and 1970s, the call to create an independent labor party could be heard again during some strikes and in the demands of some rank-and-file trade union groups such as UAW's United National Caucus. But the idea of a labor party was overshadowed this time by social movements that owed little to labor, even when congenial. Instead, other types of alternative political action were sought, such as embodied by the Mississippi Freedom Democratic Party and the Peace and Freedom Party, in instances when the Democrats were not embraced outright (Moody 2007: 241; Weir 2004: 305–306).

Between 1968 and 1974, workplace militancy spread across North America and in a number of industries: from autoworkers to postal workers, from telephone operators to teamsters. Similar rank-and-file uprisings of predominantly young workers then struck in the automobile plants of Turin, Stuttgart, Billancourt, and elsewhere (including countries as diverse as Canada, Chile, South Africa, and Brazil). These worker movements all had links to a "global" New Left and shared the New Left critique of organized labor, the anti-authoritarian mood, and militant revolutionary rhetoric (Pizzolato 2004: 423–429, 435). In those years there were also significant movements aimed at greater union democracy in America, articulated in dissident caucuses within the unions such as Miners for Democracy, Steelworkers Fight Back, Teamsters for a Decent Contract, and in the UAW, the United National Caucus (Cohen 2008: 408–409). In addition, there were movements as diverse as the United Farm Workers' national grape boycott, the struggle to organize the (mostly Latina) garment workers at the Farah Garment Factory in El Paso, Texas, and the movement among Boston office workers that revived the Service Employees International

Union. This activity seemed to indicate a new dawn for labor in the United States.

During this period of industrial unrest, young workers in industry chafed against supervision on the assembly line, clogged up the system with grievances, demanded improvements in the quality of work life, walked out in wildcat strikes and organized to overthrow bureaucratic union leadership. Observers often referred to the restiveness on the assembly lines as the "Lordstown syndrome," named after the strike in 1972 by a group of young, hip, and interracial autoworkers of a General Motors (Chevy Vega) plant in Lordstown, Ohio, which allegedly had the fastest, and most psychically deadening, assembly line in the world (Cowie 2010: 7–8, 23–68).

At Lordstown and in some of the other labor protests, the issue of "alienated work" surfaced as a major grievance. The issue of alienation in the work setting had been introduced by some labor leaders, influenced partly by the findings of Robert Blauner's comparative sociological study of the implications of "automation" on work satisfaction or deprivation (in terms of powerlessness, meaninglessness, isolation and estrangement), which indicated relatively high alienation levels among workers in the auto industry (Blauner 1964).[6] Furthermore, labor-oriented radical students brought into unions the attacks of critical intellectuals on the machine-paced work that reflected human alienation in capitalist industry. At the background was the rediscovery of Marx's early writings on alienation by a new generation of philosophers and social thinkers in Britain, France and America, as well as dissidents and revisionists in Eastern Europe (Bell 1959; Ollman 1971; Aronowitz 1973: 26).

The issue of "alienated work" also involved a change in values among workers—a move away from some characteristically "bourgeois" values, notably the belief that work is the main business of life for the male (work-centeredness). Other value patterns that took root in those years included an emphasis on one's quality of life, including a "hedonistic" preference for leisure to work and an environmentalist resistance to the cult of economic growth at all costs. The "post-bourgeois" values held by a substantial number of younger workers implied hostility to impersonality, to being used purely as an instrument or resource, and to any form of autocratic direction or supervision. Strong resentment against rationalized work emerged among the workforce, which was manifested in the erosion of industrial discipline evident from figures for turnover, absenteeism, and timekeeping, as well as a growing disrespect for the authority of foremen and managers (Rose 1988: 307–308, 356–366).

The Lordstown workers became a collective national symbol of the new kind of worker and emblematic of a widespread sense of alienation in the workplace. Journalists wrote about "blue-collar blues" resulting from workers who felt "robotized" by Taylorism. This in turn incited a moral panic among economic and political elites about the alleged decline of the work ethic. Many American commentators saw this revolt against work as a rejection of economic values thought essential to sustaining a dynamic capitalist economy. The Lordstown rebellion therefore drew national political attention. The local union president testified at the Democratic Party's platform committee, and a Senate subcommittee convened hearings on "alienation." The Nixon administration appointed a national commission to study the problems it raised, which led to the federal report, *Work in America* (Special Task Force 1973). This culminated in the "quality of work life" movement that sought to redesign work, introduce automation differently, and invest in "human relations" strategies, most of which continued to empower management, not workers, albeit with the appearance of a gentler style (Cowie 2010: 47).

The broader wave of labor unrest also involved a radical left-wing movement of black workers in the auto industry. By the late 1960s and early 1970s, discontent among black autoworkers spawned serious conflicts within the UAW, especially in Detroit. The economic boom stimulated by the Vietnam War (and the enhanced military Keynesianism it implied) led to an expanded auto workforce. General Motors, Ford, and especially Chrysler hired thousands of black workers. Many were young men who combined the toughness of life in the ghetto with the rising expectations fomented by the civil rights movement. Detesting the casual racism manifested by white supervisors and co-workers, and often having to work with antiquated and malfunctioning equipment in decaying plants, young black workers turned against the hierarchies of power and authority that had traditionally ruled the auto plants. Through the late 1960s, there were dozens of incidents whereby angry young workers challenged harassing foremen, disdainful co-workers, and aging union officials. This in-plant conflict did not remain confined to individual fights and protests but also took the form of collective action.

In many of the plants in Detroit, as well as some in Chicago and other northern cities, young black workers formed embryonic workplace groups aimed at "workers' control," with a cadre of black radicals providing ideological and organizational support. Radical students at Wayne State University together with shop-floor activists helped create workers councils; the largest and most active emerged at the Dodge main plant, which employed thirty thousand workers. Next to protest against intolerable working conditions, members of the Black Power movement honed in on racial discrimination tied to a dual internal labor market. The Dodge group adopted the name Dodge Revolutionary Union Movement (DRUM), and similar bodies popped up at other Detroit-area factories. In 1968, these various groups joined hands to form the League of Revolutionary Black Workers (LRBW), whose leaders connected the conditions faced by black autoworkers to the struggles of southern blacks in the United States as well as to the plight of people of color throughout the world who were rising up against capitalism and colonialism.[7] Black Power spokesmen such as Stokely Carmichael asserted that African Americans historically were super-exploited, sharing racial and economic bonds with their "soul brothers" in the

Third World.[8] They argued that the surplus wealth on which America was built was created by enslaved blacks. And as the United States became an industrial power, African Americans continued to play a vital role. According to the League of Revolutionary Black Workers, blacks had "finally gotten the news" that white capital derived from their blood, sweat and tears, from the colonial and antebellum plantations to the more modern steel forges, slaughterhouse yards, and automobile assembly lines (Levy 1994: 77, 115–116). Both the Coalition of Black Trade Unionists (CBTU, founded in 1973) and the A. Philip Randolph Institute of the AFL-CIO were heavily opposed to this new generation of black militants with their Marxist-Leninist critique of mainstream unions (Cowie 2010: 59).

In Detroit, militant black workers did attack the auto companies' management and the city's corporate elites, but much of their anger was concentrated on the UAW, which union shop contracts required them to join. They accused union leaders, who were well paid and enjoying great fringe benefits, of paying little attention to serious workplace problems at the increasingly inhospitable and dangerous auto plants. Within the auto sector, the revolutionary union movements (RUMs) were staunchly critical of the UAW because of its bureaucratic complicity in the companies' speedups, unsafe working conditions, authoritarian supervision at the plants, and institutional racism. The white-dominated UAW leadership ignored black workers' demands to abolish racist language and demeaning treatment. Grievance officers downplayed those workers' complaints, responding at times with their own racist remarks. While the UAW may have offered solutions to workers' problems in the past, now LRBW activists charged it had become an integral part of the problem (Zieger 2007: 199–200). This radical protest in the auto industry drew national media attention and provoked a crisis at the company headquarters about lost production, as well as in the UAW, whose leadership feared it was losing its grip on the workforce. The latter was understandable since the radical leaders of the protest considered the local and international officers as being part of the same machinery as the company management. They were convinced that the union's bureaucracy would co-opt African Americans who merely sought to improve their own status and salary, preempting the possibility of an independent black leadership within the UAW.[9]

Like many other left-wing labor activists in the late 1960s and early 1970s, the benchmark of these radical black workers' analysis was the 1930s. Just like the rank and file of that era had joined forces as a bottom-up movement to form the CIO throughout the country, the time had arrived for similar action to push for union democracy. The black radical movements in industry had very limited impact, however. The RUMs found it virtually impossible to win union elections—even in locals with black majorities.[10] Their Black Power posture and contempt for liberals, reform-oriented black leaders, and above all white workers involved in the white backlash, tended to evoke more fear than solidarity, and they wound up alienating the older generations of black workers. Black Power influence in the plants quickly faded; after a brief flurry of wildcats in the auto plants in 1973, it disappeared altogether (Cowie 2010: 60; Boyle 1995: 254).

How about New Left labor activism, which evolved independently for the most part from the black radical movements? There was a brief period in which the theory of the "new working class" held some sway within the New Left. By 1967 a segment of the New Left (including SDS leaders Greg Calvert and Carl Davidson) had adopted this theory as put forward in the works of French socialists Serge Mallet and André Gorz and applied it to the American "multi-university." The new working class, which supposedly had replaced Marx's industrial proletariat as the potential revolutionary vanguard, consisted of those individuals who similarly lacked control over the means of production yet performed society's essential functions. This group of technocrats, engineers, and knowledge workers was a class in and of itself. According to Mallet, the position of the new working class in contemporary society was analogous to that of skilled manual workers in a less developed economy. Through its own contradictions, capitalism was creating a new radical agent, one that could shake society simply by withdrawing its labor. The operator-technicians of the advanced technology industries would adopt a new brand of unionism — or rather, an updated form of syndicalism aimed at gaining control over management's prerogatives, winning the right to set objectives and to check on their achievement. The demand for workers' self-management (*autogestion* in French) would produce a "revolution from below" rather than the top-down pattern favored by the old working class (as envisioned in traditional Marxist literature) that required the prior seizure of state power (Mallet 1963).[11]

In what became known as the "Port Authority Statement" (a reference to its authors' New York origins and to the more famous Port Huron Statement), the SDS activists Robert Gottlieb, Gerry Tenney and David Gilbert likewise theorized the emergence of the relatively recent social layer of salaried professionals and technical workers. They suggested that in advanced capitalist societies the labor question was now a struggle for emancipation, not from labor itself, but from the authority of capitalist society. They argued that the social position of educated workers, especially in the advanced technological sectors, should be understood as a new working class rather than adjuncts to management and members of the middle class. What distinguished the demands of this social formation from those of industrial workers was that they were most preoccupied with the quality of their working lives — whether they had autonomy in the performance of their work that matched their education and knowledge — rather than mainly with job security and with wages and benefits (Gottlieb, Tenney, and Gilbert 1967).[12]

The new working-class theory as received among this faction of the New Left surpassed the prevailing student power idea in that it more clearly defined the role of radical students after they left the university. Since today's engineering, science, social science, and humanities students were tomorrow's technocrats, bureaucrats, teachers, and managers, the role of student activists remained the same. Students could stay in college or graduate school, and the New Left could continue its college campus focus, based on the assumption that "university uprisings served as training grounds for future revolts against society at large" (Levy 1994: 120).

But for many New Left activists, this theory was problematic since it was not confrontational enough to contest the status quo. Its stature within the SDS also rested to a large degree on the ascendancy of National Secretary Greg Calvert, not on widespread understanding of the theory itself. The idea of the new working class remained vulnerable to attack, especially by well-organized factions, such as the Progressive Labor Party, which saw it as a direct repudiation of its own neoclassic Marxist theories. Consequently, when the leadership of SDS changed, this theory fell out of favor. Yet after the demise of SDS, there were still some interesting New Left efforts to account for the politics of students, professionals, and other intellectual workers in terms of a "new class" (Ehrenreich and Ehrenreich 1977; Walker 1979).

Many in the New Left were inclined to see unions as "part of the problem, not part of the solution." And some activists considered the working class as totally "integrated" by affluence — it had lost all interest in societal transformation, merely seeking "more" from the system. Herbert Marcuse's ideas about the all-pervasive power of technical rationality in quashing protest through co-optation in advanced industrial societies were influential here. In *One-Dimensional Man* (1964), which offered a wide-ranging critique of both contemporary capitalist societies and Soviet communist societies, Marcuse outlined the parallel rise of new forms of social repression in both types of societies as well as the decline of revolutionary potential in the West. He argued that "advanced industrial society" created false needs, which integrated individuals into the existing system of production and consumption via mass media, advertising, industrial management, and prevailing modes of thought. This resulted in a one-dimensional world of thought and behavior in which ability and opportunity for critical thinking and oppositional behavior wither away. Against this prevailing climate, Marcuse promoted the "great refusal" as the only adequate opposition to all-encompassing modes of control, along with a defense of "negative thinking" as a disrupting force against the prevailing positivism. In asserting the complete integration of the industrial working class into capitalist society, Marcuse questioned the Marxist belief in the revolutionary potential of the proletariat. Instead, he hung his hopes for revolutionary change on non-integrated minorities, outsiders, and radical intelligentsia who attempt to fuel oppositional thought and behavior (Kellner 1991: xi). Proponents of this view among the New Left suggested that social change would come from blacks and other people of color, women, youth, and people in the Third World. For a decade, they drew the most attention, overshadowing others who were building new unions, reorganizing the older unions, and forming caucuses that campaigned inside unions for union democracy (Aronowitz 1998: 199).

In the early 1970s, the latter New Leftists began moving into workplaces as a political act — "colonizing" or "industrializing" as they called this strategy. In the ongoing upsurge of labor unrest these young activists saw a new route to political power denied them on university campuses as they looked for a democratic socialist future. They hoped that the labor activism epitomized by Lordstown and Miners for Democracy, along with the United Farm Workers and the Farah strikers, represented something greater than the simple business unionism that had been at the center of much of labor history — that a revolutionary transformation might be at hand. In 1973, Staughton Lynd, a key figure, explained that movement organizers had become aware that the weak link in the chain of campus politics was their inability to make common cause with working people. So they had shifted gears and had recently started to reach out to working-class America.

> Collectives of former students who have taken jobs in offices and factories are dotted across the nation. Others have sought to reach the same constituency from outside the workplace, organizing around issues like pollution and taxation. Miners for Democracy and [movements like that at Lordstown] symbolized the new restlessness. Unsure as yet about who the enemy is, what the goal is, workers have begun to sense their power and make their feelings known [Lynd 1973: 28].

Thus, young militants who entered the workplaces joined forces with rank-and-file workers interested in transforming the union leadership, while creating a source of annoyance to the union leadership, which turned around and blamed them for whatever lay beyond their control. And, instead of being involved in bringing about a revolutionary transformation, the New Left activists ended up being pragmatic reformists (Cowie 2010: 68–69). As one veteran, Steve Early, suggested,

> Most New Leftists who entered the labor movement had hoped to win converts to socialism. But where radicals had been most successful in building a rank-and-file base, it has often been through downplaying their politics and winning acceptance on the basis of their performance as dedicated and effective trade unionists [Early 2003: 9].

The primary target of those radicals was the autocratic labor bureaucracy, which to them was the sole force blocking the dynamism of working-class revolution. New Left radicals like Stanley Aronowitz, Alice and Staughton Lynd, and Jeremy Brecher aggressively criticized what they saw as the collaborationist character of the mainstream trade unions. They echoed C. Wright Mills's denunciation of the Old Left's faith in organized labor — what he called "the labor metaphysic," the notion that the working class would be the primary agent of historical change — in his famous 1960 "Letter to the New Left."[13] In his last book, *The Marxists* (1962), Mills stated that wageworkers in advanced capitalism had seldom become a "proletariat vanguard" acting as the agency of any revolutionary societal change. Instead, they had to a considerable degree been incorporated into "nationalist capitalism — economically, politically, and psychologically." The same was true of trade unions and labor parties (Mills 1962: 126–128; Levy 1994: 111–112).[14] As Jim Green would later remark about his experiences as a member of the *Radical America* collective, the understanding of the union bureaucracy by the New Left activists involved "was not balanced with an explanation of why union members often accepted business unionism or why they abandoned the social [movement] unionism radical and progressive leaders advocated" (Green 2000: 44, 48). It became clear to the New Left by 1975 that the mishmash of labor insurgencies, along with their alleged potential for radical transformation, were stagnating and were not going to coalesce into a new kind of radical movement. They also became aware that the emphasis on shop-floor activism failed to address important political questions about gender, culture, sexuality, and race relations (Cowie 2010: 69–70).

Needless to say, the idea that the working class was on the brink of fundamental societal change and kept away from this only by the detested "union bureaucrats" did not dovetail with reality. This realization led to great disappointment among those who had held tightly to this belief. But the New Left generation that entered the labor movement with high hopes about fundamental societal change often ended up as good reformist organizers as they made the long march through organized labor's institutions. A number of student-movement veterans became activists in unions such as Hospital Workers Local 1199, the United Electrical Workers, the United Farm Workers, and the American Federation of State, County, and Municipal Employees (AFSCME), where they did not necessarily oppose the leadership (Lichtenstein 2002: 170).

Overall, the various insurgencies achieved little lasting institutional presence in the labor movement and left almost no legacy in American politics. Rather than being institutionalized as, for example, the intense workers' struggle in Turin, Italy, in the fall of 1969, called *Autunno Caldo* (which opened the path to many pieces of progressive labor legislation over the next decade), the American labor insurgencies were often more heavily suppressed, until the movement faded away (Pizzolato 2004: 424–427). Similarly, Mike Davis argues,

> In contrast to Western Europe, where the insurgencies of 1968–1973 led to profound upheavals that set new agendas for the labor movement and recomposed its activist leadership, the American rank-and-file struggles did not succeed in re-orienting the unions towards "qualitative" demands nor did they produce a distinct new layer of worker-militants. As often as not, the defeat of local insurgencies, or, conversely, their immediate cooption into the status quo, only left enduring legacies of frustration and demoralization [Davis 1986: 127].

Organizations like the Coalition of Black Trade Unionists and the Coalition of Labor Union Women (founded in 1974) continued to function as the moral conscience of the official labor movement, while a small number of determined

New Leftists eventually attained leadership positions in a movement that had long been on the defensive. Organized labor in America moved on to become one of the most diverse institutions in American society, but, at the same time, its energies cracked under the harsh economic climate marked by the great stagflation crisis in the second half of the 1970s (Cowie 2010: 70–71). The failure of the above-mentioned insurgences to make a lasting imprint on American life would handicap future attempts at establishing a labor-based left party.

The Upsurge of Pro-Business, Right-Wing Politics and the Weakening Working-Class Allegiance to the Democrats

Neoliberalism as the updated version of classical economic liberalism became increasingly important from the 1970s on, in which yet another round of ideological warfare played a crucial role. The American Chamber of Commerce expanded its base from around 60,000 firms in 1972 to over a quarter of a million ten years later. Together with the National Association of Manufacturers, the Chamber amassed an enormous campaign chest to lobby Congress and engage in research. The Business Roundtable, founded in 1973, became the centerpiece of pro-business action, uniting over one hundred of the nation's biggest corporations — from U.S. Steel and General Motors to AT&T and Bank of America — in a concerted bid to sway both government and public opinion.

Unlike older business lobbying groups, the Business Roundtable was more than simply a player in the political arena; it sought to define the playing field (Cowie 2010: 231–232). As David Vogel argues, it was more akin to a vanguard party than a simple trade union, advancing the larger issues of the business class rather than the narrow concerns of any particular interest or sector. It could modify its demands, help shape legislation to its advantage at the earliest stages, and most importantly, bring CEOs of major corporations to Capitol Hill instead of paid lobbyists (Vogel 1989: 198–199). The corporations involved accounted for about one half of the GNP of the United States during the 1970s, and they spent close to $900 million annually (a huge amount then) on political matters. Think tanks such as the Heritage Foundation, the Hoover Institute, the Center for the Study of American Business, and the American Enterprise Institute were formed with corporate backing. As in the case of the National Bureau of Economic Research (NBER), their primary goal was to generate technical and empirical studies and political-philosophical arguments broadly in support of neoliberal politics (Harvey 2005: 44). The Business Roundtable connected high-profile CEOs to those think tanks and academic studies, as well as popular outlets like *Reader's Digest*, all aimed at its principal political adversary — the entire labor movement.

Closely linked to the academic community, the NBER was to have a crucial impact on political-economic thinking in the economics departments and business schools at major research universities in the following years. With vast amounts of money furnished by wealthy individuals (such as the beer brewer Joseph Coors) and their foundations (including Oline, Scaife, Smith Richardson, and Pew Charitable Trust), a flood of tracts and books espousing neoliberal values were produced — with Robert Nozick's *Anarchy, State and Utopia* (1974) perhaps the most widely read and appreciated. In addition, a TV version of Milton Friedman's *Free to Choose* was produced, funded with a grant from Scaife in 1977. The latter ten-part PBS mini-series (first telecast in 1980) was underwritten by some of the largest corporations in the world, including Getty Oil, Firestone Tire & Rubber, PepsiCo, General Motors, Bechtel and General Mills (Friedman and Friedman 1980; Harvey 2005: 44).[15]

The management offensive at Capitol Hill during the second half of the 1970s was paralleled by corporate assaults on labor in the workplace as firms hired anti-union consultants in unprecedented numbers. Union busting became a sophisticated big business: mass market seminars and crash courses abounded; anti-union law firms drove workers into legal quagmires; industrial psychologists sought to contain the hearts and minds of the rank and file; consulting firms taught employers how to defeat an organizing drive step by step; and trade associations customized each step for a particular industry. The AFL-CIO contended that the corporations' enhanced use of anti-union tactics was "double-barreled." First there was the fact that the NLRA had been contorted to the extent that it became little more than a "management tool," as one historian later phrased it (Brody 2004). Then there were the attempts to influence the workers' viewpoints through direct anti-union appeals. Social scientists concluded that the figures on union decline had less to do with the changing labor market, but much more with management aggressiveness and increased wrangling over unionism on the shop floor (Cowie 2010: 233–234; Goldfield 1986).

However, next to the increased popularity of "free-market" ideas after the collapse of the reigning Keynesian orthodoxy, there were two other factors that came together to produce a broader base for pro-business, right-wing politics in the 1970s. One was an upsurge of cultural-religious defense, particularly in conservative evangelical and fundamentalist Protestant denominations. The other was a conservative backlash against the civil rights, anti-war and other popular movements of the 1960s that made it possible for the right to oppose the social gains accomplished by those movements by framing themselves as opponents of "big government," which was depicted and perceived as siding with blacks, women, homosexuals, welfare recipients and so on (Phillips-Fein 2009).

Moreover, as Frances Fox Piven explains, working-class allegiance to the Democratic Party had weakened rapidly after the Second World War as a result of the failure of the party to shore up a union infrastructure or to promote welfare state policies oriented to the working class.[16] The economic and demographic trends of the first three postwar decades aggravated the weaknesses that had already developed in the centerless Democratic Party. These trends were not merely the product of external market forces, but also of policies promoted by a Democratic Party indebted to sectional and interest group forces. A series of federal policies tilted economic development toward the South. These included welfare and labor policies that sanctioned regional disparities in labor costs, as well as a range of federal activities that accelerated in the 1960s, including military installations, defense and aerospace contracts planted in the districts of powerful southern congressmen. These and other enterprises were enabled by an expensive, federally financed infrastructure, particularly highways and water projects. While the shift of mass-production industries to low-wage areas was a global trend, these federal — and Democratic — policies created additional incentives specifically stimulating the flows of new investment and people away from the conurbations of the Northeast and Midwest toward the South and Southwest.

A similar point can be made about the shift of economic activity from urban centers to outlying suburbs, now containing a majority of the nation's voters who were turning into a major base for the Republican Party. Federally subsidized highways and water and sewer grants tilted the geographical advantage to those suburban areas, while federal tax laws created incentives for investment in new facilities rather than overhauling old ones. Meanwhile, federal housing policies that provided low-cost mortgages and tax benefits for mainly suburban home owners towered over the modest programs for low-cost housing in the cities (Piven 1992: 237, 256–257). A crucial aspect is that cities obtained urban renewal programs promoted by local "pro-growth" coalitions of real estate and downtown business interests and their local political allies. This led to the decimation of entire neighborhoods, often Democratic ones, because those who could moved to the suburbs, and those who could not crowded into remaining slums (DiGaetano 1992). These policies eroded Democratic support among older constituencies and exacerbated deep-seated constituency conflicts. Racial tension was worsened further still by the scale and steep rise of the displacement of blacks from the South, which in turn had much to do with Democratic agricultural and welfare policies. A white working class that felt itself on the short end of its party or governmental stick was much more likely to resent programs directed at blacks. Finally, the combination of programs that spurred the great migration to the suburbs may also have worsened race conflict, both by divesting the older cities of employment opportunities and public revenues, and by reifying racial separation in political jurisdictions, so that race polarization came to be seen as a conflict between devastated black municipalities (or downtown areas) and prosperous white suburbs (Piven 1992: 257).

So how did the Democratic Party respond at this historical juncture? At the same time the right was waging a massive campaign to advance neoliberal economic policy and breathing new life into its political organization, there was little coordinated counter-offensive waged by the new cohort of Democrats for protecting the material interests of working people. During the electoral landslide victory of 1974, after Nixon's resignation, Democrats made large gains in the House, taking forty-nine seats from the Republican Party and increasing their majority above the two-thirds mark. But this did not translate into strong pro-labor or pro-worker policies. The new Democrats, including a significant number of ex-New Leftists, were young, well-educated and pro-civil rights, and most belonged to the new middle class. They had come out of the anti-war protests and McGovern campaign, the Peace Corps, and the women's movements, the professions and the suburbs, but not the union halls or the wards of the political machines. These suburban, post-sixties Democrats were different politically and ideologically from the postwar cohort of New Deal liberals. Their turn toward the Democratic Party coincided with the liberal retreat from the Great Society programs and the start of the retreat from the reformism that included the black poor (Cowie 2010: 236).

There was also the group of Cold War anti-communist Democrats, with Senator Henry "Scoop" Jackson taking the lead by 1973. At that year's AFL-CIO convention, Jackson insisted that only a rightward turn away from McGovernism would put the Democrats on the winning track again. He and his neo-conservative allies actually paved the way for the AFL-CIO leaders' future working relationship with Ronald Reagan. Jackson's most ardent supporters, concentrated in Social Democrats USA, continually called for the recapture of the Democratic Party from the grips of the anti-war, feminist, and environmentalist "New Politics" crowd. Moreover, the steady decline of the industrial workforce and the many plant shutdowns that disrupted communities during the 1970s left the AFL-CIO leadership with fewer resources. Less able to deliver votes to Democratic candidates, labor found itself increasingly dependent on backroom allies and deals. Labor politics in those years more and more represented the rage and resentment of older union members against younger ones, the privileging of pension packages over internal reform, pitting working-class whites against underemployed non-whites. At the same time, the AFL-CIO leadership kept up the international politics of aggressive Cold War action against the non-interventionist tendency encouraged by the new liberal Democratic Congress (Buhle 1999: 194–195).

The more general abandonment of the New Deal order was reflected in the Carter administration's domestic and foreign policy shifts of 1977–1978, which included precursors to virtually all the major components of Reaganism that would dominate throughout the 1980s (Davis 1986: 296–297). It was during Carter's presidency in the late 1970s that the first steps toward "deregulation" were made and neoliberal measures introduced that foreshadowed Reagan's more draconian measures.[17]

A Notable Exception: Public-Sector Unionism

There was one major exception to the overall trend of weakening union power in America. While the permanent federal workforce doubled in size, the state and municipal workforces tripled, or even quadrupled, in the first twenty-five years after the war. During the 1950s and 1960s, only 10 to 12 percent of workers in the public sector were members of unions, and fewer still were covered by collective bargaining contracts in this sector. Most experts and even a trade union leader such as AFL-CIO president George Meany regarded public employees as intrinsically nonorganizable, premised on the idea that it was "impossible to bargain collectively with the government" (Kramer 1962: 14). Nevertheless, public-sector unionism expanded rapidly during the next two decades.

The birthplace of modern public-employee unionism was New York City, which had remained a bulwark of New Deal liberalism and supported a strong private-sector union movement at the time. At most levels of government, however, wages and benefits lagged behind those of unionized blue-collar work in the leading private sectors. Public employment became increasingly black and brown, as administrators sought to recruit a low-wage workforce, and racial minorities, still excluded from many private-sector service jobs, valued the steady work and the protections provided by civil-service work rules (Aronowitz 1998: 59–85; Freeman 2000). On January 17, 1962, President Kennedy signed Executive Order 10988, which legalized collective bargaining between the federal government and its clerical and technical workforce and facilitated the growth of public-sector unions. Many northern and western states soon followed the federal government's lead.

Although the power and autonomy of these unions were inferior to those of the Wagner Act model—they were forbidden to strike, bargain for wages, or negotiate over the organization and assignment of personnel—the law governing public-sector unions avoided the conceptual pitfalls inherent in private-sector law. It was clearly understood that the expectation that a self-contained, pluralist system might structure labor relations did not apply in the public sector, where both management and the unions were agents of larger political processes and the union leadership recognized that political mobilization of the membership and surrounding community was critical to their bargaining effectiveness. In addition, a kind of due-process rights culture offered much protection and even some legitimacy to union activists. Few state agencies operated according to employment-at-will doctrines—individuals had to be dismissed for "just cause." Because company unions had never been such a noxious threat in the public sector, and because of the civil-service protections that were maintained, issues such as union recognition, jurisdiction, and security were much less important. The federal law in question stated that a union could emerge in at least three forms: as the representative for its members only, as the exclusive voice representing all workers in a union when it had attained a stable membership of more than 10 percent, and as the signatory of an actual bargaining contract in a unit where it had majority support from the employees (Lichtenstein 2002: 183; Bernstein 1991: 215–216).

Given the civil rights discourse that prevailed during that period and management's tendency to remain relatively neutral, this unionism served as an effective lobbyist, educator, grievance facilitator, and interpreter of the civil-service rules. Over time the government unions came to resemble private-union organizations, especially in sectors such as the post office, public schools, prisons, hospitals, and blue-collar municipal employment. Wages, seniority issues, and fringe benefits were all dealt with in the collective bargaining process. Important experiments in health care and public-sector organizing began to emerge in the U.S. South in the 1960s and early 1970s. Led by Local 1199 of the National Union of Health and Hospital Workers and the American Federation of State, County, and Municipal Employees, these efforts (including the well-known Memphis sanitation workers' struggle involving Dr. Martin Luther King Jr.) fused economic struggle for workers' rights with political struggles for black freedom. These efforts tapered off, however, and a great opportunity to reshape union organization in the South was lost (Fletcher and Gapasin 2008: 202). To date, the union movement has not resumed this challenging task.

The Corporate Culture Movement, "Flexible Specialization" and the Undermining of Unionism

Amid the turbulent environment of the 1980s with its heavy international competition, there was growing concern with organizational culture among top executives of corporations. The much-discussed decline in U.S. economic performance was attributed to the failure of U.S. firms to monitor and manage the cultural dimensions of organization, seen in sharp relief against Japanese companies. The 1985 report of the President's Commission on Industrial Competitiveness, in tandem with a number of other studies by the U.S. Commerce Department, concluded that America had lost its competitive edge in a range of industries, including steel, motor vehicles, textiles, electronics, robotics, and telecommunications. The American auto industry's declining performance was a poignant reminder of slippage when compared to its Japanese counterpart. By 1980, Japan had overtaken the United States as the world's leading car producer. Similarly, Japan began outpacing the United States in the computer industry thanks to a ten-year government-sponsored program launched in 1981. Within a decade Japan pulled away from the pack, becoming the world's leading supplier of advanced computer systems.

U.S. exponents of the so-called corporate culture movement saw this threatening state of affairs as a result of the deficiencies of American-style management, organization, and production and the virtues of the Japanese approach, which they often attributed to the distinctive features of "Japanese culture" and its emphasis on ensuring cultural consensus as a form of managerial control. This they contrasted to American corporations' reliance on bureaucratic or assembly-line control and discipline, depicted as destroying commitment (Ouchi 1981; Pascale and Athos 1981; Salaman 1997: 246).[18]

It was generally assumed that organizational cultures could be assessed, managed, constructed and manipulated in the pursuit of organizational effectiveness. Employees' norms, beliefs, and values could (and if necessary should) be changed so that they might demonstrate appropriate behavior, committing themselves wholly to the organization and supporting management strategy. The guiding aim of managers' attempts to define a culture of work for employees was to achieve an internalization of regulation, "to win the 'hearts and minds' of employees: to define their purposes by managing what they think and feel, and not just how they behave" (Peters and Waterman 1982: xvii).

Corporate culture initiatives formed part of a long-standing management interest in ensuring the "morality" and discipline of the workforce: to inculcate employees with the "appropriate" attitudes and values in the work setting. Corporate culture projects represented this interest in a particularly energetic and self-conscious form. What changed in the 1980s was that top managers, persuaded by management writers and consultants acting as cultural intermediaries (and sometimes as management gurus), began to try to manage the culture of the organization — to influence how staff related to the organization, its structure and purpose, and their employment. The corporate culture trend appealed to top managers because of its implied celebration of their dramatic and heroic role as "transformative leaders." Influential management gurus such as Rosabeth Moss Kanter and Tom Peters sensed the new "postmodern" zeitgeist and its emphasis on appearance, image, and superficiality. They expediently played into it by demonstrating impressive mastery of the management of symbols and occasions in their writings and public appearances, with an emphasis on show-business elements and presentation skills — skills, they asserted, that were crucial to managers' performance (Kanter 1984; Salaman 1997: 236–241, 263).

Corporate culture projects offered to rescue the country from the dangers posed by foreign competition by unearthing and revitalizing basic American values and enabling their reassertion in the workplace. Members of this corporate culture movement made enormous claims for cultural change as a conscious managerial policy. They presented corporate culture as the preeminent managerial key to business success. When cultures were strengthened, they reasoned, organizational performance improved as staff demonstrated greater commitment, involvement, and flexibility (Deal and Kennedy 1982). More generally, gains in performance, quality, productivity, innovation, and customer orientation were credited to those corporate cultures where individual employees closely identified their own purposes and personal values with those of the organization. During the 1980s these corporate culture practices were likewise imbibed by the labor movement, in particular the Service Employees International Union (SEIU), fostering the deliberate development of a new corporate unionism seeking union-employer "partnerships" that emerged by 2000, as we shall see in the next chapter.

Along with this magnified emphasis on the "culturing of work," team-based production methods became more important in manufacturing industries. This was much enhanced by the technological and organizational shifts that took place at about the same time, which allowed for more flexible and footloose manufacturing (Piore and Sabel 1984). These changes were linked to the proliferation of advanced information and communication technologies. In contrast to mass-production techniques (the basis of the so-called Fordist regime) in which products were manufactured in large batches on assembly lines requiring large investments in inflexible production technology, novel forms of flexible, micro-electronically based automation technologies now made small-batch production possible. These new techniques were geared to short-run production for segmented markets rather than long-run production of standardized products for mass markets so characteristic of mass production.

The flexible manufacturing techniques were also more directly marketing led and "customer oriented" than traditional mass production, and were characterized by a tighter integration of the stages from design and production to distribution or circulation. What became known as "just-in-time production" or "lean production" enabled the manufacturer to operate with minimal quantities of inventory — with components arriving as close as possible to the moment when they were required. It also allowed production to be undertaken and completed, as far as possible, through orders from customers (e.g., retailers) based on information about actual sales. Flexible specialization relied on decentralizing production to small subcontractors who were capable of providing the diversity of output and the flexibility demanded by the market, registered by and filtered through the main producer. This process also demanded a more flexible deployment and performance of the workforce than under a Fordist-style regime.

Although flexibly specialized craft firms and decentered sections of larger firms became increasingly significant, core areas of capitalism were still dominated by Fordist centralized, top-down bureaucracies that employed new computer and informational technologies to more effectively control behavior, bringing about a degradation of work (deskilling) in several domains. And even where significant changes in the division of labor had been introduced — such as the "flexible teams" in the Japanese transplants or companies that imitated them — these typically involved rotating workers over a series of conventionally deskilled production jobs rather than changing the basic nature of the work (Milkman 1991: 142).

4. Corporate Assaults and Limits of Postwar Liberalism   129

According to union-affiliated labor experts Mike Parker and Jane Slaughter, the Japanese-style system of "team production" and "flexible work rules" that was installed in several U.S. factories during the 1980s was not a new system of participatory management or democratic reorganization.[19] In their analysis, the team production regime with its emphasis on continuous improvement idealized in the Japanese notion of *kaizen* (in relation to quality control and so-called quality circles) was a system based on "management by stress." This undercut worker autonomy and retook many of the most negative elements of the early twentieth-century drive system of punitive supervision exercised by foremen. Despite the rhetoric of worker participation, the team concept and other participatory schemes were basically strategies to enhance management control. Far from offering a humane alternative to Taylorism, workers at such plants mainly "participated" in the intensification of their own exploitation, mobilizing their detailed firsthand knowledge of the labor process to help management speed up production and eliminate wasteful work practices.

Parker and Slaughter contended that the team concept was insidious in that it undermined unionism through a dubious form of participation in management decisions. The erosion of negotiated work rules in the auto industry, for example, resulted in a deterioration of the rights-based quality of the workplace. Workers were well aware that failure to cooperate with management often led to economic and organizational penalties in the form of layoffs, work transfers, and plant closures (Parker and Slaughter 1988; Parker 1993). Moreover, a regime of flexible specialization implied the employment of growing armies of flexi- and temporary workers who experienced job insecurity and lacked important job benefits and social provisions, working side by side with a core of tenured personnel with seemingly secure prospects.[20] These kinds of arrangements would more generally come to characterize large sectors of American working life in the ensuing years.

5

Labor Renewal and the Issues of Immigration, Globalized Production and Erosion of Workers' Rights

Ironically, during the 1980s and 1990s the labor movement, which had for decades regarded race and gender as side issues that distracted from its primary aim to advance the interests of its core white male membership, increasingly championed interracial solidarity and cultural diversity. As employment in the traditional areas of labor's strength declined, a weakened labor movement struggled to find new members in the expanding service and governmental fields with disproportionate representations of women, blacks and other minority workers. By 1986, over a third of the workforce in the public sector was unionized, and some 40 percent were covered by collective contracts. The massive expansion of unionism in the public sector was mirrored by a huge contraction in the private sector.

The proportion of workers in unions shrunk from a third of nonagricultural wage and salary workers and over half of blue-collar workers in the 1950s to 14 percent of all wage and salary workers by 1986 — a level comparable to that during the Great Depression. Now only a tiny number of workers joined workers through NLRB elections, while national companies openly expressed their intent to establish a "union-free environment."[1] Public-sector unions such as the American Federation of State, County and Municipal Employees (AFSCME), National Education Association (NEA), Service Employees International Union (SEIU) — which became largely public sector in those years — and the American Federation of Teachers (AFT) were the largest in the country. Union density among schoolteachers reached an extraordinary 80 percent, which was higher than in coal mining and auto production. With one in three union members working in the public sector, women with master's degrees (largely schoolteachers) better organized than male high school graduates, and police and firefighters now being major exemplars of craft unionism, the union movement had a very different constituency than that led by Meany in the 1960s. By the end of the twentieth century, public-sector unionism, counting over four million members, represented almost 40 percent of all organized workers (Freeman 1988: 63–64; Lichtenstein 2002: 183, 185). Substantial gains in union organizing in the public sector were made most notably in health care among professionals, such as doctors[2] and nurses, as well as the sector's lowest paid workers, home health care workers. But by the end of the twentieth century, there was also a surge of unionization among engineers and computer experts (once considered union immune) in some of the largest corporations (Aronowitz 1998: 228, 235–236).[3]

Even as black union members were disproportionately affected by plant closures, union-busting campaigns, and job relocations, African Americans continued to be among the most union-minded workers. And politically, African Americans for the most part remained the most reliable bloc of voters for liberal and labor-endorsed candidates and in state referenda on labor issues. Union reformers recognized the crucial role played by people of color and women in their efforts to rebuild and revitalize the labor movement. Various constituency groups, most notably the Coalition of Black Trade Unionists (CBTU, founded in 1972), articulated the perspectives of women and people of color within the house of labor itself. Reaching out to other minorities, the CBTU helped to support other constituency organizations such as the Coalition of Labor Union Women, the Labor Council for Latin American Advancement (LCLAA), and the Asian Pacific American Labor Alliance(APALA). Some unions, notably the SEIU, held innovative organizing campaigns that focused on blacks and other workers of color.[4] During this period the balance of numbers (and power) in the AFL-CIO shifted decisively from the old industrial, transport, and construction unions to organizations such as the SEIU and the AFSCME, which represented service and governmental employees, many of them African American (Zieger 2007: 208–209, 223, 227).

A leadership revolt in the AFL-CIO in 1995 catapulted a group of reform-minded unionists to top positions as a result of the first contested election since 1894 (when the AFL existed as a separate organization). The CBTU played a crucial role in the successful effort to reflect the new realities of membership, appointing more women and people of color to the AFL-CIO Executive Council and to staff positions in the Federation and its affiliated unions. This team led by John Sweeney, previously president of the SEIU, promised to initiate projects revolving around the recruitment of people of color with the help of women's rights activists and progressive racial and ethnic civic organizations. Thus, Sweeney's team galvanized a liberal makeover of an ossified union apparatus, premised on guarantees to renew organized labor.

The "New Voice" team made organizing the unorganized its top priority. Other initiatives aimed to develop a more independent and powerful political presence and to give workers a voice in the community as well as the workplace. Politically, the AFL-CIO began to abandon its traditional role of endorsing and giving money to Democratic candidates no matter how conservative or pro-business they might be. The Federation claimed it was trying to become a more independent political force requiring greater accountability from politicians, who were expected to adhere to a "working families" agenda.

The AFL-CIO was simultaneously experimenting with approaches drawn from social movement experiences and others characterized by a non-adversarial business-friendly "participative" style. An eclectic pragmatism replaced ideological consistency, and the mainstream unions were expected to adopt on a wide scale only those approaches that proved to be effective within a relatively short time span. As Bruce Nissen notes, it was "a welcome advance over the hardened Cold War business union perspective of [Sweeney's] predecessor Lane Kirkland, but it should not be misread as a firm commitment to left-wing ideology or practice" (Nissen 2002b: 272).[5] In local communities throughout the country (San Diego, Los Angeles, Seattle, Milwaukee, and other cities), the new AFL-CIO worked to revitalize its central labor councils.[6] The Union Cities program, initiated in 1997, attempted to make these local central bodies more effective in organizing, mobilizing, local political action, and voicing community concerns. By 2000, a combination of strategies appeared to have some effect; these included coaxing by the national Federation, financial incentives to central bodies undertaking innovations, and conferences and meetings to spread "best practice" information.

Greater voice for workers at the work site was to be achieved in several ways. Through new institutions such as the Center for Workplace Participation and the Working for America Institute, the AFL-CIO was trying to influence workforce development policies and create union-employer partnerships that would lead to greater union clout over the running of enterprises and the training afforded to union workers (Nissen 2002a: 5–6). The effort to create partnerships was by far the most controversial aspect of the AFL-CIO's new policy among left-wing union activists and allied academics. But it was highly appreciated by many liberal and moderate social democratic unionists and academics (Lazes and Savage 1997; Parker and Slaughter 1997).

During Sweeney's tenure, in the late 1980s, the SEIU had launched a "Justice for Janitors" campaign aimed at organizing custodial workers, especially those employed in the downtown office complexes of large cities. The leitmotiv was that unions must organize an entire labor market and not just the set of workers currently employed by any given firm. Organizers combined the traditional strike with innovative tactics and well-designed appeals to gain public sympathy for these low-wage workers, most of whom were African American and Latino. In Denver, Los Angeles, Boston, Houston, and other cities, the union won and attained contract benefits. The strategy deployed in SEIU's "Justice for Janitors" campaigns built on the legacy of radical unions and the rich history of community mobilization, using the influence and talents of the unemployed, stay-at-home mothers, and young people outside the wage-labor market. This was the role played by the neighborhood-based unionism of the needle trades in the Progressive Era as well as that of the CIO two decades later, when rent strikes, boycotts, demonstrations by the unemployed, ethnic mobilizations, and political insurgencies generated an organizing culture that permeated working-class communities. The "living-wage" movement that emerged after the 1996 "welfare reform" (focused on "welfare-to-work" programs) and that aimed to raise the wages of lower-income groups and labor standards, is a more recent embodiment of this impulse, pioneered by left-wing unionists, the Progressive-Era Consumers League, and liberal Catholic clerics. The living-wage movement has targeted the high-profile department stores that sell brand products, the owners of office buildings that contract for janitorial services, and the state and city governments that subcontract so much of their work (Lichtenstein 2002: 264–266).

Other successful SEIU campaigns concentrated on hospital workers, home-care workers, and nursing home employees, bringing a strong activist dynamic to the larger project of increasing the numbers of African Americans and other people of color into the labor movement. These successes fueled hopes that marginalized low-wage minority workers might become the spearhead of a broad revitalization of the AFL-CIO. But the prospect of translating the SEIU's successes into a more general advance of the labor movement proved elusive. Although the new organizing model embodied in the "Justice for Janitors" campaign constituted a genuine advance — substituting activist mobilization and issue-based organizing for the bureaucratic grievance procedures of postwar business unionism — it also had serious flaws. Especially troublesome was the singular focus on technocratic organizing without addressing crucial elements of union renewal: those of representation — Who should do the organizing? — which perpetuated top-down union practices; the definition of the overall goals of trade unionism; and membership education to give members an active sole in the renewal process (Fletcher and Gapasin 2008: 199–207).

The increased representation of black unionists on the AFL-CIO Executive Council did not bring about the reforms desired by African-American workers either, given that there were no black leaders among the large unions that dominated the decision-making process. Moreover, the AFL-CIO's relations with constituent groups, notably the CBTU, were increasingly problematic. In the first years of the twenty-first century, sharp differences of opinion emerged among labor activists about how to build on black workers' union-mindedness to reverse labor's decline. At the same time, the influx of large numbers of immigrant workers ignited fierce debates about their role in the economy generally, their place in the labor movement, and their relationship to African-American workers.

In 2004, AFL-CIO political campaign operatives decided to quit funding constituency groups such as the CBTU, which partly reflected the changes in election funding mandated by passage of the McCain-Feingold Act in 2002. Leaders of the CBTU and other constituency organizations charged that they were frozen out of voter mobilization projects despite their proven track record. CBTU activists asserted that the AFL-CIO's new political program wasted vast sums of money in trying to mobilize disaffected white male voters while denying funding to groups such as itself that had already proven successful in generating high percentages of pro-labor votes. The subsequent debate over proposals to restructure the AFL-CIO also drew strong opposition by black unionists.

SEIU's head Andy Stern (a former New Leftist), charging that the Federation under President Sweeney had neglected organizing in favor of increasingly futile political action, proposed a drastic restructuring that would slash the number of separate affiliated unions so that a handful of mega-unions could emerge. This meant that the AFL-CIO Executive Council of fifty-four members would be streamlined to a body of just sixteen. In addition, the central staff would be sharply reduced, with the financial savings going to the newly restructured affiliated unions for a massive campaign to organize the nonunionized. When Stern and his supporters in four other unions—the International Brotherhood of Teamsters (IBT), the United Food and Commercial Workers (UFCW), the Laborers International Union of North America (LIUNA), the Union of Needle, Industrial and Textile Employees-Hotel and Restaurant Employees (UNITE-HERE)—found out that their effort was stymied by the AFL-CIO leadership, they announced their secession from the Federation (Zieger 2007: 228–229).

In September 2005, these and two other major unions, the United Brotherhood of Carpenters and Joiners (UBC) and the United Farm Workers (UFW)—together representing 40 percent of the national Federation's membership—left the AFL-CIO to form the Change to Win (CTW) coalition. Garnering widespread media attention, some commentators likened the division within the labor movement to the CIO breakup in 1935 (Kelber 2010: 1). It should be noted that the CTW unions tended to organize in "landlocked" industries less affected by globalization or offshoring, giving them an advantage over many AFL-CIO private-sector unions, especially those in manufacturing, where success rates in NLRB representation elections were much lower (Moody 2007: 172).

The response of black activists to these developments was mixed. They recognized that the SEIU was carrying out innovative programs to organize low-skilled black and other minority workers. William Lucy, head of the CBTU, and others pointed out that the plans to change the governing structure of the AFL-CIO would mean the loss of black and other minority representation on the Executive Council, which had only been achieved after a generation-long struggle by black unionists. Moreover, AFSCME, whose leaders rejected the CTW initiative, remained in the AFL-CIO and provided a base for Lucy as the

CBTU's highly respected leader. Many African-American activists, and many white supporters too, were convinced that blacks and other people of color represented the only real hope of reviving and revitalizing the labor movement. Black workers, with their disproportionate union-mindedness, their massive presence in the rapidly expanding service sector, and their energetic political action that regularly mobilized overwhelming majorities for liberal candidates, were at the forefront of the struggle to resist the conservative political tide.

Black activists appealed to both the AFL-CIO and the CTW to recognize the distinctive problems that African-American workers faced and the unique opportunities for progressive revival that they offered. The rhetorical celebration of diversity notwithstanding, they charged that neither the CTW nor the AFL-CIO leadership adequately addressed the problems and possibilities associated with black workers. This also partly explained the decrease of black union membership. Other important factors that impinged more generally on workers concerned the decline in employment in industrial and extractive industries, aggressive union busting by private employers, the impact of economic globalization, and anti-union governmental policies. Although African-American workers continued to be unionized at higher rates than their white, Latino, and Asian counterparts, there was a dramatic decrease of the number of black unionists as well. The Bureau of Labor Statistics reported that by 2004, U.S. unions had lost 300,000 members, a disproportionate number of them African American. Although just 13 percent of union membership consisted of black workers, no less than 55 percent of the union jobs lost had been held by African Americans, 70 percent of them women. The figures are telling: in 1983 almost 32 percent of all black workers were members of a union; by 2004 that figure was almost halved (Zieger 2007: 209, 224–225, 228–229).

The Immigration Issue

It was within industries such as construction, meatpacking, hotels and restaurants, manufacturing, transportation, and health care that immigrant workers played a major role in revitalizing the labor movement at the turn of the new century. They then became the major union growth engine. Reflecting changing attitudes in the unions and militancy among the workers themselves, the proportion of unionized immigrant workers grew by 23 percent between 1996 and 2003. By 2006, the SEIU had become the largest and fastest growing labor union in the United States, claiming a membership of 1.8 million, with immigrant workers accounting for two-thirds of that figure (Akers Chácon 2006: 6). Many labor activists had vested their hopes of future revival precisely in people of color, along with women. The AFL-CIO was by now far removed from the mainstream labor movement with its racist and immigration-bashing tendencies a century earlier. After a long history of opposing immigration (and the rights of immigrant workers), the AFL-CIO reversed its position in 1999, calling for a general amnesty and the right of undocumented workers to join unions.

Thirteen years earlier was the last time that amnesty had been granted to undocumented immigrants, under the Immigration Reform and Control Act (IRCA). This led to legalization and citizenship for about 2.8 million immigrant workers. It was the outcome of labor struggles on several fronts. Within the labor movement, the United Farmer Workers had led other unions in a fight against the Bracero program, which culminated in the termination of guest worker contracts in agriculture. Opinions within the labor movement had started to shift when unions such as the International Ladies Garment Workers Union (which merged with another garment union to form UNITE in 1995) had begun to organize undocumented workers in the early 1980s. Amnesty thus became the only acceptable means to guarantee workers' rights, since a necessary precondition for maintaining a viable union was freedom from retribution by immigration authorities. However, the AFL-CIO at that time officially supported immigration restrictions, which meant there was a limit to how much pressure the ILGWU and other unions who favored amnesty could garner from the rest of the labor movement.

Furthermore, social justice, Latino, and church organizations had played a significant role in defending the interests of migrant workers in the early 1980s. They built a national "sanctuary movement" that aided and sheltered undocumented refugees from Central America during the civil wars there. This fostered the rise of border-based human rights networks that advocated for migrant border crossers (Akers Chacón 2006: 2, 8; Akers Chacón and Davis 2006: 288).

Containment and restriction of immigration, especially of Mexican workers, became increasingly prominent after the terrorist attacks of September 11, 2001. This tragedy occurred just as a new generation of immigrant worker-leaders, the global justice movement, and the unions began to politically align. It allowed right-wing forces to regain the upper hand against an advancing immigrant rights agenda. The "War on Terror" singled out Arabs, Arab-Americans, Muslims, and others labeled as "potential terrorists." The imagined omnipresent terrorist threat to the homeland, along with the xenophobic imagery of "invading hordes," led to an opportunistic alliance between die-hard proponents of border protection (and intensified surveillance operations against immigrants) and anti-immigrant restrictionists. This rightward shift was aided by key Democrats whose strong support of the "War on Terror" helped turn the spotlight on the U.S.-Mexico border.

After the passage of the PATRIOT Act, the Immigration and Naturalization Service (INS) was revamped into two prongs: Immigration and Customs Enforcement (ICE) and Customs and Border Protection (CPB), both under the Department of Homeland Security. At the same time, well-funded political action groups, conservative "think tanks"— such as the Federation for American Immigration Reform (FAIR) and the Center for Immigration Studies (CIS)— federal and state legislators, and a large number of extreme-right activist organizations coalesced into a national anti-immigration front. This translation of immigration into a national security issue has allowed powerful anti-immigration forces, particularly in the Republican Party, to tighten control over all aspects of immigration policy, especially those regulating the role of Mexican immigrant labor. The domestic "War on Terror" eliminated the amnesty issue from the dominant political discourse and replaced the concept of human rights with the "terrorist" profiling of undocumented workers (Akers Chacón and Davis 2006: 217–218).

Generally speaking, most African-American labor activists opposed the imposition of harsh penalties on illegal immigrants in favor of legislation that would facilitate undocumented immigrants' transition from illegal to legal status. Like other inclusive trade unionists, they wanted to transcend the divisiveness over immigration among the American working class. In this they deviated however from the views of most African Americans as reflected in public opinion polls.[7] Many black labor leaders believed that organized labor should welcome workers of all colors and backgrounds, expand efforts to organize them, and provide educational and other public services that would raise their standards of living and reduce the competitive edge of immigration. Black unionists repeatedly deployed the notion of "black and brown" to suggest the advantages of an alliance between all people of color to build a stronger labor movement and to foster progressive political developments. Proponents of this approach, for example, referred to the success of the Los Angeles labor movement in building black-brown coalitions and electing a strongly pro-labor mayor, Antonio Villaraigosa, in 2005. They could point more generally to the fact that as time went by and immigrants became more accustomed to their new home or established documented status, they were at least as likely — and often more so — to join or organize a union in comparison with native-born workers (Milkman 2006: 13; Zieger 2007: 230–231).

Workers' Centers

Union density is not a complete measure of labor movement vitality, of course. Today Los Angeles is often held up as a city with a strong labor movement, but its union density is lower than that of New York and Chicago. Los Angeles is a major site of a broader labor movement among low-wage workers predicated on strategic combinations of organizing by workers' centers and organizing by unions in the workplace (Lesniewski 2011). Workers' centers have become an important vehicle for immigrant workers to organize and act. A center can be industry-specific or locally based so that no matter in what industry workers are employed, they can join. Worker-centered organizing overlaps with community-based organizing, so organizing is rooted in the community and not limited to the work site. Most workers' centers are preoccupied with a combination of service delivery, advocacy, and organizing. All three tend to focus mainly on issues related to work: pay and failure to pay, health and safety, immigration status, and various employment rights. But non-work concerns such as housing, transportation, education, police harassment, and other immigration issues are addressed as well (Gapasin and Bonacich 2002: 174). It is through their organization function, however, that workers' centers have the potential to play a significant role in the development of unionization and a broader social and political movement. As community-based organizations, they are geographically bound. Most of the workplaces in which their members are employed are located within or near the communities involved. However, in some cases, like those of day laborers or farm workers whose workplaces may be distant, the center concentrates on the sites where workers obtain jobs: street corners, contractors or agencies (Fine 2006: 2–3, 11–14).

The workers' centers evolved from the many changes in work itself that have occurred since the mid–1970s. These involved subcontracting, sweatshops, expanding food service and hospitality industries, relocated and de-unionized industries, new retail stores (both large and small), and so forth. All these sites of employment had common features: low wages, poor benefits, and workers of color. Increasingly the latter also were recent immigrants. By 2005, there were by one count 137 workers' centers, 122 of which dealt specifically with immigrant workers. Geographically they reflected concentrations of immigration: 41 were in the Northeast, 36 on the West Coast, 34 in the South, 17 in the East North Central region and the rest spread out over the West. Close to 80 percent of the workers involved were immigrants. About 40 percent of the workers who then participated in workers' centers came from Mexico and Central America, another 18 percent from South America, 15 percent from East Asia and the Caribbean, 8 percent from Africa, 3 percent from Europe, and 1 percent from the rest of Asia (Moody 2007: 216–217; Fine 2006: 7–21).

Because of their presence in immigrant communities, many workers' centers had the capability to reach out to workers in targeted plants and legitimize the idea of unionism in their communities. Their emphasis on leadership training offered potential for furthering the process of grassroots unionization. The workers' centers may also play a significant role in bringing black and immigrant workers together. South Carolina's Alliance for Fair Employment (CAFE) has done exactly that, and North Carolina's Black Workers for Justice (BWFJ) has worked with the Farmer Labor Organizing Committee (FLOC) in North Carolina to form the Black/Brown Alliance (Moody 2007: 232–233; Andrews 2006: 43–46).

Like other workers' organizations, workers' centers have their problems and limitations, though. Workers' centers can attain things like back pay, at times help to organize unions, and even unite to win a labor victory of national significance. But they often lack real power vis-à-vis the employers they are dealing with most directly, because (with some notable exceptions) they seldom have more than a few members in any one workplace. This means that they lack the direct workplace power that a union has, so direct disruption (as a major power source) is not possible. They usually take recourse to pressure tactics of a legal sort, making them dependent on lawyers. They rely also to a large degree on foundation funding and consequently on professionals who write grant proposals and on those who make the grant decisions.

Nevertheless, workers' centers do serve a central role in developing linkages between progressive unions and community-based organizing efforts that can potentially strengthen both organizing areas. A good example is the successful campaign to organize 4,000 workers at four big meatpacking plants in Omaha, Nebraska, in 1999 and 2000. It was initiated by the Omaha Together One Community (OTOC), a faith-based community organization affiliated with the Saul Alinsky-inspired Industrial Areas Foundation, later in alliance with the UFCW.[8] Another good example is the establishment of a workers' center in North Carolina as part of a long-term, successful effort by UFCW leaders to organize the 5,500 workers of the Smithfield hog-processing plant in Tar Heel, North Carolina, in 2003. Importantly, in August 2006, the AFL-CIO also took a significant step toward greater unity between trade unions and workers' centers when it reached an agreement with the National Day Laborer Organizing Network, a nationwide network of community-based day labor organizations that would allow workers' centers to affiliate with state and local labor councils (Moody 2007: 220–221).

Union organizing itself also involves a number of fresh strategies in the new inclusive approach. These encompass multi-union organizing to tackle globally structured production networks, non-majority unionism (as a means to build power in sectors or geographical regions where collective bargaining is absent), and political-geographical projects incorporating nonunion organizations to bolster the rights of black and immigrant workers. Central labor councils (AFL-CIO bodies operating at state, county, and city levels) are identified as crucial agencies here: local coordinating forces that can help build workers' economic power. The CLCs have a broader role, too, in social justice unionism than in conventional AFL-CIO trade unionism. They become the base for efforts to create institutional structures (working people's assemblies, strategic political blocs) that advance the wide-ranging agenda of social justice unionism and sustain its organizational alliances in the arena of local politics. In the ideal case, it is the key platform for unifying the progressive forces involved around a common set of objectives and strengthening working people's power and influence in society — a vision that goes far beyond the narrow electoral politics of traditional unionism.

In order to be successful, it is important that the local affiliates of the Federation effectively embrace the idea of social justice unionism, functioning as a component of such a movement. A major reason why the "New Voice" reformist leadership failed to overcome the structural weakness of the Federation vis-à-vis its affiliated unions was that the latter retained the power to direct their own organizing strategies and refused to take up new initiatives that the "New Voice" tried to launch. Fletcher and Gapasin point to the lack of sufficient support among local affiliates for promising attempts to encourage new forms of multi-union and geographically based organizing, in particular through reviving the central labor councils. The case of Los Angeles is instructive here. While the AFL-CIO at county level was able to book new union success and to broaden its political reach and agenda (as noted earlier), plans for a multi-union organizing project in the manufacturing sector of the Alameda Corridor[9] were stymied by local affiliates' lack of cooperation. This implies that merely providing technical resources for members does not suffice; the union must also adopt a continuous organizing practice (both internally and externally). Moreover, it must embrace a genuinely inclusive and non-discriminatory policy in terms of race/ethnicity, gender, sexual orientation, and immigration status—unencumbered by the limitations imposed by "pure and simple business unionism"—while at the same time being truly international or global in its outlook and practice (Fletcher and Gapasin 2008: 100–110, 212).

A Continued Predominance of Business Unionism

The AFL-CIO under Sweeney's leadership developed a strategy consisting of four basic components: encourage mergers with other unions to offset shrinking membership; organize in industries that cannot be moved overseas, such as health care, hotels, and construction; collaborate with management to try to gain employers' neutrality in union elections; and spend vast sums and energy (through member activism) to elect a Democratic president and Congress in the hopes of sponsoring pro-labor legislation. This approach has been pursued by the Change to Win coalition as well, and matches foremost the needs of the top echelons of the union bureaucracy.

Today the top union officials function as a buffer between capital and labor and, in the United States, most enthusiastically embrace that role. Far removed from the shop floor, leading U.S. union officials have a lifestyle and social connections that tie them more closely to management and well-established politicians than to the rank and file. Their top-down bureaucratic approach does not offer a solution to union decline. As a critical analyst and advocate of democratic social movement unionism put it recently,

> While crises and splits in the union hierarchy can open the door to reform candidates and pressure from the membership, the union bureaucracy will at best vacillate unless pressed forward by rank-and-file action. And that's exactly what today's union leaders are keen to prevent [Sustar 2009: 9].

Recent exemplary cases of this tendency include the ways in which UAW president Ron Gettelfinger in the AFL-CIO and SEIU president Andy Stern in the CTW coalition have pursued essentially the same goal, albeit though different methods, which is to create a union apparatus that is unaccountable to, and to a great extent insulated from, the rank and file.

Stern's approach has been to create gigantic "locals," often composed of more than 100,000 workers that span one or more states, led by people who were appointed or installed through electoral maneuvers orchestrated by union headquarters. In this way, Stern has reasoned, SEIU can have the necessary clout to force employers into neutrality agreements. But this most often involved top-down organizing in which the workers were passive, and at times even unknowing, recipients of union membership. In defense of these organizing methods, Stern and his supporters claimed that workers were more interested in power than democracy. The SEIU policy of "bargaining to organize" has led to strict limits on traditional union workers' rights, including the right to speak out about bad conditions (for both patients and workers) in nursing homes. The agreements also included bans on strikes and a low wage increase (Moody 2007: 195).

In more recent years, Stern has taken a hard look at some aspects of economic globalization (which he saw as inevitable) and has incorporated them in his view of partnership. Deploring the failure of employers to see the potential in partnership, he held wake-up calls for them, emphasizing that they needed to recognize that the world had changed and that there were people (unionists like Stern and his allies) who would like to help them provide solutions in ways that were up to date and that added value. Stern, then leader of the second largest union in the United States, even went so far as to assert that unions should allow employers "to operate more efficiently with better quality" by using a particular form of outsourcing. His concept of "partnership" involved the idea that the union acts as an outsourcing vehicle by taking over benefits and other provisions for workers from employers "so that there are common benefit plans or common training programs or common ways to deal with workers who lose their jobs and need a bridge until they find new employment" (Mendonca 2006). This would mean that unions are "labor contractors," perhaps providing hiring halls like the building trades. This latter-day, more corporate-oriented conception of partnership envisions that corporations hive off their firm-based social benefits, training programs, and other social provisions, which would then be administered by the unions to soften the negative effects of outsourcing and the corporations' idea of efficiency in general.

The UAW under Gettelfinger's leadership has also sought ways to preserve the union bureaucracy by making it as independent from the rank and file as possible. This was accomplished largely by striking a deal in 2009, when the retiree health care trust fund was handed over to the union by GM, Chrysler, and Ford under the terms of the new contract. The UAW took its long-established strategy of partnering with employers to an extreme this time by becoming a major shareholder in GM alongside the U.S. government and the majority (55 percent shareholders) in Chrysler. In exchange for this peculiar form of "employee ownership"—with the union trust fund getting only one seat on the company board—the union agreed to ban strikes for six years, eliminate work rules negotiated over decades, cut overtime pay, and allow further concessions. The result was the virtual elimination of the difference between UAW-organized plants and nonunion ones. While the UAW once steadily increased the standard for wages and benefits for the entire U.S. working class, it now was leading the way toward a downward trajectory. One should not forget, however, that the Obama administration was the driving force in obtaining these concessions, stating publicly that it had been tougher on the UAW than the George W. Bush White House.

Needless to say, the lack of accountability coupled with hostility to rank-and-file militancy have long been characteristic features of the U.S. labor bureaucracy. But union authorities like Stern and Gettelfinger have pushed corporate unionism control to new extremes. They justified this strategy by arguing that the union machinery had to do whatever it took to survive. According to this fatalistic view, unions must help make companies profitable and minimize, if not eliminate, union democracy. This would enable the unions to survive and build a new base among various sections of workers in nonunion industries (Sustar 2009: 2, 10–11). In his insightful overview of the current state of affairs, *U.S. Labor in Trouble and Transition*, Kim Moody calls Stern's program "corporate unionism," which goes beyond even the class collaboration of traditional American business unionism:

> To the strategies of retreat in the 1980s and 1990s, we can now add the rise of bureaucratic corporate unionism and the embrace of shallow power. The new direction is a step beyond business unionism in its centralization and shift of power upward in the union's structure away from the members, locals, and workplace; its fetish with huge administrative unions; and its almost religious attachment to partnerships with capital. We call it corporate unionism because its vision is essentially administrative, its organizational sensibility executive rather than democratic, and its understanding of power market-based and, hence, shallow. What we are confronting today in the US and world economies is a clash of social forces between labor and capital in which the power of labor, of the working class, must be derived from mass mobilization based on deep organization. This implies a very different direction than either federation offers at the moment [Moody 2007: 196].

The rest of the union bureaucracy has not gone as far in this direction as Stern and Gettelfinger, but many union leaders would probably do so if given the opportunity.

In retrospect, the major issue in the CTW's split from the AFL-CIO had more to do with control over money and other resources than any clear-cut differences over labor or political issues. Stern and the leaders of the other CTW unions—including workers in health care, food, farming, trucking, and construction sectors—no longer wanted to be dragged down by the declining manufacturing unions that remained in the AFL-CIO. But splitting the Federation did not resolve those issues either. By 2009, as a result of a pitched internecine battle, the SEIU-dominated Change to Win coalition of unions was in disarray and veering toward some kind of reunification with the AFL-CIO. This occurred under pressure from the Obama administration, which insisted on the convenience of one major representative institute when dealing with the unions (Sustar 2009: 11). When Stern resigned in April 2010, the CTW lost its prime mover. Joseph Hansen, UFCW president, became the chair of a demoralized CTW that had not lived up to its promises. By October 2010, only four CTW unions were left from the original seven: the Service Employees, Teamsters, Food and Commercial Workers, and the Farm Workers (Kelber 2010: 2).

Meanwhile, in September 2009, Richard Trumka, former president of the United Mine Workers of America and secretary-treasurer of the AFL-CIO under Sweeney, had been elected president of the AFL-CIO. Trumka took office at one of the worst times in the history of organized labor (at least since the 1920s). As Bill Fletcher Jr., former education director and later assistant to the president of the AFL-CIO, put it,

> Unions represent approximately 12% of the workforce (down from 35% in 1955); workers are under near continuous assault by employers, whether in the form of demands for concession or in the form of repression of efforts to join or organize unions; economic restructuring over the last thirty years has turned previously thriving working-class communities into ghost towns; and Black and Chicano workers have suffered devastating employment losses as major manufacturers deserted the cities and either closed down, moved into rural areas or moved overseas [Fletcher 2009b: 1].

Yet, the problems facing organized labor were not only the result of external assaults—many of which had been openly backed by anti-labor elected government officials—but of internal problems as well. Fletcher saw the CTW split as "misguided and ill-informed," which "did nothing to revitalize the union movement or even to clarify the nature of the crisis it faced. Instead it promoted confusion and despair" (ibid.: 1).[10] The AFL-CIO's financial hardship was also largely due to this split. Another important factor was organized labor's weak response to the "Great Recession" as it affected working people in the form of massive home foreclosures and layoffs accelerating by the fall of 2008. Instead of mass demonstrations, labor's response took the form of press statements, e-mails and web postings. (A notable exception was the New York City Central Labor Council, which did carry out public demonstrations.) This failure to respond ceded the political ground to right-wing populists who tapped into the intense anger felt by many white workers and professional-managerial employees. It remained an open question whether Trumka could lead a renewal effort on behalf of organized labor that could reshape the mission and form of the union movement. Fletcher suggested supporting efforts to organize the unemployed in fighting for jobs and livable wages (as happened in the 1930s and in the first decade of the twentieth century). And he called more generally for the linking up to practical social justice-based solidarity with labor movements in other parts of the world so that U.S. workers would not be pitted against non–U.S. workers. He also suggested putting more pressure on the Obama administration "to make sure it did not collapse in the face of pressure from corporate America and the political Right" and developing a forceful response to the rise of right-wing populism (ibid.: 1–2).

These remain pivotal issues at the time of this writing. But in the short period that Trumka has been president, one change is already noticeable: the AFL-CIO's sponsorship of rallies near Wall Street and the American Bankers Association conference in Chicago to protest bankers and investors who helped create the financial meltdown and to demand financial reform. Several other rallies have been held as well in cities across the country, calling for economic stimulus programs to create jobs, always with Trumka as keynote speaker.[11]

The Latest Labor Party Initiative and Unions' Continued Allegiance to the Democrats

The idea to establish an independent labor party resurfaced again in the 1990s. Surprisingly, the new initiative originated in the Oil, Chemical and Atomic Workers (OCAW), a rather conservative union of relatively well-paid white workers, many in the southern oil fields and refineries. Its champions pushed beyond the limits of business unionism on health and safety and other issues since the 1970s. Through internal education and debate, the OCAW membership was won over to the labor party position advocated for many years by its secretary-treasurer, Tony Mazzocchi. In the 1990s, this organization led the effort toward a labor party. In 1996, energized by the initial backing of four national unions (OCAW, United Electrical Workers [UE], Brotherhood of Maintenance of Way Employees [BMWE], and the International Longshore and Warehouse Union [ILWU]), Labor Party Advocates became the Labor Party at a convention held in Cleveland. These four sponsors were soon joined by the United Mine Workers, the American Federation of Government Employees, the Farm Labor Organizing Committee, the California Nurses Association and dozens of local unions. This was fueled by the desire to counter the Clinton administration's political agenda (Moody 2003: 361). It was under Clinton's watch that the Democratic Party veered starkly toward the right. Long taking labor and black voters for granted, Clinton's "New Democrats" sought to conquer the "political center" by beating the Republicans at their own game. This involved the introduction of an economic program with neoliberal tenets that exacerbated social inequality throughout the 1990s boom and dismantled significant components of the welfare system for the poor (Smith 2003: 435–436).

The AFL-CIO functioned de facto as a faction of the Democratic Party but without a public voice of its own. Some labor leaders were reluctant to speak on behalf of all working people, fearing that some union members were against parts of labor's program. This may partly explain the AFL-CIO's reluctance to publicize its opposition to the 1996 welfare reform package. Many union members had been influenced by the mainstream media's constant hammering on the conservative theme that welfare recipients abuse the system and that single parents, especially mothers, are sexually irresponsible and should suffer for their sins. On the other hand, only very little positive information about the poor was distributed by organized labor. The Executive Council kept silent about the abortion issue, and labor's spokespersons seemed not to be willing to make audible statements on the question of public assistance. Thus, there was little reason for the general public to assume that labor's political beliefs were any different from those of the Clinton administration. Only if one examined convention resolutions, the labor press, and some of Sweeney's speeches could one see the difference.

Yet gender and race issues still needed considerable improvement from a social-emancipatory perspective, and there was enough in the program of the Federation and most of its affiliates to form the basis for a new labor-based party. But the political will was missing; many in the top leadership feared that such a course would severely hurt the labor movement by alienating it from mainstream America. One indication of the AFL-CIO's political reticence was that it did not make any tangible effort to correct a glaring flaw in its approach to political education — namely, its virtual invisibility in the public sphere.[12]

A significant additional problem was that many unions became health and life insurers (for historical reasons), and some actually recruited members largely on the strength of these benefits. While some unions, like the needle trades, were staunch supporters of universal health care, others chose to stay away from the 1993 push for health care reform — they thought the Clinton health insurance plan was not in their interest. Indeed, many labor organizations had much to lose by risking their financial and other resources on confrontational activities like strikes. Labor's complex institutionalization, such as its deep legal involvement in insurance, federal management, and reporting requirements, put conservative brakes on progressive union leaders as well (Aronowitz 1998: 191–192).

Several scholars and union activists, who were highly critical of labor's close association with the Democratic Party, argued that unions in the past had received little in return for their support. Some of these critics contended that unions should consider supporting minor parties such as the New Party or the Labor Party (Brecher and Costello 1998; Buhle 1999; Lichtenstein 1998; Slaughter 1999: 52). Others, including several union leaders, suggested that labor withdraw its support to Democrats who voted against labor on key issues, such as free trade (Victor 1994: 2576). The AFL-CIO would begin to pursue this strategy in the following years.

With 1,367 delegates and 200 observers at the 1996 convention, the Labor Party seemed a promising alternative to labor politics as usual. However, the convention rejected the idea of running their own slate of candidates, opting instead to act as a pressure and campaign group for the time being. In 1998, the Labor Party held its first constitutional convention in Pittsburgh, attracting 1,209 delegates and the same six national unions. Attempts were made to resolve the questions about candidate selection and party structure. But the consensus view was to focus on issue-based campaigning, particularly a new Just Health Care campaign for a national single-payer health care system, according to Moody (2007: 262). Three major factors help to explain the party's reluctance to engage in independent electoral national politics: the central strategy of growth, the structure of the party, and the existing ties between labor leaders and the Democratic Party. The Labor Party leadership saw the key to growth in the affiliation of local and national unions, while much of the party's activist base came from the local chapters.

The hope that more national unions would affiliate proved to be misplaced, which was predictable. Although affiliation did not require a union to cease endorsing or working for Democrats, the leaders of most of the larger international unions were too institutionally intertwined with various Democrats and too concerned with recapturing Congress and the White House to jump aboard the Labor Party experiment. Many in the Labor Party favored a more "bottom-up" approach to organizing, and registered the problem of stagnated increase of affiliations as so many unions were dominated by business unionism. Only the OCAW, UE, and BMWE held recruitment drives among their own locals for the Labor Party. Campaigning among locals of other unions would have meant encroaching on the turf of international union leaders who would not appreciate such efforts among their members. Moreover, the OCAW and BMWE were both subject to separate mergers with larger unions that were not committed to the Labor Party.

Secondly, as the Labor Party mirrored the hierarchical structural norms of the prevailing top-down business union bureaucracy of the labor movement itself, the affiliated national and regional unions received the tide swell of votes at its conventions. Meanwhile, the role and nature of the local chapters remained unresolved, with no connection to national or local unions. Thus the party actually split, with the local chapters frequently dominated by the far left on the one hand, and national and other official organizations by top union officials on the other. With hardly any unions in between, this gap might have been filled by greater influence for local unions as well as more aggressive organizing among them.

Thirdly, problems surfaced with regard to electoral politics. Most importantly, the affiliation strategy of growth and the party structure itself worked heavily against the new party running its own slate of candidates in opposition to the Democrats. While leaders of the UE, OCAW, and ILWU favored limited experiments in elections, most national labor leaders objected because of ties to Democrats, which were very strong in some cases. For example, both the political director and president of the affiliated American Federation of Government Employees were members of the Democratic National Committee in 1996 and opposed running independent candidates. Richard Trumka, then secretary-treasurer of the AFL-CIO, was deeply involved in Democratic politics and dead set against running Labor Party candidates.

Consequently, the Labor Party did not take part in elections until an experimental campaign in South Carolina in 2005–2006. Of course, a "party" that abstains from the electoral process will not be seen as a party at all, and as a pressure group it has to compete with numerous other issue-oriented organizations, coalitions, and interest groups (ibid.: 242–243). Obviously, the latest effort toward independent labor-based political action was severely hampered, as usual, by the existing party duopoly, particularly the affiliations and semi-institutional connections of major parts of the U.S. labor movement with the Democrats (Chester 2004: 193–194).[13]

As Moody suggests, the alliance with the Democratic Party, the liberal-capitalist party most open to compromise, is the logical extension of business unionism to the political realm due to features that fit well with such an arrangement. These include the lack of ultimate or even long-range goals, the embrace of the U.S. capitalist system with some modifications, and the businesslike relation to limited goals (sought especially through lobbying for legislation), as well as the top-down nature of political decisions and tactical choices, the self-importance that comes from associating with those in power, and the notion of measured advances through a semi-institutional partnership with those who administer the system. The problem in a nutshell is that these very same attributes do not dovetail with organized labor as an interracial social movement focused on workers' class interests. It would be difficult to inspire African Americans or Latinos to vote in larger number for candidates who are reluctant to address their issues. The same applies to the challenge of how to turn immigrants into citizens and working-class voters. Furthermore, how can one attract working-class whites, particularly those with lower incomes, to vote for their real interests? "Clearly the Democratic Party cannot do these things. But can a business union leadership that shares many of the same ideas, cautions, and fears of class conflict and mass mobilization?" (Moody 2007: 166). The answer to this rhetorical question was obviously no.

AFL-CIO's Changed Communication Strategies and Unceasing Support of Democrats

Under Sweeney's leadership, the AFL-CIO replaced the *AFL-CIO News*, an old-style newspaper, with a more colorful magazine called *America@work*, which shifted its focus to encouraging social activism and promoting organized labor's public policies. The AFL-CIO also sent the magazine to the media to alert them of critical labor activities and issues. In addition, the Federation issued a weekly fax and e-mail, called *Work in Progress*, that provided information about organizing efforts, political mobilization campaigns, legislative victories, and news concerning visits or public appearances by AFL-CIO leaders. With the change in communication strategies, the AFL-CIO leaders were more willing to confront corporate abuses in their rhetoric and public speeches, and the AFL-CIO was also becoming better adept at disseminating its message through various informational channels (Francia 2006: 26). Yet, the problem of conservative and business-oriented think tanks supplying large numbers of "experts" to talk shows and news programs persisted, while the AFL did not support a broadly based institute of its own comparable with any of those think tanks that could counter the ongoing dissemination of the gospel of "free enterprise" and conservative social and economic policies.[14]

The steadfast support of Democratic candidates has remained the dominant union practice in state and local politics as well as at the national level. During the congressional elections from 1996 to 2002, labor PAC campaign contributions and expenditures under Sweeney continued to allocate similar proportions of their funds to Democrats as under Lane Kirkland during the elections from 1988 to 1994. Union PACs gave more than 90 percent of their U.S. House contributions to Democratic candidates. Union PAC contributions to U.S. Senate candidates likewise went disproportionately to Democrats both before and after Sweeney's election. But labor began to use the primaries to punish those who supported free trade or other anti-union policies. The AFL-CIO under Sweeney also devoted a much higher proportion of its resources to competitive congressional races than in the past. This meant that fewer resources were spent on challengers and open-seat candidates who were likely to lose, and more money went to non-incumbents in competitive races. The AFL-CIO even was aggressive in races involving incumbents, with most of the money likewise going to those whose seats were most at risk. This shift in strategy was at least partly due to the Republican takeover of Congress following the 1994 election; the AFL-CIO aimed to help Democrats regain majority control of Congress.

The AFL-CIO leadership also took other steps to rebuild labor's political power. It put a greater emphasis on independent expenditures and internal communications to mobilize its membership, especially through get-out-the-vote activities and political education efforts regarding Democratic candidates in congressional elections. The activities of the AFL-CIO alone constituted only a fraction of organized labor's overall political efforts, however. More important was the behavior of the labor movement as a whole, which followed the lead of the AFL-CIO under Sweeney by directing its resources into competitive congressional contests as well. But it continued to invest relatively more in safe incumbents (ibid.: 31–39, 50–51, 60–65).[15]

Union campaign contributions and expenditures showed a huge increase during the latest elections. In the 2008 federal election, the AFL-CIO enlisted 250,000 members to campaign for politicians, while the Federation and CTW and their political action committees spent nearly $450 million (a historical record of the U.S. labor movement) to win the U.S. Congress and presidency for the Democratic Party. In the 2010 mid-term elections, unions were worried about a drastic rollback of workers' rights by a possible Republican-controlled House or Senate, spending more than $200 million — along with the mobilization of a record number of canvassers going door to door — in a massive attempt to safeguard the Democratic majorities in both chambers of Congress (Gay Stolberg and Greenhouse 2009; Greenhouse 2010e).[16]

Labor's Responses to Corporate Globalization

In the context of enhanced economic globalization, there has been increased pressure on American unions to bend over backward to those U.S. corporate businesses operating at home and exposed to heavy competition from abroad. A key issue remains the postwar shift in production to the South, which is also part of globalization writ large as foreign capital has moved in and local companies have sought more profitable opportunities abroad (including relocation and outsourcing). Here the aftereffects are still felt of labor's historic failure to confront racism directly during the era of Jim Crow segregation. The CIO's "Operation Dixie" organizing drive in the late 1940s failed as southern employers used both racism and anti-communism to attack any and all efforts to organize black and white workers. The CIO at that time was preoccupied with purging the left-led unions that were willing to take on that challenge, and its support for the Democratic Party made it incapable of challenging the party's segregationist southern wing (Smith 2006: 189–192, 197–198). As a result, the South became an attractive locale for both U.S. and foreign capital in the postwar years. The only other real opportunity to break the anti-union barriers posed by right-to-work laws, intense overt racism, and a culture that successfully equated unionism with communism was toward the end of the 1960s when Dr. Martin Luther King Jr. shifted his attention to economic inequality and the Poor People's Campaign.[17] Some gains were made in the public sector in southern cities, and later in textiles, but few unions took up the gauntlet to unionize the region, particularly after King's assassination. The South consequently has become home to most of the auto transplants owned by German and Japanese companies, which are nonunion despite repeated efforts by the UAW to organize these workers. The pattern was repeated in other industries, which had a significant national impact given that by 2000, 30 percent of manufacturing jobs were located in the South (Moody 2007: 226, 45).[18]

Global differentiation of production processes has led to divergent strategies and interests in different parts of the world. These structural differences tend to hinder effective global solidarity among workers (Eder 2002). Global alliances between unions and long-term battles against transnational corporations such as the worldwide campaign against South Africa — with Royal Dutch/Shell as the first target of a global boycott — from 1986 onward, involved short-term costs that affected workers and unions differently in different countries.[19] The most difficult challenge for global campaigns was how to identify common goals and balance interests of the various participants.

Over the past twenty or so years, the South Africa disinvestment campaign has not been replicated by similar global campaigns elsewhere, while the collusion of governments and transnational corporations in depriving workers of fundamental political, social, and economic rights has become even more entrenched today. In most cases, the trade unions involved left the field, returning to their own particular struggles. Occasionally one group or another asked for external support in their individual contract or organizing battles with employers. The help they received tended to be sporadic and temporary at best. Some of these struggles reached a truly global scale such as the Steelworkers' fight against Bridgestone Firestone in the early twenty-first century to retain their union and hold on to pattern bargaining in the rubber industry, which ultimately involved solidarity actions in 83 countries (Bronfenbrenner 2007: 3–4).

Difficulties in achieving cross-border alliances had to do with international realities as well as the internal state of American unions. Labor movements in other countries showed a wide variety of types and roles. Many were dependent on their government in varying degrees, calling into question their independent role in defending workers' rights. Others were split into mutually antagonistic blocs, complicating efforts of cooperation. On top of this, many U.S. unions were so anemic that solidarity with other unions in the United States was hard enough, let alone finding common cause with those in other countries (Nissen 2002a: 7). Yet some American unions have developed links with workers and unions abroad who are employed in the same industries and transnational corporations. Unions such as the SEIU, Communications Workers of America (CWA), United Steelworkers of America (USWA), UAW and UE have forged more or less permanent ties to their counterparts in various countries for the purpose of sharing information and exchanging actual support of one kind or another (Slaughter 2005: 339–350).

There have been movements to build cross-border alliances between unions as part of organizing campaigns. These included the AFL-CIO, Teamsters, and Union Network International (UNI), which supported a global campaign to organize workers at Quebecor in the United States, Europe, and Latin America; the global organizing campaigns at Nestlé and Coca-Cola by the International Union of Food, Agricultural, Hotel, Restaurant, Catering, Tobacco and Allied Workers' Associations (IUF); and UNITE-HERE's Clean Clothes

Campaign of 2002 to organize Pinault-Printemps-Redoute (PPR) subsidiary Brylane (Bronfenbrenner 2007: 5). There has also been cross-border cooperation between U.S. unions and those attempting to organize maquila plants in Mexico, Central America, and the Caribbean (Frundt 2002). This direct contact was in addition to existing relations within the international trade secretariats and the worldwide federations of national unions for many major industries. Moreover, there have been unofficial links at a more grassroots level, such as those organized by the Transnational Information Exchange (TIE) in the 1990s. These concerned efforts to organize face-to-face contacts and create more meaningful, rooted relationships of solidarity between unionized workers in a number of industries, including automobile and telecommunications across borders in North America and Europe. This occurred through cross-border meetings by industry as well as through continued contact and information exchanges (Moody 1997: 227–268).[20]

But these various endeavors by labor to constrain globalizing capital have been few and far between. A crucial factor is the difficulty labor experienced in matching capital's speed and mobility and its capacity to restructure its organization. The current challenges exceed those of the 1980s, according to Kate Bronfenbrenner, a leading expert on union strategies, both in the United States and internationally:

> Where before transnational corporations seemed at least somewhat bounded by loyalty to product, firm, industry, or country, today the largest of these firms increasingly supersede most government authority and are constrained only by the interests of their biggest investors, lenders, and shareholders [Bronfenbrenner 2007: 4].

Especially with regard to industries that are more mobile and can shift around production, the major challenge remains: how to organize in these industries, which are able to flee? (Gapasin and Bonacich 2002: 171).

Still, globalization and lean production exhibit vulnerabilities for corporate businesses, which may offer possibilities of labor power. Industrial restructuring, with its extended chain of production, can make employers more vulnerable to work stoppages. In a number of cases, workers have demonstrated their willingness and ability to reach across borders and inspire secondary actions that increased the leverage of work stoppages in one country. For example, the 1998 United Parcel Service Workers strike prompted job actions and demonstrations by UPS workers across Europe and even in India and the Philippines (Piven and Cloward 2000b: 424). On the other hand, globalization of production need not be met by a globalization of union strategies to be contained. Local strategies, such as the United Auto Workers' strike against General Motors in 1998, can sometimes effectively interrupt global production processes in ways that were not possible before the emergence of widespread market integration.[21] In these instances workers need not be connected internationally to others around the world in order to effectively influence the behavior of a transnational corporation (Herod 2002). But such disruptions do not necessarily imply solidarity with the workers abroad, and may actually remain far removed from global social justice unionism.

It is at this point that the notion of empire in relation to U.S. foreign policy becomes relevant. Longtime labor activists and union advisors Bill Fletcher and Fernando Gapasin argue in their insightful diagnosis of the current state of affairs of U.S. organized labor that

> U.S. organized labor's silence on questions of empire has made the movement largely complicit in the actions of the U.S. government on the international stage. This collusion has come at great cost, both domestically and internationally....
> Although American union leaders often cloak their acceptance of U.S. foreign policy in patriotism, something far deeper and more troubling is at work: *acceptance of empire*. The U.S. trade union movement has come to accept the legitimacy of the U.S. de facto international empire and has decided that such an empire is not inconsistent with democracy. As such, it is caught in a fundamental contradiction between the notion of international working-class solidarity and silence about or support for empire [Fletcher and Gapasin 2008: 192–193].

This failure to question U.S. imperialism has many roots, not the least of which is the employment relationship that many workers have with the U.S. military and U.S.-based corporations doing business abroad.

There is also the legacy of the Cold War, when the communism-anticommunism rift put a heavy stamp on every international activity of unions, leading many labor movements on each side of the divide to support repressive governments aligned with their political camp. The personal histories of many top union leaders in the 1950s-1980s were closely tied to this historic divide as well. Moreover, U.S. union successes from the 1950s to the early 1970s without international solidarity bolstered the inclination to ignore this potential source of strength. Finally, the apparent payoffs of U.S. workers from the growing economic empire from the 1950s to the 1970s and the dominant business unionism during those same years further reinforced an outlook far removed from international class solidarity (Nissen 2002a: 7).

Generally, the U.S. trade union movement tends to see globalization merely in terms of transnationalizing corporations and economics, thereby dismissing U.S. military and political imperialism. Therefore when the United States intervenes militarily and politically elsewhere in the world (as it has in Iraq and Afghanistan in recent years and in Central America in the 1980s), the union movement often cannot respond, or at least not adequately. This is because its leaders see governmental foreign policy as separate from the aims and objectives of trade unionism, unless the policy is blatantly one-sidedly pro-corporate business, and even then, unions often tolerate the U.S. position assuming this is in their members' interest. American unions generally consider foreign policy in the narrowest sense, for example, by focusing on the implications of the North American Free Trade Agreement (or kindred agreements such as the Dominican Republic-Central American Free Trade Agreement and the recent free-trade pact with South Korea) for identifiable groups of American workers rather than considering its impact on democracy, self-determination, and human rights both at home and abroad. Thus, U.S. unions view foreign policy issues in light of their impact on their membership or, in more enlightened moments, their effects on U.S. workers in general. For this reason, the global justice movement in the United States has largely developed separately from the trade union movement, which has a negative impact on the remnants of socialism in America.

There was a moment during the Seattle demonstrations against the World Trade Organization in 1999 when "teamsters and turtles" (unionists and environmentalists) among others joined hands, which showed that unity is possible. But this did not last long, and the movement was unable to translate its lessons into theory and practice. In hindsight, the Seattle protest was an example of tactical unity rather than strategic alliance, which is not surprising given the serious disagreement within the AFL-CIO about the World Trade Organization at the time. Neither the AFL-CIO nor the CTW Federation had consistent views on international affairs; the CTW, for instance, has refrained from taking a position on the wars in Iraq and Afghanistan. Led by the SEIU, its approach to international affairs combined case-by-case analysis with the viewpoint of a trade association. In this regard the CTW did not differ qualitatively from the AFL-CIO, which traditionally has hesitated to take any position on international affairs that might challenge U.S. foreign policy, unless that policy had an impact on members of one of its union affiliates (Fletcher and Gapasin 2008: 194–195).

At the time of writing, American labor unions are generally taking a strong protectionist stance.[22] To save jobs, the AFL-CIO leadership has made calls for tariffs on rubber and steel goods, which Washington has answered by imposing a penalty tariff on Chinese tires and tubular steel. China in return targeted U.S. poultry with its own tariff. United Steelworkers filed a 5,800-page complaint detailing how China has been scheming to control most of the global market in green technologies, which the Obama administration has under investigation. On the verge of an all-out trade war, in September 2010 the House voted 348 to 79 to authorize tariffs on nearly all Chinese imports if Beijing did not give up its manipulation of its currency to underprice Chinese exports and thus hamper U.S. exports to China. Of course, other governments also routinely manipulate their currency when it suits their purpose. The United States has been doing the very same thing to the dollar through the interventions of the Federal Reserve Bank.

The trade imbalance between the United States and China is currently the largest in the world. America's trade deficit with China peaked at close to 6 percent in 2006. In 2009 it was $227 billion, which means that the U.S. exported $69.5 billion in goods and services to China, while it imported a whopping $296 billion (down significantly from 2008).[23] The U.S. economy has been buying a lot more than it produces, borrowing from foreign creditors, most notably from China, to do so. The heart of the matter is that this is the result of collaboration between the two countries over the past three decades, driven by different but mutually reinforcing motives. While American multinationals sought access to China's market, where they would be able to produce low-cost goods that Americans wanted, the Chinese were interested in acquiring factories and the modern technologies needed to develop a first-class industrial base. American companies agreed to the basic trade-off in which China would let them in to manufacture and sell products, and in exchange they would share technology and teach Chinese partners the ins and outs of the production processes in question. (Japan and then South Korea, Taiwan and Singapore basically pursued similar development strategies after World War II.) Over the course of time, U.S. corporations also gained enormous bargaining power over workers back home by threatening to move abroad if unions demurred over wage concessions. Washington gave its blessing to the deals that were proffered. Both major parties assumed that improving the fortunes of globalizing banks and businesses was in the broad national interest (Greider 2010: 21).

William Greider, national affairs correspondent for *The Nation*, argues that shrinking the trade deficits (possibly through taking unilateral action by the United States), important in itself, is not sufficient to resolve the problems that have arisen. He hits the bull's eye in emphasizing the need to change the rules under which globalizing American business and finance operate:

> Only in America do multinationals get to behave like free riders, with no strings attached. They harvest public money as subsidies and investment capital, they are protected by US armed forces and diplomacy, and they are rescued when they get into trouble.... US corporations and banks remain free to move jobs and production whenever and wherever corporate strategy dictates, regardless of the consequences for the economy. Government can stop this by forcing them to serve the broader national interest. This is not as radical as it may sound. Every other leading industrial nation does it, one way or another. They impose limits on corporate strategy, either in formally binding ways or through political and cultural pressure, to ensure that good jobs and the best value-added production remains at home. Washington can accomplish this only through multilateral action, not free-trade agreements. It has to rewrite trade law, tax law and policies on workforce development and subsidy [ibid.: 22].

Predictably, such an integrated set of regulatory measures and policy changes would meet severe resistance on the part of large corporations and big banks. But given opinion poll results in recent years, a majority of the American public is likely to support efforts to force big industrial and finance capital to serve the nation's "well-being" in the broader sense meant here. It is at this point that the American labor movement might make valuable contributions in educating its members about the relevant issues and supporting legislative efforts at the federal and state levels to win the necessary reforms.[24] These changes would also curb the tendency of pitting American workers against foreign workers by U.S. corporations relocating (or threatening to do so) and offshoring production through direct investment or contracting, all in a relentless race to the bottom.

Concerns about the Erosion of Collective Workers' Rights

The further destruction of collective workers' rights in America in recent years is a matter of much concern among critical observers on the labor left. They signal that systematic and often illegal tactics on the part of corporate business block workers from exercising their rights, particularly their right to organize — a critical factor in the ongoing deterioration of wages and working conditions. Over the past few decades a number of union leaders (including Lane Kirkland in 1984) have attacked the NLRA as being anti-labor. They followed in the track of earlier postwar NLRA critics among established labor leaders, including John L. Lewis in 1949 and the Typographers in 1954. A generation later, several academic analysts in the 1980s came to the same conclusion (Goldfield 1986; Rogers 1984; Tomlins 1985a, 1985b; Weiler 1983, 1984).

America's labor laws have attracted fierce criticism internationally from organized labor. In a detailed exposé submitted to the International Labor Organization (ILO) Governing Body in March 2002, the International Confederation of Free Trade Unions (ICFTU) argued,

> The right to organize and the right to strike are not adequately protected under US labour legislation. American law is unable to protect workers when the employer is determined to destroy or prevent union representation. Weak laws and enforcement also inhibit the practice of collective bargaining. A series of far-reaching measures need to be taken in order to establish genuine respect for core labour standards in the US, particularly with regard to trade union rights [ICFTU 2002].

At the turn of the new millennium, U.S. labor law also came under severe attack by Human Rights Watch, a respected international watchdog. In a special report published in 2000, it noted that U.S. labor law violates international standards in numerous respects, including inadequate procedures and remedies for unfair labor practices; failure to protect economic strikers against permanent replacement; and a flat ban on secondary action and withholding legal protection concerning freedom of association to agricultural workers, domestic workers, and other broad categories of workers (foremen and supervisors, and independent contractors). Human Rights Watch signaled that thousands of American workers were laid off each year or suffered other reprisals for trying to organize unions. Among other things, employers could resist union organizing by dragging out legal proceedings for years (Human Rights Watch 2000).

A comprehensive analysis of employer behavior in representation elections supervised by the NLRB from 1999 to 2003 (published in 2009) showed a significant intensification of employer opposition to organizing, including an increase in more coercive and retaliatory tactics such as plant closing threats and actual plant closings, dismissals, harassment and other discipline, surveillance, and alteration of benefits and working conditions. It was standard practice in the NLRB election process for workers to be subjected to threats, interrogation, surveillance, and retaliation for union activity. At the same time, employers were less inclined to offer "carrots" such as granting unscheduled raises, making positive personnel changes, promises of improvement, offering bribes and special favors, sponsoring social events and employee involvement programs.

The overall situation was more labor friendly in the public sector, however, where workers were relatively free from the negative tactics prevalent in the private sector. Most states in the public-sector sample during the period in question had card check certification as the primary means through which workers were organizing. In this case, the employer was required to recognize the union if the majority of workers signed cards authorizing the union to represent them.[25] The author of the 2009 report concluded that the findings suggested that

> the aspirations for representation are being thwarted by a coercive and punitive climate for organizing that goes unrestrained due to a fundamentally flawed regulatory regime that neither protects their rights nor provides any disincentives for employers to continue disregarding the law. Moreover, many of the employer tactics that create a punitive and coercive atmosphere are, in fact, legal. Unless serious law reform with real penalties is enacted, only a fraction of the workers who seek representation under the National Labor Relations Act will be successful. If recent trends continue, then there will no longer be a functioning legal mechanism to effectively protect the right of private-sector workers to organize and collectively bargain [Bronfenbrenner 2009: 3].

The penalties for violating labor laws are so slight that companies often treat them as routine costs of doing business. As Human Rights Watch pointed out, millions of workers (including farm workers, domestic household workers, low-level supervisors and "independent" contractors who are really dependent on a single employer) are deliberately excluded from the aegis of laws on organizing and bargaining rights. Human Rights Watch called on the U.S. Congress to ensure rapid reinstatement and full back pay for workers fired for organizing, faster election procedures for determining union representation in a workplace, expedited appeals to resolve unfair labor practices more quickly, proper union access rights to workplaces, stronger remedies against bad-faith bargaining by employers, and U.S. ratification of ILO conventions on freedom of association and collective bargaining.[26] Such measures would undoubtedly improve American labor's organizing successes (Human Rights Watch 2000: 18, 31, 171–190; Graham 2002).

However, the federal courts and regulatory agencies have remained reluctant to police the corporate illegalities associated with management anti-union activity—called "unfair" labor practices under the law—while workers and unions are judicially prohibited from using certain tactics mentioned in the law. In September 2007, the National Labor Relations Board (since 2002 led by a pro-business majority of George W. Bush appointees) issued a succession of decisions that were heavily biased against organized labor. One ruling made it harder to join a union through majority sign-up procedures, which is the preferred organizing method used by many unions that do not expect fair and timely NLRB elections. Another ruling even permitted employers to decertify existing unions using the very same forms of majority recognition now denied union organizers themselves. Other rulings made it even easier for employers to discriminate against union supporters and limit opportunities available to workers who are illegally fired for engaging in union activity.

In fact, the NLRB made such drastic changes to the law that it became virtually impossible for workers to receive fair treatment, either in the labor practices arena or in the elections arena. The AFL-CIO demanded the board to be "shut down" until less partisan appointments were made to three recently vacated posts on the five-member board. But this would not have addressed the deeper problems that the labor movement had to face since at least 1947, when the Taft-Hartley Act drastically curtailed workers' ability to strike and otherwise pressure employers to recognize unions. Since then, Democratic labor board majorities have hardly made a positive difference to organizing either. Although the Reagan years were particularly devastating, organized labor did not thrive under the board during the Carter and Clinton administrations (Fraser 2008).

In March 2010, President Obama appointed two union lawyers to the NLRB; this was expected to tilt the board toward a more balanced position regarding workers' rights to organize and bargain collectively (Greenhouse 2010a). Early in the next year, however, labor faced a well-orchestrated, massive anti-union offensive by corporations and their political allies, aided by conservative media coverage. In states across the country, elected officials and right-wing pundits began clamping down on organized labor, calling for wage concessions and cuts to health and pension benefits for government employees. In several cases—mostly in states where Republicans controlled the governor's office and both chambers—they were also pushing for new legislation to curb the power of unions in collective bargaining and politics, using budget woes as a pretext to undermine unions.[27] What was new in comparison with previous attacks (over almost four decades that also involved neoliberal Democrats) was their scale and intensity, as well as the real possibility of success.

It was in Wisconsin that, in February 2011, one of the boldest frontal assaults on public-sector unions was launched by a newly elected Republican governor, seconded by Republican majorities in both houses of the legislature. Governor Scott Walker's proposal to drastically scale back benefits and to virtually eliminate collective bargaining rights for most public-sector workers outraged the Democrats in the state legislature, triggering massive protest rallies at the state capitol by union supporters, public employees, and students.[28] At the time of writing, it is unclear how these events will unfold. If this anti-union assault succeeds, it would bring a dramatic turnabout in Wisconsin, which in 1959 became the first state to permit collective bargaining for public employees and was the birthplace of the AFSCME. Meanwhile, governors in several other states (most notably Ohio and New Jersey) have mounted similar attacks against state and local government employees. Those workers and their unions have followed the example set by their counterparts in the Badger State, organizing and protesting against the austerity measures and union busting they are facing (Greenhouse 2011a; McAlevey 2011).[29]

Attempts at Improving Workers' Rights

At the end of 2003 the AFL-CIO backed the introduction of the Employee Free Choice Act (EFCA) as a way out of the existing impasse regarding workers' rights. It did so in tandem with Jobs with Justice and American Rights at Work, groups that aimed to build popular support for collective bargaining rights. The CTW likewise focused on trying to pass the EFCA. A key provision — modeled after the Canadian labor law, which is more favorable to workers and their unions — allows union recognition based on majority sign-up. This would circumvent a whole category of employer abuses by abandoning certification elections. In its present form, the National Labor Relations Act allows an employer to demand a secret ballot election administered by the National Labor Relations Board when a union requests recognition based on signed authorization cards or petitions. Under the current law, only secret ballots are binding. The proposed act would authorize the NLRB to certify a union as the exclusive bargaining representative of employees based on a majority of valid signed authorizations obtained by union organizers (Lafer 2008).

In 2005 the bill had nearly a majority of House members as co-sponsors as well as thirty co-sponsors in the Senate (Cohen 2005: 70). On March 1, 2007, the House of Representatives passed the act by a vote of 241 to 185. But on June 26, 2007, the bill was stalled in the Senate, and would certainly have received George W. Bush's presidential veto had it cleared that hurdle (Stern 2008). Predictably, employers will do their utmost to kill this act, as the head of the U.S. Chamber of Commerce has made clear. On the other hand, early on in his presidency, Obama pledged to support the measure. The EFCA bill was reintroduced in Congress in March 2009, but it was halted in the Democratic-controlled Senate that summer. The most important asset of EFCA or similar legislation would be that it could reinforce the notion that there is a federally protected right for workers to organize. As in the 1930s, when organizers used New Deal legislation to claim "The President Wants You to Join the Union," today's union officials and rank-and-file activists could use EFCA to build workers' confidence to organize. The United Food and Commercial Workers (UFCW) took a decisive step in this direction when it used the EFCA debate to relaunch its effort to organize Wal-Mart (Sustar 2009: 11–12).

The push for this particular means of union recognition is an expedient response to the negative impact on union elections of Section 8(c) of Taft-Hartley, which legitimates an employer's right to wage a full-time, enduring anti-union campaign at any place in the workplace. In the event this legislation passes, its actual effect on new organizing would still be uncertain, because by itself it would do little to change the broader anti-labor climate that causes many campaigns to fail. It would also leave many key Taft-Hartley restrictions intact, including a provision that allows individual states to pass right-to-work laws, which account for the extremely weak union influence in the South (Fraser 2008).

Some in the labor movement have criticized the EFCA as an attempt to substitute a legal mechanism for the hard work of organizing the unorganized. The EFCA in itself would not overcome all the problems that for decades have impeded union organizing: bureaucratic top-down methods that use arbitrary checklists and timelines rather than cultivating and encouraging rank-and-file activists in the long run, jurisdictional disputes that pit rival unions against one another as they compete for "hot" shops, and a reluctance to use job actions and other militant tactics in the workplace to pressure employers. Moreover, the EFCA would not necessarily lead to the kind of strategic focus that these critics deem necessary to rebuild the U.S. labor movement (Sustar 2009: 12). Most importantly, however, the EFCA is unlikely to reappear on the Democrats' legislative agenda without strong intervention by the Obama administration, which, at the time of writing, was not expected to happen anytime soon.

A variety of legal scholars, labor historians, and trade unionists have called for a more far-reaching shift away from the NLRB framework toward a judicial framework revolving around an expansive interpretation of the Thirteenth Amendment (1865). This would build on a labor-infused tradition of civil rights. In the late 1940s and early 1950s, lawyers of the Civil Rights Section, a unit within the Justice Department (created in 1939 and originating out of 1930s concerns with labor rights) came to use the Thirteenth Amendment as a vehicle for instituting "free labor," broadly defined, and for prohibiting various kinds of legal and economic coercion. Until the mid-twentieth century, workers regularly took recourse to this reading of the amendment banning "slavery and involuntary servitude" to legitimate their rights to organize and strike. When employers or the government interfered with these rights, labor leaders and activists routinely invoked the Thirteenth Amendment. They argued that "yellow-dog" contracts, labor injunctions, and anti-strike laws were unconstitutional, and sought labor legislation to enforce the amendment. They claimed that without the ability to form unions and threaten employers with collective action, wage workers did not have the power to improve working conditions and were, in effect, bound to a contractual servitude. The amendment — known then as "the glorious labor amendment"—obliged the government to eliminate any such system (Goluboff 2001: 1609–1610, 1614).

Several of today's union supporters apparently want to revive this tradition of civil rights in seeking a viable alternative to the NLRB framework, and they argue that the Thirteenth Amendment could once again be a valuable organizing tool (Dudzic 2005).[30] They contend that the core of this movement's Thirteenth Amendment interpretation — that labor freedom necessarily includes the right to organize and strike — has sedimented in international labor standards. And they also argue that the model of freedom of association fits well with twenty-first-century industrial conditions:

> Unlike our current labor law, which tries to force workers into fixed bargaining units, a labor law built on the freedom of association can encompass a wide variety of promising organizational forms including community unionism, occupational unionism, and revived industrial unionism [Pope, Kellman, and Bruno 2008: 139].

Their approach is based on the idea that the labor movement should act as a real rights movement (combining workers' rights, citizenship rights, human rights, and civil rights), which conducts the labor struggle over a long-term time frame and fights over issues of basic principle. And that basic principle would apply equally to all workers, including those provided little or no protection by the NLRB.[31]

Organizing immigrant workers is arguably a major priority for the labor movement today, but their often irregular status makes them ill-suited for NLRB-certified organizing methods and vulnerable to exploitative employers. As advocates of the Thirteenth Amendment approach argue, undocumented workers today can be compared to black workers under slavery who were denied citizenship rights, whose human rights were abused and whose work placed them at the very bottom of the labor hierarchy, underneath the floor established for free labor. Legal expert Maria Ontiveros claims that an expansive (or "holistic") interpretation of the Thirteenth Amendment would provide a compelling moral and legal rationale for extending to undocumented workers full labor rights. This in turn would improve conditions for American workers at the bottom of the labor market. Violations of the Thirteenth Amendment would include current and future guest worker programs that provide for deportation of workers upon termination of employment, limitations on the social participation rights of a worker's family members, and prohibitions on workers who apply for citizenship (Ontiveros 2007). Advocates of this Thirteenth Amendment strategy also suggest that a worker's right to organize would be protected from the volatility of partisan politics and would fuel a movement aimed at making labor rights a basic and unassailable feature of American democracy (Fraser 2008).

Under the current circumstances, however, this proposal for a wholesale, radical restructuring of U.S. labor law, backed by the Labor Party, is even less likely to win passage through Congress than the proposed Employee Free Choice Act (Freeman 2005: 73). It is also telling for today's dismal state of labor power that labor activists feel obliged to fall back on a constitutional amendment banning slavery and indentured servitude dating from the early Reconstruction era (and revived during the late New Deal era) rather than seeking inspiration in labor laws that, at least for the time being, remain in place in those advanced industrial countries where labor is still *relatively* more empowered vis-à-vis capital and management.

Some U.S. labor unions have begun to draw on international labor rights in their struggles for the right to organize. For example, in December 2005, the United Electrical, Radio and Machine Workers of America (UE), which in recent decades has focused heavily on immigrant workers, filed a complaint with the International Labor Organization (ILO), the UN's labor agency, charging the U.S. government and the state of North Carolina with violations of international law protecting workers' rights to association and collective bargaining. This was part of a campaign to repeal a North Carolina state act dating from the Jim Crow era of racial segregation, General Statute 95–98, that prohibits public employees from bargaining labor contracts. (In the mid–1990s, UE had begun organizing state and municipal workers in North Carolina, chartering their statewide organization as UE Local 150. In recent years the UE expanded its public-sector organizing to two other states in the Upper South that lack public employee bargaining rights, establishing EU Local 160 in Virginia and EU Local 170 in West Virginia.)

The complaint brought to the ILO held that North Carolina General Statute 95–98, making it illegal for state, county, and other divisions of the state to sign contracts with unions, violated international labor rights (Brecher, Costello, and Smith 2007). In March 2007, the ILO ruled in favor of UE and called upon the United States and North Carolina to repeal GS 95–98 and start discussions with unions to establish "a framework for collective bargaining."[32] The fact that UE had won its case did not automatically guarantee a positive outcome for labor, since the ILO had no power to enforce its decision. But it did help to shame the employers and the governments that supported them, and gave workers the high moral ground in defending their cause.[33] Up until now however, North Carolina has maintained its ban on collective bargaining for public employees since 1959 (Jarvis 2011).

The militant and democratic approach to trade unionism that the UE pursues was also brought to the general public's attention in December 2008 during a six-day occupation at the Republic Windows and Doors plant in Chicago. The occupation was organized by workers—most of them Latino immigrants, joined by a minority of African Americans—to demand severance pay after the company announced overnight that it would close down its business. Suddenly a sit-down strike—something reminiscent of the militant unionism as described in labor history books of the 1930s—became a focal point for working-class resistance amid a profound economic crisis. It clearly resonated even with white-collar professionals who in the past might not have given a second thought to the plight of blue-collar workers like those at Republic. But they were now well aware that they ran similar risks of being unjustly treated by the bosses and laid off.[34] But this was one of the few exceptions to the overall state of affairs regarding unionism in America. Another major exception involved the vigorous actions of the independent National Union of Healthcare Workers, which could possibly establish a contemporary model for democratic, member-driven, militant unionism (Sustar 2009: 16).

The recent assaults on organized labor in Wisconsin and elsewhere have energized some of the nation's unions (including the Communications Workers of America and SEIU) to plan large-scale organizing campaigns targeting communications workers, airport security employees, and low-wage private-sector workers in many cities. Labor leaders are thereby harnessing some of the invigorated rank-and-file activism and newfound cooperation between private-sector and public-sector unions (Greenhouse 2011b). By and large, however, organized labor's prospects at this critical juncture seem bleak; especially if unions continue to fail to connect labor struggles to larger issues as most have done over the past decades.

6

The Legacy of U.S. Labor Politics and Challenges Facing the Left

The vast majority of organized labor's leadership and membership in America has rejected the class and socialist views held by trade unionists in most other developed capitalist countries—no matter how diluted those views may have become. During the greater part of its existence, mainstream organized labor dominated by the AFL, and the AFL-CIO since 1955, has been characterized by "the presence of powerful, undemocratic, and avidly anti-socialist labor leaders" (Buhle 1999: 5). And even though John Sweeney was a leading supporter of the Democratic Socialists of America, this did not mean that he was advancing the cause of socialism while he presided over the AFL-CIO from 1995 to 2009 (Selfa 2008: 184). Generally, organized labor as a movement and then as a set of institutions in the United States over time adopted a version of modern liberalism, that is, the slightly left-of-center side of capitalist ideology. It underwent the influence of larger developments in capitalist politics, notably the rise of Progressivism in the years before World War I and the New Deal in the 1930s. Sometimes, leftists did have more influence—for example, in the early twentieth century when the IWW was a significant force until its suppression by the Woodrow Wilson administration. Likewise, the CIO held clout from its inception in 1935 up to the purge of its left-led unions in 1949.

Under George Meany's leadership, the AFL-CIO institutionalized anti–communism within the union movement. Bylaws were written expressly to exclude Communists and other leftists from the AFL-CIO, and its local central labor bodies barred non–AFL-CIO bodies from affiliating with them. During the Cold War, the AFL-CIO became known internationally as the labor arm of U.S. foreign policy, which began with a large postwar offensive against the labor left in Western Europe. A long tradition of anti-communist activity—which extended to battling various other leftist movements and parties, especially in Latin America, by the CIA-backed American Institute for Free Labor Development (AIFLD)[1]—reaches as far back as the establishment of the Pan-

American Federation of Labor in the early 1920s involving Samuel Gompers's AFL (Sims 1992).[2]

Yet during the later 1960s and 1970s a new generation of college-educated leftists entered the unions and joined the few remaining leftists who had survived the Cold War purges. Many were influenced by the anti-war and civil rights movements in the United States, as well as solidarity movements in Latin America, and Marxism writ large. They would play a significant role in steering the movement toward a much greater emphasis on organizing the unorganized and reaching out to women, people of color and immigrants after 1995 (Gapasin and Bonacich 2002: 180–181). Today, a wide range of ideological perspectives exists within the U.S. labor movement, from collusion with the purveyors of neoliberalism and corporate globalization, to moderate social democratic tenets, to calls for the abolishment of the capitalist system and imperialism (Larson and Nissen 1987). But the prevailing ideology is still a liberalism somewhat tilted to the left. There is also the latter-day variant of business union ideology that has its own history.

The Heritage of Business Unionism

The business unionism of the AFL (or "pure and simple unionism" as it was first called) was not simply the result of the abandonment of ultimate goals like socialism by individual union leaders who gradually moved away from Marxism; it was forged in a long and bitter fight within the labor movement against the socialists. This fight lasted from the 1870s through the end of World War I, by which time business unionism had become virtually hegemonic in the mainstream labor movement. The rejection of social transformation would be repeatedly articulated by labor's top leaders after World War II. In 1966, Meany, writing in *The Federationalist*, admonished advocates of social transformation: "We avoid preconceived notions and we do not try to fit our program into some theoretical, all-embracing structure" (Mantsios 1998: 46). Ten years later his successor, Lane Kirkland, would echo the same ideas when he asserted that the AFL-CIO had "no visionary world, no utopia, that we're working toward" but rather the "building blocks for a society where everybody has his chance" (Buhle 1999: 211–212).

By embracing the idea of limited goals and rejecting socialism or any major social transformation, workers were led to accept a subordinate position within the capitalist system and were locked to the classic idea of liberalism: individual improvement. By 1913, Gompers expressed this belief as a spokesperson on behalf of unionized workers: "It is our duty not to work for the downfall or the destruction or the overthrow of that society, but for its fuller development and evolution." Meanwhile, another basic idea of business unionism took shape, namely the notion that the union was a business and should be run like one.

As early as 1896, Gompers had articulated this idea in his slogan that the trade unions were "the business organizations of the wage-earners to attend to the business of the wage-earners" (Laslett 1987: 84–85). The next step was to equate the role of the union leader with that of a business manager. This provided the justification for a permanent bureaucracy run by well-paid officials, as well as the de facto rejection of democracy as a guiding principle in the actual union practices. It also replicated a wider gender bias of society in assuming that "practical men" were working to get the union member "his" chance with the help of "a man" managing the union, similar to the male-centric corporate model at the time. This bias has continued to prevail, with some tapering off by the turn of the new millennium (Moody 2007: 163–164).

Two other components became pivotal to the practice of business unionism. One is its most basic belief that "a high standard of living is no more a question of mere justice.... It is essential to our system of mass production to create a consumers' demand for almost unlimited output," as Sidney Hillman, president of the Amalgamated Clothing Workers, put it in 1928 (Zieger 1995: 15). Twenty-five years later, UAW president Walter Reuther offered a more modern variant in an exchange with a Ford executive during a tour of an "automated" engine plant: "You know, Walter," said the manager, "not one of those machines pays union dues." Reuther shot back: "And not one of them buys new Ford cars, either" (Lichtenstein 1995: 291). Likewise, George Meany wrote in 1966: "Unless the ever-rising tide of goods that American enterprise can produce is matched by the real earnings of workers, these goods cannot be sold" (Mantsios 1998: 47). The implication is of course that it is in the employers' interest to provide their workers with "a high standard of living" so they can uphold the economy through their consumption. Thus, a common macroeconomic interest is allegedly established between labor and capital. The world of work is downplayed, and according to business unionism's official economic idea, it disappears completely when proponents speak of "American enterprise" rather than the workers who produce the "rising tide of goods." This business ideology embraces not only capitalism in general, but the American system in particular, meaning the belief in persistent growth, the preeminence and well-being of American business, the belief that high wages are in the interest of U.S. capital, and the belief that labor and business should "remain partners in the broad scheme of such things as economic growth, international competition, and national prosperity" (ibid.: 49–51).

The fourth component of full-fledged business unionism is the concept of a basic community of interest with capital; more specifically, the idea and practice of "partnership." Gompers was the first to lead the way as he joined the National Civic Federation (NCF), founded in 1900, and became its first vice president.[3] Its founding president was oil baron and senator Mark Hanna, who helped make the Republican Party the dominant one for the greater part of three and a half decades (after having introduced the practice of "bundling" during the crucial 1896 presidential election to beat Democrat William Jennings Bryan). Most of the NCF's members and officers were leading capitalists of the time. Gompers and Mine Workers president John Mitchell were charter members. Their class collaboration is evident, since the NCF was established in the midst of the great employers' open shop drive. This federation asserted the mutual interests of employer and employee, and advocated the end of strikes, and the overcoming of the "misunderstandings" between labor and capital. It engaged in private or company-based welfare work largely to avoid both unionization and state intervention. Gompers, Mitchell, and other labor leaders took part in the NCF committees more for the self-importance it seemed to give them than for any benefits the unions ever derived from it. While the NCF could not halt industrial struggles and strikes, it did help the employers curtail the growth of unions after 1904. But it foremost established the legitimacy of the partnership idea (Moody 2007: 165; Cyphers 2002).

This subject would return time and again in later years. In 1996, John Sweeney upon becoming AFL-CIO president addressed himself to a business group as follows:

> We want to increase productivity. We want to help American business compete in the world and create new wealth for our shareholders, and your employees. We want to work with you to bake a larger pie which all Americans can share — not just argue with you about how to divide the existing pie. It is time for business and labor to see each other as natural allies not natural enemies [Mantsios 1998: 52–53].

Sweeney often looked nostalgically back at some golden age of a social compact between labor and business during almost thirty years after World War II that never actually existed. Tellingly, he left out the mass strikes of 1945–1946, the relatively high strike levels from 1950 through 1955, the long steel and electrical workers strikes of 1959–1960, and the labor upsurge from the mid–1960s through the 1970s, as Moody points out. Gone was the fact that all of these struggles targeted corporations seeking to chip away at working conditions, shop floor organization, and wages when possible, and contain unionism: "It was a rewrite of history needed to justify the post-militant era as well as the core beliefs of the American labor bureaucracy's business union philosophy" (Moody 2007: 133).

In recent years, Andy Stern, Sweeney's successor as president of the SEIU, who led the Change to Win coalition that split off from the AFL-CIO in 2005, has taken business unionism to its extreme, espousing an even stronger corporate-oriented conception of partnership that accounts for what he sees as inexorable aspects of globalization. This means that corporations hive off their firm-based social benefits, training programs and other social provisions, which are then administered by unions to compensate for the negative effects of outsourcing and the corporations' relentless drive toward greater efficiency with an emphasis on cutting labor costs.

Socialists and Labor-Based Party Efforts

Up until now all efforts to create a labor party in the United States have been unsuccessful. Each effort at launching such a party was either quickly abandoned or co-opted, most of the time by the Democratic Party. In his historical overview of the ways socialists dealt with the labor party question in the United States, Eric Chester goes so far as to conclude that the labor party was "an artificial construct" within this context. At least for the time being, especially a left-wing labor party seems to be a pipe dream in the American political scene:

> Throughout most of U.S. history, trade unions have represented a small minority of the total workforce. Furthermore, the great majority of trade union officials have remained committed advocates of one of the two mainstream parties, usually the Democratic Party. In those few cases where a significant segment of the union officialdom has constructed independent politics, labor-based political formations have quickly shifted to become a component of a more broadly based cross-class third party. This deliberate effort to blur the class basis of an independent electoral formation reflects both the weakness of the trade union movement and the opportunistic pragmatism that characterizes officials trained in the short-run calculus of business unionism [Chester 2004: xi-xii].

From this perspective, the whole idea of a labor party in America should be abandoned as "an ideological myth." At the same time, adherents to this point of view stipulate that the progressive and anti-corporate populism of third-party politics, as epitomized by the electoral campaigns of Robert La Follette in the 1920s and Ralph Nader in 2000 and 2008, is likewise incapable of providing the necessary organizational or ideological clout for a definitive break with the firmly entrenched two-party system. According to Chester, an active member of the current Socialist Party USA, the only viable alternative for promoting the cause of socialism in America is to develop "an explicitly democratic socialist party that is open to a range of tendencies [that] can provide the organizational framework for a genuinely independent politics" (ibid.: xii). He refers to the new wave of socialist parties in Western Europe[4] for useful guidelines, but also suggests revisiting the Socialist Party of America prior to World War I. Its left wing explicitly rejected the labor party perspective and instead linked up to militant workers at the grassroots level, such as the IWW and others in a similar vein.

In his critical history of the Democratic Party and its dealings with left-wing third-party movements, socialist Lance Selfa (a regular writer for the daily website SocialistWorker.org and the *International Socialist Review*) also points to the Socialist Party under Eugene V. Debs's leadership in the early twentieth century as an important source of inspiration for building a political left alternative independent from the Democratic Party. Selfa refers to the 6 percent of the vote that Debs won in the 1912 presidential election, and the almost one million votes he obtained as presidential candidate in 1920, when he was imprisoned by the Woodrow Wilson administration for giving a speech in 1918 opposing the First World War. "The support Debs received in his active attempt to build an independent socialist alternative proved that socialism could take root in American soil. Today when the left is much weaker than it was in Debs's era, his challenge remains" (Selfa 2008: 196).

On the other hand, the more moderate Democratic Socialists of America (DSA) still remain committed to working within the Democratic Party, attempting to push it to the left.[5] In its "Where We Stand" statement, published at the end of the twentieth century, this organization contended that its members rejected an either-or approach to electoral coalition building, focused solely on a new party or on realignment within the Democratic Party. While this perspective assigned the main task of democratic socialists to building "anti-corporate social movements capable of winning reforms that empower people," these movements were largely seen in relation to their impact on the electoral arena. There was hardly any recognition of grassroots organizing and activism: "Since such social movements seek to influence state policy, they will intervene in electoral politics, whether through Democratic primaries, non-partisan local elections, or third-party efforts." The DSA's self-proclaimed aim was "building majoritarian coalitions capable of not only electing public officials on the anti-corporate programs of these movements, but also of holding officials accountable after they are elected."[6] However, the reference to "third-party" efforts appears to be perfunctory. In 2000 the DSA's National Political Committee was divided between then-Green Party candidate Ralph Nader, Democrat Al Gore, and Socialist Party candidate David McReynolds. The result was that the organization refrained from making any endorsement in the 2000 presidential race, but several prominent DSA members backed Ralph Nader.

Four years later, the DSA issued a grudging endorsement of John Kerry, even though most of its members supported Democratic candidates Dennis Kucinich or Howard Dean in the primaries and were highly critical of Kerry's voting record on trade issues as well as his support for the resolution authorizing the use of military force in Iraq. The most important concern of the DSA members was to defeat George W. Bush, and like many other progressives at the time, DSA's national director was convinced that the only way to accomplish this was to elect Democratic senator John Kerry, the Democrats' choice, as president. DSA's action in 2004 represented a familiar one for political activists bent on "fighting the good fight" every election year during the primaries, but who ultimately always end up uniting behind the Democratic nominee, no matter how conservative he might be. Once again a left-wing movement seeking to change the corporate duopoly in America had based its electoral choice on the lesser-of-two-evils principle, and been defanged by the Democrats in the process. Thus, the DSA's reliance on the Democrats tied those activists—many of whom were attracted to DSA's socialist persuasion because they aimed for fundamental change in the system — to one pillar of capitalist rule in America, the Democratic Party (ibid.: 159–160, 184–85).

During the 2008 election, the DSA "critically supported" presidential candidate Barack Obama. After learning of his plans to reform health care, right-wing pundits accused Obama of being a socialist. The criticism became even more strident when presidential candidate John McCain and vice-presidential candidate Sarah Palin likewise accused Obama and his policies of being socialistic. This focused the media spotlight on socialist organizations, such as the Socialist Party USA and the DSA.[7] When asked about the socialist movement in America, DSA spokesman Frank Llewellyn denied — in a TV interview on Fox News — that the new administration had anything to do with socialism.[8] Media attention was revved up even further when prominent members of the Republican Party and right-wing organizations accused the Obama administration and the Democratic Party of having a "socialist agenda." Naturally, the Obama administration refuted this, stating that they were neither part of nor affiliated with the socialist movement.[9]

Grassroots Movements That Raise the Relevant Issues Avoided by Major-Party Politicians

According to several critics on the left, it is organized labor's long-standing top-down union practices and predominant unwillingness to opt for democratic social movement unionism, among immigrants and more generally, that explains the unions' repeated failure to organize the unorganized. Changing track, they argue, will require a kind of politics very different from that put forward by mainstream union officials, who typically follow the dominant trends inside the Democratic Party. These critics see the need for independent working-class politics, but also warn against prematurely declaring the existence of a workers' party (or the establishment of a new labor-based party), pushing instead for building on the basis of political independence of the working class. This will necessarily be a long-term project, applying the lessons of previous generations of socialist unionists, and other radical labor activists who rejected labor-management partnership and promoted class struggle and social-movement unionism, to contemporary conditions. It would also involve taking up the new debate on socialism in U.S. politics that has emerged in the national arena within the labor movement itself (Moody 1997: 310; Sustar 2009: 18; Gapasin and Bonacich 2002: 178–180; Fletcher and Gapasin 2008: 214).

The absence of an American labor party combines with presidentialism and the nature of the U.S. party system to inhibit union power, which is further constrained by the institutions of labor law and its administration regulating labor activity. Organized labor has never been a partner in a governing coalition.

At best it was a strong interest group within the Democratic Party, functioning as a lobby and pressure group, but it did not govern per se. This has been the consequence of government opposition to such efforts, particularly in the nineteenth and early twentieth centuries, but it also reflects the attitudes and ideology of a long line of AFL and CIO leaders who continued to embrace business unionism. The major exception was the significant change in attitude toward the government's role among union leaders and rank-and-file members with the emergence of the CIO in the 1930s. Yet, by the late 1940s, the more conservative forces within and outside the labor movement had defeated even the most moderate social democratic platforms. Once advocates of industrial democracy, even more militant CIO unions moved from agitation for shop floor control and power at the firm or industry level to narrowly focused, routinized bargaining left to the higher officials and professionals.

A major problem of the existing Democratic Party–labor alliances is that "captured voters," who see themselves—and are seen—as having nowhere else to go, have little bargaining clout with party leadership or candidates. As long as the Democrats have been more responsive to their interests than the Republicans, the AFL-CIO and its affiliates continue to support the Democrats (Levi 2003: 50–51, 58).[10] But if organized labor finds that its best interests are no longer served by a government that seems intent on prioritizing corporate interests to those of working people, it could abandon the Democratic Party and retake its earlier policy of remaining outside the formal apparatus of the party system. In that case, labor could still conduct campaigns of pro-labor candidates running for Congress and other legislative bodies, and put up its own candidates in congressional, state, and local elections. Labor would also have the choice not to endorse a presidential candidate, and by refusing to commit itself to the party apparatus, it could use its independence to draw a prospective candidate to its political positions (Aronowitz 1998: 204–205).[11] This alternative course would also include electoral fusion politics—the practice whereby two or more (in the United States usually only two) political parties on a ballot list the same candidate, pooling the votes for that candidate—in those states where this practice is legal today.[12]

In the final analysis, however, it is highly questionable whether the electoral trajectory works for the labor left in the United States, given the country's political system, the crucial role of corporate money power and the conservative mass media, which the historian Paul Street aptly describes as "the United States' narrow-spectrum/big money/big media electoral process" (Street 2010c). More than ever, Thomas Ferguson's investment theory of party competition, which recognizes that in money-driven political systems like that of the United States, the influence of big business usually towers over that of voters and citizens, seems to the point. It is big financial interests—and rivalries and competition between major investor blocs—that primarily determine who parties nominate and where the candidates stand on the issues that are part of the existing political discourse (Ferguson 1995: 17–110). This is even more so now with skyrocketing campaign expenditures.

From this perspective, progressives should be careful not to fall into what the noted left social critic Charles Derber calls "the election trap"—the belief that mistakenly "equates free elections as the primary mechanism by which democracy operates." He sees the election trap as "a sign of a perversion of the electoral process and a corruption of the concept of democracy." This does not entail a critique of elections in themselves, which he believes "are a key underpinning of democracy" and a central part of "procedural democracy." Elections are a necessary democratic procedure but do not guarantee that "political leaders are accountable to ordinary citizens or that citizens ultimately control the direction of the country" (Derber 2005: 288n4). The latter are quintessential components of "substantive democracy," which needs frequent fueling and pressuring from below by social movements. As Derber notes with regard to progressive social change,

> the main catalysts for regime change in America have not been parties glued to the next election, but social movements that operate on the scale of decades rather than two- and four-year electoral cycles. Political parties have historically become agents of democratic change only when movements infuse the parties with their own long-term vision, moral conviction, and resources [ibid.: 8].

It is necessary at this point to reflect on the character of the new social movements that emerged among women, people of color and of diverse sexual orientation, and environmentalists in the 1960s and after. The cultural changes introduced by those movements occurred while a concerted attack on the economic and political gains secured in the 1930s and 1960s was underway, the old working class was dissolving, and a conservative assault against class-based organizations was emerging. Especially following the death of Dr. Martin Luther King Jr., organizing in the United States began to take shape around particular identity claims. Initially, the new social movements focused on civil rights, welfare rights, and the political mobilization of minorities and women, which were concerns of direct interest to working people. But during the late 1970s and 1980s the emphasis increasingly came to rest on the unique experiences of various oppressed groups and isolated preoccupations with as many particular issues. This shift was a manifestation of the original radicalism's decline, which generated an ever greater specificity of identity claims. At the same time, interest groups mushroomed, and their bureaucracies sought organizational autonomy. Each logically aimed to privilege the problems and interests of its own constituency. Thus, while new forms of cultural expression and anti-discrimination measures were introduced in everyday life, a broader political fragmentation of progressive forces took place. "Postmodern" theories and ideologies emerged that contested universalism and legitimated the new politics (Bronner 2001: 158).

Attempts to create a progressive alternative from the early 1990s onward relied on reiterating the "common dreams" or legislative issues around which "the people" could unify (Gitlin 1995; Tomasky 1996; Rorty 1998). But a crucial flaw of this tactic has been that the role of class, the striving for autonomy by interest groups, and the legitimate emphasis on diversity raised by the new social movements have not been taken into account. Obviously, the notion of a common purpose itself needs redefinition so that women's rights, racial and ethnic as well as sexual identity issues, and environmentalist concerns are all part of a class agenda. Still, no social theory or practice can guarantee the resolution of all future conflicts between particular groups organized around gender or race and others based on class interest: "Whether to privilege the former or latter, one group or issue over another, depends upon circumstance as well as the given organization in which an individual chooses to work" (Bronner 2001: 159). This raises the question about whether or not the best way to promote the more inclusive progressive principles is through some type of movement coalition or a political party transformed to meet new needs.

Michael Harrington, co-founder of DSA, called upon socialists in the United States to serve as gadflies within the Democratic Party. The drawbacks of this strategy and the repeated failures of those who took this road were noted earlier. At this juncture it is probably more useful to exert pressure on the Democrats (*relatively* the most progressive party of the two major parties) in a publicly demonstrative way. Sociologists Frances Fox Piven and Richard Cloward have underlined that in America, important expansions in what they call the social democratic role of the state have occurred during periods of political crisis in response to mass disruption, defiance, and protest by ad hoc social movements in the 1930s and 1960s. As they point out, "Even in the midst of the electoral instabilities of the Great Depression, voter allegiance was not the key to influence" (Piven and Cloward 2000a: 11). What changed the course of the New Deal foremost was escalating protests—the alarming growth of grassroots rebellion in the early years of the Roosevelt administration embodied by organizations of tenants and the unemployed, movements of self-help, mass demonstrations, factory occupations and general strikes in several cities. These protests were fueled not only by economic distress and hardship but by "the sense of possibility" that the Rooseveltian rhetoric about the common man championed:

> Loyal voters by themselves changed nothing; it was the rise of a disruptive strike movement that forced labor issues onto the political agenda. The movement and the turmoil and dissension it caused, threatened to do precisely what Democratic politicians were trying to prevent, to cleave the unstable New Deal majority [ibid.: 12].

According to Piven and Cloward, major initiatives in social policy are the product of such special times and activities, but the internal logical of such movements leads to their demise and to a very limited residue of reform. They stress that irregular action, not organization, is the key to understanding the development of the welfare state and that the organizational phase of irregular movements produces to a large extent the close of the period of reform (Piven and Cloward 1977). Historian Ira Katnelson has commented that their work is only persuasive within the American context:

> In the absence of a regular vehicle for social democratic reform the achievement of a social democratic surplus is rare, and when it occurs it is an outcome of elite fears and concessions to ad hoc movements. Their limited impact is likewise largely assured by the absence of more regular and enduring mass organizations [Katznelson 1978: 93].[13]

However, in recent years things have changed considerably, and the United States does not seem to be so much an outlier internationally anymore. In most other advanced capitalist societies with social democratic traditions (in Europe and elsewhere), both "the regular vehicle for social democratic reform" and the available "social democratic surplus" have deteriorated significantly, if not vanished completely, even though mass organizations (especially trade unions) may still exist that are involved in protest movements and street rallies against one-sided economic reform and austerity plans.

It should also be noted that Piven and Cloward were no die-hard fans of disruption in each and every case. They saw protest politics first of all in terms of contingencies— sometimes there was no other viable course. They recognized that for the poor and dispossessed, mobilizing for protest politics is often strategically smarter than organizing to build mass-membership organizations. This is because it is not possible to obtain concessions from elites that can be used as resources to sustain oppositional organizations over time (Piven and Cloward 1977: xxi). In short, their approach was about "leveraging power in particular instances, for particular movements" (Schram 2003: 716).

Kim Moody notices in this context that most periods of working-class upsurge involve not simply more of the same, but new types and forms of struggle and/or organization. When these types of organization befit the era, as was the case with industrial unions in the 1930s and the wildcat strikes and rank-and-files caucuses in the 1960s and 1970s, there is a widespread hope and belief that an effective way has been found to change the balance of sociopolitical power and force concessions on capital. The 1960s seem to have offered the opportunity for a full-scale alliance between organized labor and the civil rights movement. A major factor that prevented this from happening was labor leadership's retreat in the face of the rank-and-file militancy from its own membership. What was missing were the underlying conditions for a general insurgence like in the 1930s when the unemployed joined with the employed, and neighborhood organizations and unions often provided logistical support for workplace action.

The "new" forms of organization also need not be new in history, Moody argues. What matters is that types of organization such as workers' centers, non-majority unions, union reform and democracy movements, worker-based organizing drives, and deeply rooted workplace organizations are "new" to the era in question. What is important about new forms of organization is precisely their ability to disrupt unexpectedly at crucial times. According to lessons of the past, in order to be effective, movements must interrupt the "business as usual" course at key times and places (Moody 2007: 7–8).

Protest movements thrive on conflicts that mainstream politicians avoid by raising the contentious issues that leaders of the two-party system do not want to deal with, Piven and Cloward contend. And these movements raise issues by staging dramatic events, by generating noisy protests and even causing institutional disruption, all of which can sometimes enter the political discourse of communication associated with the two-party monopoly and the corporate-dominated mass media. Moreover, once a social movement manages to generate the turmoil that injects new issues into public discourse, it also threatens to fracture the consensus of majority coalitions. This means that rather than delivering votes and money to a party coalition, protest movements raise the issues that threaten to cause discontent as some party members and supporters turn against the protesters and their demands while others rally to the protest cause. Some electoral constellations are more favorable to protest movements than others. According to Piven and Cloward, a strategy that concentrates on theatrical performance, conflict, and disruption is more likely to be effective at times when significant blocs of voters are already volatile and dissatisfied. This was what survey data by the turn of the twenty-first century indicated about large numbers of white working-class voters. These findings showed a marked shift in public opinion in favor of strong government programs, especially in areas that traditionally benefit the Democrats such as health care, Social Security, and education — in short, a classic New Deal–type Democratic program.

The historical record shows that workers were not the only ones who benefited from the influence of a grassroots movement on national politics:

> From the abolitionists to the populists to the civil rights protesters, the moments of reform in American history have followed when masses of angry people posed the threat of institutional disruption and electoral dissensus, not when they followed the electoral path. As inequalities in the United States spiral, as business domination of American government and politics becomes more total, and as public disillusion sinks deeper, the stakes grow steadily higher [Piven and Cloward 2000a: 18].

Such conditions are in place at the current juncture and offer, at least in principle, opportunities to build an independent protest movement as an alternative to the conventional coalition-building strategies characteristic of the two-party system. But a major problem remains that, since at least the mid-1970s, the American right has been far more adroit than its counterpart when it comes to understanding the pitfalls of the election trap and the need to organize and agitate between and across elections. In addition, much of the remaining American left has been significantly pacified, demobilized and/or co-opted by Obama and corporate-captive Democrats (Street 2010b: 111, 211). It therefore seems unlikely that, in the short term, a massive left-wing grassroots uprising will emerge to put strong pressure on the current administration to live up to the high expectations raised by the "Yes We Can" change rhetoric articulated by Obama and his allies in the 2008 presidential campaign (Borosage and Vanden Heuvel 2009).

The Tea Party Movement and Its Challenge to the Labor Left

At the time of this writing, the Tea Party movement — with its highly vocal opposition to the "liberal" and "big government" policies of the Obama administration — appears to be drawing larger numbers of disgruntled Americans, thus diminishing popular support for the Democrats and pushing the Republican Party even further to the right. Several observers on the left consider the Tea Party (which emerged in February 2009) as an "astroturf" phenomenon, a fake grassroots movement run by lobbyists of big corporations and conservative Republicans alike. This criticism recognizes that the cable channels, especially the conservative network Fox News, have given Tea Party protest events a level of exposure far out of proportion to the actual number of participants. At the tax day protest demonstration on the National Mall, April 15, 2010, only about 10,000 people showed up, far fewer than the tens of thousands who demonstrated the previous month in support of immigration reform. A few years earlier hundreds of thousands of Americans rallied against the Iraq war, but got nothing like the extensive media attention assigned to the Tea Partiers (Martin and Smith 2010; Selfa 2010b). Similarly, in May 2009, some 10,000 people marched on city hall in Chicago, displaying a multiracial and multigenerational popular opposition to the corporate-privatized school agenda promoted by Barack Obama, U.S. education secretary Arne Duncan, Chicago-based corporations, and Chicago mayor Richard M. Daley. This left-wing demonstration with its SOS slogan "Save Our Schools" hardly drew media coverage, another example of "left invisibility in the age of Obama," as Paul Street has called it (Street 2010a).

In the meantime, Tea Party activities have become a broader, nationwide phenomenon, however; they are not just media amplifications of minor events. At a rally in Washington, D.C., on August 28, 2010, summoned by Glenn Beck, a conservative Fox News radio and TV host and political pundit, a crowd of anywhere between 300,000 and 500,000 members showed up. The participants, overwhelmingly white, consisted of a mix of groups under the Tea Party umbrella, who came together to "reclaim the civil rights movement" (Beck's words), apparently oblivious to the structural, institutionalized racism that still exists in America today. Instead, conservative paranoia and reverse-racism conspiracy theories, long a staple of the right, have resurfaced, as, for example, in Beck's accusation that Obama and his liberal allies share "a deep hatred" of white people. Ironically, Beck called for a religious rebirth in America at the very site (the steps of the Lincoln Memorial) where Dr. Martin Luther King Jr. delivered his famous "I Have a Dream" speech on the same day in 1963 during the historic March on Washington for Jobs and Freedom. Along with Beck, Sarah Palin, the other major speaker, called for a campaign to "restore America." She tapped into right-wing patriotic sentiments among the crowd in defending the U.S. military as "a force for good" in America and suggested that Americans involved in, or supporting, the ongoing U.S. foreign wars had moral courage comparable to that of Washington, Lincoln, and Martin Luther King. Evidently, the Beck-Palin attempt to co-opt Martin Luther King and the civil rights movement as part of their heavily distorted reading of U.S. history represents an inversion of everything that King stood for (DiMaggio 2010; Stark 2010; Zernicke and Hulse 2010).

To counter this misappropriation of King's dream, about 10,000 (mostly African-American) people took part in a "Reclaim the Dream" march in Washington, D.C., on the same day as Beck's right-wing rally. And in Detroit about 5,000 people participated in an issues-oriented march organized by the United Auto Workers union (a key supporter of the 1963 march) and the Rainbow PUSH Coalition led by Rev. Jesse Jackson, a former King aide. The Detroit march, which also involved the SEIU and AFSCME, the NAACP, the Urban League, as well as various ministers and civil rights activists, marked the beginning of a larger "Rebuild America: Jobs, Justice and Peace" campaign. This latest push focuses on

> 1. Jobs: economic reconstruction driven by targeted stimulus, reindustrialization and trade policy that will create jobs, supporting manufacturing in America and put workers first; 2. Justice: enforcement of the law regarding workers rights, civil rights, industrial regulation and creation of strong urban policy, and a fair and just education, economic, and health policy; 3. Peace: ending the ongoing wars in Afghanistan and Iraq, saving lives and redirecting the war budget to rebuilding America [Nichols 2010].

The Detroit march did not attract any mainstream media attention — yet another example of corporate-owned media's shutting out of progressive politics from the prevailing political discourse.

The prominent public intellectual Noam Chomsky has suggested that the Tea Partiers represent a right-wing popular uprising that could be moving in a more positive "peace and justice" direction if the left would start listening with more empathy to their legitimate working-class concerns. He considers the Tea Party phenomenon a clear sign of the failure of the left. Tea Partiers are a mixed group, but many of them are the very people who should be organized by the left. They are people with genuine grievances, reflecting the fact that their wages have stagnated or decreased over the past thirty years and benefits, which were never great, have declined as well. Given the unemployment figures, which are always understated in the manufacturing industries, and the fact that many of the jobs lost will never come back, these Americans have every right to be angry, but the left is not reaching out to them. A common reaction (even on the left) is simply ridiculing the "Tea Baggers," which is not the right response. These Americans do have bona fide grievances, and in a very real sense they are getting "shafted." Instead of ridiculing them, the left's reaction should be self-criticism: "Why aren't we organizing them? ...We are the ones that should be organizing them, not Rush Limbaugh," according to Chomsky (Krauthamer 2010).

In some respects, Chomsky's viewpoint sounds like Thomas Frank's analysis in *What's the Matter With Kansas?* (2004) written early in this century. He raises the specter of an angry white working class abandoned by elitist liberal Democrats, creating a vacuum filled by a manipulative, pseudo-populist right wing serving the plutocratic agenda of the Republicans and the wealthy few. If reasonably angry social democratic progressives do not exist to give forthright and action-oriented answers to justifiably incensed and truly oppressed people, it is left to some very dangerous and reactionary forces to capture and channel their popular anger for their own ends. Frank sees vicious Republicans steering working-class Americans away from the Democratic Party with "cultural issues" like gun control, school prayer, gay rights, and abortion (thereby underexposing race and militarism). Chomsky, in contrast, emphasizes the right's use of economic issues (jobs, taxes, trade deficits, and so forth) to seduce ordinary working people in the midst of a Great Recession that Obama inherited from the George W. Bush administration.

In Chomsky's view, the Tea Party threat increases the urgency of effective action by the American left. This means the latter needs to engage the public with credible messages and practical programs addressing their concerns and needs. In this regard it has been argued that the anti-globalization beliefs of rank-and-file Tea Party members present an opportunity for the left here. A majority of Tea Party adherents hold strong views against corporate globalization and the offshoring of U.S. jobs, which up until now has been a cause taken up primarily by organized labor and the left. Yet their views are rejected out of hand by the elites of both major political parties and even by virtually all leading Tea Party spokespersons themselves.[14] This patch of common ground could potentially be a starting point for efforts to influence the Tea Party's base. Furthermore, if progressive solutions to the nation's ongoing economic crisis are to win real momentum, the Tea Party's constituency represents at least part of those who need to be won over (Bybee 2010).

But do these insights actually apply to the Tea Party movement? Do they really come from particularly distressed working-class backgrounds? And if so, can they indeed be brought into the liberal (let alone left) fold? According to an April 2010 CBS-*New York Times* poll, self-identified Tea Party adherents are older, better-off (although not spectacularly wealthy), more educated, "whiter," more conservative and more Republican than the population as a whole.[15] A report by Devin Burghart and Leonard Zeskind of the Institute for Research & Education on Human Rights reiterates that the Tea Partiers are an overwhelmingly white and solidly middle-class segment of the population, slightly older and also financially less troubled than many other Americans. They are not economically dispossessed Americans, or populists of any stripe, but ultra-nationalists (or super patriots) who are defending their special privileges and power. The authors see the Tea Party as a broader grassroots phenomenon, consisting of three concentric circles. At the center is a hard-core group of over 250,000 enrolled members who are located across fifty states, organized into six national factions, along with hundreds of thousands who are signed up only at their local Tea Parties. At the next ring is a larger, less clearly defined group of a couple of million activists who attend meetings, buy the literature and attend many local and national protest events. And then there is the outermost ring consisting of Tea Party sympathizers who say they agree with what they believe are the Tea Party's goals. They make up as much as 16 percent to 18 percent of all voters, according to several national opinion polls. This would put the number of sympathizers in the tens of millions.[16]

Most of the media attention has honed in on the FreedomWorks faction because it is headquartered in Washington, D.C., and because it is run by Dick Armey, former Republican House majority leader. But FreedomWorks is not one of the larger Tea Party groups; ResistNet and Tea Party Patriots are actually the largest of the six national factions. The others are Tea Party Nation, which held the national convention in Nashville in February 2010 where Sarah Palin as a "real American" gave a talk; the 1776 Tea Party, whose leadership originates directly from the Minuteman Project, an anti-immigrant vigilante group; and the Our Country Deserves Better PAC, responsible for organizing the cross-country Tea Party Express bus tours (Burghart and Zeskind 2010; Zeskind 2010).

The findings of combined *USA Today*/Gallup polls conducted from March to June 2010 show that the Tea Party's major constituency overlaps heavily with the Republican "base" consisting of older, male, conservative Christian white voters—groups that were the most inclined to vote against Obama in 2008—organized through conservative networks, with encouragement from Republican operatives and Fox News. This means that the new energy and organization is primarily a function of an inflamed social grouping already aligned basically with the GOP. They represent what was the young generation of the New Right of the 1970s and 1980s that by now is middle aged or older. Lance Selfa emphasizes they are a minority of a minority but comprise one-fifth of the electorate, and about two-thirds of the Republicans. And Tea Partiers have been able to introduce into the national political discourse such absurd notions as the idea that Obama is not a U.S.-born citizen, that the Obama administration advances a "secret" socialist agenda, and that health care reform will promote euthanasia of the elderly through the federal establishment of "death panels" (Selfa 2010a; 2010b).

The results of the CBS-*New York Times* April 2010 poll among Tea Party supporters show a massive disapproval of Obama (88 percent of Tea Party supporters compared to 40 percent of the population as a whole), and 55 percent think that the Obama administration's policies "favor the poor" (against only 27 percent of the overall population). No less than 80 percent of Tea Partiers consider it a "bad idea" to "raise income taxes on households that make more than $250,000 a year to help provide health insurance for people who do not already have it." Almost three-fourths (73 percent) of them think that "providing governmental benefits to poor people encourages them to remain poor" and does not "help them until they begin to stand on their own." (This belief is shared by just 38 percent of the less affluent broader population.) More than three-fourths (77 percent) of the Tea Party respondents (compared to just 31 percent of the overall population) consider Obama "very liberal," while a striking 92 percent say that the president is "moving the country to socialism."

An interesting finding from the same poll is that 62 percent of the Tea Party adherents support Medicare and Social Security — programs from which they either benefit at the moment or will in the near future — while most of them strongly oppose Obama and the Democrats' initiatives for health care reform which were designed (despite the bill's overall corporate-friendly nature) to extend some protections to the poor and uninsured. Most Tea Partiers oppose the expansion of government in order to pay for social welfare services: 63 percent believe that "we should be reducing the size of federal government" rather than expanding it. They do not wish to see those parts of the welfare state whose benefits they themselves (expect to) enjoy dismantled, however (Street and DiMaggio 2010: 7).[17]

An analysis of the Tea Partiers' anti-government rhetoric by Anthony DiMaggio and Paul Street leads to their conclusion:

> [This] amounts largely to a selfish and significantly race-biased call for a government that sustains their own petit-bourgeois benefits and privileges while slashing services and programs for the disproportionately non-white lower and working classes [DiMaggio and Street 2010: 1].

Tea Party people oppose the government providing assistance — economic, legal, educational, real or imagined — to those who are "undeserving," which category in their worldview consists mostly of people who can be defined by race, language or religion (described in code words when required by polite society). Those parts of the government that punish the disproportionately non-white poor, are involved in U.S. imperialist enterprises abroad, and protect wealth and privilege at home do not draw much ire from the Tea Party crowd. They do not oppose the massive expenditures of the military-industrial complex (which accounts for almost half of the world's total military spending, maintaining over 1,000 military bases spread across 130 nations), nor are they against tax cuts for the rich. This is in line with their understanding of what is undermining the nation's economic prospects and saddling future generations with unsustainable debt (Street and DiMaggio 2010: 1–2).

Tea Partiers express a sense of peril regarding their own precarious position. They report high levels of anxiety about the future, although typically not based on firsthand economic hardship experience. But they do fear that shifts in the political economy will leave them vulnerable.[18] One way to look at this is that Tea Partiers perceive a threat to their share of the New Deal economic legacy the closest approximation to social democracy that Americans have, although it does not receive due recognition in the Tea Partiers' rhetoric, according to political scientist Lisa Disch. From this perspective, Tea Partiers are mobilizing in defense of property interests that are directly inherited from New Deal public policy. Insofar as the social welfare programs of the New Deal order have been racialized, they have a stake in these programs as white people.

Popular New Deal benefits such as Federal Housing Administration (FHA) mortgage loans, college educations for veterans and, especially, Social Security have been materially and symbolically framed as white. The way these programs were designed and administered made it difficult if not impossible for African Americans to access them. This was most obvious in the case of Social Security for which farm workers and domestics were initially not eligible, a provision that effectively excluded most black workers.[19] At its inception presented as "old age insurance," early proponents of Social Security campaigned to present it as a benefit that does not compromise the independence and self-sufficiency of the recipient. It was and continues to be framed as a just return for work and investment, features that are stereotypically attached to white racial identity, and contrasted to social "welfare," which is characterized by qualities of dependence, wastefulness, and laziness that are attributed to the black poor (Disch 2010).

A similar mechanism has been at work in the case of other social benefits of the New Deal order, such as Medicare, introduced during the Johnson administration. What is at stake for Tea Partiers is that they perceive government programs to be extending middle-class status to "undeserving people" by means of new social benefits (well exemplified by the 2010 Health Care Reform Bill) that they will have to foot the bill for. Thus, Tea Party mobilization amounts to defending its supporters' share in what George Lipsitz has called "racialized social democracy" (Lipsitz 1995).

Evidence in support of this interpretation may be found in the signs that Tea Partiers carry and the rhetoric they deploy.[20] This rhetoric draws upon a cultural scenario that envisions relationships between the poor, an elite class of intellectual do-good social engineers, and the hard-working "forgotten man" who pays all the costs. This political framing was first introduced in the 1890s by the "free-market" advocate and social Darwinist William Graham Sumner, but his narrative was not racialized (Sumner 1883). That was to happen in the wake of the New Deal and the decades-long campaign to label black poverty in tandem with social welfare as black pathology; this really took off in the 1960s when, in response to social movement activism that called attention to black poverty, news media moved to represent black poverty in those terms (Disch 2010).[21] This also explains why today the term "welfare," used to indicate federal social provisions, has such a negative connotation among the general public, and especially among whites.

The Tea Party protests are not just about entitlements, taxes and budgets. Tea Party activists oppose almost everything that liberals and many of those further on the left stand for; from health care and immigration reform to gun control, from a jobs program to unemployment benefits to union check-off. They also object to federal civil rights legislation, as strongly articulated by the libertarian Tea Partier Rand Paul, who won a Senate seat from Kentucky in 2010. Major strands of the Tea Party movement also reject the Fourteenth Amendment and equality before the law, manifested, for example, in their opposition to birthright citizenship for the children of undocumented immigrants. The Tea Party set is tainted with overt racism (despite vociferous denials to the contrary), as well as homophobia, Islamophobia and anti-immigrant prejudice (particularly focused on undocumented immigrants). At its fringes it gives space to gun-toting right-wing extremists, including members of nationalist and white supremacist movements such as militias and Minutemen (Zeskind 2010; Burghart and Zeskind 2010).

Despite Tea Partiers' claims to represent independent, non-partisan politics, there are close ties between Tea Party financiers and leading activists, and major sections of the Republican Party. Standing behind the purportedly spontaneous and leaderless "populist uprising" are super-rich businessmen who are bankrolling the Tea Party movement. One is Rupert Murdoch, the billionaire owner of a media conglomerate, whose contributions are mostly in-kind donations through the free promotion by Fox News, where both Beck and Palin are on the payroll. But two other significant financiers are the even wealthier brothers David and Charles Koch, whose combined assets are exceeded only by those of Bill Gates and Warren Buffett (among Americans). These three tycoons are the latest exponents of the conservative movement since the New Deal that historian Kim Phillips-Fein has called "Invisible Hands"—corporate power holders who have financed the far right ever since the Du Pont brothers founded the American Liberty League in 1934 to bring down Franklin D. Roosevelt (Phillips-Fein 2009). There is a straight line from the Liberty League's crusade against the New Deal "socialism" of Social Security, the Securities and Exchange Commission and child labor laws, to the John Birch and Barry Goldwater assault on John F. Kennedy and Medicare, to the Koch-Murdoch backed movement against the "socialist" president, Barack Obama. Only the financiers change, not their methods, nor their favorite targets (taxes, corporate regulation, organized labor, and government "handouts" to the poor, unemployed, ill and elderly).[22]

The hard-line right-libertarianism of the Koch brothers and that of kindred elements among the Tea Partiers tilts completely toward big business, aiming to dismantle even the most basic government safety nets designed to protect the unemployed, public health, workplace safety and the subsistence of the elderly. Increasingly becoming influential within the GOP, this agenda is articulated by Republican members of Congress, including the majority speaker of the House, John Boehner, and several congressmen who won their recent seats by running on a Tea Party slate (Rich 2010). When the Tea Party Caucus held its inaugural meeting with the blessing of House GOP leaders on July 21, 2010, this essentially involved a merger between certain Tea Party activists and a number of Republican officeholders, led by Minnesota representative Michele Bachmann (Milbank 2010).

According to DiMaggio and Street,

> the Tea Party represents a concession from the Republican Party elites that they (along with their Democratic counterparts) no longer enjoy much legitimacy among the American people. Their only way of appealing to voters is to appear as if they are not political leaders but "average people" taking part in a populist uprising against a corrupt political system [DiMaggio and Street 2010: 7].

Apparently, Charles Derber's observation about "pseudo-populism" with regard to the New Right, and the rise of what he called "fascism lite" during the George W. Bush presidency, holds true in this particular case as well: "a movement heavily comprised of elites, who are disguising themselves as champions of the people." Partly echoing Thomas Frank's view (mentioned earlier), Derber asserted that pseudo-populism "undercuts populism and progressivism by redirecting popular anger away from corporate power toward the power of an imagined alien liberal Establishment and the civilizational threat of evil enemies" (Derber 2005: 184). But he also suggested that those elites aligned themselves with religious and other grassroots groups that were "genuine right-wing populists" (ibid.: 299n3). The incidence, strength and endurance of such groups among the rank and file of the Tea Party movement remain as yet unclear.

Greater Challenges for Progressive Liberals and Those Further to the Left

The amplification of the Tea Party phenomenon in the media may have led to the false impression that Americans overwhelmingly hold conservative beliefs. Chomsky, among others, has pointed to the deeply rooted "social democratic" views of the majority of Americans, which are far more significant than what he sees as ephemeral, momentary shifts in party identification or candidate preferences. Public opinion polls in the United States have consistently shown majority support (64 percent) for both a single-payer health insurance system and opposition (78 percent) to the relocation or offshoring of jobs to sites like Mexico and China. Polling data likewise indicate majority support for a strong social safety net, as long as the term "welfare" is not associated with it (Chomsky 2007: 225). An April 2010 Pew Center Poll on Americans' political attitudes reaffirmed these patterns more recently:

> On nearly every major issue, from support for the minimum wage and unions, preference for diplomacy over force, deep concern for the environment, belief that big business is corrupting democracy, and support for many social programs including Social Security and Medicare, the progressive position has been strong and relatively stable. If "socialism" means support for these issues, the interpretation of the Pew poll is a Center-Left country [Derber 2010: 2].

Moreover, a public opinion poll in January 2011 for *60 Minutes* and *Vanity Fair* that asked Americans which policy they would choose to reduce the deficit found that the most popular option — chosen by 61 percent of the respondents — was to increase taxes on the rich. The next most popular, chosen by 20 percent, was to cut military spending. Few respondents wanted to cut Medicare (4 percent) or Social Security (3 percent). Other polls registered similar results (O'Brien 2011).

These popular views, however, have little political outlet for expression, much less action, because of the weakness of progressive institutions and the difficulties of translating majority opinions into electoral politics and election results. The union movement today represents 11.9 percent in general and just 6.9 percent in the private sector (the lowest level since 1901). The comparable figure in the public sector has held steady at about 35 percent since the late 1970s and is now 36.2 percent. But there are five times more wage and salary workers in the private sector.[23] And, as noted earlier, labor's last stronghold is facing a massive counter-offensive across the nation that aims to curb, if not destroy, public-sector unions. The unions have responded with large-scale protest rallies, whose overall outcome is uncertain at the time of writing. From the perspective of the labor left, the Democratic Party leaders tend to take weak, if not conservative, stands on critical economic issues. Furthermore, the progressive media have a miniscule reach compared to the massive conservative media complex, while left-wing populists hostile to growing corporate power remain too scattered to exert such influence (Bybee 2010). This contrasts sharply with the current situation in Britain, where a left-wing Tea Party-like populist movement has emerged after the new Conservative-led government came into power in the autumn of 2010 and quickly announced its plans for draconian cutbacks in public spending along with increased taxation. Activists of "UK Uncut" from all walks of life and age groups carry out direct action protests against the cuts, targeting tax-dodging corporate executives and their businesses in the process.

At this writing, these enraged citizens gather in cities across the country on a weekly basis, demanding their government to strongly regulate the behavior of corporations and the super-rich hiding fortunes in tax havens, forcing them to start paying their fair share of taxes. These British protestors have held demonstrations and peaceful sit-ins in front of shops and offices of companies known for most aggressively pursuing tax evasion. Crowds sang songs of solidarity and announced they had come as volunteer tax collectors. They also have picketed branches of the banks that caused the financial meltdown and blocked the entrances to these establishments, using Twitter and other new social media to organize and publicize the actions. Surprisingly, the *Daily Mail*, Britain's most right-wing newspaper, apparently sensing the mood among its Middle England readers (outraged about their paying more taxes than the super-rich), has been highly sympathetic in its coverage. The only part of the media that attacked UK Uncut full on was Rupert Murdoch's media complex (Hari 2011).

In the United States, the so-called Majority Agenda Project, which organized the One Nation March for Jobs, Justice, and Education on the National Mall on October 2, 2010, currently seems to be the closest approximation of a broad-based movement seeking to move American politics in a more progressive direction. This massive rally, which attracted roughly 200,000 people, garnered a variety of media responses: Fox News was predictably cynical, and more mainstream media reactions ranged from lukewarm to curious to ignoring the event completely. This seems shocking, given that participants from five hundred organizations were on hand, led by SEIU 1199, a New York health care union local, and the national NAACP. Other groups included the AFL-CIO, the National Council of La Raza, the National Gay and Lesbian Task Force, United for Peace and Justice, Green for All, and a broad range of civil rights, labor, anti-war and social justice organizations from around the country. The rally was further supported by the DSA and the U.S. Social Forum. Organizers hoped to replace what they saw as the Tea Party's negativism, extremism, and divisiveness with a message of unity to promote jobs, social justice, and education. Several sponsors said that the rally was not an endorsement of President Obama or the Democrats, but was intended to hold all Washington politicians—Democrats and Republicans alike—accountable for not doing more to resolve the nation's problems.

Some sponsors, however, clearly took a partisan position, seeing the event as an opportunity to get out the vote for the Democrats on the eve of the midterm elections. They hoped that the march would help transform some of their liberal wishes into legislative reality, partly by giving the Democrats some highly visible and vocal backing to push through stalled legislation (Greenhouse 2010c).[24] Organizers called it "an emergency mobilization of all our forces at this critical moment before the fall elections," using the following slogans:

> Take our government back from big oil and the banks; Stand up for the well-being and economic security of all our families; Stand up against hatred, intolerance and

immigrant-bashing; Stand up for a society that works for all of us; Demand the change that we voted for in 2008.[25]

The initiators of the Majority Agenda Project referred to recent public opinion polls that would indicate that most Americans support principles on the basis of which they could be mobilized to unify around an inspiring vision of the nation based on social justice.[26]

This emerging formation may perhaps best be identified as a "mass association" (to use political scientist Stephen Bronner's term) comparable to the civil rights movement and the poor people's movement earlier in the twentieth century. Such an association can focus on multiple issues, and it can also induce "a uniquely broad and universal form of ideological enthusiasm" (Bronner 2001: 160–161). Its organizational form is more structured and broader in scope than a single-issue coalition but less structured and less prone to compromise than a party. Its position between a party and an interest group, however, leaves the nature of its constituency at the base indeterminate. From a pragmatic standpoint, there is a risk of it reaching either too far in the quest of challenging the system or reverting to a more traditional coalition. In the aftermath of the 2010 mid-term elections (with major Democratic defeats in congressional and state elections and Republicans again in control of the House), it is unclear to what extent the project will morph into an enduring large-scale social movement with enough political momentum to move Washington into a more progressive-liberal direction.[27]

There can be little doubt, however, that such a grassroots movement pressuring the Democrats—"history's second most enthusiastic capitalist party," as the former Republican strategist Kevin Phillips once put it—will not suffice to bring about the sociopolitical changes desired by the anti-capitalist left (Phillips 1989: 32). As David Harvey has persuasively argued in his recent analysis of "organizing for the anti-capitalist transition" (prepared for the tenth anniversary of the World Social Forum), it is impossible to create an anti-capitalist social order without seizing state power, radically transforming the constitutional and institutional framework that shores up private property, the market system and never-ending capital accumulation. This necessarily includes a transnational focus on the dynamics of the inter-state system:

> Inter-state competition and geoeconomic and geopolitical struggles over everything from trade and money to questions of hegemony are also either far too significant to be left to local social movements or cast aside as too big to contemplate. How the architecture of the state-finance nexus is to be reworked along with the pressing question of the common measure of value given by money cannot be ignored in the quest to construct alternatives to capitalist political economy [Harvey 2010: 256].

So far, most of the U.S. trade unions' attempts to understand capitalist globalization have resulted in a one-sided analysis that focuses on the activities of transnational corporations and their ability to move around the world, outsourcing jobs and downsizing workers. Although these are certainly important elements of globalization, this analysis does not capture the complete picture of what is going on. The best way to tackle global capitalism is for the international working class to forge solidarity across borders, which likewise requires the unity of workers with non-workers who are also becoming victims of neoliberal globalization (Fletcher and Gapasin 2008: 194). Traditionally, the workers in factories, mines and other major workplaces of industrial capitalism figured prominently in the Marxist view of proletarians struggling to liberate themselves from their chains, serving as vanguard in movements to establish socialism or communism. Their conditions of exploitation and their assembly within common spaces allegedly fostered the rise in class consciousness and their organization of united action. They also had the collective power to disrupt capitalism temporarily by withdrawing their labor. This focus on factory labor as the primary site of "true" class consciousness and class struggle has always been problematic, because it considers those working in forests and fields, the "informal sectors" of casual labor in sweatshops, domestic services or in the service sector more generally as secondary actors, together with those workers involved in the production of space and built environments and/or the creation of infrastructures for urbanization. They work under different conditions, often including low-wage, temporary and insecure labor, while features such as mobility, spatial dispersal and individualized conditions of employment tend to make it more difficult to develop class solidarity or collective forms of organization. Their political muscles are more often flexed in spontaneous riots and voluntarist uprisings rather than sustained organization.

These other categories of workers have always been a large segment of the total labor force.[28] But in the advanced capitalist world, and certainly in the United States, they have become more prominent over the past three decades because of changing labor relations due to neoliberal corporate restructuring and deindustrialization. The struggles of all these other workers must be taken into account when embarking on broader anti-capitalist projects, according to Harvey. This means that the community life and social movements occurring outside of the industrial workplaces should not be ignored. Today, the city is as much a site of class movements, and the focus should be raised at least to this level and scale of political organization and political alliances. This also means, wherever applicable, alliances with rural and peasant movements (Harvey 2010: 243–244). Proponents of social movement unionism in the United States have clearly recognized this; they have been developing workers' centers and a new inclusive approach with central labor councils as crucial agencies in political-geographic projects at the city and regional levels. They seek far-reaching social reform in alliance with a variety of other social movements and left-wing political organizations locally, regionally, and (as yet to a lesser extent) across borders.

The second broad category of the deprived and the dispossessed is much more intricate both in terms of composition and class character. Included here are all those who suffer from what Harvey calls "accumulation by dispossession" and the enclosure of the commons, both in its traditional and latter-day variants.[29] This category takes a wide variety of forms in different places and times, and includes peasant and indigenous populations who are driven from the land, deprived of access to their natural resources and ways of life by illegal and legal (that is, state-legitimated), colonial, neo-colonial or imperialist means, and forced to take part in market exchange (as opposed to barter and other forms of customary exchange) by the imposition of monetization and taxation. These forms of dispossession had their heyday in the early stages of capitalist development but still exist today. There are many modern equivalents; for example, capitalists open up spaces for urban redevelopment by taking high-value spaces away from low-income people in the cheapest way possible. In places without secure private property rights, such as China or the squatter settlements of Asia and Latin America, violent expulsions of low-income populations by state authorities occur with or without minimal compensation. In countries with firmly established private property rights, such as the United States, for instance, seizure by so-called "eminent domain" can be arranged by state authorities on behalf of private capital. Moreover, legal and illegal means can be deployed to exert financial pressures (in the form of rising property taxes and rents) on vulnerable populations.

It is the credit system, however, that has become the major modern vehicle of choice by finance capital for the extraction of wealth from those in financial need, which includes many among the population at one time of another. All kinds of predatory as well as legal practices are deployed in pursuit of dispossession of people to the advantage of the rich and powerful: extremely high interest rates on credit cards, weak or fraudulent underwriting of subprime mortgages and home foreclosures, bankruptcies and closings of businesses by the denial of liquidity at key moments, and so forth. The massive wave of financialization since the mid–1970s has been marked by its strong predatory tendencies in the form of deceptive stock promotions and market manipulations; Ponzi schemes and corporate fraud; asset stripping through mergers and acquisitions; and dispossession of assets such as the pillaging of pension funds and their devaluation by stock and corporate collapses (ibid.: 244–245).[30]

From this broader perspective, it should be clear that more than ever the cause of socialism in America cannot be divorced from political developments elsewhere in the world. The chances of a left-wing movement in the United States ever becoming a sustained, significant political force are likely to be higher when stronger links are forged with kindred groupings abroad through transnational alliances. (This also means joining anti-imperialist forces that oppose imperialism in all of its forms, including those of the United States itself.) Needless to say, this is a huge challenge given that the material interests of workers in one nation need not converge with those in other nations. The interests of the whole are not simply the sum of the interests of each component. This holds true even if universal labor standards were to be introduced, because this would most likely result in costs for the richest workers in the richest nations while further industrial development would produce hardship for the poorest workers in the poorest nations. The same holds true for factions within classes. New unifying forms of class consciousness will not simply result from the advocacy and combination of particularistic forms of self-identification. Solidarity is fragile, whether between unions or potential coalition partners in community-based, immigrant and non-governmental organizations, domestic and international. Even intra-union solidarity can be problematic. Solidarity among workers is stalled by divide-and-rule strategies of employers and governments, and by the racism and sexism characterizing some unions and their rank and file. There is also the competition with the working poor and unemployed who do not belong to unions in the United States, as well as with workers abroad, unionized or not (Bronner 2001: 178–179; Levi 2003: 55).

Furthermore, it remains the case that right-wing populism and "imperial consciousness" exert a strong pull on white Americans. This has much to do with various myths about U.S. exceptionalism that have been inculcated in Americans over the generations and the blind spots that have continued to exist when it comes to racism; internal oppression of "nations" such as Native Americans, Chicanos, Puerto Ricans, et cetera; and American empire. "Challenging these myths and embracing what can be described as a *counter-narrative* regarding U.S. history will be central to uniting with a left historic bloc by whites in America," Bill Fletcher Jr. writes in a recent exposé on socialist strategy in the United States. This means that such a historic bloc may involve a majority of its people, but not necessarily a majority of whites (Fletcher 2009a: 8).

Effective new forms of internationalism will not arise without support for their institutional expression. Even if revolution would transform the political system and cultural values of most nation-states, the new regimes would still have to negotiate the conditions under which an intrusion on national sovereignty might be countenanced. This concerns the idea of a representative form of "global government" and the question of how this would be connected politically to local governments at various levels, for which only few concrete suggestions have been made thus far. This internationalism is not simply a matter of political strategies and tactics, but also of convictions. Its acceptance requires a commitment to redistribution of global wealth and a notion of human rights that includes economic and social rights. The implications of this kind of internationalism call for recasting the socialist project.

A new approach must highlight the ways in which the fluctuations of the global economy, along with the power of transnational corporations, increasingly are outside the control of any state. It should also emphasize how planetary life is deteriorating in the name of economic progress (Bronner 2001: 177–183). Since 2001, participants in gatherings of the World Social Forum (and its local version, the U.S. Social Forum, since 2007) of the global justice and solidarity movement have been doing just this as they were envisioning a different world shared in common with others: economically, politically, and culturally.

The International Socialist Organization (ISO), with branches across the country and its daily website SocialistWorker.org, locates itself within the Marxist tradition, focusing on day-to-day labor struggles and campaigns for social change and economic justice in the United States and around the world. The ISO takes the position that in order to achieve socialism, the most militant workers must be organized into a revolutionary socialist party (thus holding on to the notion of workers as primary agent to spark the revolution). The ISO is committed to playing a pivotal role in laying the foundations for such a party. It aims to build an independent socialist organization, rooted in workplaces, schools and neighborhoods, hoping that by taking part in today's struggles for justice and liberation, larger numbers will be won to socialism — defined as "a society based on workers collectively owning and controlling the wealth their labor creates."[31] ISO members have allied with anti-capitalist groups internationally, among other things, by participating in the global social justice movement.

The U.S.-based website ZNet is especially important regarding debates on concrete societal transformations in a socialist mode, one way or another. It hosts several networks of writers and activists on the left and provides many facilities, including audiovisual communications, educational materials, and publications, as well as debates, interviews, and reviews. The current Reimagining Society Project organized by ZCommunications on this website aims to share ideas about vision and strategy among activists/writers, shifting "the focus of activist attention away from merely identifying what is wrong in societies toward emphasizing what we want and how to achieve it" (Albert 2009).[32] It involves participants from around the world (some two thousand by December 2010), including a substantial number of American leftists of various stripes.[33] Among those who take part in the various discussion platforms and movement activities are key conveyers of contemporary socialism and social justice unionism in the United States. They are definitely facing enormous challenges in trying to realize their dreams about a good society in this country.

Chapter Notes

Introduction

1. Between January and October 2010, average unemployment rates for workers in the lowest income decile (those with a household income of $12,499 or less) fluctuated around 29.4 percent, which figure surpasses the Great Depression's nationwide unemployment high of 25 percent. Among those in the second-lowest income decile ($12,500 to $19,999) unemployment hovered at 20.1 percent. Among those in the third-lowest ($20,000 to $29,999) it was 14.9 percent — and it fell steadily and steeply as the income position of the household improved, with those in the top two deciles ($100,000 to $149,999 and $150,000 and above) enjoying unemployment rates of 4.1 percent and 3.4 percent. Similar analyses were made for underemployment rates and underutilization rates (a figure that combines the unemployed, the underemployed and those who are not looking but still want to work). In each instance the same pyramid pattern was found (figures calculated by Andrew Sum and Ishwar Khatiwada, as mentioned in Ratner 2011: 13–14; for comparable figures over 2009, see Sum and Khatiwada 2010: 3–4, 8).

2. The Financial Crisis Inquiry Commission concluded in its report of January 2011 that two faulting administrations (Democratic — the Clinton presidency — and Republican — the George W. Bush presidency), the Federal Reserve, the New York Federal Reserve and other regulators had permitted a disastrous mixture to emerge: careless mortgage lending, excessive packaging and sale of loans to investors, and risky bets on securities backed by the loans (including credit default swaps, a kind of insurance sold to investors seeking protections against a drop in the value of securities backed by risky home loans). A speculative binge, in which the banks hid their excessive leverage using derivatives, off-balance entities and other devices, was incited by a giant "shadow bank system" in which the banks relied heavily on short-term debt (Chan 2011). This government report had "one glaring omission — the massive fraud [both civil and criminal] that occurred on Wall Street"— according to critical observer William Greider; he mentions as the biggest players regarding "old-fashioned investor fraud" in this context, Citigroup, JPMorgan Chase, Bank of America, Morgan Stanley and three (unnamed) "leading European banks" (Greider 2011).

3. The economic inequality that prevails in America's new Gilded Age is most blatantly manifested by the income difference between the super-rich and all other U.S. citizens. In 2006, this difference was even higher than in 1928, just before the stock market collapse and the U.S. economy went into a deep depression. While in 1928 the top 0.01 percent of U.S. families had on average 892 times more income than America's families in the bottom 90 percent, the comparable figure in 2006 was 976 times more income (*The Nation* 2008). The top 1 percent had earnings growth of 144 percent from 1979 to 2006, while the bottom 90 percent saw an earnings growth of just 15.6 percent. The top 1 percent more than doubled their share of the total U.S. income in those years, from 10 percent to 23 percent. Corporate executives in 1977 earned just under 30 times the amount of their average employee; by the mid–1990s, this had increased to 115 times. Between 1962 and 2004 the share of wealth by the bottom 80 percent of the wealth distribution fell from 19 percent to 15 percent. From 1947 to 1979, the top 1 percent of wage earners made

about 20 percent more than the bottom 90 percent; by 2006, that difference had risen by 77 times (Mishel, Bernstein, and Shierholz 2009: 8, 44). The rates for the estate tax, the only federal levy on inherited wealth, followed a similar historical trend line. The rate on wealth in the top estate tax bracket hit 77 percent in 1941 and remained at that level through 1976. In 2008 the top estate tax rate was 45 percent (*The Nation* 2008), and by the end of 2010, Congress lowered it to 35 percent.

4. In this context "single-payer" refers only to how health care is financed, not how it is delivered. Medicare is a single-payer system. The Veterans Administration is socialized medicine; its doctors are on the federal payroll. All state single-payer bills (with Vermont currently leading the way) as well as the national legislation (HR 676) that have been proposed thus far allow free choice of providers, whether public or private.

5. The term "lemon socialism" is used to refer to government support for private-sector companies whose imminent collapse is perceived to threaten broader economic stability. It points to a corruption of "free-market" capitalist systems, which would normally allow defective companies ("lemons") to fail. The Emergency Economic Stabilization Act of 2008 in the United States has been cited as an example of lemon socialism.

6. Analyses of attitudes registered in polls toward concrete issues over the last thirty years by Charles Derber, summarized in books such as Derber and Magrass (2008) and Adam and Derber (2008), provide "at minimum, ... evidence of a Center-Left country" (Derber 2010: 2).

7. A national poll by Rasmussen Reports, conducted April 6–7, 2009, among a random sample of 1,000 American adults, found the following results with regard to the question "Which is better, capitalism or socialism?" Only 53 percent chose capitalism. Among younger adults (eighteen to twenty-nine), just 37 percent preferred capitalism, 33 percent opted for socialism, while 30 percent were undecided (Rasmussen Reports 2009). A survey by the Pew Research Center, carried out in late April 2010, found that a bare majority (52 percent) of Americans responded positively to "capitalism," while 37 percent gave a negative reaction and the rest were undecided. Meanwhile 29 percent in this poll viewed "socialism" positively, but this rose to 43 percent of Americans between eighteen and thirty, exactly the same percentage as those with a favorable view of capitalism. In the Pew poll, 47 percent of Democrats saw capitalism as positive, while 53 percent did not. And 44 percent of Democrats defined socialism as positive. Moreover, many other sub-groups reacted negatively to capitalism. Less than 50 percent of women, low-income groups and less-educated groups described capitalism as positive (Pew Research Center 2010). It is not clear how individual respondents actually interpreted these terms. The questions asked involve forced-choice items, and of course the abstract notion of "socialism" can cover a wide variety of meanings. The results have to be interpreted with caution and in the context of more specific attitudes on concrete issues.

8. Bronner (2001: 145–183); Panitch (2001); Panitch and Gindin (2008); Parenti (2007); Maass (2010); Shawki (2006); Ehrenreich and Fletcher (2009a, 2009b); Lebowitz (2010); Nichols (2011). See also other contributions to the forum in *The Nation*, March–May 2009, from leading voices of the American left, including Mike Davis, Immanuel Wallerstein, Tariq Ali, John Bellamy Foster, Kim Moody, Saskia Sassen, Vijay Prashad, Doug Henwood, and several others; as well as contributions by Michael Albert, Mark Evans, Tom Wetzel, Gregory Wilpert, Robin Hahnel, Bill Fletcher Jr., and many others, to the *Reimagining Society Project* hosted by ZCommunications on the website ZNet since 2009.

9. Union density, the proportion of union members to the number of workers, reached its highest point in 1953, at 32.5 percent, and then decreased to 27.3 percent in 1970. While general union density remained relatively stable in the 1970s, it dropped rapidly in the 1980s (19.1 percent in 1984) and continued to fall in the 1990s (16.7 percent in 1994) and into the new century (12.0 percent in 2006). This decline is almost fully accounted for by the private sector. Union density in this sector had dropped to a mere 7.4 percent by 2006, while the average public-sector figure went up in all those years, to reach 36.2 percent in 2006 (Moody 2007: 98–100; Warren 2007). In 2010, the union density was 11.9 percent in general, 6.9 percent in the private sector, and 36.2 percent in the public sector. "Union Members Summary—2010," Bureau of Labor Statistics, January 21, 2011.

Chapter 1

1. For example, both of the two proponents of far-reaching institutional change in the

twentieth century White House, Franklin Roosevelt and Ronald Reagan, overemphasized historical continuity. Roosevelt argued that his proposal for a reform of the Supreme Court, nicknamed the "court packing plan," was "a way to take an appeal from the Supreme Court itself" and that he wanted "an independent judiciary as proposed by the framers of the Constitution" (Roosevelt 1937). Reagan claimed "to restore the division of governmental responsibilities between the national government and the States that was intended by the Framers of the Constitution" (Reagan 1987). Both quoted in Alesina and Glaeser (2004: 95).

2. Lowi (1984: 37–38, 45–50); Oestreicher (1988: 1270–1272); Steinmo (1994: 120–121).

3. By the end of 1911, in state and local elections the Socialist Party had elected 1,141 officials in some 324 municipal governments in thirty-six states. Several major cities had Socialist mayors or high-ranking officials in this period: Milwaukee; Berkeley, California; Butte, Montana; Flint and Kalamazoo, Michigan; and Schenectady, New York. However, the more typical Socialist victories were in much smaller cities and towns: Winnfield, Louisiana; Conneaut and Martin's Ferry, Ohio; Hazeldell and Roulette, Pennsylvania; Coeur d'Alene, Idaho; Nederland, Colorado; Winslow, Arkansas; Tukwila, Washington; Antlers, Oklahoma; Pillager and Ten Strike, Minnesota; Red Cloud, Nebraska; and Arma, Kansas (Weinstein 1984: 116–118). In 1912 (at the peak of the Socialist Party's electoral strength), 174 Socialist candidates ran in U.S. congressional races, and 61 got more than 10 percent of the vote, including 27 who ran in highly industrial districts and 12 in districts with hardly any industry (Sanders 1999: 67–68). The only two Socialist representatives in the U.S. House were Victor Berger, representing a Milwaukee constituency in 1910, 1918, 1922, 1922, and 1926, and Meyer London, who was elected from the Lower East Side of New York in 1912, 1914, 1916, and 1920 (Lipset and Marks 2000: 45).

4. Bridges (1986: 192); Olssen (1988: 442–449); Lipset and Marks (2000: 58–63, 267–268).

5. Kathleen Barber argues that "The election of two Communist party members in New York City in 1945, and of African Americans in Toledo and Cincinnati, figured prominently in repeal campaigns that eliminated proportional representation" (Barber 1995: 166).

6. Initially, however, proportional representation in European countries was typically introduced by political opponents of labor-based parties as a response to the rise of such parties. In a few cases, proportional representation was introduced prior to the First World War to ensure minority representation in culturally/linguistically divided societies like Belgium and Finland. But in the large majority of cases it was introduced at the request of established "bourgeois" parties bent on protecting their ability to win seats in the face of a rapidly growing labor-based party (Lipset and Rokkan 1967: 32–33).

7. Archer (2007: 78); Carstairs (1980: 9–10, 213).

8. Schattschneider (1942: 83); Marks (1989: 218).

9. The French system, in place since 1962, allows small parties to gather votes in the first round and trade support to the larger parties or candidates for the final round (Lipset and Marks 2000: 303n12).

10. The earliest state was South Dakota, which introduced the first anti-fusion law (that is, a law that prohibited a candidate from being nominated by more than one party) in 1893. In Illinois an anti-fusion law was introduced in 1897 (Archer 2007: 270n32).

11. In the name of reform, advocates of non-partisanship attacked the "corrupt" (largely Democratic) machines, and supported the city manager system. The political machines were indeed hardly exemplary organizations, and some were heavily dominated by business interests, but most of them were no more corrupt than the city manager systems that replaced them. The machines were local neighborhood phenomena that involved voters in politics, and they tended to be far more responsive to working-class voters and organized labor than the groups that took their place. They could be effective advocates of their immigrant constituencies by organizing people, serving their everyday needs, recruiting volunteers, offering public patronage jobs (usually low-level ones) to party activists, and getting out the vote. The abolition of patronage for party activists in the form of low-level public service jobs was certainly pertinent in the case of low-level patronage in the form of no-show jobs or jobs offered to people who were incompetent to hold them, which violated the public interest. However, abolishing such patronage altogether has been detrimental to working-class-oriented politics that depended on volunteers who sought the lower-level jobs (Sexton 1991: 169–170).

12. For a statewide candidate to get on the ballot in New York today, the candidate must collect fifteen thousand valid signatures, in-

cluding one hundred signatures from each of half of the state's congressional districts. An individual voter's signature cannot count for more than one statewide candidate, and signatures can be invalidated if the voter reports his or her city or town incorrectly (Selfa 2008: 178).

13. Since the New Deal, liberals and progressive activists have at times suggested that popular forces of "the left" can democratically take over the Democratic Party. The most recent advocates of this idea are the members of the Progressive Democrats of America (PDA), which was founded in 2004. It was also the original intention of the Democratic Socialists of America (DSA), which organization aims to create a U.S. social democracy (Selfa 2008: 158–159, 182–185).

14. The introduction of universal male suffrage in Germany in 1867, coinciding with the development of a significant rift between capital and labor, provided favorable political conditions for the Social Democratic Party's success. The Anti-Socialist Laws that were passed in 1878 aimed to cripple the party through various repressive measures. But the party circumvented these measures in various ways by fostering a network of informal ties and an alternative culture, and continued to grow in popularity, becoming more successful after the expiration of the laws in 1890 (Guttsman 1981; Lidkte 1985).

15. For further details, see chapter 3.

16. "Hard money" concerns contributions directly to a candidate of a political party, which is regulated by law in both source and amount, and monitored by the Federal Election Commission.

17. In Barack Obama's case, the overwhelming majority of presidential campaign contributions came from executives and employees of large technology corporations such as Google, Cisco, Apple, Oracle, Hewlett-Packard, Yahoo! and Ebay, as Mike Davis has pointed out. This also resonated well with the idealism and computer and Internet savvy of many of the campaign's volunteers and the expectations of supporters in the big tech centers with their captive universities and myriad Internet cheerleaders. Davis has also suggested that Obama's particular realignment of politics by economics fits perfectly with Thomas Ferguson's theory, "which privileges political economy and class struggle *within* capital as modes of explanation" (Davis 2009: 37).

18. Needless to say, such realignment of politics by economics does not sit well with the Burnham paradigm, which asserts the primacy of political opinion and the durability of voter blocs (Burnham 1982).

19. "Summary Citizens United v. Federal Election Commission (Docket No. 08–205)." Cornell University School of Law, http://topics.law.cornell.edu/supct/cert/08–205; Liptak (2009, 2010); Hasen (2010); Carney (2010).

20. This meant that thirty-nine senators representing a minority of the population sufficed to prevent disclosure of corporate election spending (Neuborne 2011).

Chapter 2

1. It is obvious that these craft unions were not syndicalist in the broader meaning of the term associated with revolutionary syndicalism. Syndicalism as it emerged internationally (especially in France, Germany, Britain, and North America) in the late nineteenth and early twentieth centuries has five distinguishing features. It favored federalism over central forms of organization and thus emphasized local autonomy. It opposed political parties and replaced political work with economic action and organization. Its supreme revolutionary strategy was the general economic strike, not the overthrow of the bourgeois state. After the general strike, workers would abolish the political state altogether and replace it with a federal, economic organization of society. Finally, this new social organization would be based on *syndicats*, basic local units derived from the structure of craft and industry. Although many syndicalists supported industrial unions, industrial unionism itself was never a universally accepted part of syndicalist philosophy, and many syndicalists continued to envision the syndicats of the new society as craft-based (not industry-based) units. On the other hand, revolutionary industrial unionists, though often in agreement with individual syndicalist positions, never accepted the syndicalist philosophy as a whole (Peterson 1983: 65).

2. As commonly acknowledged, this transatlantic move was partly instigated by Marx and his followers' strategy to prevent the IWA from falling into anarchist hands. But, as Marx himself claimed, the time seemed to be ripe for the International to begin to sink real roots in North America. By the early 1870s, the IWA counted fifty sections in a dozen urban areas, ranging from Boston and New York to Chicago and San Francisco. And a section of the International played a leading role in the

first citywide general strike, organized in St. Louis in 1877 (Blackburn 2010: 159–160).

3. The New York State bill to prohibit the manufacturing of cigars in tenements was passed in 1883.

4. Foner (1974: 66); Schneider (1994: 95, 98); Weir (1996: 257).

5. Archer (2007: 44–45); Laslett (1970: 200); Stromquist (1987: 104–115, 121–122).

6. Supporters of "free silver" included owners of silver mines in the West, farmers who believed that an expanded currency would increase the price of their crops, and debtors who hoped it would enable them to pay their debts more easily.

7. This tax had been proposed by Schuyler Colfax, a radical Republican representative from Indiana, who later became vice president in the Grant administration. He had also put forward a radical tax proposal that entailed a levy on all shareholding capital (Brownlee 1996: 26; Blackburn 2010: 172).

8. Compare, for example, the results for the city council in Los Angeles during the 1911 municipal election. Although the Socialists gained almost 38 percent of the total vote, they were unable to get a single candidate in office because of the municipal charter amendment that Progressive activists had pushed through in 1909. In its revised form, the charter provided for citywide elections for council seats—a system that severely limited the ability of minority groups to achieve representation in city government. This severely handicapped the Socialists, whose constituency was geographically concentrated in the working-class districts in the eastern part of the city (Johnson 2000: 42).

9. American Federation of Labor (1902: 183), qtd. in Lipset and Marks (2000: 103).

10. This bill also included legislative ambitions regarding immigration restrictions, a cabinet-level labor department, and a government employee eight-hour workday (since government officials could not strike for that end). Immigration restriction, bans on child labor, eight-hour workday laws for civil servants and, at the state level, for women — all were meant to put a floor on the labor market. Along with the desired anti-injunction statutes, they were the visible manifestation of AFL voluntarism (Forbath 1991).

11. In 1912, three presidential candidates (Eugene Debs, Theodore Roosevelt, and Woodrow Wilson) contended for the labor vote, and Wilson won the election. There was much affinity between Wilson's "new freedom" and the anti-statist proclivity of Gompersism. Ironically, however, it was independent labor reformer Frank P. Walsh and various Progressive-minded AFL leaders at the state level who helped most to shape Wilson's appeal to labor. When shortly before the 1916 election a national railroad strike loomed, it was Walsh who persuaded Wilson (with no track record of labor legislation to speak of) to support a federal eight-hour workday law for railroad workers, which became the defining labor statute of Wilson's first term. But this was precisely the kind of state regulation that Gompers and the national AFL strongly opposed (Forbath 1999: 199).

12. The platform contained a long list of demands for workers: an eight-hour workday and prevailing union wages on government work; unemployment assistance paid to labor organizations; loans to state and municipal governments for extensive public works; in industry, a shorter workday, a guaranteed day and a half of rest, public health and safety inspection, prohibition of child labor, and compulsory health, life, and unemployment insurance. Railroads, telephones, telegraphs, steamship lines, mines, forests, oil wells, water-power facilities, and "all land" should be collectivized. However, only those industries "organized on a national scale" and in which competition had "ceased to exist" were targeted for socialization, This despite the fact that "trustification" (monopoly power) had proceeded much more slowly in agriculture than in industry (Sanders 1999: 63–64).

13. At first its main leaders were Bill Haywood, Vincent Saint John, Daniel De Leon and Eugene V. Debs. In 1908 the Wobblies split into two factions. The group headed by Debs advocated political action through the Socialist Party and the trade union movement to attain its goals. The other faction, led by Haywood, believed that general strikes, boycotts and even sabotage were the preferred means to achieve its objectives. Haywood's views prevailed, and Debs, and others who shared his ideas, left the organization.

14. This does not mean, of course, that the IWW and the AFL were identical in their union practices, for clearly they were not. Especially important were the contrasting logics of collective action: the AFL's craft unions' reliance on small numbers, reserve power, and contractualism versus the IWW's dependence on mass mobilization, situational power, and unrestricted direct action. These contrasting approaches represented the different disruptive

capacities of skilled and unskilled workers (Kimeldorf 2005: 548–549).

15. In the years 1914–1917, when the IWW had gained influence as a consequence of contending power at the point of production and beyond, it may have effectively reached about 120,000 workers—the number mentioned by Kim Voss (Voss 1993: 242n13)—but most likely many of them were only dues-paying members for a brief period. Afterward, the membership diminished because at the start of the war the IWW moved away from the large factories of the East to concentrate on the Midwest wheat fields, the mines of the West and Southwest, and the timber ranges of the Northwest (Shor 1999: 69).

16. Most of the great strikes in which the IWW was involved were forceful expressions of discontent among unskilled and semi-skilled workers who were excluded from, or did not want to join, AFL unions: Hungarian machinists in Bridgeport (1907–1908); Hungarian, Croat, Slovenian, Austrian, and Serb steelworkers in McKees Rocks (1909); Italian, Austrian, Russian, and Turkish textile workers in Lawrence (1912); southern Italian and Eastern European Jewish textile workers in Paterson (1913). IWW activists managed to successfully lead these militant strikes by recognizing that ethnicity can, under certain circumstances, generate particular forms of radical protest. The IWW leadership's tactic of establishing strike committees composed of democratically elected representatives of each ethnic group optimally used the strength of the pre-existing network of immigrant institutions. So long as each group believed no one group was receiving favored treatment, the bonds of ethnicity did not prevent workers from the different groups from working together (Foner 1978; Dubofsky 1969; Conlin 1969).

17. IWW influence also persisted in a place like Cleveland into the 1940s (where the IWW demonstrated a rival style of unionism to that of the CIO in the metalshops) and was reincarnated in Minnesota in the 1930s as the Independent Union of All the Workers (Montgomery 1999: 359).

18. Also incorporated in the new Social Democratic Party was the independent socialist party that Austrian émigré Victor Berger had established in Milwaukee, which was allied both with local unions and a Milwaukee People's Party started by local Knights of Labor. The new party's thirty-three founding members were from Illinois, Indiana, and Wisconsin, and its membership base lay among SLP defectors in Milwaukee, Massachusetts, and St. Louis (Sanders 1999: 58–59).

19. In 1910, Victor Berger reiterated his view that unions should limit their activity to economic matters and leave to the Socialist Party the task of articulating the demands of the working class in the political arena. In the same year the National Executive Committee praised the Los Angeles branch for the "splendid work" it had done in preventing the formation of a labor party as a rival to the Socialist Party, and suspended the Arizona branch for helping to launch a labor party. In Washington, the state party did the same to locals and members for participating in a labor party convention (Kipnis 1952: 126).

20. However, at the 1913 AFL convention, Socialists opposed a resolution, introduced by George Berry, the president of the Pressmen's Union, calling for the formation of a labor party (Fine 1928: 295).

21. Halpern (1997: 48–72); Brody (1998: 244–262); Zieger (2007: 70–105).

22. The Republican Party's presidential candidate was Calvin Coolidge, who as president had helped roll back labor's gains from the war, whereas the Democratic Party passed over William G. McAdoo, who as federal railroad administrator in 1917–1919 had been sympathetic to labor, in favor of corporate lawyer John W. Davis, later the defense attorney for the segregationists in *Brown v. Board of Education* (Lipset and Marks 2000: 106; Aronowitz 1998: 196).

23. Bill Haywood often spoke of the IWW as "socialism with its working clothes on," although the union did not wage political struggles apart from those for free speech and legal defense (Haywood 1966: 158).

24. A more inclusive and broader public sphere of this kind would emerge during the industrial union upsurge of the 1930s and 1940s, when unions that included both semi-skilled and skilled workers in mass-production industries established their own union halls. The Auto Workers, Electrical Workers, Textile Workers, and the older needle trades union halls became spaces of public and social life for hundreds of thousands of workers (Aronowitz 2008: 228). Denning describes the "movement culture" that sustained the cultural front of the Popular Front social movement by the mid-1930s—a world of working-class education, recreation, and entertainment built by the Communist Party, the new industrial unions, and the fraternal benefit lodges, in particular those of the International Workers Order (IWO) (Denning 1997: 67–83).

25. Many Socialists also took recourse to the concept of industrial democracy as a substitute for socialism, as a way of promoting their vision in an extremely conservative age. In 1919, the Intercollegiate Socialist Society (ISS) changed its name to the League for Industrial Democracy (LID). This reflected its leaders' awareness that the term "socialism" had by then obtained highly negative connotations in American political discourse. The word "socialist" was also dropped from the title of its chief publication; *The Socialist Review* was renamed *Labor Age* in 1921 (Gerstle 1986: 87–88).

Chapter 3

1. Roosevelt and other New Dealers deliberately opted for the label "liberal" over possible alternatives. Prior to the 1930s, "liberalism" had been used occasionally as a synonym for "progressivism." The term could draw on progressive support yet still indicate innovative departures. Importantly, "liberalism" was also as a label a good antidote to "socialism" and allowed New Dealers to counter accusations of bureaucratic coercion and rigid collectivism while competing with Herbert Hoover and other conservative critics of the New Deal for the claim of best representing the traditional American values of individualism and liberty. For a while, critics of the New Deal from the right insisted on calling themselves "the true liberals," but from the late 1930s on they accepted the label "conservative" for their position (Rotunda 1968).

2. Rather than functioning as a divisive factor, ethnicity laid the basis for the type of cooperation that would be necessary for the eventual success of the CIO, which was structured along the lines of ethnic federations. In this the CIO's inclusive Americanism played a pivotal role. It brought together workers of very different political, ethnic, and religious backgrounds in one large movement for industrial unionism (Gerstle 1986: 90–91). However, the CIO's "interracial" unionism was a highly inclusive *white* unionism (that is, it included the Southern and Eastern European immigrants of the early twentieth century and their children) and for the most part excluded African Americans, Asians, and other people of color (Roediger 2005: 207–224).

3. In 1933 and 1934, the Marxist magazine *Modern Quarterly* also made calls for an American labor party along with an Americanized Marxism. A number of dissident Communists had become associated with this magazine. In December 1933, several of them (including V.F. Calverton, editor of the magazine, Sidney Hook, and James Rorty) joined the radical labor leader A.J. Muste and his Conference for Progressive Labor Action in founding the American Workers Party (AWP). This party never numbered more than a few hundred members, yet it played an important role in the militant labor upsurge in 1934, organizing unemployed leagues as well as the Toledo Auto-Lite Strike which triggered a general strike. However, in late 1934 the AWP merged with the Trotskyist Communist League of America to form the Workers Party of the United States, led by James Cannon and Max Shachtman. Muste and most of the AWP intellectuals (including Calverton, Hook, and Rorty) left the new party, which was absorbed into the mainstream Trotskyist movement (Denning 1997: 431–432).

4. Although Hillman had provided financial and organizing support to the defeated textile strike of 1934 and throughout the 1930s remained an unwavering proponent of the CIO's organizing drives, by 1936 Hillman no longer believed that socialist politics served organized labor. His defection from the Socialist Party to the Roosevelt coalition, along with a similar move by the ILGWU's David Dubinsky, was an important step in the process of the incorporation into the New Deal of organized labor's more radical groupings. John L. Lewis, by contrast, was an old business unionist with ties to the Republican Party. He became a fervent New Dealer primarily because he believed that government intervention in labor relations was both inevitable and desirable. He thought the threat to the labor establishment posed by Communists and other leftists would grow unless the moderate leaders of organized labor and enlightened members of the business elite took the initiative to hold them in check (Aronowitz 2003: 82–83).

5. The NRA strikes were led by shop nuclei of militant workers, the most important of which were the Communist Party's factory cells, its separate unions (created during the party's ultra-sectarian Third Period—1928–1935) affiliated to the Trade Union Unity League, and its Slavic, Finnish, Magyar, and Yiddish language federations and cultural organizations, which gave it easy access to the second generation, semi-skilled "new immigrants," who constituted the majority of the militant base for the new industrial unionism. In addition, there were the much smaller but

locally significant groupings of Trotskyists, Wobblies, and Musteites (members of the American Workers Party). On the other hand, one could find informal groupings of highly skilled workers (including machine makers and maintenance technicians) who conserved neo-syndicalist craft traditions of a more radical kind than the AFL mainstream and played crucial roles in the organization of the NRA strikes. The left's capacity to act as an alternative pole of leadership was also enhanced by the de facto industrial united front between the Communists and Socialists that emerged in 1935 and lasted, at least in the auto industry, until the spring of 1937, during a phase of the Communist Party's development on its way from Third Period to Popular Front phase (Davis 1986: 57–60).

6. Sinclair won the Democratic primary for the governorship in California on a progressive platform to "End Poverty" in California during the Depression years. Sinclair proposed for the state to take over idle factories and farmland and turn them over to cooperatives. He also proposed to levy a state income tax on corporations. But the Democratic establishment, including President Roosevelt, did not show any loyalty to the Democrats' democratically elected candidate. Democratic big business money shifted to the Republican candidate, formed a one-time third party to draw votes away from Sinclair, and financed a red-baiting scare campaign. As a result, Republican Frank Merriam was reelected with only 48 percent of the vote, compared to the 37 percent that Sinclair received (Mitchell 1992: 214; Selfa 2008: 167).

7. AFL president William Green used the same terminology when he welcomed the Wagner Act at the time. And it would shape the dominant narrative of the labor struggles and the new labor law in the 1930s until recently (e.g., Schlesinger 1988). This narrative hides the fact that the events of 1933–1937, which shaped labor relations for most of the remainder of the twentieth century, occurred outside the purview of the law. It took more than two years for the Supreme Court to reject constitutional challenges to the NLRA, during which one could witness some of the most militant and far-reaching demonstrations of labor's power to act outside the law's guarantees (Aronowitz 2003: 80–81).

8. See also Klare (1978, 1981); Atleson (1983); Tomlins (1985a, 1985b).

9. These critics included the ACLU, Abraham Muste, the IWW, Trotskyists from the Communist League of America, and intellectuals like Robert S. Lynd. The NLRA was also criticized by the NAACP and the Urban League for having little to offer to black workers (Goldfield 1989: 1278n3). There is little evidence that the Communist Party articulated criticism of the act or its winner-take-all provision (Aronowitz 2003: 85).

10. This is a hiring agreement in which a worker disavowed membership in, and agreed never to join, a labor union in order to get a job (Goldfield 1989: 1258).

11. Staughton Lynd has argued that the CIO's conservative bureaucracy prevented the further development of an alternative unionism that was more innately democratic and radical during the wave of U.S. labor militancy in the early 1930s (Lynd 1996). It was during a period of autonomous unemployment councils and a rising tide of worker self-organization expressed in wildcat strikes and various slowdowns that the CIO — whose formation coincided with the establishment of the federal government's NLRA in 1935 — represented instead a "business unionism" (Lynd 1992).

12. This was the major reason why CIO's leader John L. Lewis fiercely opposed Roosevelt's interventionist policy in 1940 and 1941; it also explains partly his decision to support the Republican candidate, Wendell Willkie, in the 1940 presidential election. Lewis was afraid that war would destroy whatever chances remained for progressive change (to be brought about by enhanced labor power) at home (Brinkley 1995: 203).

13. This agreement was no dead letter. When, for example, the Coal Miners' Union refused to honor the pledge by organizing several brief strikes in May and June 1943 to demonstrate the union's determination in a crucial wage dispute, the courts fined the union and indicted its leader, John L. Lewis.

14. As national trade union executives became virtual representatives of the government, the secondary leadership (stewards, committeemen and local officials) increasingly took up the complaints of the rank and file and coordinated the labor actions. In the rubber industry, the new layer of militant labor leaders took control of key Akron locals. In the auto industry, Briggs Local 212, led by Emil Mazey, played this role (Davis 1986: 78–79).

15. Byrnes was a member of the House of Representatives (1911–1925), a senator (1931–1941), a justice of the Supreme Court (1941–1942), and would later become secretary of state (1945–1947) and governor of South Carolina (1951–1955).

16. Mills, following suggestions by political theorist Robert Michels, admonished a union leadership increasingly attracted to oligarchic rule, to avoid class compromise and instead embrace democratic and militant unionism. He argued that the "main drift" was away from the collaboration between business and labor made necessary and viable by the war, and suggested that labor leaders of "great stature" should step forward before labor was weakened. A conservative counter-movement was already gaining force at the bargaining table. Corporations steadily translated economic strength into effective and united political power. The power of the federal state was increasing enormously and so heavily in the grip of big business that "unions could no longer seriously expect even the traditional short-run gains without considering the conditions under which their demands are politically realizable." Mills straightforwardly suggested that the labor leader become the basis for the formation of a "new power bloc." "Rather than make deals on the top with powerful interests he will have to accumulate power from the bottom. If the democratic power of members is to be used against the concentrated power of money, it must in some way create its own political force ... the left would create an independent labor party" based on labor's economic strength. But Mills hastened to add that it must enlarge its own base to include the "underdogs," few of whom were in the unions (Mills 1948: 260). He meant the working poor, the unskilled, who were largely left out of the great organizing wave of the 1930s and the war years. He also called for the organization of elements of the new middle class and the rapidly growing white-collar strata, whose potential power, he argued, would remain unrealized unless they were organized into the union movement. As Aronowitz points out, Mills was mistaken — at least for the short run — that unions would have to become an independent political force to meet the elementary economic demands of their membership. During the first three decades after the war, unions did deliver to a substantial minority of the American working class. But the "underdogs," as well as the new middle class of professional and technical employees, and white-collar workers were mostly forgotten by the postwar labor movement (Aronowitz 1998: 298–299).

17. Lichtenstein (2002: 117); McAuliffe (1978); Levenstein (1981: 208–229); Schrecker (1992).

18. A major part of the U.S. offensive to "liberalize" postwar Europe was the campaign, not just aimed against Communists, but against all broad and inclusive forms of working-class unity, both in the political and trade union domain. Throughout the Allied zones of occupation in Germany, for instance, left Social Democrats as well as Communists were purged from elected positions, local "united fronts" were outlawed, and strikes were forbidden. The AFL, the U.S. intelligence services and the State Department considered moderate, trade union-based social democratic and labor parties as the best barrier to Communist advance in France and Belgium especially. In Italy, where the political situation was different, they vested their hopes and most of their funds in Christian Democracy. Following the expulsion of Communist parties from government in France, Belgium and Italy in the spring of 1947, and especially after the Prague coup by Communists in February 1948, Western European Socialists and Communists drew apart. There were violent clashes between Communist and Socialist workers' unions, and between Communist-led strikers and troops ordered in by Socialist ministers, while news arrived from Eastern Europe of Socialists arrested and imprisoned. Many Western European Social Democrats turned into determined enemies of the Soviet bloc and ready recipients of covert American funding (Davis 1986: 186–188; Judt 2005: 156–157, 218–219).

Chapter 4

1. In the political arena, unions were seeking to expand programs — national unemployment insurance, higher minimum wages, and full employment laws — that would add to the gains already made through collective bargaining (Jacoby 2004: 205).

2. A few large firms (including American Motors, Kaiser Steel, and Armour Packing) were an exception to this trend and sought to solve their competitive problems by establishing less adversarial relations with their unions through experiments in union-management cooperation in the late 1950s and early 1960s.

3. This was to become dramatically clear in connection with the assassination of a prominent union dissident. In 1969, Jock Yablonski, the leader of a democratic reform movement in the United Mine Workers who sought to challenge incumbent Tony Boyle for the union presidency, was murdered along with his wife and daughter. Mike Trbovich, who had man-

aged Yablonski's campaign, sent a request to George Meany asking that Miners for Democracy (organized by Yablonski's supporters immediately after his murder) be allowed to argue their case to the AFL-CIO Executive Council so that labor might clean its own house without government intervention. Meany would have none of this and indicated that he disapproved of labor and government assistance in cleansing a union of corrupt officials (apparently including even those who hired hit men). Such assistance, in his view, would constitute a violation of a union's "democratic structure" (Buhle 1999: 165).

4. The 1970 Racketeer Influenced and Corrupt Organizations Act (or RICO Act) provides for extended criminal penalties and a civil cause of action for acts performed as part of an ongoing criminal organization.

5. More recent important pieces of "labor legislation" of this kind are the Americans with Disabilities Act (1990) and the Family and Medical Leave Act (1993).

6. Blauner argued that since industrialization began, alienation had followed the path of an "inverted-U curve": non-alienating pre-industrial craft work was superseded by alienating machine-minding and mass production, which in turn would be superseded by automated industry in tomorrow's world — process work in the petrochemical industry offered an advance example of this. Blauner predicted that full-fledged automation would remove human alienation (Blauner 1964; Rose 1988: 227, 230). Earlier interest in alienation among the postwar labor left can be found in the popular writings on the dehumanizing effects of the never-ending assembly line by Harvey Swados (ex-Trotskyist and member of the anti-Communist left), based on his observations while temporarily working in a factory. Especially the key essay "The Myth of the Happy Worker" in his collection *On the Line* (1957) was one of the first literary expressions of U.S. worker discontent during the 1950s.

7. Even though much of this analysis had traces of Marxist-Leninist revolutionary thinking, most Black Power advocates insisted that race, not class, defined their status. As Stokely Carmichael put it, "Racism, for black people in this country, is far more important than exploitation, because no matter how much money you make in the black community, when you go into the white community you are still a nigger" (qtd. in Levy 1994: 116).

8. Black Power theorists were much inspired by the outburst of Third World revolutions that took place in the 1960s. The overthrow of European colonial powers and the success of the Viet Cong fueled their idea that a revolution of non-whites could succeed. Black radicals traveled to Africa, Latin America, and Asia to meet with "freedom fighters" and their new revolutionary heroes, such as Fidel Castro, Ho Chi Minh, and Kwame Nkrumah. The alleged support of these soul brothers was important in black militants' refutation of the claim made by black activists like Bayard Rustin and A. Philip Randolph that black nationalism was an impractical panacea. Black Power spokesmen also pointed to the blackening of America's inner cities and the wave of rebellions that broke out in black ghettos during the mid-1960s. While the former revealed the latent strength of the African-American community, the latter demonstrated the willingness of urban blacks to take a revolutionary stance. If organized, it was argued, militants could transform the ghettos and the southern black belt into strong political bulwarks (Levy 1994: 116–117).

9. Georgakas (1975); Geschwender (1977); Jefferys (1984); Thompson (2001); Widick (1989).

10. Although Chrysler and the UAW made no concessions to DRUM, within two years of its appearance Local 3 elected a black president (and so did other locals), and Chrysler appointed black supervisory staff in its plants. But by 1973, during a subsequent wave of wildcat strikes at Chrysler's Detroit plants, conditions on the shop floor were equally bad for blacks and whites, and rank-and-file protest then was markedly interracial (Pizzolato 2004: 435).

11. Levy (1994: 119–120); Mallet (1975); Gorz (1967); Guarasci (1980: 110–113); Rose (1988: 231–232).

12. In 1967, Calvert elaborated this new theory in a speech at Princeton University. He suggested that students were themselves part of a "new working class," created and exploited by "this super-technological capitalism." The system of "corporate capitalism" was challenged not by "new insurgents" and "alternative institutions" but by the working class heading toward revolution. At the core of this theory was the idea that modern society had created a new proletariat composed of middle-class and professional workers. The "new working class" was presented as a class not because of its relation to the means of production but because of conditions of "unfreedom" in society, conditions affecting deprived minorities;

high-salaried, middle-class professionals; and students in "factory-like multi-universities" (Calvert 1969: 415, 417). Calvert left the SDS when it split into the Progressive Labor Party and Weathermen factions at the summer convention in 1969.

13. Michael Denning points out that Mills did *not* abandon the "labor metaphysic" in his sociological work. In an analysis of what he called "the cultural apparatus" (the world of "mass culture," the culture industry and the new class of intellectuals)—a book project he began around 1955 but never completed— Mills consistently attempted to replace the term "intellectual" with his phrase "cultural workman," rejecting the notion of the "committed intellectual," with its connotation of autonomous advance guard, and replacing it with a sense of the politics of cultural work. His call on cultural workers to "repossess" the cultural apparatus was based on an ideal of workers' control. For Mills, the "cardinal value" of "arts, science and learning" was "craftsmanship" (Denning 1997: 110–113; Mills 1963).

14. By now, Aronowitz had abandoned his earlier belief that the American labor movement could be regenerated, with the expectation that the rank-and-file membership could still act as an agent of change (Aronowitz 1964). He asserted that the modern labor agreement is the essence of "class collaboration," while the union is "chiefly a force for integrating the workers into the corporate capitalist system" (Aronowitz 1971). The Lynds shared this idea, as evidenced by the general tenor of *Rank and File*, published in 1973, which was a clear attack on institutional unionism in its then-prevailing form. They stated that contemporary labor unions had become "a new kind of company union, financially independent of the rank and file because the company deducts union dues from the worker's pay check, and politically all-powerful because the contract takes away from rank and filers the right to strike" (Lynd and Lynd 1973: 3–4). Similarly, in *Strike!* Jeremy Brecher presented a U.S. labor history in which "the main actors in the story are ordinary people," whose struggles against capital and the state were stymied by "unions and labor leaders [who] have most often striven to prevent or contain them" (Brecher 1972: 10). By the early 1980s, New Left activist Mike Davis had lost all hope in American labor's contribution to a more inclusive and more egalitarian society. This was largely because of what he saw as the Reaganite success in solidifying racial divisions within the working class. The unions acted only to the benefit of workers with secure jobs under the seniority system. This defense of employment privileges risked "the creation of a reactive anti-solidarity," as the unemployed turned into strikebreakers, or the "second-class citizens of the lower wage tiers decertify unions that have failed to represent them" (Davis 1986: 153).

15. The PBS series was rebroadcast on public television in 1990, then with personal introductions by Ronald Reagan, George Schultz (U.S. secretary of state from 1982 to 1989), film actor Arnold Schwarzenegger and TV personality/comedian Steve Allen.

16. Working-class support for the Democrats (76 percent in 1948) dropped steeply during the presidential contests of the 1950s (52 percent in 1952 and 44 percent in 1956), recovered briefly in the 1960s (75 percent in 1964), and then dropped again: 50 percent in 1968, 32 percent in 1972, 58 percent in 1976, 44 percent in 1980, 42 percent in 1984 (Piven 1992: 235–236).

17. In 1978 Carter deregulated the airline industry, and two years later he began deregulating trucking as a practical solution to the chronic crisis of "stagflation" in the U.S. economy throughout the 1970s (Harvey 2005: 22–25). In 1978, Congress also passed a tax reform bill cutting the top capital gains by more than 40 percent, from 48 percent to 28 percent. In addition, Carter oversaw the Chrysler bailout and did the advance planning for crushing the 1981 Professional Air Traffic Controllers Organization (PATCO) strike. A year before the PATCO contract was due to expire, Carter created the Management Strike Contingency Force to run air traffic without the controllers were they to go on strike (Smith 1992: 10).

18. One must not forget, however, that American welfare capitalism of the 1920s was nowhere more avidly admired than in Japan where it was extensively copied, becoming the model to which Japanese business returned in the early 1950s after the anti-communist purge of the labor movement.

19. Parker and Slaughter's observations (and much of the controversy over worker participation at the time) focused on the New United Motoring Manufacturing Inc. (NUMMI) plant in Fremont, California, a joint venture of Toyota and General Motors that opened in 1984. Most of the workers had been employed by GM in the same plant before it was closed two years earlier. Unlike Toyota's Kentucky plant and the other fully Japanese-owned transplants, the workers at NUMMI were UAW members (Milkman 1991: 144).

20. There was a crucial difference between the original Japanese model and the one that was selectively adopted by the U.S. companies in the auto industry, which did not promise job security to their core labor force. The cost-cutting measures of Japanese lean production were adopted without the related employment policies, which model has rightly been called "lean and mean" (Harrison 1997). In contrast, the original "Toyotist" model—that offered employment security to a core labor force in exchange for cooperation, but at the same time created a large buffer of less-privileged workers without the same rights and benefits—might be called "lean and dual" (Silver 2003: 67).

Chapter 5

1. The general decrease in union membership in the United States was not unique, however. With the notable exception of the Scandinavian countries, Finland, and Canada, union density declined in almost every industrialized Organisation for Economic Co-operation and Development (OECD) country, although no other economically developed country has had such a continuous and dramatic decrease in the post–World War II era. Union density for nineteen OECD nations fell from an average of 46.1 percent in 1980 to 40.1 percent in 1994. Leaving out the four highly unionized northern countries in the count, the decline was from 39.6 percent to 30.3 percent. In Canada, union membership grew from the 1960s to the 1980s, and increased slightly from 36 percent in 1980 to 38 percent in 1997. The proportion of unionized workers in France was lower than the U.S., but unions received good majorities of the votes in elections to various boards and most workers were covered by collective bargaining contracts (Lipset 1998: 123). In 1992, when the next lowest countries on the scale were at 24.5 percent (Japan) and 25.9 percent (New Zealand) density, the United States was at 15.3 percent and France at 9.4 percent. Australia and the United Kingdom, countries that had experienced strong anti-union governments, were at 39.6 percent and 41.3 percent, respectively. The share of workers covered by collective bargaining agreements showed a somewhat different picture: the United States at 18 percent, Japan at 21 percent, the United Kingdom at 47 percent, Australia at 80 percent, and France at 92 percent. There are multiple dimensions of political and economic power, as the French case makes clear. In France and in several other continental European countries, remnants of Roman law required legal extension of collectively bargained wages to all contracts in the same sector. In France, as well as in Austria, Belgium, and Portugal, the state was particularly active in extending coverage. In Germany, Austria, and the Scandinavian countries, employers' associations were likely to extend coverage. Work councils could further strengthen the influence of unions, even where, as in France, union density was very low; their major effect was to provide rank-and-file representation in the workplace. They were mandatory in Australia, Belgium, France, Germany, the Netherlands, and Spain, and guaranteed through collective bargaining in Scandinavia and Italy (Levi 2003: 48–49; Wallerstein and Western 2000).

2. In 1999, for example, some 15,000 doctors formed a union, the National Doctors Alliance, while the powerful and influential American Medical Association announced the formation of its own union (Francia 2006: 57).

3. A good example is the category of engineers originally organized in the Society of Professional Engineering Employees in Aerospace (SPEEA), which was founded in 1944 to become the collective bargaining agent with Boeing in 1946. It was primarily a professional association composed of the highest-educated, highest-paid, and highest-status employees at Boeing. SPEEA was used to the periodic layoffs in the industry and was prepared to deal with them. However, when the corporate culture changed after Boeing's merger with McDonnell Douglas, SPEEA affiliated with the International Federation of Professional and Technical Engineers, becoming IFPTE Local 2001, in 1999, and the next year organized a major strike that led to victory. In the 1990s, the "permatemps" of Microsoft and other high-tech companies began to object to their second-class and insecure status. Microsoft classified them as employees of temporary staffing firms, denying them health benefits, investment in the company, advancement opportunities, etc., even though they did the same work as the permanent employees. In 1998, they formed the Washington Alliance of Technology of America and affiliated with the Communications Workers of America (CWA), AFL-CIO. In the same year they began to win major settlements in a suit initiated against Microsoft (Levi 2003: 54–55).

4. During the 1980s and 1990s, Sweeney hired mostly college-educated veterans of the 1960s and 1970s, former leftist activists with

community organizing, industrial "colonizing" or union staff backgrounds (Moody 2007: 165–166).

5. Yet during the early years of his presidency, Sweeney gave a different perspective on organized labor's purpose than that of traditional business unionism. He then emphasized traditional progressive causes, notably the increasing wage and income disparities separating workers from corporate executives. Sweeney began his tenure as president of the AFL-CIO with his "America Needs a Raise" campaign, which consisted of a series of town hall meetings in which he discussed issues surrounding low-wage workers and did not shy away from addressing the economic inequalities of capitalism (Francia 2006: 23–25).

6. In the nineteenth century, central labor councils (CLCs) were formed to coordinate political, social, and economic action by the working class within an urban area. CLCs were central agencies in campaigns for the eight-hour day and labor rights and to some of the major actions in U.S. labor history; the Seattle General Strike of 1919 is a preeminent example. As early as the 1910s, the AFL enacted rules and policies to limit the power of central labor councils in order to inhibit their potential competition with national unions. They became even less important as labor markets became more national and the shift from geographic to occupational mobilization was completed (Levi 2003: 51).

7. African Americans — influenced by the individualistic ethos of the dominant culture — often expressed annoyance and hostility toward Latinos and Asians who relied on close networks of family members and old-country friends and neighbors to control certain categories of jobs and to promote group-oriented entrepreneurial activities. A large majority of Latinos, when asked in polls about their ethnic identity, opted for "white," thus clearly distinguishing themselves from blacks. Other polls and surveys showed that levels of anti-black sentiment in the United States were even higher among Latinos and Asians than among white respondents (Waldinger and Lichter 2003: 205–217).

8. However, the contract that the UFCW officials negotiated in this case neglected many of the workers' most deeply felt workplace problems or the question of immigrant status. This is due to a remaining gap between the cultures of most unions and many workers' centers. Moody suggests that union officials and staff need to consider workers' centers as part of the same movement, but with unique functions (Moody 2007: 221).

9. The Alameda corridor is a 120-square-mile corridor that stretches from downtown Los Angeles to the port of Los Angeles and contains almost two-thirds of the manufacturing jobs in the city. It also contains a number of residential communities with the workers who are employed in the plants concerned.

10. According to Nelson Lichtenstein, CTW was "an organization that never really got off the ground.... Everything Change to Win did could have been done inside the AFL-CIO," adding that the rival federation was a vehicle for Andy Stern's own ambitions (Horowitz 2010).

11. A rally near Wall Street in April 2010, with the AFL-CIO as major sponsor, urged Congress and the president to be tougher on the banks. It called for significantly higher taxes on bankers' bonuses and the earnings of private equity managers, as well as a new tax on short-term financial transactions (Greenhouse 2010b).

12. Since the 1950s, when the AFL sponsored nightly radio news broadcasts, there had been no regular presentation of labor's views on network television or radio. Nor were there serious plans to begin publishing a national labor daily, a long-held dream of the progressive labor movement (Aronowitz 1998: 191). But the rise of the Internet would offer new opportunities in the ensuing years, and the AFL-CIO's new Department of Public Affairs, which was part of a major reorganization completed in 1996, would contribute an extensive, improved communication and public relations effort (Hurd, Milkman, and Turner 2003: 110).

13. By the turn of the twenty-first century, at the local level, some individual unions had also become involved in other third parties such as the New Party, the Greens, the Vermont Progressive Party, and New York's Working Families Party. The basic problem facing union political action continued to be that too many corporate-friendly politicians in both major parties were elected to public office. Today, the Democratic Party presents labor with a complex mixture of political influences ranging from strong pro-labor to the overt embrace of corporate America's political agenda. The party as a whole fails to provide an adequate vehicle for effective progressive labor politics (Reynolds 2000; Greider 2009: 181–184).

14. But even with such a pro-labor think tank, there might still be a great chance that its experts would not — or only sporadically — be

invited to present their views in the mainstream media.

15. The unions occasionally sought political allies among Republicans. One "new" tactic has been called the "politics of the deal" by its union advocates. But this tactic at any level of politics is hardly new. What is somewhat new in recent years is that both the union's "bottom line" and the reward come up front. Two prominent examples come both from New York. In the 2002 governor's election in New York State, SEIU local 1199 endorsed the conservative Republican incumbent, George Pataki, over African-American Democrat Carl McCall. The reward came in the form of the Health Care Worker Recruitment and Retention Act, which passed the state legislature under pressure from Pataki well before the election. The act set aside $1.8 billion for raises for state health care workers, and Pataki won the election. In the 2005 mayoral election in New York City, AFSCME District Council 37 endorsed incumbent Republican mayor Michael Bloomberg over Latino Democratic contender Freddy Ferrer. The 2005 deal involved a 1 percent pay hike for DC 37 members, which hike came from a provision in the 2004 agreement that allowed for an additional 1 percent if productivity gains had been made (Moody 2007: 167–168).

16. Labor's role was especially significant to the Democrats because it succeeded in 2008 in making inroads with a crucial demographic segment: blue-collar white men. While white male non-union workers voted against Obama by a margin of 16 percentage points in 2008, he won among white male union workers by 18 percentage points. Moreover, these voters were in the swing states that mattered—for instance, about 30 percent of Pennsylvania voters came from union households, as did 35 percent of Ohio voters, and both states had tough, crucial races for governor and U.S. senator (Greenhouse 2010d).

17. With the Memphis sanitation workers' strike in 1968, King came to see the unionization of the South as a key to ending poverty. If King would not have been assassinated in Memphis, he would have gone to Charleston, South Carolina, in support of Local 1199's efforts to win a contract for hospital workers there.

18. Yet, despite the extremely low union density of the South (an average of 5.8 percent for the region in 2006), Moody agues, there are important pockets of unionism from which support could be drawn for broader unionization efforts. The CWA in telecommunications, the two postal unions in the communications sector, the Teamsters in many national trucking firms, and in railroad companies as well, can be found throughout the South; the ILA in the ports and the AFSCME, AFT, and ATU in various municipalities and the building trades in the expanding urban centers—these and other unions provide a core, particularly in cities, of potential support (Moody 2007: 231–232).

19. In 1986, the United Mine Workers of America (UMWA), under the leadership of Richard Trumka, joined with the National Union of Mineworkers (NUM), other South African Unions, the Free South Africa Movement (FSAM), and the rest of the U.S. labor movement to launch this campaign against the apartheid regime in South Africa.

20. The latter included the Communications Workers of America's (CWA's) efforts in support of Colombian workers. Moreover, there was the boycott of Coca-Cola organized by Corporate Campaigns Inc. because of its support for the Colombian government and its suppression of trade union rights (Moody 2007: 238).

21. In this case, 3,400 UAW union members walked away from their jobs making auto body parts at GM's metal stamping plant in Flint, Michigan, on June 4, 1998. Seven days later they were joined by another 5,800 UAW workers who struck at the Delphi parts plants also in Flint. The resulting parts shortages caused a ripple effect leading to the shutdown of 90 percent of GM's facilities in North America.

22. A conspicuous exception is the support of the recent free-trade pact with South Korea by two powerful unions, the United Auto Workers and the United Food and Commercial Workers in December 2010. The UAW was pleased that the agreement would increase auto exports to Korea and also keep a 2.5 percent American tariff on Korean autos for four years and a 25 percent tariff on Korean SUVs for six years. The UFCW welcomed the pact as it would bolster meat exports to that country (because, among other things, it eliminated a Korean 40 percent tariff on beef imports) and was expected to create over 20,000 jobs in the U.S. meat export-producing sectors. On the other hand, the Machinists' union and two other powerful unions, the Steelworkers and the Communications Workers, denounced the Korea deal, as did anti-free trade activists, arguing that the Korea agreement promoted "free trade" but not fair trade by increasing im-

ports made by lower-paid workers in other countries. This unusual split in the labor movement disrupted the unified labor opposition that helped block ratification of trade agreements with Colombia, Panama, and, until then, South Korea (Greenhouse 2010e).

23. U.S. Census Bureau, Foreign Trade Division, Data Dissemination Branch, *Trade with China 2009*, http://www.census.gov/foreign-trade/balance/c5700.html#2010.

24. The Creating American Jobs and Ending Offshoring Act (S. 3816) that was introduced by Senator Richard Durbin (D-IL) in September 2010, and was endorsed by the AFL-CIO, could have been a significant step in this direction. The bill would close two tax loopholes (introduced during the Reagan era in the 1986 revisions of the Internal Revenue Code) and encourage companies to move their overseas jobs back to the United States. It would end the practice of tax deferral of overseas earnings by outsourcing U.S. corporations and eliminate the tax deductions they receive for the cost of an American jobs offshoring transaction (that is, when they close down a trade or business in America in connection with the establishment or expansion of such trade or business abroad). The bill also provided a two-year break to companies from paying their share of Social Security payroll taxes on wages of employees who replace other employees who are not citizens or permanent residents of the United States and carry out similar work overseas. However, after a barrage of criticisms from the side of big business, including the U.S. Chamber of Commerce and the National Association of Manufacturers, and an intensive campaign by high-powered lobbyists to defeat the bill, it was killed soon after its introduction in the Senate due to a united Republican filibuster and the defection of a handful of Democrats, as a result of which the bill failed to achieve cloture and the Democrats were unable to bring the bill up for vote (Working America and AFL-CIO 2010: 5; official summary of the bill). Critics on the labor left criticized the Democrats for treating the exporting of U.S. jobs issue as "a political afterthought, asserting it into the legislative debate at the last minute before the [2010 midterm] election in order to simply 'rally the base'" (Dean 2010).

25. In the public sector, unfair labor practices concerned the interpretation of state bargaining laws — whether a particular topic was subject to collective bargaining or was a management prerogative — not opposition to unionism per se. Public-sector managers rarely hired consulting firms to prevent organization by their employees. Because of changes in state laws, there was even a trend toward less management opposition to collective bargaining in the public sector during the 1980s (Freeman 1988: 79). This situation would change dramatically by 2011, however, due to a massive right-wing assault on public-sector unionism.

26. In 1992, the United States ratified the International Covenant on Civil and Political Rights, which provides that "everyone shall have the right to freedom of association with others, including the right to form and join trade unions for the protection of his interests." As a member of the International Labor Organization (ILO), the United States is obligated to respect ILO conventions. However, the United States has not ratified the relevant conventions (Bellace 2001: 269–87; Pope, Kellman, and Bruno 2008: 136, 142n58). The ILO's Committee on Freedom of Association has determined that various features of U.S. labor law — including the permanent replacement rule, the flat ban on secondary boycotts, and the failure to protect the right to organize with effective remedies — violated those standards (Human Rights Watch 2000: 18, 31, 171–190, 209–213).

27. At this writing, right-to-work legislation has been filed in twelve states — in addition to the twenty-two (mostly in the South and West) that already have such laws on the books. Three more states — Montana, Ohio, and Wisconsin — are expected to have bills introduced converting their legal status to right-to-work (McAlevey 2011).

28. The proposed bill would strip public-sector workers of the right to bargain collectively over anything other than wages. It would also end the automatic payment of union dues and compel unions to hold elections each year to "recertify" their status as bargaining units. This legislation would also force public employees to pay 12.6 percent of their health insurance costs (instead of about 6 percent that most pay now), and contribute 5.8 percent of their paychecks to their pensions — instead of less than 1 percent that most pay now (Sustar 2011). Contrary to assertions that abound, public employees, in both state and local government, are not overpaid compared to private-sector workers according to a recent study conducted at the Economic Policy Institute: "Comparisons controlling for education, experience, hours of work, organizational size, gender, race, ethnicity and disability, reveal no significant overpayment but a slight under-

compensation of public employees when compared to private employee compensation costs on per hour basis" (Keefe 2010). Many journalists and pundits have parroted Governor Walker's and like-minded government officials' claim that unionized state workers get their pensions and health insurance plans "subsidized" by the state. This ignores the fact that those public workers themselves contribute 100 percent to their benefits in deferred wages (rather than taking immediately in cash) on the basis of negotiated contracts (Johnston 2011). The struggle is first of all over power rather than over benefits. Governor Walker's campaign platform also called for sharp cuts in corporate taxes, while his "budget repair bill" proposes to allow the state to sell energy plants "with or without solicitation of bids, for any amount that the department determines to be in the best interest of the state" and goes on to say that "any such purchase is considered to be in the public interest." The ultimate outcome of all the intended measures is therefore not necessarily one of lower deficits. But it would lead to a situation where power is distributed very differently, with significantly strengthened corporate power and weak labor power (Klein 2011). At the time of writing, polls show the public leaning in favor of government workers having collective bargaining rights and maintaining the essence of a union. A *New York Times*/CBS News poll conducted February 24–27, 2011, found that Americans opposed weakening the bargaining rights of public employee unions by a margin of nearly two to one: 60 percent to 33 percent (and 71 percent opponents among Democrats). The respondents also said they opposed, 56 percent to 37 percent, cutting the pay or benefits of public employees to reduce deficits (Cooper and Thee-Brenan 2011).

29. Democratic governors, like Jerry Brown of California and Andrew Cuomo of New York, have come up with their own demands for cuts in wages, pensions and jobs of public-sector workers. But they and other Democratic governors across the country have tried to avoid Wisconsin-like confrontations with public-worker unions, a key constituency (and their most loyal and financial supporters), by quietly cutting deals with labor leaders. The difference with Republicans is that Democrats have a vested interest in leaving public-sector unions mostly intact, as they want labor's fundraising and get-out-the-vote operations at election time (Sustar 2011; Wallsten and Dennis 2011).

30. It is in the same vein that William Greider has proposed to "free the workers" of the current regulation, that is, to eliminate the NLRA and replace it by a very different labor law. The newly to be enacted labor law he has in mind would be grounded in constitutional rights—free speech, freedom of assembly, and the Thirteenth Amendment prohibiting involuntary servitude—rather than regulatory law vulnerable to direct political influence. Ralph Nader has likewise proposed to view labor rights as civil rights, whereby workers seeking to unionize could sue under the Civil Rights Act of 1991 and secure various financial compensations and reliefs (Nader 2004). Creating a broader set of rights that apply to all employees regardless of union status would provide an opportunity to build bridges across class differences in Greider's view. It would entail basic protections against managerial abuses, and also new rights of self-expression and the right to participate in decision making within the firm (Greider 2006). Needless to say, the latter is at right angles with the persistent preoccupation, if not obsession, of American employers with their "managerial prerogatives" in having complete control of their operations, supported by their massive economic and political resources, which is also backed by various U.S. Supreme Court decisions.

31. Mark Dudzic, National Organizer of the Labor Party, likewise has argued that the First Amendment might also offer protection for attempts at unionization. However, according to critics, like the Thirteen Amendment, the First Amendment is "no magic bullet," evidenced by the very limited protection that the U.S. Supreme Court has provided for free speech in the quasi-public space of the shopping mall. It seems unlikely that a First Amendment–based law would provide stronger free speech rights than the Wagner Act to workers inside a workplace, which is normally considered a much more private space than a shopping mall (Freeman 2005: 73–74).

32. In addition, in October 2006, UE's Mexican ally the FAT (Frente Auténtico del Trabajo, the Authentic Labor Front), an independent Mexican union, with the support of fifty-two other U.S., Mexican, Canadian and global labor organizations, filed a complaint with the Mexican National Administrative Office, a body established to address complaints of labor rights violations under NAFTA. The complaint charged that the North Carolina bargaining ban violated the North American Agreement on Labor Cooperation (NAALC), the labor-rights side agreement to NAFTA. In

November 2007, the Mexican National Administrative Office began an investigation into those charges, http://www.ueunion.org/.

33. "Global Labor Strategies: Ideas and Resources for the Global Labor Movement," May 2007, http://laborstrategies.blogs.com/global_labor_strategies/2007/05/glo.

34. Shortly after having received a $45 billion bailout from the U.S. government, Bank of America canceled its line of credit that kept the Republic Windows factory operating. The executives, who knew that this would happen, had been sneakily moving machinery out. They then closed the factory and sent the workers home. The sit-down strike and its aftermath had a surprising ending. After a settlement had been reached with the company over severance, vacation time, and temporary health care benefits, it filed for bankruptcy on December 15, 2008. The property was put under the control of its major creditors, Bank of America and JPMorgan Chase (who on December 10, 2008, had agreed to create a $1.75 million fund to pay the workers their back pay and benefits and to provide two months of health insurance coverage). Under public and political pressure Bank of America extended a $1.35 million loan. In February 2009, Serious Materials, a California-based company, announced it would purchase the building and assets of Republic Windows, and that it intended to hire back all of the former factory workers (Lydersen 2009).

Chapter 6

1. It should also be noted that in the 1960s and 1970s, the U.S. government's favored tactic for dealing with the popularity of developmentalism and democratic socialism was to try to equate them with orthodox communism, deliberately blurring the marked differences between the two worldviews. A prototypical example is the CIA-funded propaganda campaign depicting Salvador Allende as a Soviet-style dictator after he won the 1970 Chilean presidential election as leader of the *Unidad Popular* ("Popular Unity") coalition (Klein 2007: 452).

2. AIFLD became fully established in 1962. Its offshoots, within a few years, included the African-American Labor Center (AALC) and the Asian-American Free Labor Institute (AAFLI). All were funded partly out of the AFL-CIO budget, as well as by government agencies ranging from the Agency for International Development to the CIA. But later they increasingly acquired financial sources of wealthy CEOs and foundations, thus foreshadowing the "privatization" of militarized foreign policy during the 1980s. AIFLD/CIA training of CIA-sponsored (pro-American and pro-business) unions was abandoned only in 1995. The AFL-CIO under Kirkland's presidency was also involved in the political and economic changeover throughout Eastern Europe after the collapse of Communist regimes. From 1989 to 1995, strategic takeover (including attempts to create unions loyal to the "American system" in Eastern Europe) became even the AFL-CIO's foreign policy raison d'être and almost its whole domestic policy as well (Buhle 1999: 151–154, 230–231).

3. After observing the hostility of Kansas Populists and Chicago Socialists toward corporate domination, Ralph M. Easley, a conservative Republican, organized the NCF with the intention of bringing top business and labor leaders together in harmony. Other NCF founding members from trade unions included Daniel Keefe (International Longshoremen's Association) and J.J. Sullivan (Typographers). Prominent public figures, including former U.S. presidents Grover Cleveland and William H. Taft, also joined this project of class cooperation. After the death of Gompers in 1924, the NCF's relationship to the labor movement largely ended, and business leaders, too, withdrew their financial backing (Tomlins 1985b: 73; Cyphers 2002).

4. Chester mentions as examples the Scottish Socialist Party and the Red-Green Alliance of Denmark but overlooks such parties as *Die Linke* in Germany and the New Anti-Capitalist Party (NPA) in France. Remarkably, he also does not recognize the populist left parties (with various mixes of socialist and indigenist ideologies) that have come to state power in Latin America as possible sources of inspiration and possible allies for American and European socialist parties in the context of a globalizing left-wing movement. It has been suggested that the Bolivarian Revolution (spearheaded by Venezuela) has the potential to lead the global working class in a renewed challenge to transnational capitalism (Robinson 2008).

5. In 1972, writer and political activist Michael Harrington and the Coalition caucus (including a number of Norman Thomas–era Socialists, younger activists and ex-Shachtmanites) founded the Democratic Socialists Organizing Committee (DSOC). It was

the largest group to emerge from the splintering of the Socialist Party of America in 1972–1973. Harrington and his supporters believed that the third-party road to democratic socialism had been a failure, and instead sought to work within the Democratic Party as an organized socialist caucus to bring about that party's "realignment" to the left. In 1982, Democratic Socialists of America (DSA) was formed by a merger of the DSOC and the New American Movement (NAM). The latter was a non-partisan socialist organization, carried by a coalition of writers and intellectuals with roots in both the New Left movements of the 1960s and the more traditional parties of the Old Left. In 1983, Michael Harrington and socialist-feminist author Barbara Ehrenreich were elected as DSA's co-chairs. In its early years, DSA backed relatively mainstream liberals such as Walter Mondale, even though there was a dramatic growth of a left wing associated with Jesse Jackson and the Rainbow Coalition. But subsequently DSA strongly supported Jackson's second presidential campaign in 1988. DSA's position regarding U.S. electoral politics has since evolved. From 1993 onward its official position is that Democratic Socialists reject an either-or approach to electoral coalition building, focused solely on a new party or on realignment within the Democratic Party. During the 1990s, DSA took inspiration from the Religious Right's activism within the Republican Party as a model for how the left could gain a stronger foothold within the Democratic Party, which then was dominated by President Clinton's "New Democrats" in the Democratic Leadership Council. The DSA is the principal U.S. affiliate of the Socialist International (a federation of social democratic, democratic socialist and labor parties and organizations), but it acts less like a traditional U.S. political party and much more like a political education and grassroots activism organization. The DSA's leadership believes working within the Democratic Party is necessary because of the nature of the American political system, which rarely offers third parties a chance politically. However, DSA is very critical of the corporate-funded Democratic Party leadership, especially the Democratic Leadership Council. DSA's website emphasizes that electoral politics are only a means for democratic socialists; the main objective is the building of a powerful anti-corporate coalition. The DSA's 2005 convention focused on Bernie Sanders's campaign as an independent candidate for the U.S. Senate. The DSA never fielded candidates for office until 2006 when a candidate for the Pennsylvania statehouse qualified for the ballot under the banner of the Social Democrats of Pennsylvania (Judis 1983; Marable 1996: 61); *Democratic Left*, Spring/Summer 2000: editorial; Winter 2006: 4, http://www.dsausa.org/dl; "Directory of U.S. Political Parties," Ron Gunzburger's Politics1.com, http://www.politics1.com/parties.html.

6. DSA, "Where We Stand," http://dsausa.org/about/where.html, accessed on November 3, 2008.

7. In some cases, DSA has continued to partner with local county chairs and other Democratic Party officials to promote progressive candidates to the state legislature. This occurred, for example, in Detroit, Michigan, since 1998. But the DSA activists involved, who participated in phone banking and e-mail campaigns, were instructed by their local DSA leadership not to identify themselves as DSA members, to avoid the predictable response many have toward people who call themselves "socialists." Detroit DSA has come under attack by Republicans and Democrats for being a "socialist" organization. Detroit DSA candidates have been red baited by both Republican opponents and mainstream newspapers. Moreover, progressive Democratic candidates in two congressional races in 2008 — Gary Peters and Mark Schauer, both of whom went on to win — were pleased to have Detroit DSA's involvement, but "handlers" from the Democratic National Committee (DNC) refused the support, for fear that the candidates would be red baited or branded as socialists (Maxon 2009).

8. Llewellyn made the ironic remark that, of the "four people running for national office," Sarah Palin was the most socialistic because "she administered a state that says that the oil revenues are collectively owned and used the revenue to give money to the people living in the state" (Llewellyn and Schwarz 2009b); Glenn Beck, "A Socialist's Perspective on America," Fox News, February 19, 2009, http://www.foxnews.com/story/0.2933.496446.00.html.

9. Cavanaugh (2009); Llewellyn and Schwarz (2009a).

10. There have been major exceptions among the AFL-CIO rank and file, however. Previously many voted for Ronald Reagan. Some Internationals, most famously the Teamsters, were as likely to back a Republican as a Democrat for president. There were also those who advocated the formation of a labor party

or the use of fusion politics (Levi 2003: 59). During the George W. Bush presidency, when labor faced severe challenges, including several anti-labor executive orders and anti-union administrative decisions, a number of unions broke ranks to work with the president and Republican congressional leaders on narrow issues that benefit only their specific members. For example, the Steelworkers secured import restrictions on steel, a consortium of unions led by the Teamsters supported drilling for oil in Alaska, and the Autoworkers endorsed relaxed fuel consumption standards for motor vehicles (Hurd, Milkman, and Turner 2003: 105).

11. The problem remains that union members are far from a homogeneous group in terms of voting behavior. Some are pro-choice and some are right-to-life. Some support gun control and some are violently opposed to any restrictions on the right to bear arms. Some are racist or sexist, while others are not. To create a more effective voting bloc for labor requires effective mobilization around key issues, along with voter education to enable voters to understand that their interests might actually be with a different candidate or policy than they initially believed (Levi 2003: 58–59: Moody 2007: 154–159).

12. These states are Connecticut, Delaware, Idaho, Mississippi, New York, Oregon, South Carolina and Vermont. In several other states, notably New Hampshire, electoral fusion is legal when primaries are won by write-in candidates.

13. Katznelson sees a striking resemblance here with the dynamics of social democratic policy innovation in England in the 1880s, when the resources of the new unionism were only beginning to be available to British workers, and those of the Labour Party were more than a decade away. The disruptive protests of London's casual workers were characterized by the absence of a coherent movement ideology, and by the combination of violence and protest. This expressive radicalism evoked panic among politicians and professional reformers. The prevailing feeling among them was fear rather than guilt. The response to this social crisis did produce advances for the poor, as the collective sphere of the state expanded to their benefit. But these new policies were in fact part of an effort to reassert order and social control (Katznelson 1978: 94). For every proposal to provide subsidized housing and meals, there were "parallel proposals to segregate the casual poor, to establish detention centers for 'loafers,' to separate pauper children for 'degenerate' parents or to ship the 'residuum' overseas" (Stedman Jones 1971: 314).

14. Nearly 74 percent of self-described Tea Party supporters would back a "national manufacturing strategy" to make sure that economic, tax, labor and trade policies in this country work together to help support manufacturing in the United States," according to a 2010 poll conducted by the Mellman Group and the Alliance for American Manufacturing. And 56 percent of the same respondents favored "a tariff on products imported from other countries that are cheaper because they come from a country that does not have to comply with any climate change regulations in the country where the products are made." Other polls show that 86 percent of the American people are against the notion of corporation as people, which refers to the recent *Citizens United* Supreme Court ruling that declared that corporations have the same rights as humans (Bybee 2010).

15. According to the CBS-*New York Times* poll conducted April 5–12, 2010, of 1,580 persons among the 18 percent of Americans who call themselves Tea Party supporters, 75 percent have college educations, and 76 percent have household incomes above $50,000 (including a fifth of them making more than $100,000); 78 percent describe their financial situation as "good" or "fairly good"; 65 percent of them identify themselves as either middle or middle upper class; 59 percent are men, 75 percent are forty-five or older, and 80 percent are white; 54 percent are openly supporters of the Republican Party; 66 percent (compared to just 28 percent of Americans) either usually or always vote Republican; and 72 percent describe themselves as "conservative" (Street and DiMaggio 2010: 9).

16. According to an August 2010 poll from WorldPublicOpion.org, 52 percent of Americans felt sympathy for the Tea Party, but only 31 percent of them said their main concern was that government "is becoming too big." Instead, 55 percent said their great concern was that the government "is not following the will of the people." Even among those who said that they were "very sympathetic" to the Tea Party—about 20 percent overall—only 43 percent expressed major concerns about big government. More respondents, 47 percent, expressed greater concern about the lack of democratic responsiveness by the government, which put them in a mood hostile to the incumbents, who then were largely Democrats (Kull 2010).

17. It is noteworthy that while most of the Tea Party's rank-and-file supporters do not want to do away with Medicare and Social Security, they seem not to be aware that the movement's financiers and strategists, such as the Koch brothers and Dick Armey, lead the conservative campaign to gut both programs in the name of self-reliance, freedom, and "free-market" capitalism (DiMaggio and Street 2010: 2).

18. This part of the interpretation is similar to the arguments of Barbara Ehrenreich with regard to the "retreat from liberalism" by the professional middle class from the 1950s to the 1980s in her book *Fear of Falling: The Inner Life of the Middle Class* (1989).

19. Farm workers and domestics—the two job categories where blacks were concentrated—were not covered by Social Security, unemployment benefits, or collective bargaining. In addition, FHA mortgages were disproportionately approved for white borrowers and structured to encourage purchase in suburbs with "higher residential security," away from redlined neighborhoods considered the most risky for mortgage support, which tended to be in the center of cities and were often black neighborhoods. As suburbia developed, federal and state governments invested in infrastructure to serve the commuter, routing highways through city centers in ways that physically and geographically instituted racial segregation (Massey and Denton 1993). All of this constituted "whiteness" but made it virtually invisible as such.

20. Tea Partiers speak in a language that is informed by this New Deal legacy, as the signs that they carry show: "This democracy will cease to exist when you take it away from those who are willing to work and give it to those who would not," "You are not entitled to what I have earned," or "Redistribute my work ethic" (Disch 2010).

21. Richard Nixon and Ronald Reagan were very adept in tapping racial "schemas" without explicitly mentioning race, and to stir anger and resentment among those who, despite being well represented politically, consider themselves victims of this scenario and righteously indignant (Winter 2006).

22. David Koch, who is known as a conservative Republican and is widely celebrated as a cultural philanthropist, is the founder of the Americans for Prosperity Foundation, which has helped build the Tea Party movement since its inception by giving money to "educate," fund, and organize Tea Party protesters. Historical continuity can be seen in the fact that, in 1980, David Koch ran to the right of Reagan as the vice-presidential candidate for the Libertarian Party, and many of the ideas propounded in that campaign foreshadowed those of the Tea Party movement. Another major sponsor of the Tea Party movement, Dick Armey's FreedomWorks, under its original name, Citizens for a Sound Economy, received $12 million on its own from Koch family foundations (Mayer 2010; Rich 2010).

23. These are the figures of 2010. More public-sector employees (7.6 million) belonged to a union than did private-sector employees (7.1 million). Within the public sector, local government workers had the highest union density: 42.3 percent. This group included workers in heavily unionized occupations, such as teachers, police officers, and firefighters. Private-sector industries with high unionization rates included transportation and utilities (21.8 percent), telecommunications (15.8 percent) and construction (13.1 percent). Low unionization occurred in agriculture and related industries (1.6 percent) and in financial activities (2.0 percent). Among occupational groups, education, training, and library occupations (37.1 percent) and protective service occupations (34.1 percent) had the highest unionization. Black workers were more likely to be union members (13.4 percent) than workers who were white (11.7 percent), Asian (10.9 percent) or Hispanic (10.0 percent). Black men had the highest union density (14.8 percent), while Asian men had the lowest rate (9.4 percent). "Union Members Summary—2010," Bureau of Labor Statistics, January 21, 2011.

24. At this writing, the leaders of the OneNationStandingTogether Coalition (as it has also been called) seem not to be prepared to take on the right-wing within the Democratic Party. Most likely they will not embark on this course in the foreseeable future either, according to Bill Fletcher. This while any attempt to generate a political movement that pushes from the left would necessarily mean going against some elected leaders who have often merely posed as friends of the people. It would also require "a long-term strategy that moves from the rhetoric of change to the practice of social transformation" (Fletcher 2010).

25. The rally's platform included the following planks: extend unemployment benefits, raise the minimum wage, end the foreclosure epidemic, enact legislation making it easier to join unions, increase infrastructure spending to create jobs, "fix our immigration system"

and end immigration roundups that encourage racial profiling (Greenhouse 2010c).

26. Majority Agenda Project (2010); Solomon (2010).

27. At the local level in various parts of the country there are now also initiatives to build a new majority by unions and community groups seeking a long-term alliance (Brenner 2010).

28. Harvey indicates that many of the revolutionary movements in capitalist history were broadly urban rather than narrowly factory based: the revolutions of 1848 throughout Europe, the Paris Commune of 1871, Leningrad in 1917, the Seattle general strike of 1919, and the Tucumán uprising in Argentina of 1969, as well as Paris, Mexico City, and Bangkok in 1968; the Shanghai Commune of 1967; Prague in 1989; Buenos Aires in 2001–2002; and several other cases. Even historic key movements in the factories, such as the Turin Workers Councils in Italy of the 1920s and the Flint Strike in Michigan of 1936–1937, were characterized by the critical role in the political action that the organized support in the neighborhoods played — the communal "houses of the people" in Turin and the women's and unemployed support groups in Flint (Harvey 2010: 243).

29. "Accumulation by dispossession is an updated and more fine-tuned version of what Marx called "primitive accumulation," with privatization and commodification, and more extreme forms of financialization as key elements (Harvey 2005: 159–165).

30. Furthermore, the emphasis on intellectual property rights in the so-called Trade-Related Aspects of Intellectual Property Rights (TRIPS) agreements during the World Trade Organization negotiations refers to ways in which the patenting and licensing of genetic materials, seed plasmas, and all kinds of other products, can now be used to deprive whole populations of critical assets, while their practices have played a crucial role in the development of those materials, There is also the deliberate orchestration, management, and control of economic crises to "rationalize" the irrationalities of the capitalist system. What especially comes to mind here are state-administered austerity programs, making use of the key levers of interest rates and the credit system. This may involve limited crises imposed by external agencies upon one sector or upon a territory (or nation-state) as the International Monetary Fund has been doing through its imposition of market-led structural adjustment programs (Harvey 2010: 245–247).

31. The organization explicitly states that the "socialism" associated with China and Cuba, like the former Soviet Union and Eastern Bloc, have nothing to do with socialism. ISO, "Where We Stand," http://socialistworker.org, accessed February 27, 2011.

32. According to this project's initiator, Michael Albert, in an interview in October 2009, the WSF "started with a tremendous surge" but is now "mostly a place where people vent outrage, or display great knowledge of the intricacies of injustice" at sessions "where people redundantly show that capitalism sucks. Why not have most sessions developed shared visions for culture, politics, economy, kinship, ecology, and so on — including discussing commitments that could sustain organizations and engender mass participation?" (Albert 2009: 1–2). Albert has been advocating what he calls "Participatory Economics" (or Parecon), an economic model meant to replace not only capitalism but also twentieth-century socialism. It revolves around a few key institutional features including workers' and consumers' self-managed councils; equitable remuneration for duration, intensity, and "onerousness" of socially valuable work; "balanced job complexes" (a way of organizing work that avoids class divisions based on position in the division of work); and "participatory planning for allocation" instead of either markets or central planning (Albert 2009: 2–3); see also Wilpert (2009).

33. At this writing, it is unclear what the outcome is of recent efforts of some sections of the radical left to create a new Workers' International, provisionally called the Fifth International. During an international meeting of left parties held in Caracas in November 2009, Hugo Chávez launched a call for the convoking of a Fifth Socialist International in April 2010 in Venezuela, which would bring together left-wing parties and social movements. A number of groups, mainly from South America, immediately responded that they would join such a body. In response to this call, Michael Albert, coordinator of ZNet, wrote an article "Fifth International?" (published in January 2010) that led to the draft of a "Proposal for a Participatory Socialist International," which had been signed by a large number of left-wing intellectuals and political activists, including Noam Chomsky, Vandana Shiva, Fernando Vegas, John Pilger, Trevor Ngwane, Pervez Hoodbhoy, Susan George, Boris Kagarlitsky, François Houtars, and nearly 1,320 others by April 2010 (*ZMagazine* 2010). Ac-

cording to Eric Toussaint, a member of the International Council of the World Social Forum, this could open an interesting new perspective if it would lead to reflection and dialogue between parties and social movements. But it should then not be an organization like the previous internationals, which were — or are, since there is still the Fourth International (with its World Socialist Website, wsws.org, published by the International Committee of the Fourth International) and even a separate, Trotskyist, League for a Fifth International — "organizations of highly centralized political parties" (Bonfond and Toussaint 2010). The congress intended to constitute the Fifth International in Venezuela was postponed, and, by December 2010, no comments had yet emerged from the working group in charge of the mission (New Unionism 2010). One of the signers of the draft proposal, the seasoned internationalist leftist activist Peter Waterman, has indicated possible problems of the Chávez and Albert initiatives, particularly in relation to the WSF and global social justice movement. Waterman discerns in both cases a notable silence on the role of the state (or states) in the envisioned participatory socialist international, and only passing or rhetorical reference to the international working class and the organized labor movement. These and similar other proposals also run the risk of individual or group vanguardism, "of a self-proclaimed elite or individual prophet substituting for a specified constituency, for 'real' or 'revolutionary' socialists, 'the working class,' 'the people,' or 'the world'" (Waterman 2010: 4).

Bibliography

Adam, Katherine, and Charles Derber. 2008. *The New Feminized Majority: How Democrats Can Change America with Women's Values.* Boulder, CO: Paradigm Publishers.

Akers Chacón, Justin. 2006. "Out From the Shadows, Into the Streets: The New Immigrant Civil Rights Movement." *International Socialist Review*, 47 (May–June), http://www.isreview.org/issues/47/newmovement.shtml.

_____, and Mike Davis. 2006. *No One Is Illegal: Fighting Racism and State Violence on the U.S.–Mexico Border.* Chicago: Haymarket Books.

Albert, Michael. 2009. "Interview with Michael Albert about the WSF and 'Reimagining Society.'" *ZNet*, October 21, 2009, http://www.zcommunications.org/contents/76395/print.

Alesina, Alberto, and Edward L. Glaeser. 2004. *Fighting Poverty in the U.S. and Europe: A World of Difference.* Oxford: Oxford University Press.

Amberg, Stephen. 1998. "The CIO Political Strategy in Historical Perspective: Creating a High-Road Economy in the Postwar Era." In *Organized Labor and American Politics, 1894–1994: The Liberal-Labor Alliance*, ed. Kevin Boyle, pp. 159–194. Albany, NY: State University of New York Press.

American Federation of Labor. 1902. *Report of Proceedings of the Twenty-second Annual Convention of the American Federation of Labor.* Washington, DC: Law Reporter Printing Company.

Andrews, James. 2006. "Pulling Together in North Carolina." *New Labor Forum*, 15 (2): 42–46.

Archer, Robin. 2007. *Why Is There No Labor Party in the United States?* Princeton, NJ: Princeton University Press.

Aronowitz, Stanley. 1964. "Against the Mainstream: Interview with James Mattes of the U.E." *Studies on the Left*, 5: 43–54.

_____. 1971. "Trade Unionism in America." *Liberation*, December 22–27.

_____. 1973. *False Promises: The Shaping of American Working-Class Consciousness.* New York: McGraw-Hill.

_____. 1998. *From the Ashes of the Old: American Labor and America's Future.* New York: Basic Books.

_____. 2003. *How Class Works.* New Haven and London: Yale University Press.

_____. 2008. *The Last Good Job in America: Work and Education in the New Global Technoculture.* Lanham, MD: Rowman & Littlefield.

Atleson, James B. 1983. *Values and Assumptions in American Labor Law.* Amherst: University of Massachusetts Press.

Barber, Kathleen L. 1995. *Proportional Representation and Election Reform in Ohio.* Columbus, OH: Ohio State University Press.

Bartolini, Stephano. 2000. *The Political Mobilization of the European Left, 1860–1980.* Cambridge: Cambridge University Press.

Bassett, Michael. 1973. "Municipal Reform and the Socialist Party, 1910–1914." *Aus-*

tralian Journal of Politics and History, 19 (August): 179–187.
Bell, Daniel. 1959. "The 'Rediscovery' of Alienation: Some Notes along the Quest for the Historical Marx." *Journal of Philosophy*, 56 (24): 933–952.
———. 1963. *The Radical Right: The New American Right Expanded and Updated*. Garden City, NY: Doubleday.
Bellace, Janice. 2001. "The ILO Declaration of Fundamental Principles and Rights at Work." *International Journal of Comparative Labor Law and International Relations*, 17 (3): 269–287.
Bellush, Bernard. 1976. *The Failure of the N.R.A.* New York: Norton.
Bernstein, Irving. 1969. *The Lean Years: A History of the American Worker, 1920–1933*. Boston: Houghton Mifflin.
———. 1971. *The Turbulent Years: A History of the American Worker, 1933–1941*. Boston: Houghton Mifflin.
———. 1985. *A Caring Society: The New Deal, the Worker, and the Great Depression*. Boston: Houghton Mifflin.
———. 1991. *Promises Kept: John F. Kennedy's New Frontier*. New York: Oxford University Press.
Blackburn, Robin. 2010. "Start of the Union: Marx and America's Unfinished Revolution." *New Left Review*, 61 (Jan./Feb.): 153–174.
Blauner, Robert. 1964. *Alienation and Freedom: The Factory Worker and His Industry*. Chicago: University of Chicago Press.
Bonfond, Olivier, and Eric Toussaint. 2010. "Will Capitalism Absorb the WSF?" Interview by Marga Tojo Gonzales, *Monthly Review*, February 28, http://nrzine.monthly review.org/2010/bt280210.html.
Borosage, Robert L., and Katrina vanden Heuvel. 2009. "Exacting Change: Obama, Progressives and the Fights to Come." *The Nation*, June 15, 11–12, 14–15.
Boyle, Kevin. 1995. *The UAW and the Heyday of American Liberalism, 1945–1968*. Ithaca, NY: Cornell University Press.
———. 2008. "Why Is There No Social Democracy in America?" *International Labor and Working-Class History*, 74 (1): 33–37.
Brecher, Jeremy. 1972. *Strike!* New York: Fawcett.
———, and Tim Costello. 1998. "A 'New Labor Movement' in the Shell of the Old?" In *A New Labor Movement for the New Century*, ed. Gregory Mantsios, pp. 24–43. New York: Monthly Review Press.
———, Tim Costello, and Brendan Smith. 2007. "Are Labor Rights Human Rights?" *New Labor Forum*, 16 (2): 19–25.
Brenner, Mark. 2010. "What Will Labor Learn from the Election Disaster?" *Labor Notes*, November 19, http://www.labornotes.org/print/2010/11/what-will-labor-learn-electi....
Bridges, Amy. 1986. "Becoming American: The Working Classes in the United States before the Civil War." In *Working-Class Formation: Nineteenth-Century Patterns in Western Europe and the United States*, ed. Ira Katznelson and Aristide R. Zolberg, pp. 157–196. Princeton, NJ: Princeton University Press.
Brinkley, Alan. 1995. *The End of Reform: New Deal Liberalism in Recession and War*. New York: Knopf.
———. 1998. *Liberalism and Its Discontents*. Cambridge, MA: Harvard University Press.
Brody, David. 1993. "Workplace Contractualism in Comparative Perspective." In *Industrial Democracy in America: The Ambiguous Promise*, ed. Nelson Lichtenstein and Howell John Harris, pp. 176–205. Cambridge: Cambridge University Press.
———. 1998. *Steelworkers in America: The Nonunion Era*. Urbana: University of Illinois Press.
———. 2004. "Labor versus the Law: How the Wagner Act Became a Management Tool." *New Labor Forum*, 13 (1): 8–16.
Bronfenbrenner, Kate. 2007. *Global Unions: Challenging Transnational Capital through Cross-Border Campaigns*. Ithaca, NY: Cornell University Press.
———. 2009. *No Holds Barred: The Intensification of Employer Opposition to Or-*

ganizing. Washington, DC: EPI Briefing Paper 235, May 20.

Bronner, Stephen Eric. 2001. *Socialism Unbound.* 2nd ed. Boulder, CO: Westview Press.

Brown, Michael. 1999. *Race, Money, and the American Welfare State.* Ithaca, NY: Cornell University Press.

Brownlee, W. Eliot. 1996. *Federal Taxation in America.* Cambridge: Cambridge University Press.

Bucher, Erwin. 1971. "Historische Grundlegung: Die Entwicklung der Schweiz zu einem politischen System." In *Das politische Sytem der Schweiz,* ed. Jürg Steiner et al., pp. 11–50. München: R. Piper & Co. Verlag.

Buhle, Paul. 1999. *Taking Care of Business: Samuel Gompers, George Meany, Lane Kirkland, and the Tragedy of American Labor.* New York: Monthly Review Press.

Burch, Philip H., Jr. 1973. "The NAM as an Interest Group." *Politics and Society,* 4 (Fall): 97–103.

Burghart, Devin, and Leonard Zeskind. 2010. *Tea Party Nationalism: A Critical Examination of the Tea Party Movement and the Size, Scope, and Focus of Its National Factions.* Kansas City, MO: Institute for Research & Education on Human Rights.

Burnham, Walter Dean. 1974. "The United States: The Politics of Heterogeneity." In *Electoral Behavior: A Comparative Handbook,* ed. Richard Rose, pp. 653–725. New York: Free Press.

———. 1982. *The Current Crisis in American Politics.* London: Oxford University Press.

Bybee, Roger. 2010. "Tea Party Poses Threat to Democracy: There Have Been Ugly Incidents at Tea Party Events as Well as Openings for Progressive Dialog." *ZMagazine,* November 2010, http://www.zcommunications.org/contents/173434/print.

Calvert, Gregory. 1969. "In White America: Radical Consciousness and Social Change." In *The New Left,* ed. Massimo Teodori, pp. 412–417. Indianapolis: Bobbs-Merrill.

Carney, Eliza. 2010. "Court Unlikely to Stop with Citizens United." *National Journal,* January 21, 2010, http://www.nationaljournal.com/njonline/rg_20100121_2456.php.

Carstairs, Andrew McLaren. 1980. *A Short History of Electoral Systems in Western Europe.* London: Allen & Unwin.

Caute, David. 1978. *The Great Fear: The Anti-Communist Purge under Truman and Eisenhower.* New York: Simon & Schuster.

Cavanaugh, Maureen. 2009. "Political Analysis: The New Fear of Socialism." KPBS, October 7, 2009, http://www.kpbs.org/news/2009/oct/07/political-analysis-new-fear-socialism/.

Chan, Sewell. 2011. "Financial Crisis Was 'Avoidable,' Inquiry Concludes." *New York Times,* January 25, 2011.

Chester, Eric. 1985. *Socialists and the Ballot Box: A Historical Analysis.* New York: Praeger.

Chester, Eric Thomas. 2004. *True Mission: Socialists and the Labor Party Question in the U.S.* London and Sterling, VA: Pluto Press.

Chomsky, Noam. 2007. *Failed States: The Abuse of Power and the Assault on Democracy.* London: Penguin Books.

Cobble, Dorothy Sue. 1991. *Dishing It Out: Waitresses and Their Unions in the 20th Century.* Urbana: University of Illinois Press.

———. 1999. "American Labor Politics AFL-Style." *Labor History,* 40 (2): 192–196.

Cohen, Larry. 2005. "Collective Bargaining Is the Priority." *New Labor Forum,* 14 (1): 68–71.

Cohen, Sheila. 2008. "The 1968–1974 Labour Upsurge in Britain and America: A Critical History, and a Look at What Might Have Been." *Labor History,* 49 (4): 395–416.

Conlin, Joseph R. 1969. *Bread and Roses Too.* Westport, CT: Greenwood Press.

Cooper, Michael, and Megan Thee-Brenan. 2011. "Majority in Poll Back Employees in Public Sector Unions." *New York Times,* February 28, 2011.

Cowie, Jefferson. 2010. *Stayin' Alive: The*

1970s and the Last Days of the Working Class. New York and London: New Press.

———, and Nick Salvatore. 2008. "The Long Exception: Rethinking the Place of the New Deal in American History." *International Labor and Working-Class History*, 74 (1): 3–32.

Crouch, Colin. 1997. "The Terms of the Neo-Liberal Consensus." *Political Quarterly*, 68 (4): 352–360.

Cyphers, Christopher J. 2002. *The National Civic Federation and the Making of a New Liberalism, 1900–1915*. New York: Praeger.

Dahl, Robert A., ed. 1966. *Political Oppositions in Western Democracies*. New York: Yale University Press.

Daniel, Cletus E. 1980. *The ACLU and the Wagner Act*. Ithaca, NY: Cornell University.

Daniels, Roger. 1990. *Coming to America: A History of Immigration and Ethnicity in American Life*. New York: Harper.

Davin, Eric Leif. 1996. "The Very Last Hurrah? The Defeat of the Labor Party Idea, 1934–36." In *"We Are All Leaders": The Alternative Unionism of the Early 1930s*, ed. Staughton Lynd, pp. 117–171. Urbana: University of Illinois Press.

Davis, Mike. 1986. *Prisoners of the American Dream: Politics and Economy in the History of the U.S. Working Class*. London: Verso.

———. 2009. "Obama at Manassas." *New Left Review*, 56 (March–April): 5–46.

Dawley, Alan. 1976. *Class and Community: The Industrial Revolution in Lynn*. Cambridge, MA: Harvard University Press.

Deal, Terence E., and Allen A. Kennedy. 1982. *Corporate Cultures: The Rites and Rituals of Corporate Life*. Reading, MA: Addison-Wesley.

Dean, Amy. 2010. "Moves against Offshoring Should Be More Than Political Afterthought." *In These Times*, September 29, 2010, http://www/inthesetimes.com/working/prnt/6486/moves_against_off-s....

DeChiara, Peter. 1993. "Rethinking the Managerial-Professional Exemption of the Fair Labor Standards Act." *American University Law Review*, 43 (1): 139–189.

Denning, Michael. 1997. *The Cultural Front: The Left and American Culture in the Age of the CIO*. New York: Verso.

Derber, Charles. 1998. *Corporation Nation: How Corporations Are Taking Over Our Lives and What We Can Do about It*. New York: St. Martin's.

———. 2005. *Hidden Power: What You Need to Know to Save Our Democracy*. San Francisco: Berrett-Koehler.

———. 2010. "Capitalism: Big Surprises in Recent Polls." Common Dreams.org, May 18, http://www.commondreams.org/print/56203.

———, and Yale R. Magrass. 2008. *Morality Wars: How Empires, the Born Again, and the Politically Correct Do Evil in the Name of Good*. Boulder, CO: Paradigm Publishers.

Dick, William M. 1972. *Labor and Socialism in America: The Gompers Era*. Port Washington, NY: Kennikat Press.

DiGaetano, Alan. 1992. "The Democratic Party and City Politics in the Postindustrial Era." In *Labor Parties in Postindustrial Societies*, ed. Francis Fox Piven, pp. 212–234. New York: Oxford University Press.

DiMaggio, Anthony. 2010. "Glenn Beck's Inverted America: Behind the Perversion of Martin Luther King's Dream." ZNet, September 1, 2010, http://zcommunications.org/glenn-beck-s-inverted-america-by-anthony-dimaggio.

———, and Paul Street. 2010. "What 'Populist Uprising'? Part 2: Further Reflections on an 'Astroturf Movement.'" *Monthly Review*, April 29, http://mrzine.monthlyreview.org/2010/sd290410.html.

Disch, Lisa. 2010. "The Tea Party: The American 'Precariat'?" Article based on talk given at the Tea Party Conference held by the Center for the Comparative Study of Right-Wing Movements, UC Berkeley, October 22, 2010, http://www.opendemocracy.net/print/57213.

Dubofsky, Melvyn. 1969. *We Shall Be All: A History of the Industrial Workers of the World*. Chicago: Quadrangle Books.

———. 1988. *We Shall Be All: A History of the Industrial Workers of the World.* 2nd ed. Urbana: University of Illinois Press.

———. 1994. *The State and Labor in Modern America.* Chapel Hill: University of North Carolina Press.

———. 1999. "Wobblies Past and Present: A Response." *Labor History,* 40 (3): 365–369.

———. 2005. "The IWW at One Hundred: The Return of the Haunted Hall?" *Working U.S.A.,* 8 (September): 535–543.

Dudzic, Mark. 2005. "Saving the Right to Organize: Substituting the Thirteenth Amendment for the Wagner Act." *New Labor Forum,* 14 (1): 59–67.

Duverger, Maurice. 1954. *Political Parties: Their Organization and Activity in the Modern State.* London: Methuen.

Early, Steve. 2003. "Thoughts on the 'Worker-Student Alliance'—Then and Now." *Labor History,* 44 (1): 5–13.

Eder, Mine. 2002. "The Constraints on Labour Internationalism: Contradictions and Prospects." In *Global Unions? Theory and Strategies of Organized Labour in the Global Political Economy,* ed. Jeffery Harrod and Robert O'Brien, pp. 167–185. London: Routledge.

Ehrenreich, Barbara. 1989. *Fear of Falling: The Inner Life of the Middle Class.* New York: Pantheon Books.

———, and John Ehrenreich. 1977. "The New Left: A Case Study in Professional-Managerial Class Radicalism." *Radical America,* May–June, pp. 7–24.

———, and Bill Fletcher Jr. 2009a. "Rising to the Occasion: Do Socialists Have a Plan?" *The Nation,* March 23, pp. 13–14, 17.

———. 2009b. "Change Socialists Can Believe In: A Response to Our Forum on 'Reimagining Socialism.'" *The Nation,* May 25, pp. 16, 18, 20.

Farrell, Frank. 1985. "Socialism, Internationalism, and the Australian Labour Movement." *Labour/Le Travail,* 15 (Spring): 125–144.

Ferguson, Thomas. 1995. *Golden Rule: The Investment Theory of Party Composition and the Logic of Money-Driven Political Systems.* Chicago: University of Chicago Press.

Fine, Janice. 2006. *Worker Centers: Organizing Communities at the Edge of the Dream.* Ithaca, NY: Cornell University Press.

Fine, Nathan. 1928. *Labor and Farm Parties in the United States, 1828–1928.* New York: Rand School of Social Sciences.

Fink, Leon. 1983. *Workingmen's Democracy: The Knights of Labor and American Politics.* Urbana: University of Illinois Press.

Fletcher, Bill. 2009a. "Race, the National Question, Empire and the Socialist Strategy in the U.S.A." ZNet, June 11, 2009, http://www.zcommunications.org/contents/58613/print.

———. 2009b. "Can Richard Trumka Turn Organized Labor Around?" ZNet, October 12, 2009, http://www.zcommunications.org/contents/76133/print.

———. 2010. "Reflections on the October 2nd Rallies and Where We Go From Here." ZNet, October 7, 2010, http://www.zcommunications.org/contents/172794/print.

Fletcher, Bill, Jr., and Fernando Gapasin. 2008. *Solidarity Divided: The Crisis in Organized Labor and a New Path toward Social Justice.* Berkeley: University of California Press.

Foner, Eric. 1978. "Class, Ethnicity and Radicalism in the Gilded Age: The Land League and Irish America." *Marxist Perspectives,* 2 (Summer): 6–55.

———. 1984. "Why Is There No Socialism in the United States?" *History Workshop Journal,* 17 (Spring): 57–80.

Foner, Philip S. 1974. *Organized Labor and the Black Worker, 1619–1973.* New York: Praeger.

Fones-Wolf, Elizabeth. 1994. *Selling Free Enterprise: The Business Assault on Labor and Liberalism, 1945–1960.* Urbana: University of Illinois Press.

Forbath, William E. 1991. *Law and the Shaping of the American Labor Movement.* Cambridge, MA: Harvard University Press.

———. 1999. "Not So Simple." *Labor History,* 40 (2): 196–201.

Francia, Peter L. 2006. *The Future of Organized Labor in American Politics.* New York: Columbia University Press.

Frank, Thomas. 2004. *What's the Matter with Kansas? How Conservatives Won the Heart of America.* New York: Henry Holt.

Fraser, Max. 2008. "Beyond the Labor Board." *The Nation*, January 21, pp. 6, 8.

Fraser, Steve, and Gary Gerstle. 1989. "Introduction" to *The Rise and Fall of the New Deal Order, 1930–1980*, ed. Steve Fraser and Gary Gerstle, pp. ix–xxv. Princeton, NJ: Princeton University Press.

Freeman, Joshua. 2000. *Working-Class New York: Life and Labor since World War II.* New York: Free Press.

———. 2005. "The Thirteenth Amendment Is No Magic Bullet." *New Labor Forum*, 14 (1): 72–74.

Freeman, Richard B. 1988. "Contraction and Expansion: The Divergence of Private Sector and Public Sector Unionism in the United States." *Journal of Economic Perspectives*, 2 (2): 63–88.

Friedman, Gerald. 1988. "The State and the Making of the Working Class: France and the United States." *Theory and Society*, 17 (3): 403–440.

Friedman, Milton, and Rose D. Friedman. 1980. *Free to Choose: A Personal Statement.* Boston, MA: Houghton Mifflin Harcourt.

Frundt, Henry J. 2002. "Four Models of Cross-Border Maquila Organizing." In *Unions in a Globalized Environment: Changing Borders, Organizational Boundaries, and Social Roles*, ed. Bruce Nissen, pp. 45–75. Armonk, NY: Sharpe.

Frymer, Paul. 2008. *Black and Blue: African Americans, the Labor Movement, and the Decline of the Democratic Party.* Princeton, NJ: Princeton University Press.

Gabin, Nancy. 1990. *Feminism in the Labor Movement: Women and the United Auto Workers, 1935–1940.* Ithaca, NY: Cornell University Press.

Gapasin, Fernando, and Edna Bonacich. 2002. "The Strategic Challenge of Organizing Manufacturing Workers in Global/Flexible Capitalism." In *Unions in a Globalized Environment: Changing Borders, Organizational Boundaries, and Social Roles*, ed. Bruce Nissen, pp. 163–188. Armonk, NY: Sharpe.

Gay Stolberg, Sheryl, and Steven Greenhouse. 2009. "Pace of Change under Obama Frustrates Unions." *New York Times*, September 7, 2009.

Geary, Dan. 2001. "The 'Union of the Power and the Intellect': C. Wright Mills and the Labor Movement." *Labor History*, 42 (2): 327–345.

Georgakas, Dan. 1975. *Detroit, I Do Mind Dying: A Study in Urban Revolution.* New York: St. Martin's.

Gerber, Larry J. 1997. "Shifting Perspectives on American Exceptionalism: Recent Literature on American Labor Relations and Labor Politics." *Journal of American Studies*, 31 (2): 253–274.

Gerstle, Gary. 1986. "The Politics of Patriotism: Americanization and the Formation of the CIO." *Dissent* 33 (1): 84–92.

———. 1994. "The Protean Character of American Liberalism." *American Historical Review*, 99 (4): 1043–1073.

Geschwender, James A. 1977. *Class, Race, and Workers Insurgency: The League of Revolutionary Black Workers.* Cambridge: Cambridge University Press.

Gieske, Millard L. 1979. *Minnesota Farmer-Laborism: The Third-Party Alternative.* Minneapolis: University of Minnesota.

Gitlin, Todd. 1995. *The Twilight of Common Dreams: Why America Is Wracked by Culture Wars.* New York: Metropolitan Books, Henry Holt.

Goldberg, David J. 1988. *A Tale of Three Cities: Labor Organization and Protest in Paterson, Passaic, and Lawrence, 1916–1921.* New Brunswick, NJ: Rutgers University Press.

Goldfield, Michael. 1986. "Labor in American Politics—Its Current Weakness." *Journal of Politics*, 48 (February): 2–29.

———. 1989. "Worker Insurgency, Radical Organization, and New Deal Legislation." *American Political Science Review*, 83 (4): 1257–1282.

Goldstein, Robert J. 2010. "Response in

Labor History Symposium: Political Repression of the American Labor Movement during Its Formative Years—A Comparative Perspective." *Labor History*, 51 (2): 310–315.

Goluboff, Risa L. 2001. "The Thirteenth Amendment and the Lost Origins of Civil Rights." *Duke Law Journal*, 50 (6): 1609–1685.

Gompers, Samuel. 1892. "Organized Labor in the Campaign." *North American Review*, 155 (July): 91–97; reprinted in *The Samuel Gompers Papers*, Vol. 3, *Unrest and Depression, 1891–94*, eds. Stuart B. Kaufman and Peter J. Albert, pp. 200–204. Urbana: University of Illinois Press, 1989.

———, and Frank Morrison. 1902. *Meat vs. Rice: American Manhood against Asian Coolieism; Which Shall Survive?* Washington, DC: American Federation of Labor.

González, Francisco E., and Desmond S. King. 2003. "The United States as a Divided Democracy: Competing Interpretations." In *Governing America: The Politics of a Divided Democracy*, ed. Robert Singh, pp. 32–50. Oxford: Oxford University Press.

Gorz, André. 1967. *Strategy for Labor*. Boston: Beacon Press.

Gottlieb, Robert, Gerry Tenney, and David Gilbert. 1967. "Toward a Theory of Social Change in America." *New Left Notes*, May 22.

Graham, Ian. 2002. "It Pays to Be Union, U.S. Figures Show." January 2002, http://www/ilo.org/public/english/dialogue/actrav/publ/128/.

Green, James R. 1978. *Grass-Roots Socialism: Radical Movements in the Southwest, 1896–1943*. Baton Rouge: Louisiana State University Press.

———. 1980. *The World of the Worker: Labor in Twentieth-Century America*. New York: Hill & Wang.

———. 2000. *Taking History to Heart: The Power of the Past in Building Movements*. Amherst: University of Massachusetts.

Greene, Julie. 1998. *Pure and Simple Politics: The American Federation of Labor and Political Activism, 1881–1917*. Cambridge: Cambridge University Press.

Greenhouse, Steven. 2010a. "Deadlock Is Ending on Labor Board." *New York Times*, April 1, 2010.

———. 2010b. "Unions Hold a Rally to Protest Wall Street." *New York Times*, April 29, 2010.

———. 2010c. "Liberal Groups Planning to Rally on National Mall." *New York Times*, September 27, 2010.

———. 2010d. "Democrats Look to Clout of Unions as Vote Nears." *New York Times*, October 22, 2010.

———. 2010e. "Unions Fear Rollback of Rights Under Republicans." *New York Times*, November 1, 2010.

———. 2010f. "2 Unions' Backing Helps Chances of Trade Pact With South Korea." *New York Times*, December 9, 2010.

———. 2011a. "Strained States Turning to Laws to Curb Labor Unions." *New York Times*, January 3, 2011.

———. 2011b. "Unions Hope Attacks Nurture a Comeback." *New York Times*, March 5, 2011.

Greider, William. 2006. "The Future Is Now." *The Nation*, June 26, pp. 23–26.

———. 2009. *Come Home, America: The Rise and Fall (and Redeeming Promise) of Our Country*. New York: Rodale.

———. 2010. "The End of Free-Trade Globalization." *The Nation*, November 22, pp. 20–22, 24–25.

———. 2011. "Needles in a Haystack." *The Nation*, February 21, p. 8.

Griffith, Robert. 1989. "Forging America's Postwar Order: Domestic Politics and Political Economy in the Age of Truman." In *The Truman Presidency*, ed. Michael Lacey, pp. 57–88. New York: Cambridge University Press.

Grob, Gerard N. 1961. *Workers and Utopia: A Study of Ideological Conflict in the American Labor Movement, 1863–1900*. Chicago: Quadrangle Books.

Gross, James A. 1981. *The Reshaping of the National Labor Relations Board*. Albany, NY: SUNY Press.

Guarasci, Richard. 1980. *Theory and Prac-*

tice of American Marxism, 1957–70. Lanham, MD: Rowman & Littlefield.
Guérin, Daniel. 1987. *100 Years of Labor in the United States*. London: Pluto Press.
Guttsman, W.L. 1981. *The German Social Democratic Party, 1875–1933*. London: Allen & Unwin.
Halpern, Rick. 1997. *Down on the Killing Floor: Black and White Workers in Chicago's Packinghouse, 1904–1954*. Urbana: University of Illinois Press.
Hamby, Alonzo. 1973. *Beyond the New Deal: Harry S. Truman and American Liberalism*. New York: Oxford University Press.
Hanagan, Michael. 1984. "Response to Sean Wilentz, 'Against Exceptionalism: Class Consciousness and the American Labor Movement, 1790–1920.'" *International Labor and Working-Class History*, 26 (Fall): 31–36.
Hari, Johann. 2011. "The UK's Left-Wing Tea Party." *The Nation*, February 21, pp. 11–12, 14–15, 17–18.
Harris, Howell John. 1982. *The Right to Manage: Industrial Relations Policies of American Business in the 1940s*. Madison: University of Wisconsin Press.
Hartz, Louis. 1955. *The Liberal Tradition in America: An Interpretation of American Political Thought since the Revolution*. New York: Harcourt Brace.
Harvey, David. 2005. *A Brief History of Neoliberalism*. Oxford: Oxford University Press.
———. 2010. *The Enigma of Capital, and the Crises of Capitalism*. London: Profile Books.
Hasen, Richard. 2010. "Money Grubbers: The Supreme Court Kills Campaign Finance Reform." Slate, January 21, 2010, http://www.slate.com/id/2242209.
Haywood, William. 1966/1929. *The Autobiography of Big Bill Haywood*. New York: International Publishers.
Herod, Andrew. 2002. "Organizing Globally, Organizing Locally: Union Spatial Strategy in a Global Economy." In *Global Unions? Theory and Strategies of Organized Labour in the Global Political Economy*, ed. Jeffrey Harrod and Robert O'Brien, pp. 83–99. London: Routledge.

Hofstadter, Richard. 1972. *The Age of Reform: From Bryan to FDR*. New York: Knopf.
Horowitz, Carl. 2010. "Laborers to Leave Change to Win, Rejoin AFL-CIO." National Legal and Policy Center, August 17, 2010, http://nlpc.org.
Human Rights Watch. 2000. *Unfair Advantage: Freedom of Association in the United States under International Human Rights Standards*. New York: Human Rights Watch, http://www.hrw.org/reports/2000/uslabor.
Hurd, Richard, Ruth Milkman, and Lowell Turner. 2003. "Reviving the American Labour Movement: Institutions and Mobilization." *European Journal of Industrial Relations*, 9 (1): 99–117.
Husbands, C.T. 1976. "Introductory Essay." In *Why Is There No Socialism in the United States?* by Werner Sombart, trans. Patricia M. Hocking and C.T. Husbands; ed. C.T. Husbands, pp. xv–xxxvii. London and Basingstoke: Macmillan.
ICFTU (International Confederation of Free Trade Unions). 2002. "Freedom of Association and Effective Recognition of Right of Collective Bargaining." Document for the ILO Governing Body, 283rd Session, March 2002, http://www.ilo.org/public/english/standards/relm/gb/docs/gb283.
Jacobson, Gary. 2004. *The Politics of Congressional Elections*. 6th edition. New York: Pearson Longman.
Jacoby, Sanford M. 1997. *Modern Manors: Welfare Capitalism since the New Deal*. Princeton, NJ: Princeton University Press.
———. 2004. *Employing Bureaucracy: Managers, Unions, and the Transformation of Work in the 20th Century*. Mahwah, NJ: Erlbaum.
Jarvis, Craig. 2011. "Protesters Want Collective Bargaining Restored in N.C." *Charlotte Observer*, February 22, 2011, http://www.charlotteobserver.com/2011/02/22/2081948/protesters-want-collective-bargaining.html.
Jefferys, Steve. 1984. *Management and the Managed*. Cambridge: Cambridge University Press.

Johnson, Daniel. 2000. "'No Make-Believe Class Struggle': The Socialist Municipal Campaign in Los Angeles, 1911." *Labor History*, 41 (1): 25–45.

Johnson, Donald Bruce. 1978. *National Party Platforms*. Vol. 1, *1840–1956*. Rev. ed. Urbana: University of Illinois Press.

Johnston, David Cay. 2011. "Really Bad Reporting in Wisconsin: Who 'Contributes' to Public Workers' Pensions?" Tax.com, February 24, 2011, http://www.tax.com/taxcom/taxblog.nsf/Permalink/UBEN-8EDJYS?OpenDocument.

Joyce, Charles T. 1987. "Union Busters and Front-Line Supervisors: Restricting and Regulating the Use of Supervisory Employees by Management Consultants during Union Representation Election Campaigns." *University of Pennsylvania Law Review*, 135: 453–493.

Judis, John B. 1983. "Despite Growth, DSA Is Unsure of Its Political Role." *In These Times*, October 26–November 1, pp. 5–6.

Judt, Tony. 2005. *Postwar: A History of Europe since 1945*. New York: Penguin.

Kanter, Rosabeth Moss. 1984. *The Change Masters: Corporate Entrepreneurs at Work*. London: Allen & Unwin.

Karson, Marc. 1965. *American Labor Unions and Politics, 1900–1918*. Boston: Beacon Press.

Katznelson, Ira. 1978. "Considerations on Social Democracy in the United States." *Comparative Politics*, 11 (1): 77–99.

———. 1981. *City Trenches*. Chicago: University of Chicago Press.

———. 1989. "Was the Great Society a Lost Opportunity?" In *The Rise and Fall of the New Deal Order, 1930–1980*, ed. Steve Fraser and Gary Gerstle, pp. 185–211. Princeton, NJ: Princeton University Press.

———. 2005. *When Affirmative Action Was White: An Untold History of Racial Inequality in Twentieth-Century America*. New York: Norton.

Kaufman, Stuart B. 1973. *Samuel Gompers and the Origins of the American Federation of Labor, 1848–1896*. Westport, CT: Greenwood Press.

———, ed. 1986. *The Samuel Gompers Papers*. Vol. 1, *The Making of a Union Leader, 1850–86*. Westport, CT: Greenwood Press.

———, ed. 1987. *The Samuel Gompers Papers*. Vol. 2, *The Early Years of the American Federation of Labor, 1887–90*. Urbana: University of Illinois Press.

Kaufmann, Eric P. 2004. *The Rise and Fall of Anglo-America*. Cambridge, MA: Harvard University Press.

Kazin, Michael. 1995. "The Agony and Romance of the American Left." *American Historical Review*, 100 (December): 1488–1512.

———. 1998. *The Populist Persuasion: An American History*. Ithaca, NY: Cornell University Press.

———. 1999. "What Did Gompers Start?" *Labor History*, 40 (2): 189–192.

Keefe, Jeffrey H. 2010. "Debunking the Myth of the Over-compensated Public Employee." *EPI Briefing Paper #276*, September 15, 2010, http://epi.3cdn.net/8808ae41b085032c0b_8um6bh5ty.pdf.

Kelber, Harry. 2010. "'Change to Win' Was Doomed to Failure in Effort to Build a Rival Labor Federation." *Labor Educator*, August 20, 2010, http://www.laboreducator.org/lt100820.htm.

Kellner, Douglas. 1991. "Introduction to the Second Edition." In *One-Dimensional Man: Studies in the Ideology of Advanced Industrial Society*, by Herbert Marcuse, pp. xi–xxxviii. London: Routledge.

Kimeldorf, Howard. 1999. *Battling for American Labor: Wobblies, Craft Workers, and the Making of the Union Movement*. Berkeley: University of California Press.

———. 2005. "'Joe Hill Ain't Never Died': The Legacy of the Wobblies' Practical Syndicalism." *Working U.S.A.*, 8 (5): 545–554.

Kipnis, Ira. 1952. *The American Socialist Movement, 1897–1912*. New York: Columbia University Press.

Kirkpatrick, David D. 2007. "Use of Bundlers Raises New Risks for Campaigns." *New York Times*, August 31, 2007.

Klare, Karl. 1978. "Judicial Deradicaliza-

tion of the Wagner Act and the Origins of Modern Legal Consciousness, 1937–1941." *Minnesota Law Review*, 62: 265–339.
———. 1981. "Labor Law as Ideology: Towards a New Historiography of Collective Bargaining Law." *Industrial Relations Law Journal*, 4: 450–482.
Klein, Ezra. 2011. "In Wisconsin, the Real Struggle is Over Power." *Washington Post*, February 21, 2011.
Klein, Jennifer. 2008. "A New Deal Restoration: Individuals, Communities, and the Long Struggle for the Collective Good." *International Labor and Working-Class History*, 74 (1): 42–48.
Klein, Naomi. 2007. *The Shock Doctrine: The Rise of Disaster Capitalism*. New York: Metropolitan Books, Henry Holt.
Kramer, Leo. 1962. *Labor's Paradox — the American Federation of State, Council, and Municipal Employees, AFL-CIO*. New York: Wiley.
Krauthamer, Diane. 2010. "Workers Occupations & the Future of Radical Labor: An Interview with Noam Chomsky." *ZMagazine*, February 2010, http://www.zcommunications.org/worker-occupations-and-the-future-of-radical-labor-by-diane-krauthamer.
Kull, Steven. 2010. "Big Government Is Not the Issue." *Politico*, August 17, 2010, http://dyn.politico.com/printstory.cfm?uuid=80A864D6-18FE-70B2-....
Lafer, Gordon. 2008. "What's More Democratic Than a Secret Ballot? The Case for Majority Sign-Up." *Working U.S.A.*, 11 (1): 71–98.
Larson, Simeon, and Bruce Nissen, eds. 1987. *Theories of the Labor Movement*. Detroit: Wayne State University Press.
Laslett, John H.M. 1970. *Labor and the Left: A Study of Socialist and Radical Influences in the American Labor Movement, 1881–1927*. New York: Basic Books.
———. 1987. "Samuel Gompers and the Rise of American Business Unionism." In *Labor Leaders in America*, ed. Melvyn Dubofsky and Warren R. Van Tine, pp. 62–88. Urbana: University of Illinois Press.
Lazes, Peter, and Jane Savage. 1997. "New Unionism and the Workplace of the Future." In *Unions and Workplace Reorganization*, ed. Bruce Nissen, pp. 181–207. Detroit: Wayne State University Press.
Lebowitz, Michael A. 2010. *The Socialist Alternative: Real Human Development*. New York: Monthly Review Press.
Lesniewski, Jacob. 2011. "Yes, It Is Organizing: Workers Centers and the Labor Movement." ZNet, January 6, 2011, http://www.zcommunications.org/contents/175005/print.
Levenstein, Harvey A. 1981. *Communism, Anticommunism, and the CIO*. Westport, CT: Greenwood Press.
Levi, Margaret. 2003. "Organizing Power: The Prospects for an American Labor Movement." *Perspectives on Politics*, 1 (1): 45–68.
Levy, Peter. 1994. *The New Left and Labor in the 1960s*. Urbana: University of Illinois Press.
Lichtenstein, Nelson. 1977. "Ambiguous Legacy: The Union Security Problem during World War II." *Labor History*, 18 (2): 214–238.
———. 1982. *Labor's War at Home: The CIO in World War II*. New York: Cambridge University Press.
———. 1989. "From Corporatism to Collective Bargaining: Organized Labor and the Eclipse of Social Democracy in the Postwar Era." In *The Rise and Fall of the New Deal Order, 1930–1980*, ed. Steve Fraser and Gary Gerstle, pp. 122–152. Princeton, NJ: Princeton University Press.
———. 1995. *Walter Reuther: The Most Dangerous Man in Detroit*. New York: Basic Books.
———. 1998. "Roll the Union On: Rebuilding the Labor Movement." *Institute for Public Affairs*, October 18, p. 18.
———. 2002. *State of the Union: A Century of American Labor*. Princeton, NJ: Princeton University Press.
Litdke, Vernon L. 1985. *The Alternative Culture: Socialist Labor in Imperial Germany*. New York: Oxford University Press.
Lipset, Seymour M. 1998. "American Union Density in Comparative Perspec-

tive." *Contemporary Sociology*, 27 (2): 123–125.
———. 2000. "Still the Exceptional Nation?" *Wilson Quarterly*, 24 (1): 31–45.
———, and Gary Marks. 2000. *It Didn't Happen Here: Why Socialism Failed in the United States*. New York and London: Norton.
———, and Stein Rokkan. 1967. *Party Systems and Voter Alignments*. New York: Free Press.
Lipsitz, George. 1995. "The Possessive Investment in Whiteness: Racialized Social Democracy and the 'White' Problem in American Studies." *American Quarterly*, 47 (3): 369–387.
Liptak, Adam. 2009. "Supreme Court to Revisit 'Hillary' Documentary." *New York Times*, August 29, 2009.
———. 2010. "Justices, 5–4, Reject Corporate Spending Limit." *New York Times*, January 21, 2010.
Llewellyn, Frank, and Joseph Schwartz. 2009a. "Summers Says U.S. Not in Danger of Becoming Socialist State." *Wall Street Journal*, June 12, 2009.
———. 2009b. "Socialists Say: Obama Is No Socialist." *Chicago Tribune*, November 1, 2009.
Lowi, Theodore J. 1984. "Why Is There No Socialism in the United States? A Federal Analysis." *International Political Science Review*, 5 (4): 369–380.
Lydersen, Kari. 2009. *Revolt on Goose Island: The Chicago Factory Takeover, and What It Says about the Economic Crisis*. Brooklyn, New York: Melvillehouse.
Lynd, Alice, and Staughton Lynd. 1973. *Rank and File: Personal Histories by Working-Class Organizers*. Boston: Beacon Press.
Lynd, Staughton. 1973. "Blue-Collar Organizing: A Report on CEOHC." *Working Papers for a New Society*, 1 (1): 28–34.
———. 1992. *Solidarity Unionism: Rebuilding the Labor Movement from Below*. Chicago: Charles H. Kerr.
———, ed. 1996. *"We Are All Leaders": The Alternative Unionism of the Early 1930s*. Urbana: University of Illinois Press.
Maass, Alan. 2010. *The Case for Socialism*. Chicago: Haymarket Books.

McAlevey, Jane. 2011. "Labor's Last Stand." *The Nation*, March 7/14, pp. 22–26.
McAuliffe, Mary Sperling. 1978. *Crisis on the Left: Cold War Politics and American Liberals, 1947–1954*. Amherst: University of Massachusetts Press.
McCartin, Joseph A. 1999. "Power, Politics, and 'Pessimism of the Intelligence.'" *Labor History*, 40 (3): 345–349.
McKibbin, Ross. 1990. "Why Was There No Marxism in Great Britain?" In *The Ideologies of Class: Social Relations in Britain 1880–1950*, by Ross McKibbin, pp. 1–41. Oxford: Clarendon.
McQuaid, Kim. 1994. *Uneasy Partners: Big Business in American Politics, 1945–1990*. Baltimore, MD: Johns Hopkins University Press.
Majority Agenda Project. 2010. "A Call to All Sectors of Our Movements for Justice and Peace to Mobilize October 2." August 4, 2010, http://majorityagendaproject.org/go/print/node/95.
Malbin, Michael J. 2009. "Small Donors, Large Donors and the Internet: The Case for Public Financing after Obama." Working paper, published by the Campaign Finance Institute, Washington, DC.
Mallet, Serge. 1963. *La nouvelle classe ouvrière*. Paris: Éditions du Seuil.
———. 1975. *Essays on the New Working Class*. St. Louis, MO: Telos Press.
Mantsios, Gregory. 1998. "What Does Labor Stand For?" In *A New Labor Movement for the New Century*, ed. Gregory Mantsios, pp. 44–64. New York: Monthly Review Press.
Marable, Manning. 1996. *Beyond Black and White: Transforming African-American Politics*. New York: Verso.
Marcuse, Herbert. 1964. *One-Dimensional Man: Studies in the Ideology of Advanced Industrial Society*. Boston: Beacon Press.
Marks, Gary. 1989. *Unions in Politics: Britain, Germany, and the United States in the Nineteenth and Early Twentieth Century*. Princeton, NJ: Princeton University Press.
Marqusee, Mike. 2004. "Patriot Acts." *The Nation*, December 13, pp. 30–32, 34.
Martin, Jonathan, and Ben Smith. 2010.

"The Tea Party's Exaggerated Importance." *Politico*, April 22, 2010, http://dyn.politico.com/printstory.cfm?uuid=234CBD3C-18FE-70B2-....

Mason, Robert. 2003. "Political Parties and the Party System." In *Governing America: The Politics of a Divided Democracy*, ed. Robert Singh, pp. 94–108. Oxford: Oxford University Press.

Massey, Douglas S., and Nancy A. Denton. 1993. *American Segregation and the Making of the Underclass*. Cambridge, MA: Harvard University Press.

Maxon, Seth A. 2009. "Mobilized in Motor City: How Detroit DSA Works in the Democratic Party to Effect Change." *In These Times*, December 25, 2009, http://www.inthesetimes.com/article/5317/mobilized_in_motor_city/.

Mayer, Jane. 2010. "Covert Operations: The Billionaire Brothers Who Are Waging a War against Obama." *New Yorker*, August 30, 2010.

Mendonca, Lenny. 2006. "Shaking Up the Labor Movement: An Interview with the Head of the Service Employees International Union." *McKinsey Quarterly*, 1 (February): 53–60.

Messer-Kruse, Timothy. 1998. *The Yankee International: Marxism and the American Reform Tradition, 1848–1876*. Chapel Hill: University of North Carolina Press.

Milbank, Dana. 2010. "Michele Bachmann Leads the Tea Party." *Washington Post*, July 21, 2010.

Milkman, Ruth. 1991. "Labor and Management in Uncertain Times: Renegotiating the Social Contract." In *America at Century's End*, ed. Alan Wolfe, pp. 131–151. Berkeley: University of California Press.

———. 2006. *L.A. Story: Immigrant Workers and the Future of the U.S. Labor Movement*. New York: Sage.

Mills, C. Wright. 1948. *The New Men of Power: America's Labor Leaders*. New York: Harcourt, Brace.

———. 1962. *The Marxists*. New York: Dell.

———. 1963. *Power, Politics, and People: The Collected Essays*. New York: Ballantine.

Mishel, Lawrence, Jared Bernstein, and Heidi Shierholz. 2009. *The State of Working America, 2008/2009*. Ithaca, NY: ILR Press.

Mitchell, Greg. 1992. *The Campaign of the Century: Upton Sinclair's Race for Governor of California and the Birth of Media Politics*. New York: Random House.

Montgomery, David. 1972. *Beyond Equality: Labor and the Radical Republicans, 1862–1872*. New York: Vintage.

———. 1979. *Workers' Control in America*. Cambridge: Cambridge University Press.

———. 1983. "New Tendencies in Union Struggles and Strategies in Europe and the United States, 1916–1922." In *Work, Community and Power: The Experience of Labor in Europe and America, 1900–1925*, ed. James E. Cronin and Carmen Sirianni, pp. 88–116. Philadelphia: Temple University Press.

———. 1987. *The Fall of the House of Labor: The Workplace, the State, and American Labor Activism, 1865–1925*. New York: Cambridge University Press.

———. 1999. "What More to Be Done?" *Labor History*, 40 (3): 356–361.

Moody, Kim. 1997. *Workers in a Lean World: Unions in the International Economy*. New York: Verso.

———. 2003. "Review of Seymour Martin Lipset and Gary Marks, *It Didn't Happen Here: Why Socialism Failed in the United States*." *Historical Materialism*, 11 (4): 347–362.

———. 2007. *U.S. Labor in Trouble and Transition*. London and New York: Verso.

———. 2008. "The Party That Never Was. Review of Robin Archer: *Why Is There No Labor Party in the United States?*" *International Socialism*, 119 (Summer), http://www.isj.org.uk/index.php4?id=466&issue=119.

Moss, B.H. 1993. "Republican Socialism and the Making of the Working-Class in Britain, France, and the United States: A Critique of Thompsonian Culturalism." *Comparative Studies in Society and History*, 35 (2): 390–413.

Nader, Ralph. 2004. "The Crucial Legacy of Taft-Hartley: A Labor Day Call for Rights for Working People." *Counterpunch*, September 6, 2004.

The Nation. 2008. "Plutocracy Reborn." *The Nation*, June 30, pp. 24–25.

Nelson, Bruce. 2001. *Divided We Stand: American Workers and the Struggle for Black Equality*. Princeton, NJ: Princeton University Press.

Neuborne, Burt. 2011. "The Censorship Canard." *The Nation*, January 31, p. 23.

New Unionism. 2010. "Fifth International, Eh?" ZNet, December 14, 2010, http://www.ZCommunications.org/contents?174534/print.

Nichols, John. 2010. "Sorry, Glenn Beck. But King's 'Dream' is on the March in Detroit." *The Nation*, August 28, http://www.thenation.com.

———.2011. *The "S" Word: A Short History of an American Tradition...Socialism*. London: Verso.

Nissen, Bruce. 2002a. "The Labor Movement in a New Globalized Environment." In *Unions in a Globalized Environment: Changing Borders, Organizational Boundaries, and Social Roles*, ed. Bruce Nissen, pp. 3–13. Armonk, NY: Sharpe.

———. 2002b. "Concluding Thoughts; Internal Transformation." In *Unions in a Globalized Environment: Changing Borders, Organizational Boundaries, and Social Roles*, ed. Bruce Nissen, pp. 264–273. Armonk, NY: Sharpe.

Nolan, Mary. 1997. "Again Exceptionalism. Review Essay of Seymour M. Lipset, American Exceptionalism." *American Historical Review*, 102 (3): 769–774.

Nozick, Robert. 1977. *Anarchy, State and Utopia*. New York: Basic Books.

O'Brien, Michael. 2011. "Poll: Tax Hikes on Rich the First Step toward Balancing Budget." *The Hill*, January 3, 2011, http://thehill.com/blogs/blog-briefing-room/news/135639-poll-tax-hike.

Oestreicher, Richard. 1988. "Urban Working-Class Political Behavior and Theories of American Electoral Politics, 1870–1940." *Journal of American History*, 74 (4): 1257–1286.

———. 1998. "The Rules of the Game: Class Politics in Twentieth-Century America." In *Organized Labor and American Politics, 1894–1994: The Labor-Liberal Alliance*, ed. Kevin Boyle, pp. 19–50. Albany: State University of New York Press.

Ollman, Bertell. 1971. *Alienation: Marx's Conception of Man in Capitalist Society*. New York: Cambridge University Press.

Olssen, Erik. 1988. "The Case of the Socialist Party That Failed, or Further Reflections on an American Dream." *Labor History*, 29 (4): 416–449.

Ontiveros, Maria L. 2007. "Noncitizen Immigrant Labor and the Thirteenth Amendment: Challenging Guest Worker Programs." *University of Toledo Law Review*, 38 (3): 923–939.

Ouchi, William G. 1981. *Theory Z: How American Business Can Meet the Japanese Challenge*. Reading, MA: Addison-Wesley.

Panitch, Leo. 2001. *Renewing Socialism: Democracy, Strategy and Imagination*. Boulder, CO: Westview Press.

———, and Sam Gindin. 2008. "The Current Crisis: A Socialist Perspective." *The Bulletin of the Socialist Project*, October 9, 2008, http://www.marxsite.com/crisis_socialists.htlm.

Parenti, Michael. 2007. *Democracy for the Few*. 8th ed. Boston, MA: Wadsworth.

Parker, Mike. 1993. "Industrial Relations Myth and Shop-floor Reality: The 'Team Concept' in the Auto Industry." In *Industrial Democracy in America: The Ambiguous Promise*, ed. Nelson Lichtenstein and Howell John Harris, pp. 249–273. Cambridge: Cambridge University Press.

———, and Jane Slaughter. 1988. *Choosing Sides: Unions and the Team Concept*. Boston: South End Press.

———. 1997. "Advancing Unionism on the New Terrain." In *Unions and Workplace Reorganization*, ed. Bruce Nissen, pp. 208–225. Detroit: Wayne State University Press.

Pascale, Richard Tanner, and Anthony G. Athos. 1981. *The Art of Japanese Management: Applications for American Executives*. New York: Simon & Schuster.

Patterson, James T. 1996. *Grand Expectations: The United States, 1945–1974*. New York: Oxford University Press.

Pelling, Henry. 1963. *A History of British Trade Unionism*. London: Penguin.
_____. 1965. *Origins of the Labour Party*. 2nd ed. Oxford: Oxford University Press.
Perlman, Selig. 1928. *A Theory of the Labor Movement*. New York: Macmillan.
Peters, Thomas J., and Robert H. Waterman. 1982. *In Search of Excellence: Lessons from America's Best-Run Companies*. New York: Harper & Row.
Peterson, Larry. 1983. "The One Big Union in International Perspective: Revolutionary Industrial Unionism." In *Work, Community and Power: The Experience of Labor in Europe and America, 1900–1925*, ed. James E. Cronin and Carmen Sirianni, pp. 49–87. Philadelphia: Temple University Press.
Pew Research Center for the People & the Press. 2010. "A Political Rhetoric Test: 'Socialism' Not So Negative, 'Capitalism' Not So Positive." News Release, Washington, DC, May 4, 2010, http://pewresearch.org/pubs/1583/political-rhetoric-capitalism-socialism-militia-family-values-states-rights.
Phillips, Kevin. 1989. *The Politics of Rich and Poor: Wealth and the American Electorate in the Reagan Aftermath*. New York: Harper.
Phillips-Fein, Kim. 2009. *Invisible Hands: The Making of the Conservative Movement from the New Deal to Reagan*. New York: Norton.
Piore, Michael, and Charles Sabel. 1984. *The Second Industrial Divide: Possibilities for Prosperity*. New York: Basic Books.
Piven, Frances Fox. 1992. "Structural Constraints and Political Development: The Case of the American Democratic Party." In *Labor Parties in Postindustrial Societies*, ed. Francis Fox Piven, pp. 235–264. New York: Oxford University Press.
_____, and Richard Cloward. 1977. *Poor People's Movements: Why They Succeed, How They Failed*. New York: Pantheon.
_____. 2000a. "Does the Electoral Path Work for Labor?" *Working U.S.A.*, 4 (1): 9–18.
_____. 2000b. "Power Repertoires and Globalization." *Politics and Society*, 28 (3): 413–430.

Pizzolato, Nicola. 2004. "Workers and Revolutionaries at the Twilight of Fordism: The Breakdown of Industrial Relations in the Automobile Plants of Detroit and Turin, 1969–1973." *Labor History*, 45 (4): 419–443.
Pope, James G., Peter Kellman, and Ed Bruno. 2008. "The Employee Free Choice Act and a Long-Term Strategy for Winning Workers' Rights." *Working USA*, 11 (1): 125–144.
Popper, Karl. 1945. *The Open Society and Its Enemies*. Vol. 1, *The Spell of Plato*. London: Routledge.
_____. 1945. *The Open Society and Its Enemies*. Vol. 2, *The High Tide of Prophecy: Hegel, Marx, and the Aftermath*. London: Routledge.
Preis, Art. 1972. *Labor's Giant Step: The First Twenty Years of the CIO, 1936–1955*. New York: Pathfinder.
Purcell, Theodore Vincent. 1960. *Blue Collar Man: Patterns of Dual Allegiance in Industry*. Cambridge, MA: Harvard University Press.
Rasmussen Reports. 2009. "Just 53% Say Capitalism Better than Socialism." April 9, 2009, http://www.rasmussenreports.com/public_content/politics/general_politics/april_2009.
Ratner, Lizzy. 2011. "Boom Town and Bust City: A Tale of Two New Yorks." *The Nation*, February 14, pp. 11–14.
Reagan, Ronald. 1987. "Executive Order 12612 — Federalism." October 26, 1987, http://www.presidency.ucsb.edu/ws/index.php?pid=33607#axzz1TVgzXasi.
Reynolds, David. 2000. "Labor and the Third-Party Route." *Working U.S.A.*, 4 (1): 49–72.
Rich, Frank. 2010. "The Billionaires Bankrolling the Tea Party." *New York Times*, August 29, 2010.
Richie, Bob. 2007. "Failing Electoral College." *The Nation*, October 1, pp. 4–5.
Robinson, William I. 2008. *Latin America and Global Capitalism*. Baltimore, MD: Johns Hopkins University Press.
Roediger, David R. 2005. *Working toward Whiteness — How America's Immigrants Became White: The Strange Journey from*

Ellis Island to the Suburbs. New York: Basic Books.

Rogers, Joel E. 1984. "Divide and Conquer: The Legal Foundations of Postwar U.S. Labor Policy." Unpublished Ph.D. diss., Princeton University.

Rogin, Michael. 1974. "Radicalism and the Agrarian Tradition: Comment." In *Failure of a Dream? Essays in the History of American Socialism*, ed. John Laslett and Seymour Martin Lipset, pp. 135–164. Garden City, NY: Anchor/Doubleday.

Roosevelt, Franklin D. 1937 "Fireside Chat on Reorganization of the Judiciary." March 9, 1937, http://www.mhric.org/fdr/chat9.htlm.

Rorty, Richard. 1998. *Achieving Our Country: Leftist Thought in Twentieth-Century America*. Cambridge, MA: Harvard University Press.

Rose, Michael. 1988. *Industrial Behaviour*. 2nd ed. London: Penguin.

Rose, Richard. 1974. *Electoral Behavior: A Comparative Handbook*. New York: Free Press.

Rotunda, Ronald D. 1968. "The 'Liberal' Label: Roosevelt's Capture of a Symbol." *Public Policy*, 17: 377–408.

Salaman, Graeme. 1997. "Culturing Production." In *Production of Culture/Cultures of Production*, ed. Paul du Gay, pp. 236–272. London: Sage.

Sanders, Elizabeth. 1999. *Roots of Reform: Farmers, Workers, and the American State, 1877–1917*. Chicago: University of Chicago Press.

Saxton, Alexander. 1971. *The Indispensable Enemy: Labor and the Anti-Chinese Movement in California*. Berkeley: University of California Press.

Schaefer, Nancy A. 2009. "The Left Behind Series and Its Place within the American Evangelical Subculture." In *End of Days: Essays on the Apocalypse from Antiquity to Modernity*, ed. Karolyn Kinane and Michael A. Ryan, pp. 287–308. Jefferson, NC, and London: McFarland.

Schattschneider, Elmer E. 1942. *Party Government*. New York: Rinehart.

Schlesinger, Arthur M., Jr. 1988. *The Coming of the New Deal*. Boston: Houghton Mifflin.

Schlichter, Sumner H. 1947. *The Challenge of Industrial Relations*. Ithaca, NY: Cornell University Press.

Schneider, Dorothee. 1994. *Trade Unions and Community: The German Working Class in New York City, 1870–1900*. Urbana: University of Illinois Press.

Schram, Sanford F. 2003. "The Praxis of Poor People's Movements: Strategy and Theory in Dissensus Politics." apsanet.org, 1 (4): 1–4, www.apsanet.org.

Schrecker, Ellen. 1992. "McCarthyism and the Labor Movement: The Role of the State." In *The CIO's Left-Led Unions*, ed. Steve Rosswurm, pp. 139–157. New Brunswick, NJ: Rutgers University Press.

Seidler, Murray. 1961. "The Socialist Party and American Unionism." *Midwest Journal of Political Science*, 5 (3): 207–236.

Seitz, Virginia A. 1984. "Legal, Legislative and Managerial Responses to the Organization of Supervisory Employees in the 1940s." *American Journal of Legal History*, 28 (January): 218–235.

Selfa, Lance. 2008. *The Democrats: A Critical History*. Chicago: Haymarket Books.

———. 2010a. "Can the Right Stage a Comeback?" *International Socialist Review*, 69 (January–February), http://www.isreview.org/issues/69/rep-rightcomeback.shtml.

———. 2010b. "Does the Right Have a Future?" SocialistWorker.org, April 27, 2010, http://socialistworker.org/2010/04/27/does-the-right-have-a-future.

Sexton, Patricia Cayo. 1991. *The War on Labor and the Left: Understanding America's Unique Conservatism*. Boulder, CO: Westview Press.

Shalev, Michael, and Walter Korpi. 1980. "Working-Class Mobilization and American Exceptionalism." *Economic and Industrial Democracy*, 1 (1): 31–61.

Shannon, David A. 1967. *The Socialist Party of America*. Chicago: Quadrangle Paperbacks.

Shapiro, Stanley. 1971. "The Great War and Reform: Liberals and Labor 1917–1919." *Labor History*, 12 (3): 323–344.

———. 1985. "'Hand and Brain': The

Farmer-Labor Party of 1920." *Labor History*, 26 (3): 405–422.

Shawki, Ahmed. 2006. *Black Liberation and Socialism*. Chicago Haymarket Books.

Shor, Francis. 1999. "'Virile Syndicalism' in Comparative Perspective: A Gender Analysis of the IWW in the United States and Australia." *International Labor and Working-Class History*, 56 (3): 56–77.

Silver, Beverly J. 2003. *Forces of Labor: Workers' Movements and Globalization Since 1870*. Cambridge: Cambridge University Press.

Sims, Beth. 1992. *Workers of the World Undermined: American Labor's Role in U.S. Foreign Policy*. Boston: South End Press.

Slaughter, Jane. 1999. "The New AFL-CIO: No Salvation from on High for the Working Stiff." In *The Transformation of U.S. Unions*, ed. Ray M. Tillman and Michael S. Cummings, pp. 49–60. Boulder, CO: Lynne Rienner.

_____, ed. 2005. *A Troublemaker's Handbook 2: How to Fight Back Where You Work — and Win!* Detroit: Labor Notes.

Smith, Neil. 2005. *The Endgame of Globalization*. New York and London: Routledge.

Smith, Sharon. 1992. "Twilight of the American Dream." *International Socialism*, 54 (3): 3–43.

_____. 2003. "Review of Nelson Lichtenstein, State of the Union: A Century of American Labor." *Historical Materialism*, 11 (4): 429–444.

_____. 2006. *Subterranean Fire: A History of Working-Class Radicalism in the United States*. Chicago: Haymarket Books.

Socialist Party. 1910. *Proceedings of the First National Congress, 1910*. Chicago: Socialist Party.

Solomon, Mark. 2010. "One Nation on 10/2/2010: A Major Step Forward." October 11, 2010, http://majorityagendaproject.org/go/print/node/123.

Sombart, Werner. 1906. *Warum gibt es in den Vereinigten Staaten keinen Sozialismus?* Tübingen: Verlag von J.C.B. Mohr (Paul Siebeck).

_____. 1976. *Why Is There No Socialism in the United States?* trans. Patricia M. Hocking and C.T. Husbands; ed. C.T. Husbands. London and Basingstoke: Macmillan.

Special Task Force to the Secretary of Health, Education, and Welfare. 1973. *Work in America*. Cambridge, MA: MIT Press.

Stagner, Ross. 1954. "Dual Allegiance as a Problem in Modern Society: A Symposium." *Personnel Psychology*, 7 (1): 41–80.

Stark, Mike. 2010. "Reclaiming the Dream from Glenn Beck." SocialistWorker.org, August 30, 2010, http://socialistworker.org/2010/08/30/reclaiming-the-dream.

Stedman Jones, Gareth. 1971. *Outcast London: Study in the Relationship between Classes in Victorian Society*. London: Penguin.

Steinmo, Sven H. 1994. "American Exceptionalism Reconsidered: Culture or Institutions?" In *The Dynamics of American Politics: Approaches and Interpretations*, ed. Lawrence C. Dodd and Calvin Jillson, pp. 106–131. Boulder, CO: Westview Press.

Stern, Andy. 2008. "Labor's New Deal." *The Nation*, April 7, p. 26.

Stevens, Beth. 1990. "Labor Unions, Employee Benefits, and the Privatization of the American Welfare State." *Journal of Policy History*, 2 (3): 233–260.

Street, Paul. 2010a. "Resisting Left Invisibility in the Age of Obama." *ZNet*, July 24, 2010, http://zcommunications.org/resisting-left-invisibility-in-the-age-of-obama-by-paul-street.

_____. 2010b. *The Empire's New Clothes: Barack Obama in the Real World of Power*. Boulder, CO: Paradigm Publishers.

_____. 2010c. "The Empire's New Clothes." *ZNet*, August 29, 2010, http://www.zcommunications.org/contents/170999/print.

_____. 2011. "State (of) Capitalist Absurdity: Reflections Before and After Obama's State of the Union Address." *ZNet*, January 28, 2011, http://www.zcommunications.org/contents/175465/print.

_____, and Anthony DiMaggio. 2010. "What 'Populist Uprising'? Part 1: Facts and Reflections on Race, Class, and the Tea Party Movement," *Monthly Review*, April 21, 2010, http://mrzine.monthlyreview.org/2010/sd210410.html.

Stromquist, Shelton. 1987. *A Generation of Boomers: The Pattern of Railroad Labor Conflict in Nineteenth-Century America*. Urbana: University of Illinois Press.

_____. 1990. "United States of America." In *The Formation of Labor Movements, 1870–1914*, ed. Marcel van der Linden and Jürgen Rojahn, pp. 543–577. Leiden: Brill.

Sum, Andrew, and Ishwar Khatiwada. 2010. "Labor Underutilization Problems of U.S. Workers across Household Income Groups at the End of the Great Recession: A Truly Great Depression among the Nation's Low Income Workers amidst Full Employment among the Most Affluent." Paper prepared for the C.S. Mott Foundation, Flint, Michigan. Boston, MA: Center for Labor Market Studies, Northeastern University, http://www.massworkforce.com/documents/LaborUnderutilizationProblemsofU_000.pdf

Sumner, William Graham. 1883. *What Social Classes Owe to Each Other*. New York: Harper & Brothers.

Sustar, Lee. 2009. "U.S. Labor in the Crisis. Resistance or Retreat?" *International Socialist Review*, 66 (July), http://www.isreview.org/issues/66/feat-USLabor.shtml.

_____. 2011. "Class War in Wisconsin." SocialistWorker.org, February 18, 2011, http://socialistworker.org/print/2011/02/18/Wisconsin.

Swados, Harvey. 1957. *On the Line*. Boston: Atlantic/Little, Brown.

Thompson, Heather A. 2001. *Whose Detroit? Politics, Labor, and Race in a Modern American City*. Ithaca, NY: Cornell University Press.

Tomasky, Michael. 1996. *Left for Dead: The Life, Death, and Possible Resurrection of Progressive Politics in America*. New York: Free Press.

Tomlins, Christopher L. 1985a. "The New Deal, Collective Bargaining, and the Triumph of Industrial Pluralism." *Industrial & Labor Relations Review*, 39 (1): 19–34.

_____. 1985b. *The State and the Unions: Labor Relations, Law, and the Organized Labor Movement in America, 1880–1960*. London: Cambridge University Press.

Vale, Vivian. 1971. *Labour in American Politics*. London: Kegan Paul.

van Elteren, Mel. 2003. "Workers' Control and the Struggles against 'Wage Slavery' in the Gilded Age and After." *Journal of American Culture*, 26 (2): 188–203.

Van Wezel Stone, Katherine. 1981. "The Post-war Paradigm in American Labor Law." *Yale Law Journal*, 90 (7): 1509–1580.

Victor, Kirk. 1994. "Friend or Enemy?" *National Journal*, November 5, pp. 2575–2587.

Vogel, David. 1978. "Why Businessmen Distrust Their State: The Political Consciousness of American Corporate Executives." *British Journal of Political Science*, 8 (1): 45–78.

_____. 1989. *Fluctuating Fortunes: The Political Power of Business in America*. New York: Basic Books.

Voss, Kim. 1993. *The Making of American Exceptionalism: The Knights of Labor and Class Formation in the Nineteenth Century*. Ithaca, NY: Cornell University Press.

Waldinger, Roger, and Michael I. Lichter. 2003. *How the Other Half Works: Immigration and the Social Organization of Labor*. Berkeley and Los Angeles: University of California Press.

Walker, Pat, ed. 1979. *Between Labor and Capital*. Boston: South End Press.

Wallerstein, Michael, and Bruce Western. 2000. "Unions in Decline? What Has Changed and Why." *Annual Review of Political Science* 3: 355–377.

Wallsten, Peter, and Brady Dennis. 2011. "Democratic Governors Try to Enlist Labor's Help in Dealing with Budget Crisis." *Washington Post*, February 25, 2011.

Warren, Dorien. 2007. "The Changing Climate for Union Organizing at the Turn of the Millennium." New York: Columbia University, Institute for Social and Economic Research and Policy, Fall 2007, http://www.iserp.columbia.edu/news/articles/un.

Waterman, Peter. 2010. "Five, Six, Many New Internationals! (Eight Reflections on a Fifth International)." *Links*, March 3, 2010, http://links.org.au/node/1560.

Weiler, Paul. 1983. "Promises to Keep: Securing Workers' Right to Self-Organization under the NLRA." *Harvard Law Review*, 96 (June): 1769–1827.

———. 1984. "Striking a New Balance: Freedom of Contract and the Prospects for Union Representation." *Harvard Law Review*, 98 (December): 351–420.

Weinstein, James. 1984. *The Decline of Socialism in America, 1912–1925*. New Brunswick, NJ: Rutgers University Press.

———. 2003. *The Long Detour: The History and Future of the American Left*. Boulder, CO: Westview Press.

Weir, Robert E. 1996. *Beyond Labor's Veil: The Culture of the Knights of Labor*. University Park: Pennsylvania State University Press.

Weir, Stan. 2004. *Singlejack Solidarity*. Minneapolis: Minneapolis University Press.

Widick, B.J. 1989. *Detroit: City of Class and Race Violence*. Detroit: Wayne State University Press.

Williams, Linda Faye. 2003. *The Constraint of Choice: The Legacies of White Skin Privilege in America*. University Park: Pennsylvania State University Press.

Wilpert, Gregory. 2009. "What Might Be 21st Century Socialism?" ZNet, June 23, 2009, http://www.zcommunications.org/contents/58936/print.

Winter, Nicholas J.G. 2006. "Beyond Welfare: Framing and the Racialization of White Opinion on Social Security." *American Journal of Political Science*, 50 (2): 400–420.

Working America and the AFL-CIO. 2010. *Sending Jobs Overseas: The Cost to America's Economy and Working Families*. Washington, DC: Working America—AFL-CIO.

Zernicke, Kate, and Carl Hulse. 2010. "At Lincoln Memorial, a Call for Religious Rebirth." *New York Times*, August 28, 2010.

Zeskind, Leonard. 2010. Presentation on the Tea Party to the NAACP National Convention, July 11, 2010, http://lawprofessors.typepad.com/immigration/2010/07/leonard-zeskind.

Zieger, Robert H. 1986. *American Workers, American Unions, 1920–1985*. Baltimore, MD: Johns Hopkins University Press.

———. 1995. *The CIO: 1935–1955*. Chapel Hill: University of North Carolina Press.

———. 2007. *For Jobs and Freedom: Race and Labor in America since 1865*. Lexington: University Press of Kentucky.

Zinn, Howard. 2003. *A People's History of the United States, 1492–Present*. New York: HarperCollins.

ZMagazine—various contributors. 2010. "Searching for a Democratic Alternative: A New International?" April 2010, http://zcommunications.org/searching-for-a-democratic-alternative-by-various-contributors.

Index

A. Philip Randolph Institute (AFL-CIO) 116
abolition of sweatshops 46
acceptance of empire by U.S. trade unions 152
accumulation by dispossession 187, 211n29
affirmative action 110
Afghanistan 152; war 153, 176
AFL *see* American Federation of Labor
AFL-CIO *see* American Federation of Labor-Congress of Industrial Organizations
AFL-CIO News 147
Africa 138, 200n8
African American Free Labor Institute (AAFLI) 207n2
African Americans 39, 48, 59, 66, 74, 90–91, 95, 100, 118, 122, 125, 143, 147, 161, 197n2, 203n7, 210n19; black activists' response to AFL-CIO reorganization and CTW split-off 134–135; and black radical movements in auto industry 115–117; and (dis)enfranchisement 12, 19, 23–24; and exclusion from New Deal programs 93–94; and ingrained patterns of racial discrimination within AFL-CIO 112–113; and responses to illegal immigration 137; and War on Poverty 109–110; and union-mindedness 130–131, 135; *see also* black workers
Age Discrimination in Employment Act 111
agrarian radicals 38, 46, 45, 61
agrarian socialism 62
agricultural workers 59, 93, 112, 155
airport security employees 162
Akron, Ohio 59, 81; rubber workers' labor actions 198n14
Alameda Corridor 140, 203n9
Alaska 209n10
Albert, Michael 192n8, 211n32, 212n33
Alesina, Alberto 13
alienation in the work setting 114–115, 200n6
Alinsky, Saul 139
Allen, Steve 201n15
Allende, Salvador 207n1
Ali, Tariq 192n8
Alliance for Fair Employment (CAFE) 138
alternatives to electoral trajectory 8, 171–175

Amalgamated Associates of Iron, Steel, and Tin Workers 51
Amalgamated Clothing and Textile Workers Union (ACTWU) 54, 59, 65, 67, 78, 165, 196n24
Amalgamated Transit Union (ATU) 204n18
Amberg, Stephen 106
America@Work 147
"America Needs a Raise" campaign (AFL-CIO) 203n5
American Action 105
American Bankers Association 144
American Civil Liberties Union (ACLU) 84, 198n9
American Commonwealth Federation (ACF) 79
American enterprise: and the ever rising tide of goods 165
American Enterprise Association 105
American Enterprise Institute 121
American exceptionalism 4, 188; labor exceptionalism 3–4
American Federation of Government Employees (AFGE) 144, 147
American Federation of Labor (AFL) 6, 41, 43, 47, 57, 59–60, 62–64, 68–70, 80–81, 84–85, 105–106, 164, 170, 195n14, 196n16, 196n20, 198n5, 198n7, 199n18, 203n6, 203n12; AFL advocates of left-wing politics 52–55; AFL-conservative alliance 89; Bill of Grievances 53, 67; constitutional amendments barring Communists from holding office 66; and de facto alliance with Democratic Party 54; Executive Council 45, 50, 53, 66; and hypocrisy toward race 44; internecine fighting with CIO 81, 86; as labor arm of U.S. foreign policy 163; leadership 39–40, 50, 52, 55, 76, 86, 96–97, 153, 170; membership 39, 65; organizational logic of AFL politics pre-World War I 50–52; Pennsylvanian Federation 55; and political alliances with city machines 50–51; pro-AFL congressmen 89; Progressive AFL officials 67; "reward friends and punish enemies" strategy 38, 40, 51, 53, 96; and sectional and interest groups 92;

231

Socialist- and Republican-leaning members 54; and voluntarism 50, 52, 195n10
American Federation of Labor-Congress of Industrial Organizations (AFL-CIO) 7, 113, 122, 125, 139, 141, 150, 157–158, 163–164, 166, 184, 203n5, 203n10, 203n1–12, 205n24, 207n2, 208n10; business-friendly participative style 132; Center for Workplace Participation 132; changed communication strategies 147–148; continued support of Democrats 148–149, 170; and CTW split-off 142–143; Department of Public Affairs 202n12; elective pragmatism 132; Executive Council 131, 133–134, 145, 200n3; internal disagreement about WTO 153; leadership 112, 124, 134, 144–145; lobby against Landrum-Griffin Act 108; local affiliates' lack of cooperation 140; modern pattern of political intervention 106; new reformist leadership 7, 131–132, 140; PAC contributions and expenditures 148–149; political campaigns 133–134; protectionist stance 153–154; reversal of position toward undocumented workers 135–136; virtual invisibility in public sphere 145
American Federation of State, County, and Municipal Employees (AFSCME) 120, 126, 130–131, 134, 158, 176, 204n18; District Council 37 (New York City) 204n15; Local 1733: 111
American Federation of Teachers (AFT) 130, 204n18
American Institute for Free Labor Development (AIFLD) 163, 207n2
American Labor Party (ALP) (New York State) 67, 78, 81, 91
American liberalism 70–72
American Liberty League 181
American Medical Association (AMA) 202n2
American Motors 199n2
American nationalism 19
American Railroad Employers and Investors Association 51
American Railway Union (ARU) 47, 60
American Rights at Work 158
American Security Council 105
American Workers Party (AWP) 197n3, 198n5
Americanism 100
Americans for Prosperity 210n22
Americans with Disabilities Act 200n5
Amlie, Thomas R. 79
amnesty for undocumented workers 136
anarchism/anarchists 36, 45, 194n2
anarcho-syndicalism 36
Anglophone countries see English-speaking countries
Anglo-Protestant rural districts 24
antebellum era 30
anti-capitalist left: and alliances with rural and peasant movements 186; and transnational alliances 8, 187; and transnational focus on inter-state system 185–186
anti-colonial struggles 101
anti-communism 95, 97, 124, 149, 163; labor movements 99; literature 104; purges of CIO unions 99–100
anti-corporate populism of third-party politics 167
anti-corporate social movements 168, 183–184
anti-fascism 100
anti-fusion law 193n10
anti-immigrant prejudice 191
anti-imperialism 1, 187
anti-labor legislators 85
anti-lynching bill 82
anti-monopolism 30
anti-socialism 39; Catholics 39; labor leaders 163; laws in Germany 194n14; propaganda 3
anti-statism 58, 166
anti-strike laws 159
anti-unionism 3; of alliance of northern Republicans and southern Democrats 107–108; business consultants and union busting 122; of corporations and their political allies 104–105, 121–122, 135, 157–158; open-shop drive 166
anti-war movement 106, 122, 164, 184; anti-Iraq war rally 175
Antlers, Oklahoma 193n3
apparel industries 75
Apple 194n17
Arab Americans and Arabs 136
Archer, Robin 47
Argentina 211n28
aristocrats of labor 39, 43
Arizona 196n19
Arma, Kansas 193n3
Armey, Dick 210n17, 210n22
Armour Packing 199n2
arms industry 112
Aronowitz, Stanley 70, 84, 97, 119, 199n16, 201n14
artisans 12, 29, 45, 55
Asia 138, 187, 200n8
Asian American Free Labor Institute (AAFLI) 207n2
Asian Pacific American Labor Alliance (APALA) 131
Asians 39, 135, 197n2, 203n7
assaults on union bureaucracy: by rank-and-file unionists 107–108, 119–120; by the right 106–108
Association of Catholic Trade Unionists (ACTU) 100
"at will" employment doctrines 125
AT&T 121
austerity plans 173
Australia 15–16, 19, 36, 50, 69, 202n1
Australian ballot (secret ballot) 24
Australian Labor Party 16
Austria 20, 302n1
automobile industry 77, 80, 92, 151; assembly 112; bailout 2; production 130; transplants in U.S. (German- and Japanese-owned) 149, 201n19; workers' retiree health care trust fund 141
autogestion 117

Index

automation: and implications on work satisfaction 114
Autunno Caldo 120

Bachmann, Michele 2, 182
bakeries 107
Bakers' Union 46, 65
Bangkok revolt of 1968 211*n*28
bank bailouts 2
Bank of America 121, 191*n*2, 207*n*34
Barber, Kathleen 193*n*5
Bechtel 122
Beck, Glenn 2, 175–176, 181
Beijing 153
Belgium 193*n*6, 199*n*18, 202*n*1
Bell, Daniel 96
Berger, Victor L. 62, 193*n*3, 196*n*18–19
Berkeley, California 193*n*3
Berry, George 196*n*20
big business 32, 170
Billancourt 113
biopiracy 211*n*30
Bipartisan Campaign Reform Act (BCRA) 33–35, 134
Black/Brown Alliance 138
black-brown labor coalitions 137
black freedom movement 99, 107
Black Power movement 116–117, 200*n*7; and Third World revolutions 200*n*8
black workers 7, 43, 113, 115–117, 130–131, 133–135, 160, 180; *see also* African Americans
Black Workers for Justice (BWFJ) 138
Blackburn, Robin 49
blacks *see* African Americans
Blauner, Robert 114, 200*n*6
Bloomberg, Michael 204*n*15
blue-collar work 125; "blue-collar blues" 114; dual allegiance of 105; municipal employment 126; white workers 110, 204*n*16; workers 105, 130, 162
Boehner, John 182
Boeing 202*n*3
Bohemian female tenement workers (New York) 42
Bolivarian Revolution 207*n*4
Bolshevik-style revolution in U.S., fear of 72
boot and shoe workers 55
border-based human rights networks 136
Boston, Massachusetts 29, 132, 194*n*2, 196*n*18; office workers 113
bourgeois political parties 4, 28
"bourgeois" vs. "post-bourgeois" values 114
boycotts 97, 133; Coca-Cola boycott 204*n*20
Boyle, Tony 199*n*3
Bracero program 112, 136
Brazil 113
Brecher, Jeremy 119, 201*n*14
Brewers/Brewery Workmen's Union 38–39, 54–55, 65, 69
Bricklayers Union 65
Bridgeport, Connecticut 196*n*16
Bridgestone Firestone 150
Briggs Local 212 198*n*14

Britain 19–21, 36, 38, 40–41, 46, 50, 54, 62, 64–65, 67, 69, 83, 91, 93, 114, 183–184, 194*n*1, 202*n*1
British guild socialists 72
British shop stewards' movement 57
British trade unions 4, 53, 99
Brody, David 83
"broker state" 73
Bronfenbrenner, Kate 151
Bronner, Stephen Eric 185
Bronx, New York 70
Brotherhood of Maintenance of Way Employees (BMWE) 144, 146
Browder, Earl 88
Brown, Jerry 206*n*29
Brown v. Board of Education of Topeka 196*n*22
Brownsville (eastern Brooklyn), New York City 70
Bryan, William Jennings 30–31, 53–54, 166
Brylane 151
Buckalew, Charles 19
Buckley v. Valeo (1976) 33
Buenos Aires uprising (2001–2002) 211*n*28
Buffet, Warren 181
building trades unions 48, 50–51, 54, 66, 141
"bundling" 31–33, 165–166
Bush, George W. 33, 157–158, 168; administration 2, 142, 177, 182, 191*n*2, 209*n*10
"Bush Pioneers" 33
Business Roundtable 32, 121
business unions 59, 104
Butte, Montana 193*n*3
Byrnes, James F. 90, 198*n*15

California 19, 25, 68, 198*n*6, 206*n*29
California Nurses Association (CNA) 144
Calvert, Gregory 117–118, 200-n12
Calverton, V.F. 197*n*3
Canada 19, 21, 69, 111, 113, 202*n*1; Canadian labor law 158
Cannon, James P. 197*n*3
capital accumulation: from 1870s through early 1890s 48
capitalist globalization 185; *see also* corporate globalization; economic globalization
Caracas 211*n*33
Caribbean 138, 151
Carmichael, Stokely, 115, 200*n*7
Carpenters' Union 40, 42, 65
Carter, Jimmy (James E.) 201*n*17
Carter administration 124, 156
Castro, Fidel 200*n*8
Catholics 24, 27–28, 39, 82, 110; clergy's hostility to socialism 39; Catholic hierarchy 52; and Cold War jingoism 100; unions and workers' associations in Europe 71; working class 29, 100, 110
Center for Immigration Studies (CIS) 137
Center for the Study of American Business 121
center-left views of majority of Americans 3, 8, 182–183
Central America 136, 138, 151–152

234 Index

Central Intelligence Agency (CIA) 99, 163; CIA-funded propaganda and unionism 207n1–2
central labor councils (CLCs) 7, 132, 139–140, 186, 203n6
Change to Win (CTW) 134–135, 141–143, 149, 153, 158, 166, 203n10; and its PCA 149
Charleston, South Carolina 204n17
Chartist movement 15
Chávez, Hugo 211n32, 212n33
Chester, Eric 63, 68, 167, 207n4
Chevy Vega plant 114
Chicago, Illinois 44, 47, 54, 94, 115, 137, 144, 161, 175, 194n2, 207n3
Chicago Federation of Labor (CFL) 65
Chicanos 112, 143, 188; farmers 112
child labor laws 181
Chile 113
China 153–154, 187, 211n31
Chinese workers 59; cigar makers 43
Chomsky, Noam 176–177, 182, 211n33
Christensen, Parley Parker 66
Christian Democracy in Europe 199n18
Christian right 27, 122
Chrysler Corporation 115, 141–142, 200n10, 201n17
Cigar Makers' International Union (CMIU): Local 144 40–43
Cigar Workers Union 65
Cincinnati, Ohio 193n5
CIO see Congress of Industrial Organizations
Cisco 194n17
Citizens for a Sound Economy 210n22
Citizens United v. Federal Election Commission 34–35, 209n14
city elections 14; in Los Angeles (1911) 195
City Group 191n2
civil rights: movement 12, 99, 106, 110, 112, 115, 164, 171, 176, 184–185; and unionizing impulse 111
civil rights legislation 11, 122; Civil Rights Act (1964) 110–111; Civil Rights Act (1991) 206n30; labor-infused tradition 159–161
civil service rules 126
Civil War 4, 12, 18, 67; expenditures of 49
Clarity Caucus 78
class: class-based political grievances 14–15; class-based politics 50; class conflict 4; class interest 172; class struggle 186; "class struggle unionism" 77, 169; fragmentation of collective class identity 74; international solidarity 152
class consciousness 186; labor movement 6; in the working class 74
Clean Clothes Campaign 150–151
Cleveland, Grover 80, 196n17, 207n3
Cleveland, Ohio 81, 94, 144
clientelist local parties 12; *see also* political machines
Clinton, Bill (William Jefferson) 208n5
Clinton administration 144–145, 157, 191n2; health insurance plan 145
Cloth, Hat and Cap Makers Union 59

Cloward, Richard A. 172–174
coal fields 75; coal mining 21, 130
coal miners 45, 69; Coal Miners' Union 198n12
coalition governments 22–23
Coalition of Black Trade Unionists (CBTU) 116, 120, 131, 133–135
Coalition of Labor Union Women (CLUW) 120, 131
coalition of railroad unions 67
Coeur d'Alene, Idaho 193n3
Cold War 19, 93, 97, 99–100, 112, 152, 163–164; consensus 99; jingoism 100; its legacy 152
Cole, G.D.H. 72
Colfax, Schuyler 195n7
collective action 5; power to disrupt capitalism 186
collective bargaining 3, 85, 92, 96–97, 107, 111, 139, 155, 158, 161, 202n1, 205n25, 205–206n28, 210n19; firm-centered 101–102; focus 170; public sector 126, 130–131, 156–158
Colombia 204n20, 205n22
Committee for Economic Development 103
Committee for Industrial Organization 68; *see also* Congress of Industrial Organizations (CIO)
Committee on Political Education (COPE), AFL-CIO 106
Commonwealth Federation: Oregon 27, 79, 81; Washington 27, 79
communications workers 162
Communications Workers of America (CWA) 150, 162, 202n3, 204n18, 204n20, 204n22
Communist League of America (CLA) 198n9
Communist Party USA (CPUSA) 78, 92, 96, 99–101, 196n24, 198n7; army of Communist organizers 79; election of two members in New York City council 193n5; factory cells 79, 197n5; plant daily papers 79; Popular Front phase 198n5; ultra-sectarian Third Period 197n5; *see also* Communists
Communists 75, 84, 90, 95–96, 99–101, 105, 112, 163, 197n4; leadership to social-liberal movements 99; *see also* Communist Party USA
community-based organizing 138; linkages with progressive unions 139
community unionism 160
company unions 82–83, 104
compulsory education 46
concessionary bargaining 141–142, 166
Conference for Progressive Labor Action 197n3
Conference for Progressive Political Action (CPPA) 67
Congress of Industrial Organizations (CIO) 7, 31, 68, 70, 76, 80–82, 84–85, 92, 94–95, 103, 105–106, 116, 134, 163, 196n17, 197n2, 197n4, 198n11; anti-communist statutes 100; bargaining 170; bureaucracy 100; CIO-style bargaining units 84, unionism 86, 93; ethnic mobilizations in 1930s 133; Executive Board 90; expulsion of Communist-led unions 100–101; integration into New Deal coalition 79; leadership 77–78, 86, 89–90, 96–97, 99, 170;

its left-wing unions 104; membership 100; Murray-Hillman leadership 89; proposal for Economic Bill of Rights 90; semi-institutional alliance with Democrats 96
Congress of Industrial Organizations Political Action Committee (CIO-PAC) 89–90, 95–96
Congress of Racial Equality (CORE) 92
congressional elections 31, 170, 185
Conneaut, Ohio 193n3
Connecticut 29, 209n12
conservative southern Democrats: alliance with northern Republicans 11–12, 24, 27, 92, 96, 107–108
conservative syndicalism 40
construction industry/trades 107, 135, 140, 142–143; construction trade unions 112
consumer boycott 43
consumer capitalism 110
Consumers League 133
Coolidge, Calvin 196n22
Coors, Joseph 122
corporate: culture movement 7, 126–128; educational agenda 175; flight 151; fraud 187; hostility toward regulatory state and unionism 93; influence on U.S. political system 31–35, 170; opposition to expansion of the New Deal order 7, 103–105; unionism 142; welfare 2
corporate campaign contributions 31, 35
Corporate Campaigns Inc. 204n20
corporate globalization 8, 149–154, 164, 166, 177, 185–186' labor's responses to 149–155
corporations: assigned legal status of "persons" (U.S. Supreme Court 1886) 49; mergers and acquisitions 187
corporatism 75
court: injunctions against labor 40, 53, 86, 159; invalidation 11; packing plan 193n1
courts, U.S. 10, 18, 50
Cowie, Jefferson 112
craft unionism/unions 6, 39–40, 48, 50, 62, 67, 70, 84, 131, 194n1, 195n13; and racism against blacks 66; and technological change 55; *see also* unionism/unions, exclusive
Creating American Jobs and Ending Offshoring Act 205n24
credit system 187
Croly, Herbert 72
cross-border: union initiatives and alliances 8, 150; worker solidarity 196
cross-class third party 167
cross-district school busing 110
CTW *see* Change to Win
Cuba 211n31
cultural cohesion: 99–100
cultural-religious counter-offensive 122
Cuomo, Andrew 206n29
Customs and Border Protection (CPB) 136
cutbacks in public relief 82

Daily Mail 184
Daley, Richard M. 175

Danbury Hatters case 53
Davidson, Carl 117
Davin, Eric Leif 81
Davis, David 30
Davis, John W. 196n22
Davis, Mike 80–81, 100, 120, 192n8, 201n14
day laborers 138
Dean, Howard 168
debate about establishing a labor party (1894): either-or-discourse in 40–41, 48
Debs, Eugene V. 54, 60, 63–64, 66, 167–168, 195n11, 195n13
Debsians: and anti-AFL stance 63
Deep South 94
defiant Americanism 39
degradation of work 128
deindustrialization 186
Delaware 209n12
De Leon, Daniel 45, 60, 195n13
Democratic Leadership Council (DLC) 208n5
democratic management of industry and commerce 65
Democratic National Committee 147, 208n7
Democratic Party 7–8, 16, 23, 25–26, 30, 47, 53–54, 67–68, 76–78, 81, 89, 91–92, 95–96, 105, 109, 115, 144–145, 147, 149, 167, 169, 177, 183, 196n22, 203n13, 208n5; and captured voters 170; co-optation of progressive movements 30; labor alliances 170; and its New Deal 90; right wing within the party 210n24; and sectional and interest group forces 123; primaries 168; socialists as "gadflies" within the party 172; and working-class 122; *see also* Democrats
Democratic Socialists of America (DSA) 163, 169, 172, 184, 194, 194n13, 208n5; National Political Committee 168; partnering with local Democratic Party officials 208n7
Democratic Socialists Organizing Committee (DSOC) 207–208n5
democratic syndicalist approach 97
Democrats 27–32, 44, 52, 54, 76–77, 79, 81, 90, 99, 101, 106, 113, 146–148, 157, 168, 170, 172, 179, 184–185, 204n16, 205n24, 208n7, 209n16; anti-communist 124; corporate-captive 2, 174; neoliberal 57; new cohort 124; New Deal 96; pro-labor 80; southern 12, 23, 27, 92, 96, 107–108; and working-class support 201n16; *see also* Democratic Party
Denmark 20
Denning, Michael 196n24, 201n13
Denver, Colorado 132
depoliticization: after World War II 101–102
deportation of guest workers 160
Derber, Charles 171, 182
deregulation 1, 124; of airline industry 201n17
Detroit, Michigan 59, 81, 94, 115–116, 176, 200n10, 208n7
Detroit DSA 208n7
Dewey, John 79, 96
DiMaggio, Anthony 182
direct action 63, 97, 183
Disch, Lisa 180

discrimination: in the housing market 110
disenfranchised workers and farmers 23
disenfranchising rules 49
disruptive strike movement 172
divide-and-rule strategies: of employers and governments 188
Dixiecrat control of Congress 11
dock workers 59
Dodge Revolutionary Union Movement (DRUM) 115, 200n7
domestic services 186; workers 93, 155–156, 180, 210n19
Dominican Republic-Central America Free Trade Agreement 152
Douglas, Paul 79
dual unions 60
Dubinsky, David 91, 197n4
Dubofsky, Melvyn 59, 83
Dudzic, Mark 206n31
Duncan, Arne 175
DuPont brothers 181
DuPont Corporation 80, 105
Durbin, Dick (Richard) 205n24

Early, Steve 119
Easley, Ralph 207n3
East Asia 138
East North Central region 138
Eastern Europe 58, 100, 114, 199n18, 207n2
Eastern European: Catholics 100; immigrants 39, 197n2
eastern manufacturing centers 59
Eastern U.S. 196n15; cities 38
eBay 194n17
economic: citizenship 112; inequality 149, 191–192n3
economic globalization 135, 141
Economic Policy Institute (EPI) 205n28
Ehrenreich, Barbara 192n8, 208n5, 210n18
eight-hour workday 4, 46, 65, 195n11; law for railroad workers 195n11
Eisenhower, Dwight D. 104
El Paso, Texas 113
election trap 171, 174
elections local 170; gubernatorial 21; midterm 2, 11; *see also* city elections; primary elections
electoral campaigns: fund-raising in 33
electoral system, U.S.: disproportionate representation 11, 22; Electoral College 11, 18, 21–23, 92; electoral districts 6, 17; electoral fusion politics 170; fundraising 32–35; geographical concentration of power 21–22; and majority opinions 183; and obstacles for third parties 23–25; plurality electoral system 17, 19–21, 26, 28; representation between urban-industrial and rural areas 18, 23; simple-majority single-ballot system 17; single-member plurality system 20; voter registration requirements 23–24; winner-take-all principle 6, 17, 22–23; *see also* political system, U.S.
electoral threshold 23
electrical industry/manufacture 77, 80, 92

Electrical Workers, Local 3 105
Eli Lily 105
Emergency Economic Stabilization Act (2008) 192n4
eminent domain 187
Employee Free Choice Act (EFCA) 158–159, 161
employee ownership 142
Employee Retirement Income Security Act 111
employer violence 4
enclosure of the commons 186
End Poverty in California (EPIC) 27, 79, 198n6
Engels, Friedrich 42
England 15, 209n13; *see also* Britain
English-speaking countries 20, 38, 102
environmentalists/environmentalist concerns 171–172
estate tax 192n3
ethnic diversity: of American society 26
ethnic issues 172
Europe 13, 14–15, 20, 39, 71, 138, 150–151, 173; continental 13, 20, 38, 93
European: counterparts of U.S. political institutions 12–13; labor relations practices 84; social democracy 81; socialist and social democratic parties 19–20
European-style, social democratic policies 109
Evans, Mark 192n8
Executive Order 10988 (Kennedy) 125
export-oriented agrarianism: vs. industrial capitalism 52
ex–Shachtmanites 207n5

factory occupations 84, 86, 97, 172
"failure of socialism" in America 4, 6
Fair Deal 94, 101
Fair Employment Practices Commission (FEPC) 94
Fair Labor Standards Act 94
Family and Medical Leave Act 200n5
Far West 59
Farm Equipment Workers 100
Farm Labor Organizing Committee (FLOC) 144
farm laborers/workers 47, 55, 138, 156, 180, 210n19; disconnections 55–57
farmer-labor alliance: attempts to forge 38, 55
Farmer Labor League 27
Farmer Labor Organizing Committee (FLOC) 144
Farmer-Labor Party: 1920 65–66; movement in early 1890s 6, 45–48
Farmers' Alliance 37–38, 45–46
federal: elections 170; policies on economic development in the South 123; tax laws 123; troops 45
Federal Election Campaign Act (1974) 31, 33
Federal Elections Commission 31, 33, 194n16
Federal Housing Administration (FHA): mortgage loans 180, 210n19; federal housing policies 123
Federal Reserve Bank 1, 11, 153, 191n2
Federation for American Immigration Reform (FAIR) 137

Index   237

Federation of Organized Trades and Labor Unions (FOTLU) 44
The Federationalist 164
feminist movement 111, 113
Ferguson, Thomas 34, 170, 194n17
Ferrer, Freddy 204n15
filibuster 11, 35, 205n24
Filipino workers 59
finance capital 187
Financial Crisis Inquiry Commission 191n2
financialization 187; and predatory tendencies 187
Finland 193n6, 202n1
Finnish immigrants 59, 64
firefighters 131
Firestone Tire & Rubber 122
firm-based benefits 141, 166
First Amendment 33–34, 206n31
First International *see* International Workingmen's Association
First Nations *see* Native Americans
Fletcher, Bill, Jr. 140, 143, 188, 192n8, 210n24
flexi- and temporary workers 129
flexible specialization 7, 128
Flint, Michigan 78, 80, 193n3, 204n21, 211n28
Foner, Eric 64
food service and hospitality industries 138
Ford Motor Company 80, 115, 141, 165
Fordism 74, 128
foreclosures 1; businesses and properties 187
foremen 92, 155
former Commonwealth countries 21
Foster, John Bellamy 192n8
Foster, William Z. 66
Foundation for Economic Education 103
Founding Fathers 9–10, 17
Fourierist socialist movement 30
Fourteenth Amendment 35, 49, 181
Fourth International 212n33
Fox News 169, 175, 178, 181, 184
France 4, 20–21, 36, 65, 67, 83, 93, 114, 195n1, 199n18, 202n1; two-ballot system 20–21, 193n9
Frank, Thomas 177, 182
Fraser, Steve 109
free enterprise 7, 103, 106, 148
free-market capitalism 103, 122
free-silver Populists 47
Free South Africa movement (FSAM) 204n19
Free to Choose (Friedman) 122; PBS series 201n15
free-trade: agreement with South Korea 152–153, 204n22; free-trade parties in Australia 16
Freedom Works 178, 210n22
Fremont, California 201n19
Frente Auténtico del Trabajo (FAT) 206n32
Frey, John 89
Friedman, Milton 104, 122
Frymer, Paul 111
Fur Workers union 65

Gapasin, Fernando 140
garment industry 80; unions 55

Gates, Bill 181
gay rights 177
gender: bias 165; injustice 102; issues 43, 130, 145, 172
General Confederation of Labor (Italy) 65
General Electric Corporation (GE) 76, 104–105
General Mills 122
General Motors Corporation (GM) 79, 115, 121–122, 141–142, 151, 201n19; walkouts in Flint, Michigan 204n21
George, Henry 38, 44
George, Susan 211n33
Georgia 95
German Americans 29
German revolutionary shop stewards 57
Germany 4, 20, 28, 38, 40, 49, 65, 69, 93, 194n14, 195n1, 199n19, 202n1
gerrymandering 24
Gerstle, Gary 109
Gettelfinger, Ron 141–142
Getty Oil 122
GI Bill 180
Gilbert, David 117
Gilded Age 30
Gingrich, Newt 2
Glaeser, Edward L. 13
Glass Workers Union 65
global: boycott 150; government 188; solidarity 150
globalization *see* capitalist globalization; corporate globalization; economic globalization
Goldwater, Barry 107, 181
Gompers, Samuel 6, 39, 43–47, 50, 53–55, 57, 60, 164–166, 195n11, 207n3; hostility toward SLP and independent labor-party efforts 48; prioritizing economic strategy over political strategy 40–42
Gompersian line/Gompersism 50, 61, 195n11; *see also* AFL; voluntarism
Google 194n17
GOP *see* Republican Party
Gore, Al 168
Gorman, Frank 76
Gottlieb, Robert 117
Gorz, André 117
Grant administration 195n7
grassroots movements: for new labor party in 1930s 7; and issues avoided by major-party politicians 169–175; rebellion during Roosevelt administration 75, 172; unionization 138, *see also* rank-and-file unionist activists
Great Depression 1, 68, 74, 82, 92, 130, 172
Great Migration 66
Great Recession 177
Great Society programs 7, 108–110, 124
Greece 13
Greeley, Horace 19, 30
Green, James 120
Green, William 81, 106, 198n7
Green for All 184
Green Party USA 25, 166, 203n13
Greider, William 154, 191n2, 206n30
gross domestic product (GDP) 49

gross national product (GNP) 121
Grosse, Edward 43
guest worker programs 160; contracts 136
gun control 177, 181

Hahnel, Robin 192n8
Hanna, Mark (Marcus) 30, 51, 165
Hannity, Sean 2
hard money contributions 34, 194n16
hard rock miners 59
Hardie, J. Keir 63
Hardman, J.B.S. 96
Harriman, Job 62
Harrington, Michael 172, 207–208n5
Hartz, Louis 4
Harvey, David 185–187, 211n28
hate strikes 87
Hayes, Max S. 52, 54, 66
Haywood, "Big Bill" (William D.) 63, 195n13, 196n23
Hazeldell, Pennsylvania 193n3
health care 174, 181, 192n4; benefits 112; health care industry 140, 142; Health Care Reform Bill 180; home health care workers 131, 133; profit-oriented insurance 2; professionals 131; programs 75; public option 2; reform 179; universal 2
Health Care Worker Recruitment and Retention Act (New York State) 204n15
Henwood, Doug 192n8
Heritage Foundation 121
Hewlett-Packard 194n17
Hillman, Sidney 67, 72, 77–80, 89–90, 165, 197n4
Hillquit, Morris 60, 62, 67
Ho Chi Minh 200n8
Hofstadter, Richard 29, 73
homophobia 181
homosexuals 122
Hoodbhoy, Pervez 211n33
Hook, Sidney 197n3
Hoover, Herbert 86, 96, 197n1
Hoover administration 75
Hoover Institute 121
hospital workers 133
Hospital Workers Local 1199 see National Union of Health and Hospital Workers, Local 1199
hotels and restaurants 135, 140
House Un-American Activities Committee (HUAC) 100
housing 112, 138; segregation 94; see also foreclosures
Houston, Texas 132
Houtars, François 211n33
Howe, Irving 96
human alienation 114
human rights 188
Human Rights Watch 155–156
Hungarians 100
Hunter, Robert 62

Idaho 209n12
identity politics 171–172

ideological warfare: against "collectivism" and "statism" 103–105
Illinois 47, 51, 80, 193n10, 196n18; state labor parties 65
immigrants: first-generation 49; first- and second-generation 94; Marxists 43; Mexican 137; new 19, 23–24, 59, 73, 94; second-generation new 74; and the U.S. labor movement 135–137; workers 7, 19, 24, 28, 30, 39, 42, 48–49, 51, 59, 64, 70, 105, 133, 135–139, 147, 160–161, 164, 169, 181
immigration: reform 175, 181; restrictionists 136
Immigration Act of 1924 74
Immigration and Customs Enforcement (ICE) 136
Immigration and Naturalization Service (INS) 136
Immigration Reform and Control Act (IRCA) (1986) 136
imperial consciousness 188
import barriers see protective tariff
income tax 65; progressive 49; see also tax
independent contractors 155–156
independent labor-based parties 5, 13–14
independent labor politics: constraints during World War II 86–89
Independent Labour Party (ILP, Britain) 38, 62
Independent Union of All the Workers 196n17
India 151
Indiana 80, 195n7, 196n18
indigenous populations 186
Indochina 101
Indonesia 101
Industrial Areas Foundation 139
industrial democracy 72, 85, 92, 105, 111, 170; as substitute for socialism 197n25
Industrial Revolution 28
industrial unionism/unions 38–39, 42, 48, 54–55, 57, 60–61, 66, 69, 74, 76, 80, 86, 89, 92, 160, 173, 194n1, 196n24, 197n5; United Mine Workers' autocratic model 77; see also unionism/unions, inclusive
Industrial Workers of the World (IWW) (Wobblies) 4, 6, 45, 58–59, 61, 64, 70, 100, 163, 167, 195n14, 196n15–17, 23, 198n5, 198n9; emphasis on economic action and organization 57; federal prosecution 60; free speech actions 57; National Executive Committee 63
industrialization 48–49
inequality: institutionalized 102
inheritance tax 65; see also tax
Institute for Research & Education on Human Rights 178
institutional disruption 172–174
insurgence, general: underlying conditions for 173
intellectual property rights 211n30
Intercollegiate Socialist Society 197n25
interest groups 31, 147, 170
International Association of Machinists (IAM) 45
International Brotherhood of Electrical Workers (IBEW) 196n24

Index

International Brotherhood of Teamsters (IBT) 59, 134, 143, 150, 204n18, 208–209n10
International Confederation of Free Trade Unions (ICFTU) 99, 155
International Covenant on Civil and Political Rights 205n26
International Federation of Professional and Technical Engineers (IFPTE) 202n3
international labor: rights 161; standards 160
International Labor Organization (ILO) 155, 161, 205n26; Committee on Freedom of Association 205n26
International Ladies' Garment Workers Union (ILGWU) 38, 54, 59–60, 65, 68–69, 105, 113, 136, 197n4
International Longshore and Warehouse Union (ILWU) 144, 146
International Longshoremen's Association (ILA) 59, 204n18, 207n3
International Machinists Union 60, 204n22
International Monetary Fund (IMF) 211n30
International Socialist Organization (ISO) 189
International Socialist Review(ISR) 167; *see also Socialist Review* (U.S.)
International Typographical Union 40, 46, 52, 155, 207n3
International Union of Food, Agricultural, Hotel, Restaurant, Restaurant, Catering, Tobacco and Allied Workers' Association (IUF) 150
International Workingmen's Association (IWA), or First International 30, 41, 194n2; immigrant Marxists' faction 42; Yankee reformers within IWA 42–43
Inter-Union Institute for Labor and Democracy 96
investment theory of party competition (Ferguson) 34, 170
invisibility: of the American left 3, 175
involuntary servitude 159, 161, 206n30
Iraq War 152–153, 168, 175–176
Ireland 28
Irish Americans 29, 39; as immigrants 59
Islamophobia 181
Italians 59
Italy 20, 28, 36, 65, 93, 199n18, 202n1
IWO (International Workers Order) 196n24
IWW *see* Industrial Workers of the World (IWW)

Jackson, Henry "Scoop" 124
Jackson, Jesse 176, 208n5
Jackson, Michigan 80
Jacksonian Democracy/Democrats 29–30
Japan 126, 154, 201n18, 202n1
Japanese Americans: relocation into internment camps 100
Japanese workers 59, 127, 129
Jevons, William Stanley 104
Jewish immigrants 64
Jim Crow segregation 110, 149, 161; *see also* racial segregation
jobs programs 181

Jobs with Justice 158
John Birch Society 105, 181
Johnson, Lyndon B. 7, 108, 110
Johnson administration 110, 180
Jones, Mother Mary 72
JPMorgan Chase 191n2, 207n34
judiciary 9, 13; *see also* courts
Just Health Care campaign 146
"just-in-time" production 128; *see also* lean production
"Justice for Janitors" campaign (SEIU) 132–133

Kagarlitsky, Boris 211n33
Kaiser Steel 199n2
Kalamazoo, Michigan 193n3
Kansas 207n3
Kansas City, Missouri 90
Kanter, Rosabeth Moss 127
Katznelson, Ira 109, 173, 209n13
Kautsky, Karl 63
Keefe, Daniel 207n3
Kelley, Florence 72
Kennedy, John F. 125, 181
Kentucky 181, 210n19
Kerry, John 168
Keynes, John Maynard 104
Keynesianism 104, 122; commercial 109; military 15
Kimeldorf, Howard 58
King, Martin Luther, Jr. 126, 149, 171, 176, 204n17; and Poor People's Campaign 149
Kirkland, Lane 132, 148, 155, 164, 207n2
Knights of Columbus 100
Knights of Labor (KOL) 6, 37–38, 40–41, 44–45, 47, 49, 57, 196n18
Koch, Charles 181–182, 201n17
Koch, David 181–182, 210n17, 210n22
Kodak 104
KOL *see* Knights of Labor
Kucinich, Dennis 168

Labor Age 197n25
Labor Council for Latin American Advancement (LCLAA) 131
labor councils 81; local 139
labor-farmer party 55
labor-management partnership 141, 165–166, 169; *see also* union-employer partnership
labor-management relations: cooperative 51
Labor-Management Relations Act *see* Taft-Hartley Act
Labor-Management Reporting and Disclosure Act *see* Landrum-Griffin Act
labor-market exclusion 43
labor mediator 85
labor metaphysic (Mills) 119, 201n13
labor militancy 15, 39, 74, 77, 80, 95, 113, 198n11; at the grassroots level 167; at the point of production 4–7, 57–60; militant unionism 161–162, 170, 197n3; *see also* rank-and-file, labor insurgencies
Labor Nonpartisan Political League (LNPL) 77–78, 80–81, 89

Labor Party (U.S.) 8, 144–147, 160, 206*n*31
  early efforts to establish 36–68; Labor Party Advocates 144
labor-Populist alliance 46–47; labor-Populist parties (1894) 37
Labor Representation Committee (LRC) 53
labor rights *see* workers' rights
Laborers International Union of North America (LIUNA) 134
Labour Party (Britain) 4, 5–54, 62, 64–65, 72, 90–91, 209*n*13
Labour Representation Committee 46, 62–63
La Follette, Philip 79
La Follette, Robert M., Jr. 79
La Follette, Robert M., Sr. 6, 24, 30, 65–68, 71, 167
La Follette campaign (1924) 67
La Guardia, Fiorello 67
landlocked industries 134, 140
Landrum-Griffin Act (1959) 7, 107, 108, 205*n*26
Lansing, Michigan 80
Laski, Harold 72
Lassalle, Ferdinand 41
Latin America 150, 163–164, 187, 200*n*8, 207*n*4
Latinas/Latinos 110, 112–113, 132, 135–136, 147, 161, 203*n*7
Lawrence, Massachusetts 59–60, 64, 196*n*16
League for Independent Political Action 79
League for Industrial Democracy 197*n*25
League of Nations 71
League of Revolutionary Black Workers (LRBW) 115–116
lean production 151; *see also* "just-in-time" production
left-liberal politics 112; limits of U.S. political arena 92; as third party 95
left-wing: factionalism 40–41; movements within major parties 27; populists 183; Progressives 72; union pressure on Democratic Party 91
"lemon socialism" 2, 192*n*4
"lesser evil" 18, 28, 67, 78, 168; *see also* "wasted-vote" effect
Lewis, John L. 77–80, 82, 86, 155, 197*n*4, 198*n*12–13
liberal: Catholic clerics 133; competing definitions and usages of the term 197*n*1; Democrats 31; left 92–93; liberalism in America vs. in Europe 70–71
Liberal Party 91
Liberals (Britain) 53–54
Libertarian Party 210*n*22
Lichtenstein, Nelson 82–83, 93, 107, 111, 203*n*10
Limbaugh, Rush 2, 177
Lincoln, Abraham 30
Lincoln Memorial 176
Die Linke 207*n*4
Lipset, Seymour M. 69
Lipsitz, George 180
literacy requirements for voters 23
"Little Steel" 80
living-wage movement 133

Llewellyn, Frank 169, 208*n*8
Lloyd George government (Britain) 64
lobbying 33, 53, 147, 170; corporate lobbyists 32–33, 175, 205*n*24; *see also* pressure group politics
London 41
London, Meyer 193*n*3
Lordstown, Ohio 114, 119
"Lordstown syndrome" 114
Los Angeles, California 132, 137, 140, 195*n*8, 196*n*19, 203*n*9
Louis XIV 13
Lower East Side, New York 70, 193*n*3
Lowi, Theodore 10
Loyalist Cause (Spanish Civil War) 82
Lucy, William 124
lumber industry 94; lumberjacks 59
Lynd, Alice 119, 201*n*14
Lynd, Robert S. 198*n*9
Lynd, Staughton 119, 198*n*11, 201*n*14

Machinists 45, 55
Madison, James 13
Magna Carta 82
Maine 29
maintenance of membership 86
Majority Agenda Project 184–185
male-centric corporate model 165
Mallet, Serge 117
management: by stress 129; "inviolability" 92; prerogatives 117, 205*n*25, 206*n*30
Management Strike Contingency Force 201*n*17
manufacturing industries 77, 177; output 49; workers 49
Maquila plants (*maquiladoras*) 151
March on Washington for Jobs and Freedom (1963) 176
Marcuse, Herbert 118
Marks, Gary 69
Marshall, Alfred 104
Marshall Plan 99
Martin's Ferry, Ohio 193*n*3
Marx, Karl 41–42, 194*n*2; early writings on alienation 114
Marxism 164; Americanized form 197; Marxist-Leninist critique of mainstream unions 116; theories of state planning 104; view of farmers 46, 55; view of workers 186, 189
Marxists: urban (Socialist Party members) 56
The Marxists (Mills) 119
mass demonstrations 75, 172
mass disruption, defiance, and protest 172
mass media: as conservative, corporate-dominated 2, 170, 174–176
mass picketing 86, 97
Maurer, James H. 55
May 1968 revolt (Paris) 211*n*28
Mazey, Emil 88, 198*n*14
Mazeyites 88
Mazzocchi, Tony
McAdoo, William G. 196*n*22
McBride, John 47
McCain, John 169

McCain-Feingold Act *see* Bipartisan Campaign Reform Act
McCall, Carl 204n15
McCarthyism 99
McClellan Committee hearings 106
McDonnell Douglas 202n3
McGovern, George 113, 124
McGovern campaign 124
McGovernism 124
McGuire, Peter J. 41–42
McKees Rocks, Pennsylvania 59, 64, 196n16
McKibbin, Ross 54
McKinley, William 30
McReynolds, David 168
Meany, George 106, 108, 113, 125, 131, 163–165
Meat vs. Rice... (Gompers) 44
meatpacking industry 66, 77, 135, 139
Medicare 179–181, 183, 192n4, 210n17
Memphis, Tennessee 204n17
Merriam, Frank 198n6
metal miners 45; metal workers 52
Mexican American workers 59, 94
Mexican National Administrative Office 206–207n32
Mexican workers 59, 100, 112, 137
Mexico 112, 138, 151, 183; Mexico city revolt (1968) 211n28
Michels, Robert 199n16
Michigan 19, 80
Microsoft Corporation 202n3
Midwest 59, 62, 67, 89, 123, 196n15; midwestern cities 38
militarism 177
military: expenditures in the U.S. South 93
military-industrial complex 2, 179
Mills, C. Wright 96, 119, 199n16, 201n13
Milwaukee, Wisconsin 55, 61–62, 70, 132, 193n3, 196n18
Milwaukee People's Party 196n18
Mine Safety Act 111
miners 46
Miners for Democracy 113, 119, 200n3
minimum wage 65, 94
Minneapolis, Minnesota 55, 61, 70
Minnesota 79, 182, 196n17
Minnesota Farmer-Labor Party 79, 81
minor parties 22–23, 25–26, 29; candidates 27; *see also* third parties
minority group: ideological 17
minority workers 19, 91; occupational rights; *see also* people of color
Minutemen 181; Minuteman Project 178
Mississippi 24, 209n12
Mississippi Freedom Democratic Party (MFDP) 113
Mitchell, John 166
Modern Quarterly 197n3
monarchies: hereditary 13
Mondale, Walter 208n5
monetization 187
Montana 25, 205n27
Montgomery, David 65

Moody, Kim 32, 48, 142, 146–147, 166, 173, 192n8, 203n8, 204n18
Morgan Stanley 191n2
multiparty system 17
multi-union organizing 139
multi-university 117, 201n12
municipal ownership 46
municipal socialism 61
Murdoch, Rupert 181, 184
Murray, Philip 79, 86, 89, 95
Muslims 136
Muste, Abraham J. 197n3, 198n9
Musteites 198n5

NAACP *see* National Association for the Advancement of Colored People
Nader, Ralph 25–26, 167–168, 206n30
Naderites 25
Nashville, Tennessee 178
The Nation 154
National Association for the Advancement of Colored People (NAACP) 92, 113, 176, 184, 198n9; its Legal Defense Fund 107
National Association of Manufacturers (NAM) 53, 85, 103, 105–106, 108, 121, 205n24
National Bureau of Economic Research (NBER) 121
National Civic Federation (NCF) 52, 165–166, 207n3
National Council of La Raza 184
National Day Laborer Organizing Network 139
National Doctors Alliance 202n2
National Education Association (NEA) 130
National Farmer-Labor Federation 79
National Gay and Lesbian Task Force 184
National Industrial Recovery Act (NIRA) 74–75, 77, 83; Section 7(a) 74–75, 83
National Labor-Management Conference 92
National Labor Relations Act (NLRA) 7, 74, 82, 84–85, 93–94, 97, 110–111, 122, 125, 155–156, 158, 198n7, 198n9, 198n11, 206n30–31; and collective bargaining 83; and criticism 83; exclusion of agricultural labor and domestic service 98; grievance procedures 98; jurisdiction between rival unions 83; secret ballot elections 158; and southern textile interests 95; and winner-take-all system for certification 83
National Labor Relations Board (NLRB) 80, 82–86, 97, 99, 104, 130, 134, 155–160
National Labor Union (NLU) 30, 43
National Mall 175, 184
National Nonpartisan League 65
National Recovery Administration (NRA) 75
National Union of Health and Hospital Workers, Local 1199: 120, 126, 204n17
National Union of Healthcare Workers (NUHW) 162
National Union of Mineworkers (South Africa) 204n19
National Urban League 176, 198n9
nationalization 46; *see also* Plank Ten of "Political Programme"
Native Americans 188

native-born: Americans 19, 58; Protestant workers 28; small farmers 64, 67
Nazism 19
Nederland, Colorado 193n3
needle trades 65, 133, 145; unions 78, 196n24
neighborhood-based unionism 133
neighborhood desegregation 110
neighborhood organizations 173
neoclassic Marxist theories 117
neoclassical economics 104
neo-conservatives 124
neoliberalism 3, 32, 104, 164; and corporate restructuring 186; and upsurge of pro-business, right-wing politics 121–122, 124, 144, 186–187
neo-syndicalist craft traditions 198n5
Nestlé 150; and Coca-Cola global organizing campaign 150
Netherlands 20, 202n1
New American Movement 208n5
New Anti-capitalist Party (Nouveau Parti anti-capitaliste, NPA), France 207n4
New Deal 8, 27–28, 30, 34, 47, 70, 73–74, 76, 85, 96, 158, 161, 163, 172, 174, 181, 194n13; and discriminatory housing policies 94; economic legacy of 180, 210n20; first New Deal 7, 75; and maintenance of white supremacy in the South 94; public policy and social welfare programs 180; second New Deal 7, 75, 82, 91–94; southern elites' nullification of New Deal social legislation 94
New Deal Coalition 76–77, 79, 89; co-optation of insurgent political movements into 80
New Deal liberalism 125
New Deal order 102, 112, 124
New Dealers/New Deal liberals 72, 80, 90, 101, 110, 124, 197n1
New Democrats 2, 144, 208n5
New England 76, 94
New Hampshire 29, 209n12
New Jersey 29, 158
New Left 27, 99, 112–113, 117–121, 208n5; as global 113; industrial colonizing by activists 119, 203n4; labor activism 117–121; "new working class" theory 117, 200n12
The New Men of Power (Wright Mills) 96
new middle class 124, 199n16
New Orleans, Louisiana 48, 81
New Party 145, 203n13
New Republic 72
New Right 178, 182
New South Wales Labor Electoral League 16
New United Motoring Manufacturing Inc. (NUMMI) plant 201n19
new unionism 38, 41, 209n13
New York City 29, 41–44, 55, 62, 67, 70, 78, 137, 193n5, 194n2, 204n15; docks 107
New York City Central Labor Council 143
New York Federal Reserve 191n2
New York State 25, 51, 78, 94, 193n12, 195n3, 209n12; labor parties 65
New Zealand 19, 67, 69, 202n1
Ngwane, Trevor 211n33

1930s organizations of tenants and the unemployed 75, 172
Nissen, Bruce 132
Nixon, Richard M. 31, 110, 124, 210n21
Nixon administration 115
Nkrumah, Kwame 200n18
Nolan, Mary 4
non-agricultural workers 91, 130
non-parliamentary government 17
Nonpartisan League (NPL) 27, 79
non-unionized Americans 95
Norris-LaGuardia Act (1932) 84
North American Agreement on Labor Cooperation (NAALC) 206n32
North American Free Trade Agreement (NAFTA) 152, 206n32
North Carolina 138–139; and collective bargaining ban 206n32; and General Statute 95–98 161
North Dakota 27, 79, 95
Northeast U.S. 62, 75, 123, 138
northern cities 28–29, 115
Northern Europe 57, 59
Northern U.S. 23, 50, 55, 93–94; states 125; industries 66; system of de facto segregation 94; white working class 27
Northwest U.S. 196n15
Norway 20
Nozick, Robert 122
NRA codes 75–76
nursing home employees 133

Obama, Barack 2, 34–35, 157–158, 169, 175–179, 181, 184; campaign contributions 194n17
Obama administration 2, 142–144, 153, 159, 169, 175, 178–179; relationship with the left 3, 174
occupational communities 69
occupational justice 110
Occupational Safety and Health Act (OSHA) 32, 111
OECD countries and union membership 202n1
Oestreicher, Richard 17–18
Office of Price Administration (OPA) 91
offshoring 177, 183; see also outsourcing
Ohio 47, 51, 80, 158, 204n16
Oil, Chemical and Atomic Workers International Union (OCAW) 144, 146–147
oil industry 77, 94
Oklahoma 25, 27, 56
Oklahoma Socialist Party 56
"Old Guard" 78
Oline Foundation 122
Olson, Floyd B. 79
Omaha, Nebraska 139
Omaha Together One Community (OTOC) 139
On the Line (Swados) 200n6
One Big Union 60
One-Dimensional Man (Marcuse) 118
One Nation March for Jobs, Justice, and Education 184
OneNationStandingTogetherCoalition 210n24

Ontiveros, Maria 160
open-shop drive 40, 166; employers 53
The Open Society and Its Enemies (Popper) 104
"Operation Dixie" (CIO) 149
Oracle 194n17
Oregon 27, 79, 81, 209n12
O'Reilly, Bill 2
organizing: immigrant workers 160; the unemployed 143–144; the unorganized 159, 164, 169
Our Country Deserves Better PAC 178
outsourcing 141, 149, 166, 185–186; *see also* offshoring

PAC *see* Political Action Committee
Packinghouse Workers' Organizing Committee (PWOC) 77
Painters and Molders Union 65
Palin, Sarah 2, 169, 178, 181, 208n8
Panama 205n22
Pan-American Federation of Labor 163–164
Paris Commune (1871) 41, 211n28
Parker, Mike 129, 201n19
parliamentary system 17, 26, 30; balance of power and minor parties 21–22
Participatory Economics (Parecon) 211n32
Passaic, New Jersey 59–60
Pataki, George 204n15
Paterson, New Jersey 59–60, 64, 196n16
patronage resources 11, 24, 29, 89, 193n11; *see also* political machines
Paul, Rand 181
Peace and Freedom Party 113
Peace Corps 124
Pearl Harbor 86
peasant populations 186
Pendergast machine, Kansas City 90
Pennsylvania 19, 51, 80, 204n16, 208m5
pension 75, 102, 112; cuts 2–3; funds 187
people of color 94, 112, 118, 130–131, 133–135, 164, 171, 197n2
people of diverse sexual orientation 171
People's Party (aka Populist Party) 30, 45–47
PepsiCo 122
Perkins, Frances 76
Perlman, Selig 4
Perot, H. Ross 21
Peters, Gary 208n7
Peters, Tom (Thomas J.) 127
Pew Charitable Trust 122
Philadelphia, Pennsylvania 45, 54
Philippines 101, 151
Phillips, Kevin 185
Phillips-Fein, Kim 181
Pilger, John 211n33
Pillager, Minnesota 193n3
Pinault-Printemps-Redoute (PPR) 151
Pittsburgh, Pennsylvania 94, 146
Piven, Frances Fox 92, 122, 172–174
Plank Ten of "Political Programme" 46–47
plant closings 156
Poland 28, 111
police 131

Political Action Committees (PACs) 31–32, 89, 99, 105
political machines, city-based 12, 16, 23–25, 28–29, 32, 89–90; vs. city manager systems 193n11
"Political Programme" of 1894 46
political realignment of 1896 47
political repression 15, 60, 72, 95, 98–101
political system, U.S. 15–16, 19–20, 24, 27, 29, 170; bicameral structure of Congress 17–18; changes in rules of the political game 6, 9, 31–35; constitutional compromise over slavery 10; constitutional division of powers 9–10, 13, 26; constitutionally-specified policies 10; executive branch 21–22, 25–26; executive power 10–11; federalism 9–14, 28; fragmentation of political parties 12; fragmentation of power 10–11, 13; legislative branch 22, 25; legislative power 11; majoritarian system 23; multiple points of access and exposure to interest groups 12; multiplicity of political units in federal system 14; more historical continuity in comparison with European counterparts 12–13; presidency 10–11, 13, 21–22, 28, 30; presidentialism 21–23, 30, 169; separation of powers 9–10; structural bias toward cross-class political coalitions 18; system of checks and balances 10–11; *see also* U.S. two-party system
political systems as money-driven 34, 170
political uprisings in Europe (1848, 1870–1871, 1917 and 1919) 71
Ponzi schemes 187
the poor 173, 182; poor farmers 28, 45–46; poor people's movement 185; whites 23
Poor People's Campaign 149
Popper, Karl 104
Popular Front 95, 100, 196n24
popular initiative 45
population growth 48–49
Populism 23, 61
Populists 18, 30, 46–47, 174; anger against big government 1, 179; Populist farmers 45; movements 23, 70–71
Port Authority Statement 117
Port Huron Statement 117
Portugal 13, 202n1
post-bellum era 19
postmodern theories and ideologies 171
Powderly, Terence V. 44
practical syndicalism 58
Prague: Communist coup (1948) 199n18; uprising in 1989 211n28
Prashad, Vijay 192n8
Pregnancy Discrimination Act 111
Pressmen's Union 196n20
pressure group politics 170
primary elections (primaries) 19, 24–26, 28
private-sector unionization: cooperation with public-sector unions' 162; organized by the state 86
private-sector workers 156, 205n28
procedural democracy: vs. substantive democracy 171

producer ethic/producerism 30, 36, 47
Professional Air Traffic Controllers Organization (PATCO) 201n17
progressive Americanism 72
Progressive Cigar Makers' Union 43
Progressive Democrats of America 194n13
Progressive electoral reforms 19, 24–25, 50, 195n8
Progressive Era 19, 24–25, 133
Progressive Labor Party 44, 118, 201n12
progressive liberals 79, 182
progressive media 183
Progressive movement 71–72
Progressive Party 6, 68, 79, 96
Progressive reformers/Progressives/Progressivism 19, 24, 50, 71, 163
pro-labor: legislation 140; political candidates 170
propaganda 105
proportional representation 6, 17–18, 19, 20–22, 23, 83, 193n6
protectionist parties in Australia 16
protective tariff 51–52, 153–154, 204n22, 209n14
protest: movements 173; rallies 157
Protestant denominations: conservative evangelical and fundamentalist 122
proto-feminism 99
public opinion polls and survey data 3, 80, 174, 154, 182–183, 185, 192n7
public-sector workers 112, 130–131, 149, 156, 205–206n28, 207n29
Puerto Ricans 188

quality circles 129
quality of work life movement 115
Quarry Workers Union 65
Quebecor 150

race: and class-based social inequality 109; discrimination 110; injustice 102, 109; issues 145, 172, 177
racial minorities 125
racism 85, 149, 181, 188; structural, institutionalized 175
Racketeer Influenced and Corrupt Organization Act (RICO) 108, 200n4
Radical America collective 120
Railroad Brotherhoods, independent 51–52, 65
railroad companies 47; workers 45–47
Rainbow Coalition 208n5; Rainbow PUSH Coalition 176
Randolph, A. Philip 200n8
Rank and File (Lynd and Lynd) 201n14
rank-and-file: activists and caucuses 76, 107, 119, 159, 170, 173; defiant plant committees 77; labor insurgencies 76, 85, 92, 113, 142, 173; movements within unions 7, 119–120; union democracy 79, 97, 119; *see also* labor militancy
Reading, Pennsylvania 55, 61, 70
Reagan, Ronald 104, 124, 193n1, 201n15, 208n10, 210n21–22
Reagan years 156

Reaganism 124
"Rebuild America: Jobs, Justice and Peace" campaign 176
"Reclaim the Dream" march 176
Reconstruction era 161
Red Army 100
Red Cloud, Nebraska 193n3
Red-Green Alliance of Denmark 207n4
Red Scare: First (1919–1920) 72; Second (1947–1957) 100; red-scare mongering 3
redistribution of global wealth 188
redistricting 24
Rehabilitation Act 111
Reimagining Society Project (organized by ZCommunications) 189
relocation of production 149, 183
rent strikes 133
Republic Windows and Doors factory 161–162, 207n34
Republican Party (aka GOP or Grand Old Party) 16, 18, 25–27, 47, 51, 67, 123–124, 137, 165, 169, 178, 181–182, 196n22, 208n5, 209n15; *see also* Republicans
"Republican Revolution" of 1994 27
Republicans 2, 27–32, 80, 89–90, 96, 110, 144, 148, 157, 170, 175, 177–178, 184, 204n15, 208n7; northern Republicans 23; progressive Republicans 90; *see also* Republican Party
ResistNet 178
restaurants 107
retail stores 138
Reuther, Walter 93, 95–96, 106, 113, 165
revitalization of socialism in America 169
Revolutionary Union Movements (RUMs) 116
revolutions: 1848 in Europe 211n28
Rhode Island 29
Ricardo, David 104
RICO law *see* Racketeer Influenced and Corrupt Organization Act
right-libertarianism 181–182
Right-to-Work Committee 108
right-to-work laws 149, 159, 205n27
right-wing: extremists/fringe groups 105, 181; organizations 169; populism 188; pundits 3
Rockefeller family 76
Roosevelt, Franklin D. 30, 73, 76–82, 84–85, 89–90, 94, 193n1, 197n1, 198n6, 198n12; administration 77, 84, 90, 94; coalition 97, 197n4
Roosevelt, Theodore 30, 68, 71, 195n11
Rorty, James 197n3
Roulette, Pennsylvania 193n3
Royal Dutch/Shell 150
rubber industry 77, 150, 198n14
rural migrants 90
Russia 72
Russian Revolution (1917) 210n28
Rustin, Bayard 200n8

sabotage: industrial 58
Saginaw, Michigan 80
Saint John, Vincent 195n13
St. Louis, Missouri 45, 48, 195n2, 196n18

San Diego, California 132
San Francisco, California 51, 54, 194n2
sanctuary movement 136
Sanders, Bernie 208n5
Santa Clara case (1886) 35
Sassen, Saskia 192n8
Savage, Michael 2
Scaife Foundations 122
Scandinavian countries 202n1
Schauer, Mark 208n7
Schenectady, New York 61, 193n3
Schimkowitz, Samuel 43
school prayer 177
schoolteachers 130
Schultz, George 201n15
Schwarzenegger, Arnold 201n15
Scottish Socialist Party 207n4
Sears 105
Seattle, Washington 132; anti-WTO mobilization 153
secondary action (cross-border union tactic) 151, 155
Securities and Exchange Commission 181
segregation: and housing policies 94; physically and geographically instituted 210n19; in political jurisdictions 123; in U.S. South 50; *see also* Jim Crow segregation
SEIU *see* Service Employees International Union
self-help movements 75, 172
Selfa, Lance 178
semi-skilled workers 64, 66, 69, 74, 91, 196n16
seniority rights 8, 94
September 11, 2001 terrorist attacks 136
serf labor 23
Service Employees International Union (SEIU) 113–114, 128, 130–135, 141, 143, 150, 153, 162, 166, 176
service sector 135, 186
settlement houses 62
sexism 188
sexual identity issues 172
Shachtman, Max 96, 197n3
Shanghai Commune (1967) 211n28
sharecroppers 45, 112
Sherman Anti-Trust Act (1890) 40, 53
Shiva, Vandana 211n33
shoeworkers 45
shop democracy *see* industrial democracy
shop-floor activism 115, 120
short-haul trucking industry 107
silver: free coinage of 30, 47
Simons, Algie M. 56, 62
Sinclair, Upton 27, 79, 198n6
Singapore 154
single-payer health care system 2, 146, 183, 192n4
single-tax issue 38, 44
skilled workers 15, 37–39, 42–43, 48, 52, 55, 64, 69, 74, 102, 117; distinctions between skilled and unskilled workers 15, 39, 74, 195–196n14
Slaughter, Jane 129, 201n19

slavery 10, 18, 116, 159–161; slaveholders in the U.S. South 30
Slavs 59, 100
slowdowns 58
small farmers 23, 37, 45–47, 55–57, 64, 67
Smith, Adam 104
Smith, Sharon 81–82, 99
Smith Richardson Foundation 122
Smith-Connally Act (1943) 89, 99
Smithfield hog-processing plant 139
social Darwinism 181
social democracy: in Europe 71; ideas and their appeal in the U.S. 91; as "racialized" 180; surplus 173; tenets 173; traditions 173; views of majority of Americans 182
Social Democratic Federation 78
Social Democratic Party (SPD): Germany 28, 63, 194n14; Switzerland 16; U.S. 60, 196n18
Social Democratic Workingmen's Party 41, 48
Social Democrats of Pennsylvania 208n5
Social Democrats USA 124
social justice: movement 136, 153, 189, 212n33; organizations 184; unionism 139–140, 143, 152, 189; *see also* unionism
social liberals 101
social media 184
social movement activism 8, 169, 181
social movement unionism 7, 140, 186
social movements 171–172, 186; new 7, 112, 171
social safety net 183
Social Security 93–94, 112, 174, 179–180, 183, 210n17, 210n19
Social Security Act (1935) 84
social welfare services 179
socialism: defining features 5; homegrown 61; movements 19; parties' subcultures 70; views 169; revitalization of in America 3, 192n8
Socialist International 208n5
Socialist Labor Party (SLP) 37, 41, 43–45, 60, 196n18
Socialist Party of America (SP or SPA) 6, 14, 16, 25, 28, 37, 44–45, 54–55, 62, 66–68, 92, 100, 196n19, 197n4, 208n5; divisions between radicals and moderates 61–62; and electoral success 64; farm program added 57; and the labor party question 60–64; local, state and congressional elections results (1911–1926) 193n3; militants 78; opposition to World War I 64; and Populist-stamped planks (1901) 56; rift with mainstream labor unions 7, 69–70; working program (1912) 56
Socialist Party USA 167–169
Socialist Review (U.S.) 197n25
Socialist Trades and Labor Alliance (ST&LA) 45
Socialist Workers Party (SWP) 78
Socialists 8, 14–16, 20, 26, 38, 44–45, 47, 55–56, 60, 62–63, 66–67, 69, 71–72, 75, 78–79, 84, 101, 113, 117, 164, 172; and labor-based party efforts 167–169; *see also* Socialist Party of America and other socialist parties listed in this index
SocialistWorker.com 167, 189
society as "laboristic" 103, 105

Society of Professional Engineering Employees in Aerospace (SPEEA) 202*n*3
soft money 33–34
soldiering 58
solidarity: interracial 130; intra-class among workers 102; intra-union 188; movements in Latin America 164
Sombart, Werner 4, 28, 54
Sorge, Friedrich 42–43
South Africa 111, 113, 150, 204*n*19; disinvestment campaign 150
South America 211*n*33
South Carolina 25, 90, 95, 138, 147, 198*n*15, 209*n*12
South Dakota 193*n*10
South Korea 111, 154, 204–205*n*22
Southern Conference for Human Welfare 92
Southern Europe 59; immigrants from 39, 197*n*2
Southern U.S. 12, 19, 45, 54, 66, 76, 85, 89, 92, 112, 123, 126; agricultural interests 93; cities 149; textile interests 108; white ruling class in 93–94, 98, 138, 149, 159, 204*n*17, 205*n*27
Southwest U.S. 45, 55–56, 61, 96, 123, 196*n*15
Soviet Union 211*n*31
Spain 13, 36, 111, 202*n*1
Spanish Civil War 82
Spargo, John 62
stagflation crisis 121, 201*n*17
Stalin-Hitler pact 87
Standard Oil trust 76
state labor councils 139
state militias 45, 76
state repression of labor strikes 4, 38, 45, 76, 82, 87, 95; *see also* political repression
steel industry 66, 77, 92; regions 51; towns 79
Steel Workers' Organizing Committee (SWOC) 77
Steelworkers Fight Back 113
Stern, Andy (Andrew L.) 134, 141–142, 166, 203*n*10
Strasser, Adolph 41–43
Street, Paul 170, 175, 182
street rallies 173
Strike! (Jeremy Brecher) 201*n*14
strikes 5, 8, 38–39, 40, 59, 64, 70, 72, 87–88, 92, 95, 97, 10, 111, 132, 141–142, 145, 151, 161, 172–173, 207*n*34; Auto-Lite strike (1934) 197*n*3; Dockers' strikes 48; Farah Garment Factory strike 113, 118; general strike in Seattle (1919) 203*n*6, 211*n*28; general strike in textile industry (1934) 76; general strikes 58, 75, 172; great Pullman strike (1894) 60; Homestead strike (1892) 51; maritime strikes (1923–1924) 60; Memphis sanitation workers' strike (1968) 126, 204*n*17; national steel strike (1958) 105; New York cigar makers' strike (1877) 42; NRA strikes 77, 197*n*4, 198*n*5; Sacco and Vanzetti strikes (1927) 60; sit-down strikes and factory occupation in 1930s 75–80, 82; steel and electrical worker strikes of 1959–1960 166; steel strike of 1919 64; strike wave in early 1890s 45; strike wave 1918–1922 66; strike wave 1945–1946 166; strike wave 1968–1974 113–115, 117; United Parcel Service (UPS) strike (1998) 151; wildcat strikes 84, 92, 98, 100, 114, 173, 200*n*10; *see also* hate strikes
structural adjustment programs 211*n*30
Students for a Democratic Society (SDS) 117–118, 120*n*12
Stuttgart, Germany 113
subcontracting/subcontractors 128, 138
subprime mortgages 187
suffrage 12, 30; female suffrage 71; and property qualifications 14–15; white male suffrage 6, 11, 14–17, 28–29
Sullivan, J.J. 207*n*3
Sumner, William Graham 181
supervisors 92, 155–156
Swados, Harvey 200*n*6
sweatshops 138, 186
Sweden 20, 69, 83
Sweeney, John 131–132, 134, 140, 145, 147–148, 163, 166, 202*n*4, 203*n*5
swing states 22
Switzerland 16
syndicalism 5, 66, 117, 194*n*1; AFL craft unions' conservative syndicalism 40; IWW's practical syndicalism 58; syndicalist unions in France 4; version propagated by European left-wing intellectuals 58; and workers' self-management (new middle class theory) 117

Taff Vale ruling (House of Lords, Britian) 53
Taft, William H. 207*n*3
Taft-Hartley Act (1947) 7, 96–97, 98, 101, 104, 112, 157
Taiwan 154
Tammany Hall 29
Tar Heel, North Carolina 139
tax: concessions to corporations 91; evasion 3, 183–184; havens 184; reform 201*n*17; regressive state and local 110; and the rich 2–3, 183; *see also* income tax; inheritance tax
tax day protest demonstration 175
Taylorism 74, 114, 129
Tea Party movement/Tea Partiers 2, 8, 27, 176, 179–181, 199*n*14–16, 210*n*17, 210*n*20, 210*n*22; anti-globalization beliefs among rank-and-file members 177; "astroturf" phenomenon 175; overlap with Republican base 178; pseudo-populism 182; Tea Party Caucus 182; Tea Party Express bus tours 178; Tea Party Nation 178; Tea Party Patriots 178
team-based production 7, 128
Teamsters *see* International Brotherhood of Teamsters
Teamsters for a Decent Contract 113
Teamsters for a Democratic Union (TDU) 108
telecommunications industry 151
telegraph and telephone systems: government ownership of 45
Ten Strike, Minnesota 193*n*3
tenant farmers 46
tenement shops (New York) 43

Index

ten-hour workday 29
Tennessee 25
Tennessee Valley Authority projects 93
Tenney, Gerry 117
Texas 95
textile industry 75, 94, 112, 149
Textile Workers Union 113
third parties 18–23, 26, 29–30; efforts 6, 13–14, 20–21, 29, 64–68; *see also* minor parties
Third World 116, 118
Thirteenth Amendment: expansive interpretation 159–160, 206n30–31
Thomas, Norman 96, 207n5
Thompson Products 104
Title VII of Civil Rights Act (1964) 110–111
tobacco industry 94; workers 43
Toledo, Ohio 193n5, 197n3
Toryism 71
Toussaint, Eric 212n33
Toyota 201n19; "Toyotist" model 202n20
trade: imbalance between U.S. and China 153–154
Trade-Related Aspects of Intellectual Property Rights (TRIPS) agreements 211n30
Trade Union Unity League (TUUL) 197n5
Trades Union Congress (TUC) 53
transnational corporations 185
Transnational Information Exchange (TIE) 151
transportation 135, 138
Trbovich, Mike 199n3
Trotskyist Communist League of America 197n3
Trotskyist League for a Fifth International 212n33
Trotskyists 78, 96, 198n5, 198n9
trucking industry 142
Truman, Harry S. 90, 92, 94, 99, 101; and anti-labor actions 95
Truman administration 95
Trumka, Richard 143–144, 147, 204n19
Tucumán uprising (1969) 211n28
Tukwila, Wshington 193n3
Turin, Italy 113, 120, 211n28
two-party system, U.S. 4, 18, 21, 23, 62, 167; coalitions between competing interests and value groups 26; co-optation of working-class and third-party demands and leadership 29; institutional porousness of major parties 28; major parties' conventional coalition-building strategies 29, 174; major parties' duopoly 6, 9, 28–30, 147, 168, 174; major parties' electoral opportunism and ideological diffusiveness 26; major-party flexibility and permeable channels of recruitment 26–28; the system's historical function as "shock absorber" 28; *see also* political system, U.S.

UK Uncut 183–184
ultra-nationalists (or super patriots) 178, 181
undocumented immigrants/workers 136–137, 160, 181; terrorist profiling of 137
unemployment: benefits 181, 210n19; figures 1, 177, 191n1; insurance 75, 94, 102, 195n12;

unemployed workers 73, 75, 102, 133, 144, 172–173, 182, 188
unfair labor practices 155–156, 205n25
Unidad Popular 207n1
union: bureaucracy 119, 140–141, 146, 159, 165, 169; busting 95, 122, 135, 158; check-off 86, 181; democracy 7, 14, 107–108, 165–166; density 137, 192n8, in private sector 130, 183, 192n9, 210n23, in public sector 130, 183, 192n9, 202n1, 204n18, 210n23, racial/ethnic differences 210n23; global campaigns 8; growth 59, 65, 76, 86, 91; and health and life insurance 145; label 43; as labor contractors 141; power 3, 7–8, 97, 169; and support for the Democrats 144–149; *see also* union halls; union leadership; union members; unionization
union-based vs. political party-based strategies 40–42
Union Cities program (AFL-CIO) 132
union-employer partnership 128, 132; *see also* labor-management partnership
union halls: as working-class public sphere 70, 196n24
union leadership bureaucratic 79, 107–108, 114, 200n2; *see also* union, bureaucracy
union members: bill of rights 107; foremen and supervisors 98; membership trends 3, 91, 125, 135, 202n1; voting behavior 204n16, 209n10
Union Network International (UNI) 150
Union of Needle, Industrial and Textile Employees-Hotel and Restaurant Employees (UNITE-HERE) 134, 150
unionism/unions: business 4, 8, 39, 48, 52, 119, 140–142, 144, 147, 152, 164–167, 170, 197n4, 203n5; exclusive 37, 39, 42; inclusive 6, 37, 48, 55, 57, 197n2; non-majority 139, 173; occupational 160; public-sector 125, 126, 130–131, 156, 157–158, 162; 183, 205n27, 205n28, 206n29; "pure and simple" 6, 41–42, 47, 54, 57–58, 140; *see also* craft unionism/unions; industrial unionism/unions
unionization: among professionals 131, 202n2–3
UNITE *see* United Needletrades, Industrial and Textile Employees
UNITE-HERE *see* Union of Needle, Industrial and Textile Employees-Hotel and Restaurant Employees
United Auto Workers (UAW) 77–78, 80, 86, 93, 96, 116, 141–142, 165; Local 3 black president 200n10; United National Caucus 113, 149–151, 176, 196n24, 200n10, 201n19, 204n21–22, 209n10
United Brewery Workers 59–60
United Brotherhood of Carpenters and Joiners of America (UBC) 134
United Electrical, Radio and Machine Workers (UE) 146 -147, 150, 161, 206n32
United Electrical Workers 100, 120
United Farm Workers (UFW) 111, 113, 119–120, 134–135, 143
United Food and Commercial Workers (UFCW) 134, 139, 143, 158, 203n8, 204n22

United for Peace and Justice 184
United Kingdom *see* Britain
United Labor parties (1886) 37–38, 44
United Labor Party: in New York 44; in San Francisco 51
United Labor Union 43
United Mine Workers of America (UMW or UMWA) 38, 45, 47–49, 54, 59–60, 63, 65, 67, 77, 143–144, 166, 198n13, 199n3, 204n19
United Nations (UN) 161
United Needletrades, Industrial and Textile Employees (UNITE) 136
United Packinghouse Workers 77
United States: border with Mexico 136; foreign policy 10, 97, 99, 152–153; foreign wars 176; entry into World War I 63; ideological heritage of mainstream labor 8, 164–166; imperialism 99, 152; intelligence services 199n18; labor law 83, 94–95, 98–99, 155–156, 160, 169; post-war campaign against the labor left in Europe 163, 199n18; ratification of ILO conventions 156; trade policy 176, 152–153–154; *see also* Central Intelligence Agency; electoral system, U.S.; National Labor Relations Act; political system, U.S.; protective tariff; Taft-Hartley Act; two-party system, U.S.
U.S. Agency for International Development 207n2
U.S. Bureau of Labor Statistics 135
U.S. Chamber of Commerce 76, 103, 105, 121, 158, 205n24
U.S. Congress 10, 11, 13, 18, 24, 26, 28, 32, 51, 83, 92–93, 96, 101, 140, 156, 161, 170, 201n17, 203n11
U.S. Constitution 10, 11, 17, 23
U.S. Department of Commerce 126
U.S. Department of Homeland Security 136
U.S. Department of Labor 107
U.S. House of Representatives 11, 19, 24, 27, 31–32, 53, 124, 148, 153, 158, 182
U.S. Labor in Trouble and Transition (Moody) 142
U.S. Senate 11, 17–18, 27, 32, 71, 92, 115, 148, 158, 205n24, 208n5
U.S. Social Forum 184, 189
U.S. State Department 99, 199n18
U.S. Steel Corporation 76, 121
U.S. Supreme Court 12, 18, 24, 33–35, 49, 53, 83, 86, 97, 193n1, 198n7, 198n15, 206n31, 209n14
U.S. Treasury Department 1
United Steel, Paper and Forestry, Rubber, Manufacturing, Energy, Allied-Industrial and Service Workers International Union (USWA) 77
United Steelworkers of America (USWA) 150, 153, 204n22, 209n10
United Textile Workers 76
universal health care 145
universal labor standards 188
universal peacetime military service 100
University of Chicago: Department of Economics 104
unskilled workers 15, 37–39, 47, 50, 55, 59, 64, 66–67, 69, 74, 91, 196n15; distinctions between skilled and unskilled workers 15, 39, 74, 195–196n14
urban renewal programs and local "pro-growth" coalitions 123
USA PATRIOT Act 136
Utah 66

Vegas, Fernando 211n33
Venezuela 207n4, 211n32, 212n33
Vermont 192n4, 209n12
Vermont Progressive Party 203n13
Veterans Administration 192n4
Victoria, Australia 16
Viet Cong 200n8
Vietnam War 109, 115
vigilante actions 60
Villaraigosa, Antonio 137
Virginia 161
"Viva La Huelga" 111
V-J Day 95
Vogel, David 121
von Bismarck, Otto 13
von Hayek, Friedrich 104
von Metternich, Clemens 13
von Mises, Ludwig 104
Voss, Kim 196n15
voter: apathy in industrial working class 90; democratic participation 34; registration reform 24; registration requirements 23, 50; rights 14; turnout 25
voting: malapportionment of districts 24; poll tax requirements 23–24

Wagner, Robert F. 83
Wagner Act *see* National Labor Relations Act.
Walker, Scott 157, 206n28
Wall Street 1, 144, 203n11
Wallace, Henry A. 90–91, 95–96, 99
Wallerstein, Immanuel 192n8
Walling, William English 63
Wal-Mart 159
Walras, Leon 104
Walsh, Frank P. 195n11
War Labor Board (WLB): during World War II 86–87, 91
War on Poverty 109
War on Terror 136–137
wartime nationalism 100
Washington, D.C. 175, 178
Washington Alliance of Technology of America 202n3
Washington State 27, 79, 196n19
"wasted-vote" effect 14, 20–22; *see also* "lesser evil"
Watergate affair 31
Waterman, Peter 212n33
Wayne State University 115
Weathermen factions of SDS 201n12
welfare: arrangements in U.S. 102; capitalism 74, 166; company-based work 66; recipients 122; rights 171; "welfare-to-work" programs 133

Welfare Reform Act of 1996 133, 145
welfare state 40, 172
West Africa 101
West Coast, U.S. 81, 100, 138
West Virginia 161
Western Europe 13, 57, 59, 99, 102, 111; left-wing workers' movements in 99; social democrats in 199n18
Western Federation of Miners (WFM) 48–49, 54, 57–59, 61
Western U.S. 24, 89, 93, 125, 138, 196n15, 205n27
Wetzel, Tom 192n8
What's the Matter With Kansas? (Frank) 177
Whig party 18, 30
white-collar workers/professionals 130–131, 162, 199n16, 202n3
white supremacy 24; movements 181
Why Is There No Socialism in America? (Sombart) 4
Willkie, Wendell 198n12
Wilpert, Gregory 192n8
Wilson, William B. 63
Wilson, Woodrow 63, 71–72, 80, 95, 195n11
Wilson administration 163, 168
Winnfield, Louisiana 193n3
Winslow, Arkansas 193n3
Wisconsin 24, 30, 56, 68, 79, 157–158, 162, 196n18, 205n27
Wisconsin Progressive Party 79
Wobblies *see* Industrial Workers of the World (IWW)
women 19, 43–44, 58, 65, 74–75, 90–91, 95, 112, 118, 122, 130, 135, 164, 171; and occupational rights 111; support groups in Flint 211n28; women's movement 106, 124; women's rights 65, 131, 172
work councils 202n1

Work in America (Federal Special Task Force 1973) 115
Work in Progress (AFL-CIO) 148
work stoppages 58, 151
workers': centers 137–139, 173, 186; control 72, 115, 201n13; councils 115; rights 5, 8, 29, 155–157, 158–161
Workers Party of the United States 197n3
working-class: consciousness 4, 13, 15, 28–29, 70; divisions in U.S. 12, 28, 39, 70, 102; movements 70; politics 12, 74; solidarity 43, 186
Working Families Party (New York State) 203n13
Working for America Institute (AFL-CIO) 132
working poor 188
Workingmen's parties of the 1820s and 1830s 4, 29
workplace: action 173; parochialism 101; power 139; workplace-related goals 40
World Social Forum (WSF) 185, 188, 211n32, 212n33
World Socialist Website (wsws.org) 212n33
World Trade Organization (WTO) 153, 211n30
World War II: defeat of the labor left post-war 7, 91–95; labor party explorations in aftermath of 95–97; limits of liberalism post-war 103–106, 108–110; no-strike pledge 86; social compact between labor and business post-war 166

Yablonsky, Jock 199n3
Yahoo! 194n17
yellow-dog contracts 84, 159
"Yes We Can" change rhetoric 175

Zeskind, Leonard 178
ZNet 189

www.ingramcontent.com/pod-product-compliance
Ingram Content Group UK Ltd.
Pitfield, Milton Keynes, MK11 3LW, UK
UKHW041936140426
5217IPUK00014B/508